THE CRYSTALLIZATION OF THE ARAB STATE SYSTEM, 1945–1954

Contemporary Issues in the Middle East

THE CRYSTALLIZATION OF THE ARAB STATE SYSTEM, 1945–1954

BRUCE MADDY-WEITZMAN

Published in cooperation with
The Moshe Dayan Center for
Middle Eastern and African Studies
Tel Aviv University

SYRACUSE UNIVERSITY PRESS

Copyright © 1993 by Syracuse University Press
Syracuse, New York 13244-5160

ALL RIGHTS RESERVED

First Edition 1993

93 94 95 96 97 98 99   6 5 4 3 2 1

The paper used in this publication meets the minimum requirements of American National Standard for Information Sciences—Permanence of Paper for Printed Library Materials, ANSI Z39.48-1984. ∞™

Library of Congress Cataloging-in-Publication Data

Maddy-Weitzman, Bruce.
    The crystallization of the Arab state system, 1945–1954 / Bruce Maddy-Weitzman.
       p.   cm. — (Contemporary issues in the Middle East)
    "Published in cooperation with the Moshe Dayan Center for Middle Eastern and African Studies, Tel Aviv University."
    Includes bibliographical references and index.
    ISBN 0-8156-2575-8 (cloth). — ISBN 0-8156-2580-4 (pbk.)
    1. Arab countries—Politics and government—1945–   I. Title.
II. Series.
DS63.M23   1993
909'.09749270825—dc20   92-20835

Manufactured in the United States of America

To my parents

Bruce Maddy-Weitzman is a Research Associate at The Moshe Dayan Center for Middle Eastern and African Studies, Tel Aviv University. He is the author of numerous articles in professional journals and annuals, including *ORBIS, Middle Eastern Studies, Middle East Journal,* and *Middle East Contemporary Survey,* and chapters in collected works.

CONTENTS

Preface ix

A Note on Sources, Terminology, and Transliteration xv

Introduction 1

1. Genesis 5
2. The Formative Years, 1945–1947 25
3. The System Is Tested 55
4. Upheaval and Crisis 91
5. Solidification and Transition, 1950–1954 143

Conclusion 175
Notes 185
Sources Cited 231
Index 243

PREFACE

For decades to come, Morocco's King Hasan declared before the Moroccan Parliament in October 1990, the Arab world will record two forms of history: before and after August 2, 1990, the date of Iraq's invasion of Kuwait. Indeed, Saddam Husayn's action marked the first time since the Arab League came into being in 1945 that a member state had frontally assaulted, occupied, and incorporated a fellow Arab state. In doing so, Iraq flagrantly violated every principle of collective Arab solidarity and good-neighborliness, principles enshrined in the founding Charter of the Arab League and the Joint Defense Pact of 1950. Moreover, the decision to invade was preceded by months of diplomatic activity that culminated in a week of frenetic inter-Arab negotiations, the kinds that had always succeeded in smoothing over inter-Arab disputes. The shock was therefore that much greater, and the departure from previous norms that much more pronounced.

Saddam's act, unique in the annals of modern Arab history, prompted a similarly unprecedented abandonment of long-held norms and taboos by his Arab neighbors. Saudi Arabia dropped its traditional "over the horizon" policy of opposing a U.S. military presence on its soil, even at the risk of creating an affront to Muslim sensibilities. Together with Egypt and Syria, the Saudis fashioned a majority from among the twenty-one members of the Arab League, which endorsed the military buildup. Moreover, Egypt and Syria dispatched substantial numbers of troops to stand beside the U.S.-led coalition forces which ultimately liberated Kuwait and emasculated Iraq's military machine.

Just over a decade ago, Fouad Ajami proclaimed "the end of pan-Arabism." Indeed, on one level, the crisis confirmed anew his thesis that pan-Arabism as both an idea and a movement had lost out to the polycentric reality of multiple Arab states. Iraq's incorporation of Kuwait as its "nineteenth province" was depicted as righting a historical wrong, the supposed separation of part of the Iraqi motherland from the whole. The immediate context was a bilateral dispute over an oil field, oil production and pricing policies, debt repayment, and Iraqi demands for territorial adjustments that would improve Iraq's access to the Persian Gulf. Ajami's thesis was further reinforced by the finely calibrated responses of each Arab state to the crisis, based on their particular readings of their own regional and domestic interests.

At the same time, the crisis was clearly more than just a bilateral dispute. Saddam's action was a brazen and audacious bid to gain center stage in the region, in line with his own long-held predilections, Ba'thist ideology, and Iraq's geopolitical standing and ambitions from the 1930s onward. Moreover, the favorable responses Saddam drew in some Arab quarters (particularly from the Palestinian, Jordanian, Yemeni, and North African streets) indicated a desire for relief from the genuine material hardships and psychological despair prevailing in much of the Arab world, a situation that the "triumph" of individual states has largely failed to alleviate. Ironically, these problems were profoundly exacerbated by the crisis. In fact, for those who followed Saddam's lead, the disastrous outcome of the crisis was comparable to the collective Arab failures of 1948 and 1967.

Ghassan Salame had already suggested that the fragmentation and functional division into subregional blocs (North Africa, the Fertile Crescent, the Gulf) that had characterized inter-Arab politics since the signing of the Camp David Accords in 1978 had reached their limitations, and that a more inclusive, all-Arab political reality might again be emerging. The fact that he did not foresee a more assertive and aggressive Iraq as the catalyst for this development does not detract from his original insight. Nonetheless, the essential tenor of Ajami's proposition still appears sound: Saddam Husayn may have styled himself as a latter-day Jamal 'Abd al-Nasir, but he did not possess the credentials or the appeal to back up his claim. Further, Arab states were now far less vulnerable to the kind of messianic pan-Arab appeal that had been so threatening during the 1950s and 1960s. Finally, the international environment was no longer gripped by the bipolar U.S.-Soviet rivalry.

Still, the crisis contained many of the enduring themes that have come to characterize inter-Arab politics over the past half century: a particular country bidding for regional hegemony by seeking to invoke a combination of patriotic, pan-Arab, and Islamic themes; the banding together of other Arab countries to act as a counterweight; and peripatetic efforts by various Arab parties to mediate a solution. The inter-Arab system remains an intricate web, a bundle of contradictions, to be sure, and highly dynamic, but also with a number of enduring, and too often debilitating, features and patterns. The intent here is to shed light on how this came to be, through an examination of an earlier, and in many ways formative, period, what can loosely be termed the "dynastic phase" of inter-Arab relations, between the years 1945 and 1954.

What is the existing state of the literature? The recent availability of archival materials from the 1940s and 1950s has resulted in a number of scholarly works on the Middle East dealing with this period. All of them provided meaningful insight into inter-Arab politics, but almost exclusively through the prism of the Arab-Israeli conflict. Barry Rubin's *Arab States and the Palestine Conflict* (Syracuse: Syracuse Univ. Press, 1981) expertly covers the entire Mandate period, while Avraham Sela's as yet unpublished doctoral dissertation ("The Question of Palestine in the Inter-Arab System, from the Foundation of the Arab League until the Invasion of Palestine by the Arab Armies, 1945–1948," The Hebrew University, 1986), exhaustively and comprehensively treats the last crucial years before the British departure from Palestine. Benny Morris's *Birth of the Palestinian Refugee Problem, 1947–1949* (Cambridge: Cambridge Univ. Press, 1987) addresses a central aspect of the first Arab-Israeli war. Avi Shlaim's controversial *Collusion Across the Jordan* (Oxford: Oxford Univ. Press, 1987) concentrates on the Zionist-ʿAbdallah relationship. Itamar Rabinovich's *A Road Not Taken* (New York: Oxford Univ. Press, 1991) sheds important new light on Arab-Israeli diplomacy in the first years after Israel came into being. Other recent works deal mainly with British Middle East policy, such as Ilan Pappé's *Britain and the Arab-Israeli Conflict, 1948–1951* (London: Macmillan, 1988), and William Roger Louis's *British Empire in the Middle East, 1945–1951* (Oxford: Oxford Univ. Press, 1984).

The only significant archival-based monographs written on inter-Arab politics as a whole conclude with the foundation of the Arab League in 1945—Yehoshua Porath's *In Search of Arab Unity, 1930–1945* (London: Frank Cass, 1986), and Ahmed Gomaa's *Foundation of the League of Arab States* (London: Longman 1977). Thus, up until now, Patrick Seale's *The Struggle for Syria* (London: Oxford Univ. Press 1965) has been the sole serious treatment of inter-Arab politics between 1945 and 1958. Although his was a seminal work with much continuing value, the wealth of new material now available to the researcher and greater degree of historical perspective that has come with the passage of time compelled, in my view, a fresh and, I hope, a synoptic treatment of the period.

It is my pleasant task at this point to express my thanks to a number of people and institutions for their assistance during the course of my endeavor. This work is a revised version of my doctoral dissertation at Tel Aviv University. As such I owe a special debt of gratitude to my chief adviser, Itamar Rabinovich. His generosity in sharing his expertise, his efforts to exact from me the same high standard of scholarship that characterizes his own work, and his unwavering belief in the worthiness of the project were all vital to its successful completion. I also wish to express my appreciation to my second adviser, Yair Evron, for his constructive advice and encouragement as I struggled to apply some of the analytical tools of the discipline of International Relations to a historical narrative.

Without question, my approach toward the subject has been heavily shaped by Daniel Dishon, former editor of *Middle East Record* and *Middle East Contemporary Survey*, and one of the keenest observers of inter-Arab affairs whom I know. It has been a privilege to have collaborated with him on numerous projects dealing with inter-Arab politics over the years. For his help, guidance, and friendship, and for his insightful critiques at different points of my labors, I extend my profound thanks. Numerous others have offered assistance and constructive advice at various points and in different ways, belying the notion that writing is a solitary enterprise. They include Joseph Kostiner, Martin Kramer, Barry Rubin, Ilan Pappé, Gabriel Ben-Dor, Joel Migdal, Avraham Sela, Michael Barnett, Yehudit Ronen, Ami Ayalon, and Joel Greenberg. Asher Susser provided considerable moral support. Nadav Safran provided important guidance during the early stages of my graduate studies. Gad Gilbar offered much appreciated advice in the post-dissertation phase of this work. Adam Garfinkle tendered many important suggestions. Ofra Bengio was helpful in more ways than can be enumerated. The friendship and advice of the late Uriel Dann was much appreciated; his absence is felt keenly by all whose path he graced.

The Moshe Dayan Center for Middle Eastern and African Studies at Tel Aviv University—my institutional "home" throughout my professional life—has been extremely generous in making available to me both the time and resources that have enabled me to pursue my research. A postdoctoral fellowship at the Center for Jewish-Arab Studies at Haifa University enabled me to work on revising the dissertation for publication: my thanks to the center's director, George Kanazi, the head of the university's Basic Research Authority, Ze'ev Giora, and the university's rector, Gabriel Ben-Dor. Final revisions were made in the very hospitable environment of the Carter Center of Emory University, where I was a Visiting Fellow during 1990–1991 academic year. My special thanks to Ken Stein, director of the Carter Center's Middle East Program, for his innumerable constructive suggestions and encouragement, and for hosting me in his own inimitable fashion.

The writing of the dissertation was made possible by grants from the Israel Foundations Trustees and the Faculty of Humanities, Tel Aviv University, under the stewardship of Gabriel Cohen. I also received financial support along the way from the Bronfman Program for Jewish-Arab Relations, Tel Aviv University's Basic Research Authority, the Aranne School of History at Tel Aviv University, and the Baruch HaElyon Prize.

My good friend Doug Cahn provided the best hospitality possible during my time in Washington, D.C.; he also assisted in obtaining material from the Library of Congress. Thanks also to the staffs of the various archives and libraries where I gathered my material: the Public Record Office, the U.S. National Archives, the Israel State Archives, The Moshe Dayan Center's Documentation Center, the library of the Harry S. Truman Institute at The Hebrew University, and the Middle East Center at St. Antony's College, Oxford.

Finally, there is my family. My wife, Edie, has been my partner in this, as in all ventures, even as she labored successfully to fulfill her own professional ambitions. For her love and support, as well as for bearing with me during all the ups and downs of what often seemed like an endless journey, I am truly thankful. It would be difficult to imagine more encouraging and generous parents than mine, Bernard and Harriet Maddy. From bankrolling to baby-sitting, their contributions have been indispensable. My parents-in-law, Ya'acov and Naomi Weitzman, have been helpful throughout, as well as tolerant of my occasional mania. The dignity, modesty, and *yiddishkeit* of my late, sorely missed grandmother, Dora Hordies, will always be a source of strength for me. I hope that she would see this book as being congruent with her oft-repeated dictum to "do the right thing." Finally, there are Shira and Daniel, who have competed mightily with this manuscript for my attention. In so doing, they provided me with a healthy, daily injection of the kind of energy that only one's children can generate, thus allowing me to place the heavy pressures of this type of work in proper perspective.

Bruce Maddy-Weitzman

Tel Aviv
February 1992

A NOTE ON SOURCES, TERMINOLOGY, AND TRANSLITERATION

MUCH OF MY ACCOUNT derives from material gleaned from British and U.S., and, to a lesser extent, Israeli archives. No history of this period will ever be considered definitive as long as the diplomatic archives of Arab states remain unavailable to historians. I have sought to partially compensate for this inherent limitation by making use of (1) relevant memoirs and diaries of Arab statesmen, the most important of which, by far, is the second volume of Taha al-Hashimi's diary (*Mudhakkirat Taha al-Hashimi*, vol. 2, Beirut, 1978); (2) material from what was still a pluralistic and contentious Arab press; and (3) the small amount of documentation available, such as the protocols of the Arab League Council meetings (unfortunately, most of the important League discussions were held in the League's Political Committee, whose minutes are not available). Given these unavoidable shortcomings, it is my hope that I have, nevertheless, managed to provide a credible (dare I even say original?) interpretation of Arab politics during these formative and tumultuous years.

The term "Jordan" gradually came to replace "Transjordan" in international usage beginning in 1949, even though the official name of the kingdom had been "the Hashimite Kingdom of the Jordan" since independence was proclaimed in 1946. The Arab League Council meeting of March 17, 1949, marked the first time that "Jordan," not "Transjordan," was the official designation used. On June 1, 1949, the prime minister published an official notice reiterating the kingdom's official name and instructing the foreign minister to inform all foreign legations in Amman, Jordanian legations abroad, and the United Nations of the official name. (Muhammad Khalil, *The Arab States and the Arab League,* vol. 1, Beirut, 1962, 15–16.) In this work, the name "Jordan" is substituted for "Transjordan" in any reference dealing with events subsequent to the signing of the April 4, 1949, armistice agreement with Israel.

Arabic transliteration follows the simplified system adopted in the most recent volumes of the *Middle East Contemporary Survey,* apart from Westernized spellings of certain common place names and proper names. Hebrew transliteration uses "kh" for the letter כ, "h" for the letter ח, and aʿ for the letter ע.

THE CRYSTALLIZATION OF THE ARAB STATE SYSTEM, 1945–1954

INTRODUCTION

THE EMERGENCE IN 1945 of the seven-member League of Arab states was a watershed in the modern history of the Middle East. It marked the conclusion of an almost thirty-year process that transformed the defunct Ottoman Empire's Arabic-speaking territories into separate political entities. Concurrently, Arab nationalism came to be the dominant political ideology within the Arabic-speaking world. Its emphasis on the oneness of the Arab nation tended to delegitimize, explicitly or implicitly, the newly established Arab entities. The ensuing tensions between pan-Arab ideology and day-to-day political praxis became a lasting underpinning of inter-Arab affairs, such that, as described by P. J. Vatikiotis, "inter-Arab relations cannot be placed on a spectrum of linear development, moving from hell to paradise or vice versa. Rather their course is partly cyclical, partly jerkily spiral, and always resting occasionally at some 'grey' area."[1]

Despite their often tortured course, the historical evolution of inter-Arab relations can be classified into four overlapping yet distinct periods since 1945: (1) the "dynastic" phase (1945–1954), (2) the Nasirist interlude (1954–1970), (3) the Sadat and Saudi eras (1970–1979), and (4) the decade of fragmentation (Salame's "return to geography,"[2] 1979–1989). The end of the decade was marked by Egypt's formal return to prominence and Iraq's bid for power. Although still nominally allies, as fellow members of the one-year-old Arab Cooperation Council, their sharp differences at the May 1990 Arab summit conference in Baghdad marked the renewal of an old and familiar pattern of intense competition and set the stage for the coming crisis in the Persian Gulf two months hence.

Throughout these periods, there were numerous swings of the inter-Arab pendulum marking the changing regional balance of power and shifting Arab alignments. Moreover, this unceasing dynamism was often the outcome of the massive socioeconomic and internal political changes percolating throughout the region. The former has been expertly documented and interpreted both by Alan Richards and John Waterbury and by Gad G. Gilbar: it includes massive population growth at among the highest rates anywhere; improved health and education standards, resulting in significant increases in life expectancy and literacy rates; and infrastructure development on a large scale. At the same time, as they point out, the new relative well-being for most of the region's inhabitants is not built on firm foundations, with the emergence of new economic actors not leading to a corresponding increase in the productive capacity of national economies.[3]

On the more purely political plane, regimes have been toppled, elites emasculated and replaced by rival forces, ideologies adopted and discarded, and global orientations altered with considerable frequency. During the forty-seven years after its founding, the Arab League expanded from seven to twenty-one members (actually twenty-two, until the unification of North and South Yemen in late 1989 reduced the rolls by one). Nonetheless, the underlying nature of inter-Arab politics was not fundamentally at variance with what emerged during the first decade after World War II. Indeed, much of the explanation for this continuity lies in the developments during the first postwar decade (1945–54): the crystallization of the Arab state system during these years was one of the central determining features of the political history of the Middle East over the last two generations.

For one, far-reaching changes occurred during this period in the nature of the involvement of outside powers in Arab political life. British and French domination came to an end, the latter's more swiftly than the former's, conferring on the local actors far greater autonomy of action than previously. At the same time, although meaningful Soviet penetration into the Middle East heartland would not occur until 1955–1956, the region was already being factored into Western strategic calculations, and in ways that would further complicate inter-Arab affairs. For another, it was a decade packed with regional challenges, most notably the first Arab-Israeli war and the "struggle for Syria" between the Hashimite camp (Iraq and Transjordan) and the anti-Hashimite bloc (led by Egypt and Saudi Arabia). In addition, the postwar decade was marked by the progressive weakening of the ruling elites in three key countries—Egypt, Syria, and Iraq. By the end of the decade, the first generation of modern Arab political leaders had passed from the scene—Transjordan's King ʿAbdallah, Egypt's King Faruq, Saudi Arabia's King ʿAbd al-ʿAziz Bin Saʿud, Lebanon's Riyad al-Sulh and Bishara al-Khuri, and, last but not least, the Arab League's first secretary-general, ʿAbd al-Rahman ʿAzzam Pasha.

During these years, Arab leaders faced a test of one of the central principles of Arab nationalist ideology, the imperative of unifying into a single entity those areas populated by speakers of Arabic. With the decline of foreign control, local Arab elites were now theoretically in a position to fashion a completely different regional political system. In fact, the reality of Arabism as an "expressive" as opposed to a "practical" ideology was not lost on the political leaders of the new system.[4] Still, the issues facing them were fundamental: How was the agreed-upon goal of pan-Arab nationalism to be implemented— through cooperation among the existing sovereign states, via partial geographic unification or by more comprehensive unity schemes? What was to be the scope of the Arab League's activities? How were Arab political leaders to guard and to enhance their own particular interests both domestically and within the wider Arab setting? The need to address these issues produced a state of intensive flux. The outcome was the crystallization of a state system, the resilience of which helped to inhibit the subsequent attempts of Jamal ʿAbd al-Nasir and other practitioners of radical pan-Arabism to rearrange fundamentally the regional order.

What follows partially accounts for this resilience by providing an assessment of the dynamic political interrelationships among ruling Arab elites and an analysis of the underlying implications of inter-Arab patterns for the system as a whole. More specifically, this book seeks to provide answers to the following sets of questions:

1. What were the most permanent patterns emerging from Arab political interaction and how did they serve to strengthen the regional status quo and the particularist tendencies within each state?

2. What were the effects of inter-Arab dynamics on other regional issues, for example, the Arab-Israeli conflict, and the relationship between the Arab world and the big powers? To what extent did

developments in these spheres reinforce the inter-Arab status quo and to what extent did they militate against it?

3. What were the attitudes of the ruling elites regarding both the existing political frameworks and the vision of Arab unity? What was the impact of other elites in the political-cultural community who had the vision on the governing elites?

In sum, what was the relationship between the vision of Arab nationalism and the reality of Arab particularism, and how did the latter come to block the realization of the former?

1

GENESIS

It is often forgotten that the vast majority of Arab countries are not only old societies but also old political entities in one form or another. As noted by one astute scholar, nearly all of today's Arab states are the product of indigenous and regional forces mostly related to and, in fact, predating European colonialism. Thus, they have within themselves many of the sources of their own legitimacy. There is only one, albeit crucial, exception to the above stipulation: the "colonially created" states (modern-day Syria, Iraq, Jordan, and to a certain extent, Lebanon), which were carved out of the defunct Ottoman Empire "on the basis of foreign imperial interests and in the absence of any credible local base of authority upon which to erect the new structures."[1] Thus, it is no coincidence that the ideology of Arabism was born and developed in those colonially created states in the Fertile Crescent. It was in those states that the traditional sources of authority and legitimacy were the weakest, and the challenges posed to the local socially and religiously fragmented societies were the most acute, first by the centralizing and Turkicizing rulers in Istanbul, and then by the arbitrary actions and high-handedness of the European powers that carved up the area.

Without digressing too deeply into the origins and fundamental underpinnings of Arab nationalism, it seems helpful at this juncture to refer to a number of salient points. The scholarly debate over the roots of the Arab national movement centers in part on whether it predated World War I.[2] By the mid-1930s, it was the dominant political ideology among the political elites of the Fertile Crescent and was making significant inroads in Egypt. Its attraction was based on many factors, some rooted in the history and political culture of the region, and others in the context of European intellectual and political developments. At a time of acute ideological, political, and cultural confusion, Arab nationalism promised to restore the Arab nation to what was perceived as its rightful state of power and glory that it held during the seventh century, following the Prophet Muhammad's entry onto the stage of history. Its invocation of the unity of *al-umma al-'arabiyya* (the Arab nation) was a modern variation on the populace's deeply rooted identification with the concept of a single *al-umma al-islamiyya* (Islamic nation, i.e., community of believers).

Many scholars have pointed to the Islamic base of Arab nationalism. For Ernest Gellner, the history of modern Arab nationalism is inextricable from the advent of Islamic reformism over the last hundred years, with its heavy emphasis on a central cultural tradition and rejection of more localized, syncretic forms of religious practice, all for the expressed purpose of fashioning a community better able to cope with the challenges posed by modernization and Western political domination.[3] Sylvia Haim has pointed to the features of Arab nationalist doctrine that grew out of and are compatible with the Muslim past: a deep-rooted deference to authority; the importance of maintaining solidarity, discipline, and cooperation; and the glorification of one's own group.[4] At the same time, Haim and Bassam Tibi have demonstrated how the influences of central European romantic nationalist doctrines, with their exaggerated pride in race and language, shaped the writings of Sati' al-Husri, the preeminent exponent of Arab nationalism during the interwar years.[5] Unquestionably, the mass appeal of pan-Arabism, at least on the emotional level, lay in its simplicity: An ideology grounded on perceived ethnic, linguistic, historical, and religious ties was far more comprehensible to the bulk of the populace than the competing alternatives—pharaonicism in Egypt, pan-Syrianism, and various forms of constitutional government copied from the West.

In both Egypt and the Fertile Crescent, Arab nationalists initially were agents for opposition and dissent: They sought to identify the ills of their societies, fix blame, and offer remedies.[6] Their successes were only partial, however, and their resulting frustrations and impatience acute.[7] Despite the artificiality of the new political entities that had emerged on the ruins of the Ottoman Empire, they were beginning to inculcate, almost involuntarily, a sense of political identity among its residents through a combination of "habit, vested interests, local peculiarities and sensitivities and common experiences." Naturally, these developments were intimately bound up with considerations of political power, growing state bureaucracies, the development of different economic systems, and determined efforts at governmental centralization.[8]

The process of building a "territorial state" was a slow one. Consequently, beginning in the 1920s, one of the outstanding features of Arab political life was the ongoing struggle between *raison d'état* (*wataniyya* — state nationalism) of the particular Arab entities and *raison de la nation Arabe* (*qawmiyya* — pan-Arab nationalism). In systemic terms, the combination within these entities of the lack of "stateness," on the one hand, and a rapidly developing common ideology of Arabism, on the other, resulted in the system's becoming, to a large extent "interpenetrated."[9] That is, the system was one in which the specific components, governmental and nongovernmental, were reciprocally influencing (i.e., "penetrating" and "being penetrated") each others' affairs.[10]

It was on this plane of cross-currents and competing pressures that the dominant Arab political elites operated. All sought to protect and enhance their own standing vis-à-vis their regional rivals, albeit always in the name of general Arab interests. Their policies were, of necessity, finely calibrated to the exigencies of the regional balance of power. Interstate relations were thus marked by a high degree of elasticity. Arab leaders demonstrated a high level of flexibility in both tactics and strategy, which entailed measures varying from simply keeping lines of communication open to one's rival, to the conclusion of formal treaties to regulate their mutual relations, all the while remaining acutely sensitive to any development that may have impacted on one's own interests or even survival.

FROM MANDATES TO INDEPENDENT STATES

The focal points of inter-Arab affairs during the 1920s and 1930s were the same as those in the decade after 1945: the future of Syria and the question of Palestine. Maneuvering by various Arab leaders over the possible establishment of a Syrian monarchy reflected and sharpened a number of features of the burgeoning Arab system:[11] (1) the conflict between the ruling Hashimite dynasties in Iraq and Transjordan and the non-Hashimite rulers, particularly the Saudi dynasty, (2) the less visible but at times equally competitive struggle between the two Hashimite regimes, (3) the growing interest of Egypt in Fertile Crescent affairs, and (4) the concomitant beginnings of Egyptian-Iraqi competition for leadership of the Arab world. This last aspect followed on the heels of Iraq's formal attainment of independence in 1932 and the conclusion of the Anglo-Egyptian Treaty of 1936, two milestones along the road to more assertive foreign policies by both countries.[12]

Hashimite designs on Syria were particularly disturbing to the newly crystallized Kingdom of Saudi Arabia, and no wonder. Having expelled the Hashimites from the Hejaz in 1925, the Saudis were ever vigilant as to a possible Hashimite attempt to regain their lost patrimony. Thus, Hashimite efforts to penetrate the Syrian polity and tip the regional balance of power were met by Saudi countermeasures. They, too, sought to forge links with sections of the Syrian political elite. In the diplomatic sphere, Ibn Saʿud repeatedly reminded his British patrons of the necessity to restrain their Hashimite clients. At the same time, the Saudis were concerned, as they would be again in the late 1970s, with the growing strength of Iraq and Iran and thus desirous of an arrangement that would increase their room for maneuver. The response of Iraq's Nuri al-Saʿid (the man who dominated Iraqi politics for three decades) was to seek to mollify Saudi concerns, while taking care not to renounce Iraq's Fertile Crescent ambitions. As a result of Nuri's efforts, on April 19, 1936, the two countries concluded a "Treaty of Friendship and Arab Brotherhood."[13] One year later, Nuri even briefly put forward Ibn Saʿud's candidacy to head his proposed Arab federation.[14]

Thus, the dynamics of penetration, concern with the regional balance of power, and the elasticity of interstate relations combined to underpin the convoluted Iraqi and Saudi maneuverings during the 1930s. In the process, they provided a foretaste of the post-1945 Arab system.

All of these systemic features were present with regard to the Arab world's treatment of the Palestine question. From 1936 onward, the "regionalization" of the issue on the governmental and popular levels added a further dimension to the politics of the nascent Arab system.[15] In contrast with the Syrian question, which was the concern of relatively small elites, the Arab Revolt in Palestine from 1936 to 1939 stirred genuine passions among much wider sectors of the various Arab countries. Nongovernmental groups, such as the Muslim Brotherhood in Egypt and various organizations in Syria, were ahead of their own governments in drumming up moral and material support for the Palestinian Arabs. Increasingly, a leader's position on the Palestine question came to be the litmus test for fidelity to pan-Arab ideals, in both the domestic and the regional spheres. "Public opinion" was now a further constraint to be reckoned with by Arab rulers.[16]

Sporadic attempts were made to translate the common Arab concern for Palestine into concrete policy. For example, in October 1936 there was a prearranged appeal by Iraq, Transjordan, Saudi Arabia, and Yemen to the Arab Higher Committee in Palestine to call off a six-month general strike. Egypt joined them at the February 1939 St. James Conference in London. These efforts did not result, however, in a sustained, collective Arab posture and the Palestine question became one more plane for maneuvers and competition among Arab actors. Much of the focus centered on the dissatisfaction of other Arab leaders with the ambitions of Transjordan's Amir ʿAbdallah to expand his kingdom. As part of his efforts, ʿAbdallah cultivated Palestinian Arab groups opposed to the dominance of the mufti of Jerusalem, Hajj Amin al-Husayni. His efforts highlighted the particular penetrability of Palestinian Arab society in those years, and beyond—years that marked the beginning of an inexorable loss of independence of Palestinian Arab decision making vis-à-vis the Arab states, although scholars tend to underestimate the contribution of the Palestinian Arabs to the collective Arab policy toward Palestine before 1948.[17]

By the end of the 1930s, the Arab "proto-system" exhibited many of the features that came to characterize regional Arab politics in the years after 1945: Tension between Arab nationalist ideology and particular interests, dynastic and personal rivalries, permeable, penetrable frontiers, and an increasing concern with coalition and alliance-building. Still, given the continued preeminence of Great Britain and France in the region, much had to happen before a real state system could emerge.

Developments during World War II laid the final groundwork for the postwar Arab state system. The British-French "division of labor" in the Levant gradually broke down, with Great Britain tilting, haltingly at first, decisively in the end, toward the Syrian and Lebanese nationalists against France. Accompanying this was a growing perception among British officials that a reshaping of the postwar order would be necessary, owing to Britain's own weakening due to the war and the expectation of a more assertive posture by local nationalists. They believed that British and Western strategic interests in the area could best be preserved by renegotiating Britain's bilateral treaties with Egypt and Iraq, a new arrangement with Transjordan, and perhaps even Syria.[18] Arab leaders in the Fertile Crescent were not slow in picking up on these developments, and they began their own planning and maneuvering. Finally, Egypt entered onto the Arab stage in full force.

The flurry of Arab diplomatic activity during the war years was viewed widely at the time and for years afterward as being inspired and directed by Great Britain.[19] A somewhat simplistic understanding of Elie Kedourie's seminal article, "Pan-Arabism and British Policy," reinforced this view in academia. In the article, Kedourie pointed to a widespread belief in British circles, both official and nonofficial, in the "inevitable" triumph of pan-Arabism and the resulting belief that it was in Britain's vital interests to ally itself with the movement. As a result, he states, Britain's simultaneous, if contradictory encouragement of Faruq and his "coadjutors and instruments," on the one hand, and the original pan-Arabs in the Fertile Crescent, on the other, combined with Britain's victory in el-Alamein over Rommel's forces, gave the decisive impetus to the historical process that resulted in the formation of the Arab League.[20]

More recent works have elaborated further on the entangled connection between British desires and Arab actions. As Porath and Gomaa have shown, the initiatives for fashioning the postwar regional order came mainly from various Arab quarters, albeit with encouragement from British officials stationed in the Middle East. Furthermore, British policymakers in London were divided over what course of action to adopt with regard to the various Arab federation and unity schemes being broached. One must conclude that Great Britain did not give the decisive push toward the League's creation, although if it had the capability to return British-Arab relations to the status quo before 1939, its attitude would have been far more hostile. Rather,

Great Britain was eventually compelled to follow along after an Egyptian-led thrust toward a loose inter-Arab network at the expense of the more localized Hashimite unity schemes being advocated by the Hashimites and a number of British officials in the region.[21]

During the war, the first Arab testing of Britain's intentions came from its closest client. In July 1940, Transjordan's Amir ʿAbdallah complained to the British that the Vichy French rulers in Damascus were creating additional barriers between Syria and Transjordan, and renewed his longstanding entreaties for British help in unifying the Syrian homeland—*bilad al-sham*—or "natural Syria" (*suriyya al-tabiʿiyya*), terms that by definition included Syria, Palestine, Transjordan, and Lebanon. These initial efforts may have been undertaken primarily for tactical purposes—the countering of Axis propaganda. Nonetheless, they reflected ʿAbdallah's long-standing position, and indicated that he would seek to implement it as soon as the opportunity presented itself.[22] The British brushed aside ʿAbdallah's various appeals to fulfill Winston Churchill's alleged promise to ʿAbdallah in 1920 to help him ascend to the Syrian throne. ʿAbdallah was not discouraged, however, and continued his push with considerable vigor in subsequent years despite all odds.[23] Independent of ʿAbdallah's initiative, Nuri al-Saʿid informed the chief British adviser to his government that the time had come to push for an Arab Confederation of Iraq, Transjordan, Palestine, and, if possible, Saudi Arabia. His proposal drew no reply. Nonetheless, as Porath states, one can by no means argue that the Arab demands being advanced by Nuri and ʿAbdallah, and also by the Arab historian and ex-British civil servant George Antonius, "fell on totally deaf ears."[24]

In his Mansion House speech of May 29, 1941, British Foreign Secretary Sir Anthony Eden declared his government's willingness to support any scheme to strengthen political, cultural, and economic ties that the Arabs might agree upon.[25] The speech was delivered at the low point of Britain's "moment" in the Middle East, with Rommel's Afrika Corps knocking on the Egyptian door, with Vichy France still in control of Syria and Lebanon, and with the still uncertain internal situation in Iraq, where the British had just restored the Hashimite monarch and evicted the nationalist, pro-Axis government of Rashid ʿAli al-Gaylani.[26] As such, the declaration could have only limited practical significance. It drew only a tepid reaction from the

Arab world. In any case, it had not been put forth to advance any radical changes in the region during the war. Nonetheless, it revealed Eden's reading of the Arab situation: Talk of unity was now useful because it echoed the rising tide of such sentiment among the Arab leaders.[27]

By mid-November 1942, following Montgomery's victory at el-Alamein and the British-U.S. landing on the North African coast, the situation had tilted decisively in Britain's favor. Hashimite Arab leaders were the first to begin probing London's intentions and advancing their own leadership claims in a more sustained fashion. 'Abdallah lost no time in reiterating—both privately and publicly—his claim to Greater Syria. More important was Nuri al-Sa'id's "Fertile Crescent Project," also known as Nuri's "Blue Book," which was submitted to the British minister for the Middle East, P. G. Casey, in February 1943 under the title "Arab Independence and Unity: Memorandum on the Arab Cause." Interestingly enough, Casey encouraged the preparation of the proposal, one of the numerous instances of support for Arab aspirations tendered by British officials serving in the Middle East.[28] The essence of the plan entailed the unification of "historical Syria" (Syria, Transjordan, Lebanon, and Palestine), and its joining together with Iraq in an "Arab League," whose permanent council, presided over by one of the heads of state, would be responsible for defense and foreign affairs, currency, communications, customs, protection of minority rights, and education. Other Arab states could join the League whenever they so desired, but for the immediate future the focus was clearly on the Fertile Crescent. In addition, the type of government of the enlarged Syrian state would be decided upon by the inhabitants; the clause was intended temporarily to mollify Syrian opposition to a monarchical, Hashimite-led government.

Ultimately, Nuri envisaged securing the Syrian throne for the Iraqi regent, 'Abd al-Ilah, and not for Transjordan's 'Abdallah. The Jews in Palestine would be granted a "semi-autonomous administration" in the areas where they formed a majority; the Maronites in Lebanon would be able to retain the special status they had held during the last years of the Ottoman Empire.[29]

Nuri's plan to place Iraq squarely in the center of regional Arab politics might have had a better chance of success had it not coincided with similar aspirations in Egypt. Popular agitation for the Palestinian Arabs, developing intellectual currents of pan-Arabism, the ambitions of young King Faruq and the Wafd party's pragmatic, politically inspired drift toward an Arab orientation had combined to serve notice in the late 1930s that Egypt no longer intended to remain aloof from Fertile Crescent affairs. By 1943, Mustafa al-Nahhas Pasha, prime minister since the February 1942 British ultimatum to Faruq to install a Wafd government, concluded that promoting pan-Arab causes would bolster his internal standing vis-à-vis Faruq and other domestic rivals.[30]

The pace of events quickened accordingly. On February 29, 1943, Eden responded to a parliamentary question by a pro-Arab Labour M.P. by reiterating the essence of his Mansion House speech, with the additional comment that he was not aware that any Arab scheme "which would command general approval [had] yet been worked out."[31] This time, Arab reaction was almost uniformly favorable, a reflection of Britain's successes on the battlefield.[32]

The first concrete Arab response to Eden's statement came from Nuri: He sent a close associate and former minister, Jamil al-Midfaʻi, to various Arab capitals to explore their attitudes on Arab unity. Nuri intended this to be followed by the early convening of a pan-Arab conference, which would include nonofficial groups, presumed to represent the general Arab desire for unity. In March 1943 he wrote to Nahhas, asking his views on Cairo as a possible venue for the conference and whether Nahhas would prefer officially to chair the conclave or to nominate another distinguished Egyptian to do so.[33] Nuri's "fateful decision" to approach Nahhas has never been fully explained.[34] It appears that he felt that by offering the Egyptians a ceremonial role, they would be less of a stumbling block to his own plans. As he told a worried Amir ʻAbdallah, Egypt was interested in the Arab East mainly for prestige reasons and had no political pretensions in Syria.[35]

Nuri may also have thought that Egypt would be in favor of a division of the Arab world into spheres of influence, with Iraq dominating the Fertile Crescent and the Egyptians exercising predominance in the Sudan and North Africa.[36] If so, he sorely miscalculated Egyptian intentions to promote simultaneously a geographical unity scheme in the Nile Valley and an inclusive Arab framework under its leadership. As it happened, Nahhas took the initiative out of Nuri's hands. On March 30, 1943, he proposed to convene a government-level pan-Arab congress in Cairo to discuss plans for an Arab federation, without specifying either the nature of the political structure of the federation or the fate of the more localized Fertile Crescent and Greater Syria schemes.

The proposal was, however, the first clear indication that Egypt would not look kindly on any arrangement that would entail the redrawing of the regional map and the loss of independent existence by any of the existing Arab entities. More broadly, Nahhas conceived of Egypt's role as similar to that of the United States in the Western hemisphere.[37] Thus, in structural terms, Egypt was attempting to play two complementary roles simultaneously: one domineering, the other stabilizing.

To prepare the ground for the proposed congress, Nahhas undertook preliminary, separate consultations with other Arab leaders beginning in the summer of 1943. His first round of talks was with Nuri al-Sa'id in Alexandria from July 31 to August 6. Nuri suggested two possible forms of Arab union: an integral, binding union and a nonbinding one. Nuri declared that he preferred the former. In fact, he probably felt confident that Egypt's opposition to a more binding union would free Iraq's hand in the Fertile Crescent. As for the immediate course to be pursued, Nuri strongly advocated the establishment of Greater Syria as a first step toward wider unity. Nahhas, in his ostensibly neutral role as the seeker of different Arab views, was noncommittal. He did, however, register his view that a nonbinding arrangement, being devoid of real political cooperation, was not attractive.[38]

By this time, Nuri could not have harbored many illusions about Nahhas's aims; but, apparently, he believed that he still had the advantage regarding future efforts for unity. He was reported to have found Nahhas "more enthusiastic than informed on Arab affairs,"[39] which could only increase his skepticism in regard to the likelihood that the initiative would bear fruit. As a result, Nuri chose to mark time, a choice consistent with his characteristic pragmatism in the conduct of foreign affairs.[40] If Nahhas's plans for a loose federation were to gain momentum, Iraq—and Nuri personally—could not afford to be left behind. Furthermore, if handled correctly, later efforts to implement Nuri's own program would not be precluded. If, on the other hand, Nahhas's efforts were to come to naught, which seemed likely, then Nuri's prospects for success would be strengthened.

Transjordan was the next to be approached. Nahhas met with ʿAbdallah's prime minister, Tawfiq Abu al-Huda, in Alexandria, from August 28 to September 1. The talks clarified two essential points. Like Nuri, ʿAbdallah strongly believed that the establishment of a Greater Syria federation should be the first priority for any collective Arab thrust. He was, however, not willing to countenance any alternative to his own leadership of the federation, not by his nephew, the regent of Iraq, nor by a nonmonarchical, republican regime. At the same time, ʿAbdallah had no intention of remaining aloof from the developing Arab effervescence, even if the particulars being promulgated by Nahhas did not satisfy him.[41]

Ibn Saʿud, for his part, was not keen on participating in any Arab unity scheme, fearing that it might threaten his still-insulated kingdom with the penetration of foreign (both Arab and non-Arab) influences and also tilt the Arab balance of power in favor of the Hashimites. Moreover, he was angry with Nahhas for not consulting with him before his initiative. Ibn Saʿud thus had no inclination even to send a representative to Cairo for talks with Nahhas. In the end he relented, owing to British intervention, to his realization that Hashimite operations were not being backed by either Great Britain or Egypt and to his understanding that Egypt was not going to support a real federation.[42]

The position presented by the Saudis between September and November 1943 was a difficult one for Nahhas. Ibn Saʿud agreed with the idea of a preparatory pan-Arab congress but demanded that all political discussions be avoided until the end of the war. Furthermore, he insisted that Mecca be the venue, which would exclude non-Muslim representatives, not to mention the unpleasantness it would cause the Hashimites. Eventually, with Syrian help, the Saudis were mollified, although Ibn Saʿud's personal representative and leading adviser on Arab affairs, Syrian-born Yusuf Yasin, refused to sign the minutes of his discussions.[43]

The Syrian position was the most complex. On the one hand, they alone continued to advocate political unity "as a practical goal and as a means to ensure general Arab backing in their struggle against the French." On the other hand, their impulse was to coordinate with Ibn Saʿud and Nahhas, out of a desire to resist inclusion in the Hashimite sphere. This was further reinforced by National Bloc leader Shukri al-Quwwatli's familial and commercial links to Ibn Saʿud. In fact, the contradiction was more apparent than real. Syrian advocacy of unity was primarily an exercise in Arab nationalist posturing, as they were already aware that the Nuri-Nahhas talks had, in essence, foreclosed the option of real political federation.[44]

The Lebanese leadership was consulted by Nahhas in January 1944. The Christian components were extremely suspicious of any hint of absorption into a Muslim-Arab hinterland. They were also bolstered by their own recent advancements toward full independence. In practice, Lebanese attitudes toward Arab unity coincided with those of the Syrians, despite the apparent clash between Lebanon's insistence on retaining its independence and Syria's declared willingness to give itself away to the cause of a strong central government embracing all the Arab countries. A mutual understanding had evolved over the previous two years. In June 1942, exploratory talks among Syria's Jamil Mardam, Bishara al-Khuri (the Lebanese Maronite leader and Lebanon's future first president), and Nahhas Pasha, Khuri stressed his desire to cooperate more closely with Syria and the other Arab countries. If this was to be the official Lebanese policy, pledged Mardam, then Syria would recognize Lebanon's independence within its present frontiers and renounce its claims to those areas lost by Syria to Lebanon in 1920. The Lebanese position was subsequently embodied in the "National Pact" of 1943.[45]

The first round of Nahhas's consultations ended in February 1944 with talks with a representative of Yemen's Imam Yahya. In line with Yemen's geographical remoteness from the rest of the Arab world, and with the imam's own predilection for isolation, the Yemeni representative was even more aloof to Nahhas's idea than Ibn Sa'ud had been.

Nuri al-Sa'id's response to Nahhas's initiative was not slow in coming. In January and February 1944, he undertook a long visit to Syria, Lebanon, Transjordan, and Palestine in a renewed bid to promote a Greater Syria and a Syrian-Iraqi federation. This time, he gave in to Syrian demands for a republican form of government, realizing that they were a sine qua non for their possible support of his larger schemes.[46] These steps toward unity, he suggested, could be ratified by a general Arab conference in the spring of 1944. If this proved unattainable, then Nuri proposed that the Syrians and Iraqis "go it alone" and federate. By pushing for an early convening of the proposed Arab conference and by refocusing its agenda, Nuri was attempting to bypass Nahhas. The results were discouraging. The British reproached him for moving too fast, while ʿAbdallah was angered by Nuri's placating of the supporters of the Syrian republic to the detriment of his own claims.[47] The Syrians were noncommittal. This may have had something to do with the fact that the emerging Syrian polity did not speak with one voice. Sir Edward Spears, British minister in the Levant, recognized this when he stated that Nuri may have received an overly optimistic response to his suggestions from Syrian foreign minister Mardam, "whose loyalty to the president is not above suspicion and who is a great intriguer."[48]

Nahhas made the next move in his no longer subtle tug-of-war with Nuri, attempting to achieve the release of two British-interned Palestinian Arab leaders in order to enable them to participate in his proposed conference. British officials had initially hoped that the conference would take steps compatible with British interests. Now, however, the prospects for this seemed far less likely, because placing the Palestine issue, with all of its emotive qualities, in the forefront of the conference would give it an anti-British cast. Thus, Nahhas was warned by Sir Miles Lampson—the British ambassador in Cairo, and up to that point sympathetic to Arab aspirations—not to proceed with the conference plans. The warning had the opposite effect, however, as Nahhas chose to issue invitations to the six other Arab governments to convene in Cairo for a preparatory Arab gathering. The invitations were quickly accepted by Iraq, Syria, Transjordan, and Lebanon. The British were annoyed but thought they had little choice but to go along with the new developments and to encourage a reluctant Ibn Saʿud to participate as well.[49]

Although temporarily out of office, Nuri made one more effort before the conference to alter the emerging inter-Arab patterns. He again pressed the Syrians and Lebanese to coordinate their positions with Iraq but succeeded only in annoying the Syrians, the Lebanese Maronites, ʿAbdallah, and Egypt.

The drive for some type of Arab cooperation over the previous eighteen months had not possessed any aura of irresistible momentum, nor had it been the result of broad-based ideological pressure. The competition between Egypt and Iraq for Arab leadership had more to do with the concrete specific calculations of small groups of decision makers, and the whole thrust toward closer Arab ties seemed quite shaky. Still, on September 25, 1944, the Preparatory Committee of the General Arab Conference convened in Alexandria, a noteworthy event in and of itself. Five governments—Egypt, Iraq, Transjordan, Syria, and Lebanon—were represented by their respective prime ministers, indicating the importance they attached to the meetings.

Less auspicious was the complete Saudi absence. But with the conference already under way, Ibn Saʿud chose not to be left behind; on October 1, at the third session, Yusuf Yasin took his seat as the Saudi representative. Yemen's representative was present from the second meeting on as an observer only, and was accredited as a delegate by Imam Yahya only for the final meeting. But because of Yemen's physical and political remoteness from the rest, its involvement in inter-Arab activities, or lack thereof, had little practical value. This changed only in the 1960s. The Palestinian Arabs were represented at the meetings by Musa al-ʿAlami, although not as an equal participant.

On October 7, the representatives of Egypt, Iraq, Syria, Transjordan, and Lebanon signed what came to be known as the Alexandria Protocol. The Saudis and Yemenis acceded to it in January and February 1945, respectively. Basically, it was a statement of intentions, with the details to be worked out by a subsidiary committee. The Protocol envisaged the establishment of a League of Arab States, which was intended to deepen the cooperation and coordination among themselves in the political, economic, social, and cultural spheres, and to "protect their independence and sovereignty against every aggression by suitable means." It also expressed the hope that further steps toward even closer ties would be taken in the future. In addition, the Protocol included two "special resolutions": on Lebanon, emphasizing the signatories' respect of its "independence and sovereignty . . . within its present frontiers"; and on Palestine, emphasizing their support for the Arab cause there.[50]

However vague and preliminary in nature, the Protocol was a major achievement for Nahhas.[51] But Nahhas' enjoyment of his success was short-lived: He was dismissed from office the next day by Faruq. Nonetheless, his successors remained committed to the thrust of his Arab policies. Accordingly, Egypt's new preeminence in Arab affairs was further confirmed during the following months, and movement toward a more definitive polarization of the Arab world into Hashimite and anti-Hashimite blocs also occurred. Ibn Saʿud, concerned over Iraq's intentions, drew closer to Egypt and pulled Syria and Lebanon with him. Faruq's meeting with Ibn Saʿud at the Saudi port of Yanbuʿ in January 1945, made possible by a real improvement in their personal relations, symbolized the consolidation of their ties. This was followed by Shukri al-Quwwatli's visits to both Saudi Arabia and Egypt, with the Syrians adjusting their position on the desired degree of Arab cooperation to Saudi Arabia's. In response, Nuri al-Saʿid and ʿAbd al-Ilah called on ʿAbdallah, on February 5, to coordinate positions.[52]

Followup meetings were held in Cairo in February and March 1945, resulting in the drafting and signing of the Pact of the League of Arab States on March 22. In the Alexandria talks, the Iraqis had advocated the maximum amount of cooperation possible short of a central government, to be embodied by a League Council with considerable powers, particularly in mediating and arbitrating disputes among members. Four months later, however, Baghdad reversed its stand, as it was now apparent that the Council would be dominated by Egypt.

With the help in part of Iraq's position, ARTICLE 5 of the League's charter granted the Council considerably less scope and power to settle inter-Arab disputes.[53] The Iraqis also tried to limit Egyptian dominance in another way, opposing, albeit unsuccessfully, the appointment of Egypt's ʿAbd al-Rahman ʿAzzam Pasha as the first secretary-general of the League. In general, though, Iraq was unwilling to challenge Egypt more drastically, something that would repeat itself on a number of occasions after 1945.[54] Ironically, it was the Saudis—finally convinced that the Egyptians were no more interested than themselves in real Arab unity—who now favored compulsory arbitration by the Council in case of disputes between members. They also pushed unsuccessfully for the conclusion of treaties of alliance for mutual assistance in cases of aggression from within the system.

The Pact of the League of Arab States (*mithaq jamiʿat al-duwal al-ʿarabiyya*) was signed initially by six of the seven participants, with the Yemenis acceding to it two months hence. On that same day, May 19, the League officially came into being, with Cairo its permanent location, following the Pact's ratification by four of the seven founders. The Arab states had formed an association whose object, according to ARTICLE 2, was to strengthen the ties among the participant states, to coordinate their political programs in such a way as to effect real collaboration among them, to preserve their independence and sovereignty, and to consider in general the affairs and interests of the Arab countries. This collaboration was to extend to social, economic, financial, cultural, consular, and communications spheres as well.

The participants themselves were not overly enthralled by what they had wrought.[55] Moreover, the new arrangement was a far cry from the unity ideal championed by Arab nationalist ideology, as evidenced by the criticism of the pact by pan-Arab elements in Syria and Iraq and by the Egyptian Wafd.[56] Even the vaguely worded Alexandria Protocol held out greater hope for a more powerful, united Arab world than the resulting pact.[57] The pact's limitations were illustrated by ARTICLE 7: Unanimous Council decisions would be binding on all members, while majority decisions were to be "binding only upon those states which have accepted them." In practice, this meant that without a consensus on a particular issue, a Council decision stood little likelihood of being implemented, particularly if the recalcitrant parties had the effective means to oppose it.

Still, creation of the Arab League was a milestone in Arab affairs, for it brought about the formal acceptance by all the members of each others' "independence and sovereignty" (ARTICLE 2). This was reinforced by each state's pledge to "respect the existing regime[s] in the other League States," as it was a "(fundamental) right of those states." Thereafter, no League member would "undertake any action" to alter other regimes (ARTICLE 8). In other words, the status quo in Arab politics had been formally and officially legitimized. Only ARTICLE 9 offered a loophole for those (i.e., the Hashimites) who desired further unity efforts, stipulating that member states "desirous of closer collaboration with each other and [of] stronger ties than those specified by this Covenant have a right to conclude such agreements between themselves towards the realization of these efforts as they desire."[58] The League's creation had immediate value as well: It shored up the position of Syria and Lebanon vis-à-vis the French, who were still engaged in desultory efforts to reestablish their prewar preeminence in the Levant.

However vague and varied in importance to the member states, the new framework for inter-Arab cooperation was significant simply by virtue of its creation. As an established fact, it became an address to which Arab political leaders could turn in order to bolster their own regional standing. It also became a place where they in turn could be held accountable by both their opponents and public opinion. This is related to one of the central paradoxes of the system, which occurred around 1945. At that time, Arab politics within and between the various entities was being conducted by extremely narrow elite groupings, concerned first and foremost with safeguarding and then maximizing their own particular interests, whether personal or political. (They usually viewed the two as synonymous.) It was some distance from the Ottoman Empire's "politics of notables" but was far from being a politics of mass movements.[59]

On the other hand, as has been suggested by Albert Hourani, the common Ottoman links of many of the League's founders perhaps provided a psychological underpinning, based on their memories of a lost imperial grandeur, for their vision of Arab unity.[60] The details of this vision were fuzzy, but the sense of entitlement was considerable.

Concurrently, Arab politicians could not ignore the existence of an increasingly politicized, though still numerically small, Arab public opinion, which was schooled in the tenets of Arab nationalist ideology and not hesitant about communicating its views, usually via the only avenue available, the street. Thus, Arab political leaders tended to couch their policies, however narrow or particularist in intent, in terms of the interests of the Arab nation as a whole. Too often, the result was a paralysis in decision making, or alternatively, an appeal to the lowest common denominator, something that tended to limit the decision maker's options and militate against anything approaching statesmanship.

In historical terms, 1945 marked a watershed in Arab affairs. The contrast between the post–World War I Mandate arrangements and the emergence in 1945 of a league of seven independent Arab states formally committed to advancing inter-Arab cooperation is striking. Nonetheless, the Arab League's creation marked the confluence of certain forces at a certain point in time, and no more. Furthermore, two of the three main immediate reasons for the League's creation quickly ceased to be of overriding concern: Preventing the French from reasserting themselves in the Levant was a dead issue by early 1946, and the Hashimite countries soon indicated that the League's creation had not put an end to their efforts to promote closer inter-Arab ties. At the same time, the Palestine issue remained a subject demanding some kind of collective Arab action.

One astute observer of regional politics has written that the peoples of the Middle East, chiefly the Arabs, inherited from Europe the *structure* of the state and the *idea* of the nation, generating a grim struggle between the two poles.[61] Still, the intensity of this struggle could not have been fully apparent in 1945. The Arab state system at its moment of birth was not only low in the level of "stateness" but also relatively low in the level of "nationhood." Despite the sensitivity of Arab leaders to public opinion—particularly on the issues of Palestine and on relations with Britain and France—and despite Arab successes during the previous decade and an ever-widening acceptance of pan-Arab ideology, there existed in 1945 no great public thrust for any union or cooperative schemes. As Clifford Geertz has shown, the reduction of primordial sentiments—loyalties to subnational foci of identification such as family, clan, and tribe—is rendered more difficult by the fact that political modernization, epitomized by the creation of the state, actually stimulates primordial sentiments, at least initially. These factors still play an important part of Arab political life in the 1990s.

In 1945, what Geertz calls the "integrative revolution," namely the efforts to aggregate and eventually transform primordial sentiments into the basis for a civil society, was only in its infancy.[62] Neither pure Arab nationalism nor any synthesis of Arab and territorial nationalisms had found a way to subordinate these deep-rooted sentiments and, in fact, partially reinforce them.

Thus, the newly emergent Arab state system, having reached an important milestone, possessed only the barest minimum in the way of guideposts regarding the future relations between its members. Moreover, there existed very little basis for the kinds of functional cooperation that so often serves as the basis for forging more intimate links between sovereign states. Arab League members in 1945 were most definitely not moving toward greater economic integration. This was evidenced in the evolving patterns of inter-Arab trade. In 1930, there still existed a semblance of a regional market in the Near East, inherited from Ottoman times, with inter-Arab trade constituting a substantial portion of the total trade of most countries. Even then, the market did not act as a nourisher of development, that is, a "highway of learning" as in Japan.[63] The regional market was substantially reduced during the 1930s by the worldwide depression and by the assertion of nationalist economic policies by Arab countries in such realms as tariffs, trade, and finance.[64]

The creation by the allies of the Middle East Supply Center during World War II brought a momentary halt to disintegrative trends, with inter-Arab trade and total industrial output considerably boosted. The increases and changes in the inter-Arab trade were not, however, as significant as the figures appear, owing to inflation and the small number of items involved. In any case, as controls were relaxed toward the end of the war, Arab countries quickly began to revert to prewar patterns.[65] With few exceptions, economic developments during the Mandate years strengthened the *wataniyya* tendencies in each Arab state, in contradiction to the tenets of Arab nationalism. Thus, at the dawn of the postwar era, the obstacles in the path of greater inter-Arab cooperation were not only political but economic.

2

THE FORMATIVE YEARS, 1945–1947

As World War II drew to a close, Arab leaders and the elites who underpinned their rule seemed to have some cause for optimism. After all, they had survived the war with their positions intact. Moreover, regional and international configurations now provided opportunities that had not previously existed. For the non-Hashimite countries, in particular, the new Arab League was a useful framework. Ironically, having been midwifed by the Wafd's Nahhas Pasha, Egypt's King Faruq and the non-Wafd politicians could now use the League as a vehicle to promote their interests vis-à-vis their domestic rivals, Arab competitors, and Great Britain. Syria and Lebanon hoped the League would help drive the final nail in the coffin of French rule. Together with Saudi Arabia, they also saw the League as an insurance policy against Hashimite ambitions. Conversely, neither Iraqi nor Transjordani officials thought that the regional status quo was irrevocable, nor that their ambitions were unattainable.

The ebb and flow of inter-Arab relations from the onset of the League in March 1945 to the autumn of 1947 revolved around four central issues. Two of these were purely "Arab," involving Hashimite unwillingness to accept the status quo: 'Abdallah's renewed promotion of his Greater Syria plan in the face of widespread opposition from his neighbors, and Iraq's unhappiness with the character and activities of the Cairo-centered Arab League. The third, which in part overlapped with the second, centered on Egypt's efforts to mobilize Arab support behind it in its bitter dispute with Great Britain over the future of the Suez Canal and the Sudan. The fourth was a prime all-Arab concern and a matter for mutual suspicion and rivalry: the question of Palestine, whose future political status was about to be determined. The salience of each issue varied over time, and from state to state. Nonetheless, their intertwining complicated further the chances of achieving an operative Arab consensus, much less a favorable resolution, on any one of them. 'Abdallah's and Iraq's ambitions continued to be more than a nuisance to the non-Hashimite majority. Anglo-Egyptian relations continued to be poisoned by their dispute, a malady that reverberated throughout inter-Arab and Arab-British relations. As for Palestine, the gap between collective proclamations and operative divisions became increasingly debilitating as time went on. Taken together, the result was the maintenance of an uneasy but durable inter-Arab balance of power, which reinforced the nonmonolithic, pluralist nature of regional Arab politics.

The first challenge to an Arab state's independence, and, by implication, to the League as an organization of sovereign, independent states, came from another direction. On May 7, 1945, French reinforcements landed in Beirut, inaugurating the last phase of France's losing wartime struggle to preserve its former preeminence in the Levant.[1] The ensuing clashes with Syrian nationalists led to France's shelling of Damascus on May 29 and 30. Despite hints of Egyptian and Iraqi military support, neither the League as a body nor any of the members individually were in a position to render material backing to Syria and Lebanon against the French.[2] What they did do was muster diplomatic and public pressure. For the moment, existing inter-Arab rivalries were laid aside.[3]

The end to the crisis came on June 1, with Britain's reluctant military (albeit bloodless) intervention and the retirement of French forces from most of the principal Syrian towns to their barracks. One of the prime motivations of the British cabinet's decision to intervene was to avoid leaving the Arab world with the impression that Britain had done nothing to assist Syria and Lebanon against French aggression.[4] Thus, Great Britain indicated its intention to work with, and not against, the predominant regional forces in order to preserve British strategic interests. By definition, this also encompassed a willingness to view sympathetically the activities of the newly formed Arab League—the collective embodiment of Arab aspirations.[5]

Britain's quelling of the crisis in favor of Syria and Lebanon obviated the need for more than oral action by the League. Thus, from June 4 through 7, the League Council was able to convene its very first meeting to discuss the crisis secure in the knowledge that the die had already been cast in their favor (notwithstanding later Arab claims regarding the effectiveness of "secret resolutions.")[6] Expressions of gratitude toward Britain, rare in the subsequent annals of Arab League forums, and condemnations of the French were repeated throughout the session. The Council's final communiqué demanded the "immediate withdrawal of all French forces in the Levant" and the transfer of the *Troupes Speciáles* (the French-run local military units) to the local governments. It also emphasized the "identity of the aims of the League and of the two Arab republics." This communiqué was followed on June 21 by a Syrian-Lebanese joint communiqué stating that they would implement the Council's decisions.[7]

The official acknowledgment by Syria and Lebanon of the League's authority raised at least the theoretical possibility that the League possessed some measure of supranational status. In fact, however, Arab leaders had no more intention of conferring any independent executive powers on the League than they had during the 1943–1944 deliberations. Nonetheless, the high-profile, peripatetic efforts of League Secretary-General ʿAzzam Pasha to carve out a role for himself as *the* spokesman for a collective Arab position almost immediately caused alarm bells to sound in Iraq.[8]

The matter was not only procedural. ʿAzzam's utterances nearly always dovetailed with Egypt's regional policies. For example, on January 4, 1946, ʿAzzam declared that the Arab League would demand that all foreign troops leave all Arab states. The Iraqi government, favoring continued close military cooperation with Britain, privately took umbrage with ʿAzzam's Egyptian orientation.[9] ʿAzzam's actions further confirmed what had been evident in October 1944 at Alexandria: The League's underlying character and its approach to particular issues would be decisively shaped from Cairo, and the other Arab capitals would have to adjust accordingly, one way or another.

Manifestations of Egyptian-Iraqi sparring over the League occured during the following months. The result was a further, if still partial, solidification of the Arab world into two competing blocs, a dominant "status quo" Egyptian-Saudi-Syrian grouping and a weaker "revisionist" Iraqi-Transjordanian Hashimite one. Interests within each of the groupings were far from identical. Moreover, both Egyptian and Iraqi policies were subject to vicissitudes stemming from frequent changes in leadership, which in turn led to changes in tactical orientation. Finally, dialogue with the other camp, whether for tactical or strategic considerations, never ceased, with each side refraining from taking steps that might cause the other to believe that a significant alteration in the Arab balance of power was being sought.

The initial stress signs appeared at the close of 1945. In early December, Nuri al-Sa'id threatened to depart from a League Council meeting and to induce Iraq, and perhaps Transjordan, to withdraw from the League altogether, due to the monopolization of the League by 'Azzam and by Egypt.[10] Nuri's stand was rejected by Prime Minister Hamdi al-Pachachi, but he would return to it in subsequent months.[11] In the meantime, the combination of growing Hashimite frustration with the League's modus operandi and the fact that the respective plans for aggrandizement of Iraq and Transjordan had already placed them at odds with the other Arab states, led them to examine the possibility of forging closer ties with each other.[12]

Such a development was not welcomed in the non-Hashimite camp. In an indication of their concern, Ibn Sa'ud paid an official call on Egypt's Faruq in late January 1946, after which they issued a joint declaration proclaiming the inviolable Arab character of Palestine.[13] Formally, the visit was a return of Faruq's journey to Yanbu' one year earlier. More importantly, it indicated Saudi Arabia's desire to reinforce the regional status quo.[14] Ibn Sa'ud deliberately chose to mask his concern while in Cairo by making a conciliatory statement toward 'Abdallah. 'Abdallah replied in a similar vein.[15]

In fact, these soothings counted for little. The Iraqis and Transjordanians conducted a flurry of high-level exchanges during February 1946, including journeys by 'Abd al-Ilah and Nuri to Amman and by Transjordan's Crown Prince Talal to Baghdad. Once again, the possibility of the breakup of the League was raised, this time by Iraq and Transjordan.[16]

Concurrently, Nuri demonstrated his belief that the Arab world was by itself not an adequate arena for strengthening regional defense and cooperation. On February 2, he paid an official visit to Turkey to promote closer ties. One month later, Nuri initialed a friendship treaty with Ankara, in which the two countries pledged "mutual consultation in foreign affairs, the settlement of disputes by peaceful means and cooperation in regional matters within the framework of the United Nations."[17] The treaty aroused a good deal of opposition at home, with many Iraqis seeing it at odds with Iraq's commitments to the Arab League.[18] Moreover, the fact that Iraq seemed to be legitimizing Turkey's 1939 annexation of the Alexandretta district from Syria left it open to charges of infidelity to Arab ideals. For the government's opponents inside and outside of parliament, Alexandretta became an all-Arab stick with which they could flay the government. In view of the controversy it aroused, the treaty was not ratified until April 1947.[19]

One prominent historian of Iraq claims that the Iraqi-Turkish diplomatic moves were initiated by Ankara, not Baghdad.[20] Regardless of whether this was so, the concept of strengthening the links between the Arab Fertile Crescent and Turkey was consistent with Nuri's general conceptions of an Arab world organized along more localized, geographic lines and of the need for formal multilateral security arrangements, which would include non-Arab regional participants. Nuri's Ottoman background and his own temperament contributed heavily to this view, but so did geopolitical realities. Iraq's proximity to the Soviet Union was greater than that of any other Arab state. Thus, Soviet ambitions in Azerbaijan, Kars and Ardahan, and the Bosporus caused the Iraqis considerable concern. Transjordan shared at least some of this outlook and concluded a similar treaty with Turkey in January 1947.

Nuri would have very much liked Syria to follow his lead. Consequently, he stopped in Damascus on his way home from his initial visit to Ankara, in order to explain his intentions regarding the pending Iraqi-Turkish agreement and to present the Syrians with a draft of a similar Iraqi-Syrian accord. Syria's Prime Minister Sa'dallah al-Jabiri told Nuri on February 5, 1946, that his government was in no mood to take any step that might "expose Syria to the suspicions and doubts of any Arab country and of the Arab League."

The minutes of this meeting reveal the basic divergence in the two leaders' attitudes and orientations toward Arab affairs in general, and toward the Arab League in particular. Nuri elaborated at length on Iraq's special position in the Middle East, bound on the one hand to the Arab states through the Arab League Pact, and on the other to Turkey (and Iran) by the Saadabad Pact of 1936. It was natural and vital, Nuri stated, to establish closer ties "among states connected by old ancestral ties" (this was Nuri's Ottoman background coming forth), particularly in the post–World War II era of international cooperation in "all phases of life—economic, cultural, medicine, law, engineering, youth, etc." Jabiri could rest assured that he desired to act not at the expense of the Arab League but along the lines of ARTICLE 2 of the League Charter, which called for closer cooperation among its members. Nonetheless, Nuri continued, he viewed the League from a purely practical point of view. Since its inception, he stated, it had not yet achieved "a single one of its objectives"; Iraq was thus impelled to act swiftly to "preserve its [existence] and to protect its interests."

In response, Jabiri acknowledged Iraq's, and for that matter every Arab country's, right to address its own special problems, such as the division of the Euphrates waters among Turkey, Iraq, and Syria. It was "one of the fundamental aims" of the Arab League, however, that more general, wide-ranging agreements should be concluded among the Arab states first. This was not purely a practical matter, Jabiri told Nuri. The League, "of which Your Excellency was the real creator,"*[sic]* should be regarded "from a sentimental angle as well."

Sentiment apart, Jabiri was acutely conscious of what the Egyptian reaction would be and pressed Nuri to include Egypt as well. Nuri's reply was frank: "I fear that my proposals may be hindered if I advance them to Egypt." In fact, he informed Jabiri that he had already tried in July 1940 to conclude a Turkish-Iraqi-Egyptian agreement, but Egypt had never given it further consideration, as it had promised it would.

In the end, Nuri agreed to ask the incoming Iraqi cabinet to submit his proposals to the other Arab states, as long as their collective acceptance was not a prior condition for concluding bilateral pacts. Regarding Syria specifically, he submitted to Jabiri a draft agreement on irrigation. As for the Iraqi-Turkish proposals, he pledged to submit them to Syria for study as soon as they were in their final form.[21]

The following month, in March 1946, the Arab League Council convened in Cairo. All parties were uneasy with the directions that inter-Arab affairs had gone. They thus avoided needless posturing and also shelved the question of Hashimite withdrawal from the League. Consequently, the celebration of the first anniversary of the League was held in a festive atmosphere.[22]

Perhaps the most pertinent aspects of the gathering were the number of manifestations of an emerging pattern of behavior in Arab League forums that stemmed from the League's serving as an arena for inter-Arab rivalry and competition. They included the raising of nonserious proposals, in this case Faruq's suggestion to establish a common Arab citizenship designed to remove customs and passport restrictions between Arab states;[23] the emphasis on "secret resolutions" and the tendency toward unjustified credit-taking, both of which underlay the League secretariat's extravagant claims that its secret resolutions in June 1945 had been the "main factors" in solving the crisis with France;[24] and "outbidding," or the fear of it, and the overall hyperbole of "unified action," which was deemed so important in presenting the League's activities to the Arab public.

Notwithstanding the positive atmosphere engendered by the League's anniversary session, inter-Arab differences remained close to the surface. The Anglo-Transjordanian Treaty of Alliance of March 22, 1946, under which Transjordan achieved independence, was looked upon critically from a number of Arab quarters. Foremost among their stated reasons was its confirmation of Great Britain's military presence in Transjordan.[25] The Egyptian and Lebanese governments initially held back from issuing congratulatory messages; the Lebanese also made a desultory effort to forestall an official congratulation from the Arab League because Transjordan had not submitted the text of the treaty to League scrutiny.[26] In addition, Egypt boycotted 'Abdallah's May 25 coronation ceremony as king of Transjordan. That same day, Syria went one step further and closed its borders with Transjordan for twenty-four hours. It also declined to send any official delegation from Damascus and rigorously enforced exit permit regulations during the immediately preceding days, fearing that the presence either of any important Syrian dignitaries or large numbers of ordinary Syrians would be used by Transjordan to promote its Greater Syria plan.[27]

Not surprisingly, Ibn Sa'ud felt that Great Britain had been hasty in granting independence to Transjordan and that London had neglected his interests (a reference to the desert *wadi* previously used by Saudi tribes to cross into Syria that was now under Transjordanian control).[28] Moreover, the Saudis were nervous about a projected Iraqi-Transjordanian agreement, a draft of which was circulating at the end of May 1946.[29] Underpinning much of the Saudi-Hashimite mutual hostility was the legacy of the Hashimite expulsion from the Hejaz by the Saudis twenty years earlier. On this point, the Saudis were further angered by the concurrent publication of 'Abdallah's memoirs, in which he declared that the central problem for all the Muslim world was that the Kingdom of the Hejaz was still attached to the Najd. 'Abdallah also scalded the ruling Saudi dynasty as a "fanatic minority" (al-aqalliyya al-muta'assiba), which has contributed nothing to Islam, either in the past or present.[30] At the same time, the Saudis were not above advancing their own territorial claims on Ma'an and Aqaba in Transjordan, another of the unresolved matters of the post–World War I settlement.[31]

It was at this juncture that the Palestine question and British-Egyptian differences exacerbated existing Arab divisions, further complicating the calculations of Arab decision makers. One immediate consequence was that it gave Egypt a more direct stake in exercising a leadership role in the region and in cultivating Arab allies. Ironically, this occurred partly during the tenure of Isma'il Sidqi Pasha, who was the strongest advocate for minimizing Egypt's Arab links of any Egyptian prime minister of the postwar period.

The Palestine question was first "regionalized" in 1936. In 1945, the Arab League Charter included a special annex on Palestine, conferring on Council members the authority to designate a Palestinian Arab representative to take part in the League's activities (but not as a voting member) until independence could be fully exercised. Once the issue of France's postwar status in the Levant was settled, the Palestine issue became the all-Arab issue confronting the entire system, and the League devoted the overwhelming majority of its formal deliberations to it.

The gap between the real feelings of Arab solidarity over the basics of the Palestine issue and the difficulty of developing an operative consensus on how to go about saving Palestine had already begun to bedevil the Arab states from the mid-1930s. This did not, however, result in total paralysis. Every so often, they were able to present a common front.[32] Joint diplomatic meetings with and demarches to United States and British officials were designed to give the impression that the Arab states were of one mind on Palestine. So was an agreement to speak with one voice (that of 'Azzam Pasha) before the Anglo-American Commission of Inquiry in March 1946.[33]

As for British-Egyptian differences, Egypt's demand to replace the treaty was first made on September 23, 1945, and acceded to by Great Britain on January 25, 1946. Throughout the month of April 1946, numerous informal British-Egyptian contacts were held on the future of their bilateral military and political relations and of the Sudan. On May 7, Great Britain officially declared its agreement in principle to withdraw its forces from Egyptian territory, and on May 9, in an atmosphere of simultaneous tension and expectation, formal talks commenced. On May 22, however, they were suspended in a welter of mutual recriminations.

Concurrently, on May 1, the Anglo-American Commission of Inquiry report on Palestine recommending the immediate admittance of 100,000 Jewish refugees into Palestine was made public, occasioning widespread Arab protests on popular and official levels.

INSHAS AND BLUDAN

In the wake of this confluence of events, Egypt's King Faruq was able to carry out an idea that had been percolating in Egyptian circles for some time. On May 28 and 29, he convened the first official meeting of Arab heads of state, at his Inshas estate near Cairo.[34] In doing so, he signaled his rivals both abroad and at home that he intended personally to play a leading role in shaping the future of the region. To further drive the point home, Faruq acted without first consulting his government.[35] This was neither the first nor the last time that Faruq would exercise his royal prerogatives in such a high-handed fashion. He dismissed Nahhas from the premiership the day after issuing the Alexandria Protocol in October 1944. In May 1948, he bucked the wishes of his government again, leaving his singular imprint on collective Arab policy in regard to the Palestine question.

Not all Arab heads of state actually attended the Inshas summit: Ibn Saʻud delegated Faruq to act as his spokesman and dispatched Crown Prince Saʻud to the sessions as an observer.[36] Similarly, the Yemeni imam delegated a personal representative to the meeting. ʻAbd al-Ilah represented Iraq's young King Faysal II, but neither he nor his uncle ʻAbdallah was enthusiastic about the meeting. After all, the meeting's expected call for a British troop withdrawal from Egypt would be more than a little embarrassing, given the fact that British troops also were stationed in their countries. Nonetheless, they could not afford to appear in arrears regarding the Palestine question, which was to be the primary focus of the formal sessions.[37]

The gathering took place outside of the Arab League's official framework. It was agreed, however, that the final statement of the conference was to be issued through the secretary-general of the League, who was also present at the sessions, and that the deliberations would officially serve as guidance for an upcoming extraordinary League Council session in Bludan, Syria, on the Palestine question. Nonetheless, the very convening of the summit illustrated the limitations of the League's year-old institutions.[38]

The final statement issued at Inshas had a decidedly general, even bland, character. On Palestine, the operative decision was a rejection of the Anglo-American Commission's recommendation on immigration because it violated the limitations imposed by the British government's 1939 White Paper on Palestine, "to which Britain was honor bound." On British-Egyptian differences, the statement was confined to proclaiming that the Egyptian cause was one common to all Arabs, and that therefore the summit participants supported Egypt's "rightful demands." At the same time, they took care to express their pleasure at Britain's agreement in principle to withdraw its forces from Egyptian territory, hoping that this would presage the beginning of a "new era" in Anglo-Egyptian relations."[39]

The communiqué's blandness belied the considerable disagreement that occurred privately and in the public sessions. On the Palestine issue, Quwwatli and Faruq led the way in declarations of steadfastness. According to ʿAbdallah, Faruq quoted Ibn Saʿud, for whom he officially had the right to speak, as saying that he and his sons would shed their blood in defense of Palestine. ʿAbdallah was deprecating in reply, noting that they were now living in "the age of atom bombs and air raids," not of Saladin and the Crusades.[40] Instead, he declared, the Arabs should concentrate on developing and strengthening a fund for the preservation of Arab lands.[41]

No less central to the summit was the Anglo-Egyptian question. On the official level, the Egyptian leadership made sure to enter the matter on the agenda in order to obtain the desired endorsement of their position.[42] Informally, both Sidqi Pasha and Faruq explained that the reason behind Egypt's refusal to be more flexible in the talks was the acute political and public opinion constraints under which they were operating. To Nuri al-Sa'id, who accompanied 'Abd al-Ilah to Cairo (but not to the official meetings), Sidqi emphasized that only the most general sort of Anglo-Egyptian treaty, which would leave all of the details to be worked out later, could wash with the Egyptian public.[43] Sidqi and Faruq asked for 'Abdallah's trust, acknowledging at the same time that Great Britain offered the only realistic bulwark against Soviet expansionism. Furthermore, Sidqi entreated 'Abdallah to intercede with Britain in the negotiations.[44]

Nuri left Inshas both depressed and angry with the Egyptians for "trying to get 100 percent and not give 1 percent." The impasse reinforced in his mind the need to consolidate the "kernel" of the region, the Fertile Crescent, in order to defend it against the "danger from the North." That emphasizing Iraq's role in consolidating a defense line against the Soviets would ring nicely in British ears was not lost on him. Still, it remained an authentic reflection of Nuri's geopolitical outlook.

Regarding its effect on the Arab system, Iraq's application of the "kernel" approach would involve, by definition, a deemphasis on the Arab League, in that it stressed the more local, geographic aspects of Arab cooperation, and that it was not even a purely Arab vision. Concerning the impact this might have on Saudi-Hashimite relations, Nuri dismissed Ibn Sa'ud's "groundless . . . personal fears and jealousies." Egypt, on the other hand, caused more concern. The possible impact of the "kernel" approach on Egypt's regional role and on Egyptian-Iraqi relations was not at all clear to Nuri.[45]

'Abdallah, in contrast, left Inshas feeling himself to be in an improved position, for his relations with the non-Hashimite bloc were less chilly. Sidqi's request for intercession with Britain seemed to him to be advantageous. (Subsequently, his tentative mediation efforts came to nought.)[46] His interactions with Crown Prince Sa'ud had been cordial, to the point that 'Abdallah even invited him to stop in Amman on the way home (he declined).[47] Finally, notwithstanding the ringing declarations of devotion to the cause of Palestine from Quwwatli, Faruq, and the Saudis, 'Abdallah detected no resoluteness on the Palestine issue that might interfere with his own projected plans to expand his kingdom's domains westward across the Jordan River, in one form or another. While preferring in 1946 to actively participate in the various British federal or cantonment plans for Palestine, ʿAbdallah was developing the fallback position of accepting some form of partition and Transjordan's annexing of the adjacent Arab part of western Palestine. This desire was integral, not an alternative, to ʿAbdallah's long-standing Greater Syria plans. The flexibility in the stages of its implementation derived from a concern with the possibilities of the moment.[48]

One week later, from June 8 to 12, 1946, the Arab League Council met in Bludan, Syria. The debates and resulting resolutions considerably sharpened the collective Arab positions on the Palestine and Anglo-Egyptian questions. But an operative consensus was not achieved on either issue.

The Palestine question occupied, *de rigeur*, the bulk of the discussions. Three distinct Arab positions were discernible. "Pseudo-interventionist" Iraq militantly championed immediate action against Britain and the United States, including boycott measures. Its actions were underpinned, as always, by domestic motivations, and in the case of the boycott call, by a desire to embarrass the Saudis. For their parts, Egypt and Saudi Arabia held that Arab policies should conform with their limited capabilities. Finally, Syria and Transjordan, despite their opposing strategic objectives, held more activist approaches than Egypt and Saudi Arabia, tempered by their counseling of patience until after the British withdrawal.[49]

On ʿAzzam Pasha's suggestion, the Council reached a consensus on a number of steps to be taken. These included (1) the reconstitution of an expanded, Mufti-dominated Arab Higher Committee, (2) the pledging of measures to tighten the Arab boycott of Zionist goods and to forestall the selling of land to the Jews, and most importantly, (3) the adoption of "secret" resolutions that no new economic concessions were to be granted to Great Britain and the United States, and that the withdrawal of existing concessions would be considered were they to attempt to implement the Anglo-American Commission proposals.[50] These were intermediate steps that were disparaged as such by Iraq's Foreign Minister Fadil al-Jamali, who at the conclusion of the conference declared his intention to recommend that his government retain its freedom of action toward the Palestine problem.[51] Still, in the words of one historian, the Bludan conference proved to be, without the participants knowing it, "a first step towards the 1948 war."⁵²

By contrast, it had not been certain that the Anglo-Egyptian dispute would even come up for discussion at Bludan. The Egyptians took advantage of the gathering to lobby for further political backing against Great Britain.⁵³ The result was that the Council members went considerably beyond the Inshas statement in declaring their "full support for Egypt's national aspirations," the complete evacuation of British troops, and, most significant for Egypt, "the unity of the Nile Valley." Furthermore, they conditioned their future relations with Great Britain on the full satisfaction of Egyptian demands "in such a manner as to guarantee to Egypt and [the] Arab countries the international position they deserve."⁵⁴ This point was reiterated with a flourish by ʿAzzam at a June 27 press conference, in which he also shed light on Egyptian thinking regarding the relationship between Egypt's particular bilateral dispute and its relationship to the Arab system. "The cause of Egypt," he said, "is the one which is at present preoccupying the Arab nations. Everything else is secondary. The existence of the Arab League depends on the achievement of Egypt's independence. In this way the League's edifice can be completed."⁵⁵

Notwithstanding ʿAzzam's claim that Arab governments were united on this position, most remained uncomfortable with a straightforward anti-British posture, but they felt powerless to modify it. In more unguarded or frustrated moods, ʿAbdallah could privately declare that the real answer for Transjordan was to withdraw from the League and thus regain its freedom of action.⁵⁶ Lacking clear signals of approval from London, however (which would have meant a fundamental reorientation of British policy), this remained purely in the realm of "letting off steam."

ʿABDALLAH'S GREATER SYRIA MANEUVERS

The absence of British backing on inter-Arab issues did not prevent ʿAbdallah in the following months from reviving plans that, if implemented, would have decisively altered the regional balance of power. For one, he raised the possibility of developing closer ties with Iraq. These were envisaged as entailing both the retention of independence for each party, and the pursuit of common foreign, defense, and financial policies. Diplomatic representation abroad was to be pooled; moreover, the Hashimite flag of the Hejaz was to be flown alongside their respective flags.[57] Most important for ʿAbdallah was the effect this plan would have on Syria: One senior aide expected Syria to fall into line within six months of its implementation.[58]

The lack of immediate progress with Iraq did not deter ʿAbdallah from continuing to pursue his Syrian ambitions. Periodically, he issued declarations of intent, as he continued to search for political support within Syria.

ʿAbdallah was not totally persona non grata there. At various times during 1946 and 1947, many of the regime's opponents, including elements of the *ulama*, small landowners, Christian minorities, the Druze, and tribal groups, thought that support for ʿAbdallah might enhance their own standing. ʿAbdallah periodically dispatched emissaries to Syria and Lebanon to test the political waters and to dole out sums to supporters.[59] On the other hand, he was either unwilling or unable to take real risks in support of his dream. To be sure, the ground in Syria was not fertile. Opposition elements never jelled into any kind of coherent backing for ʿAbdallah. Moreover, their own conceptions of a Greater Syria often remained obscure or at variance with ʿAbdallah's. An apt illustration of his hesitation was his rebuff to the Atrash faction of the Syrian Druze, who in the summer of 1947 sought arms and money from him for a revolt against the central government in Damascus. Part of their efforts included suggesting the incorporation of Jabal Druze into Transjordan, but ʿAbdallah was skeptical as to their capabilities and intentions, and thus held back.[60]

In September and October 1946, the anti-Hashimite press in Syria engaged in a vitriolic, government-supported campaign against ʿAbdallah for his coveting of both Syria and Palestine. Neither ʿAbdallah's ambitions, his links with Britain, his personal life, nor the alleged illegitimacy of Transjordan was spared.[61] Undeterred, ʿAbdallah launched a new broadside of his own, on the occasion of his November 11 speech from the throne at the opening of the Transjordanian Parliament's regular session. Disclaiming any personal ambitions, he reiterated however that the historical ties between Syria and Transjordan, his own long-standing interest in Syria's struggle for independence, and the pressing need for regional stability all necessitated the early attainment of unification between the two countries.⁶²

'Abdallah's speech marked the beginning of a new round of inter-Arab polemics on Greater Syria. The first response came two days later from Lebanon's foreign minister, Phillipe Takla. "Such illusory plans," he said, "explicitly conflict with the Arab League Pact." His Jordanian counterpart, Muhammad al-Shurayki, promptly responded that ARTICLE 9 of the Pact legitimized any efforts to achieve a greater degree of unity, and that the calls for unity served as a "decisive reply to those who want us to acquiesce absolutely to the partition of our dear homeland."⁶³ Shurayki allowed that the inclusion of Lebanon was for the Lebanese people themselves to decide. Shortly afterward, however, he angered the Lebanese even further by declaring that Lebanon had been artificially enlarged in 1920 by the incorporation of Syrian territory into it.⁶⁴

Thanks to a Syrian initiative, and over the vigorous opposition of the Transjordanian delegate, the whole matter was acrimoniously discussed at the Arab League Council's fifth session, held in Cairo on November 26, 1946.⁶⁵

Egypt's concern was, as always, to preserve the Arab status quo under its leadership. Thus, both its new prime minister, Ibrahim 'Abd al-Hadi Pasha, and Faruq worked to dampen the emotions that had been triggered. Both of them, the former during the Council debates, and the latter in a number of tête-à-têtes at the palace stressed the importance of maintaining the League's capability to function smoothly.

The debate concluded with a unanimously approved council statement issued on November 28, which contained something for everyone. It reaffirmed the members' adherence to the League Charter, particularly their agreement not to dispute each other's independence and sovereignty (an implied rebuff to 'Abdallah) nor to attack the existing governmental regimes (which applied to all sides). In addition, it was agreed that the Greater Syria issue should not be further discussed by the League in accordance with Transjordan's previous opposition to League involvement.⁶⁶ The resolution did little to ease things. Shurayki immediately submitted a note to the secretary-general declaring that his government reserved its point of view on what it regarded as a "national principle, based on our own local interests and national program."⁶⁷

'Abdallah continued to issue periodic pronouncements on

Greater Syria. On May 6, 1947, his Royal *Diwan* issued the *Jordanian White Book (al-Kitab al-Urduni al-Abyad)*, a compilation of documents and exchanges relating to the subject over a thirty-year period. To be sure that the point was not missed, copies were distributed to all the members of the Syrian Parliament. Shortly thereafter, he took two further steps. Encouraged by an erosion of support for the Quwwatli government, as evidenced in the Syrian general elections, 'Abdallah issued his Ramadan Proclamation of August 11, inviting "the regional Syrian governments" jointly to convene a constitutional assembly to lay down a constitution on a union or federative basis for Greater Syria.[68] He followed this up with a letter to Shukri al-Quwwatli on August 14, in which he urged him to "review our present situation . . . the diffusion and separation of our union and a dispersion among the sons of [the] one Arab country."[69]

The mutual mud slinging and polemical exchanges in 1946 and 1947 over Syria highlighted three important features of inter-Arab politics during these years: (1) the intertwining between ideological considerations and political power struggles, (2) the intensely personal nature of Transjordan's policies, and (3) the intimate relationship between domestic, and even intra-elite, politics and foreign policies. Within 'Abdallah's inner circle, the flames for Greater Syria were periodically fanned by Shurayki ('Abdallah's "evil genius," in the words of Britain's chargé d'affaires in Amman, C. M. Pirie-Gordon). As part of his struggle to oust Prime Minister Samir al-Rifa'i, Shurayki consistently adopted a more extreme position on Greater Syria and then attempted to undercut Samir in the eyes of the king for his less-than-total enthusiasm for the project and for his periodic endeavors to smooth out ruffled Arab feathers. Aware of the importance of both of them, 'Abdallah tilted to one, and then the other, according to his desire of the hour. In the end, however, Samir remained within 'Abdallah's inner circle, while Shurayki lost his influence. The irony is obvious. Samir, along with the bulk of the Transjordanian civilian elite, was actually closer in ideology to the stream of Arab nationalism best represented by the Syrian political establishment, a kind of counterversion to Hashimite Arab nationalism. Yet it was precisely Samir and others, most notably Tawfiq Abu al-Huda, who were indispensable to 'Abdallah for the governing of Transjordan.[70]

As for 'Abdallah's "obsession," namely his vision for the Levant, he remained consistent. The Hashimite-led "Great Arab Revolt" (*al-thawra al-'arabiyya al-kubra*) against the Ottomans in World War I conferred on his family, and on him as its senior surviving member, a preeminent status in the Arab national movement. The principles of the revolt, and his family's preeminent status, had been ordained by the General Syrian Congress on March 8, 1920, which had established his brother Faysal as king of a united Syrian state. In his view, they remained the only legitimate basis for political life, unless all the representatives of the "regional governments" of Syria chose to update them (exactly his suggestion). Conceptually, 'Abdallah held fast to the notion of Greater Syria as the core area of the Fertile Crescent, which in turn was one of three geographic components of the Arab world, alongside the Arabian Peninsula and the Nile Valley. In this regard, he did not hesitate to point out the contradiction inherent in his opponents' advocacy of Nile Valley unity and simultaneous rejection of Syrian unity.[71] The continuing division of Syria had been "maliciously planned by foreign imperialism." Those who claimed that it was sanctified by the Arab League Charter, he said, were in fact in violation of it.[72]

This was exactly what 'Abdallah's opponents did say. His Ramadan Proclamation's call for "this false federation," declared Shukri al-Quwwatli, "violated the sacredness of the Arab League Charter . . . by meddling in our affairs." Syria's own republican regime had been ratified a number of times by the populace. By contrast, he continued, it was 'Abdallah's "princely throne," which, having been "detached from the motherland," installed by a foreign mandate and "based on neither constitution nor law," was illegitimate. Thus, if it was a plebiscite that 'Abdallah desired, he was welcome to hold one in Transjordan in order to permit its reunification with Syria under a republican regime.[73]

That was neither the first nor the last time that the Syrians took up the Greater Syria cudgel and reformulated it to place themselves in the controlling position. This must be understood almost solely as a propaganda tactic, however, not as a reflection of policy intentions nor as an attempt to make an additional contribution to Arab nationalist ideology. That was not be the case until the 1970s and 1980s, when the force of pan-Arabism as an ideology had waned, and Syria emerged as a regional power in its own right.[74]

Syria's allies adopted a similar stance regarding 'Abdallah's alleged violation of the League Charter. For example, an official Saudi statement profoundly regretted the "collapse in the Arab League" brought about by 'Abdallah's pronouncements because they were in strict contradiction to the charter's "contents, soul, principles and purposes," and specifically ARTICLE 8.[75] 'Abdallah's repeated declarations raised doubts in Saudi minds about Britain's true intentions. No amount of disclaimers from London could assuage the Saudis for long, and they repeatedly pressed U.S. diplomats to exercise pressure on Britain to declare more forthrightly their opposition to his schemes. They even tried to elicit a U.S. commitment to the Saudis in the event of a military move by 'Abdallah against Syria or Saudi Arabia.[76] Overall, Saudi nervousness on this issue, however exaggerated, provided an accurate barometer of Riyadh's weak and vulnerable status in the region.

For 'Abdallah's rivals, the timing of 'Abdallah's latest move could not have been more disturbing and cast doubt on 'Abdallah's commitment to the principles enshrined in the League Charter. Syrian Prime Minister Jamil Mardam stated it most baldly.

> We oppose the Greater Syria project because we know it is a Zionist project which is connected with the partition plan for Palestine and the establishment of a Jewish state therein. . . . King Abdallah should have considered the critical discussion of the Egyptian question before the Security Council and the Palestine problem which will be discussed soon at the General Assembly, and should have realized that the Arabs should stand all in one rank to face their joint problems.[77]

Many Arab politicians and publicists carried the allegations of coordination between the Zionist movement and 'Abdallah a step further, linking Great Britain to the scheme. This in itself pointed to another of the sensitive spots of Arab nationalists: a continued sense — long after the reality had changed — that outside powers were perpetually conspiring against them. A statement issued on September 2, 1947, by twenty-two Syrian members of Parliament stated their explicit belief that 'Abdallah's Greater Syria project was "aimed to bind Syria and Lebanon, two independent republics, with the same ties which bind Transjordan, and to pave the way for Zionist influence over the country."[78]

In truth, the British representatives in Amman, Sir Alec S. Kirkbride and C. M. Pirie-Gordon, epitomized their government's caught-in-the-middle posture between conflicting Arab forces. Far from actively encouraging ʿAbdallah, they periodically tried to moderate his utterances. These attempts were made with extreme caution in order "not to drive him to some act of folly on the spur of a moment of irritation." More often than not, their attempts to "cool down" both sides were done in conjunction with like-minded Arab politicians, such as the Transjordanian and Iraqi premiers in 1947, Samir al-Rifaʿi and Salih Jabr.[79]

Overall British policy at this juncture was underpinned by a number of interlocking perceptions:

1. A minimum level of inter-Arab harmony was still in Britain's interest;

2. A posture of strict neutrality was the best attitude to take regarding all Arab unity schemes, as long as they were advanced peacefully;

3. For ʿAbdallah, the issue had "ceased to be a policy, and [had] developed into something in the nature of an obsession"; but

4. His periodic statements were considered "relatively harmless," and the outraged reactions in Damascus and Riyadh "filled King Abdallah with impish satisfaction and [did] much to sustain his activities in this matter."[80]

The Syrian government's response to ʿAbdallah was what Stephen Walt calls the "balance of threat" mode, which frequently dominates inter-Arab politics.[81] President Quwwatli immediately dispatched a special envoy, Muhsin al-Barazi, to Ibn Saʿud and Faruq to coordinate stands. Ibn Saʿud, who was no less concerned than the Syrians with ʿAbdallah's ambitions, promised to lobby both London and Washington to restrain him. Faruq, for his part, encouraged Damascus to expose the "Zionist character" of ʿAbdallah's schemes.[82] The Syrians also inquired about Iraq's position, to which a potentially new element had been added some months earlier.

On April 14, 1947, Baghdad and Amman had concluded a treaty of Brotherhood and Alliance between them, "pursuant to the terms of ARTICLE 9 of the Charter of the League of Arab States."[83] The treaty was a much watered-down version of the pact that ʿAbdallah had been seeking the previous year. Initial reaction from both Saudi Arabia

and Syria was extremely negative, in that they feared it signified Iraqi
(and British) backing for ʿAbdallah's Greater Syrian endeavors.[84]

Iraqi leaders had no intention of giving any kind of teeth to the
agreement, which would encourage ʿAbdallah's regional ambitions.
Thus, in September 1947, the Iraqi response to Syrian inquiries regarding ʿAbdallah's Greater Syria moves belied the notion of a united Hashimite front. The Syrian minister to Baghdad was told that the Iraqis
agreed neither with ʿAbdallah's methods nor with the unwarranted
attacks on him by the Syrian media and politicians. In Jamali's view,
they only motivated ʿAbdallah further.[85] The Iraqis followed up on this
by assuming a mediating role between Transjordan and the anti-Hashimite camp. In doing so, they were spurred by their own opposition
to ʿAbdallah's ambitions and their discomfort with the anti-Hashimite
implications of the broadsides being leveled against Transjordan.[86]
This pattern would repeat itself even more acutely in 1950, when
Transjordan was being threatened with expulsion from the League.

More important than Iraqi endeavors in tempering ʿAbdallah,
however, was the fact that the Palestine issue was coming to a head
at the United Nations. On November 3, 1947, ʿAbdallah declared to
the opening session of the Transjordanian Parliament that the Palestine problem now eclipsed all the other issues confronting the Arab
world, which marked the end of this particular phase of ʿAbdallah's
pursuit of a Greater Syria. The acrimony aroused on all sides, however, did not totally dissipate.[87]

THE BRITISH-EGYPTIAN CRISIS AND
THE U.N. SECURITY COUNCIL

Meanwhile, British-Egyptian relations worsened. A draft agreement
drawn up by Sidqi Pasha and Ernest Bevin in October 1946 broke down
almost immediately amid public uproar in Egypt over conflicting interpretations of the clauses defining the future status of the Sudan.[88]
Sidqi resigned in exhaustion and was replaced by Muhammad Fahmi
al-Nuqrashi Pasha. Nuqrashi's ideas on how to break the stalemate
were directed toward the United Nations: on January 27, 1947, he told
Parliament that his government would submit its dispute to the Security Council. In the words of one scholar, his decision marked "a major

change in the pattern of bilateral Anglo-Egyptian relations and the first attempt by a minor power to shake off the British connection by appealing to the new world organization."[89] The Arab world was not being neglected, however. The Egyptian press and the Arab League broadcasts on Egyptian State Broadcasting served notice that the Arab states would be expected to line up behind Egypt and that any hesitancy in doing so would be looked on severely.[90]

Egypt's behavior, and the resulting prospect of a head-on confrontation with Great Britain at the United Nations created a considerable degree of unhappiness among the other League members. On January 3, 1947, ʿAzzam Pasha again tested the limits of his authority when he declared on behalf of the League that the Arab states were committed to the unity of Egypt and the Sudan. As he had done before, ʿAzzam spoke without consulting Arab League members. Not surprisingly, the Iraqis and Transjordanians were the most irritated. To their disappointment, albeit not to their surprise, the British again refrained from advocating their withdrawal from the League, although the British ambassador to Baghdad did raise the names of possible candidates to replace ʿAzzam as League secretary-general.[91]

On February 5, the Syrian and Lebanese governments, still conscious of Britain's role in counterbalancing France, discreetly tendered a joint offer to mediate the dispute. Egypt delivered a rebuff, as this was not the kind of collective Arab behavior that Cairo had in mind. The fact that the Egyptians distrusted Prime Minister Jamil Mardam of Syria did not improve the chances of their accepting Syrian mediation. The Saudis then tried their hand, also unsuccessfully.[92]

Matters came to a head at the regular Arab League Council session, which opened on March 17, 1947, in Cairo. On March 19, Nuqrashi Pasha forcefully presented the Egyptian case before a just-formed ad hoc policy committee of a number of prime and foreign ministers. A resolution was then drawn up, albeit not without some difficulties, by the Political Committee; and on March 23, it was adopted by the League Council.

As originally formulated, the resolution was based on but went somewhat beyond the previous Inshas and Bludan statements. Noting that Egypt had declared its intention to submit its case to the Security Council, the proposed resolution reiterated the League Council's support for Egypt's claims, namely "immediate and total evacuation and everlasting unity *(wahda al-da'ima)* of the Nile Valley under the Egyptian Crown." None of the other Arab delegates were enthusiastic about the draft resolution's direct challenge to Great Britain, nor about its seeming endorsement of Egyptian dominance of the Sudan. To ease these fears, ʿAzzam argued that the resolution was important only because of its timing because the substance had already been addressed at Inshas and Bludan. Nuqrashi, for his part, made an effort to ease qualms that Egypt was intending to rob Sudan of its independence. He also made a case, convincing even to the Iraqis, that Britain had wronged Egypt in barring them from co-administration of the Sudan as stipulated in the 1899 Anglo-Egyptian agreement and should rectify the situation forthwith.

Despite their misgivings, the other Arab representatives took the path of least resistance and publicly toed the Egyptian line. To do otherwise, in both Saudi and Iraqi eyes, was to risk the breakup of the League. In doing so, they were consoled by the belief, nurtured by several Egyptian delegates, that the issue would never actually reach the Security Council but would be addressed by renewed Anglo-Egyptian negotiations.

One final hitch developed as the resolution was being prepared for submission to the League Council: A member of the Egyptian delegation, Hafiz Ramadan Pasha, leader of the opposition *Kutla Wataniyya*, created an uproar when he suddenly rose and demanded that the wording be amended to "absolute" *(mutlaq)* support for Egyptian aspirations. The reactions among the delegates were almost uniformly negative, even though the same phrase appeared in the Bludan resolution supporting Egypt of a year earlier. After two hours of further arguments, Ramadan stormed out of the meeting, threatening publicly to denounce the cowardice of all present. This threat was more effective than all the arguments put forward up until that point: He was quickly brought back to the chamber, and the amended resolution was unanimously approved and sent on to the Council for final ratification. The background for this episode was the intricate tug-of-war within the Egyptian political arena; that these dynamics could intrude so forcefully on the activities of the League says much about the existing weaknesses of both Arab governments and the collective Arab forums.[93]

In the fewer than five months that remained before the regularly scheduled Security Council session, Great Britain attempted to channel Arab dissatisfaction with the Egyptian line into what it considered to be constructive avenues, first possibly to forestall the United Nations Security Council from taking up the dispute, and then, when that failed, to influence the outcome of the debate. The focus of these efforts was on Syria, for two reasons: (1) it formed the heart of the pro-Egyptian, anti-Hashimite block in the Arab East, and it was thought that if it could be pried away from Egypt on this issue, Saudi Arabia and Lebanon would follow; and (2) Syria held a seat on the Security Council. As such, it was understood to tacitly represent the entire League. Moreover, its representative, the veteran Syrian politician Faris al-Khuri, would be presiding over the Security Council during at least the first portion of its sessions and would thus be in a position to influence the course and tenor of the debate. The nature of his instructions from the Syrian government was thus deemed extremely important. Syria's key role was demonstrated also by the unwillingness of Iraq and Transjordan to urge Nuqrashi to abandon the U.N. path and to reopen talks with the British unless Syria and Lebanon were to do so simultaneously.[94]

Faris al-Khuri's instructions were the subject of intensive consultations during the second half of July, first between the Lebanese and Syrian prime ministers, and then the two of them plus Iraqi and Saudi representatives.[95] Two sets were issued: The first, in mid-July, vaguely directed Khuri to adopt a conciliatory attitude and to facilitate a satisfactory solution between two friends, Egypt and Great Britain, of all the Arab states.[96] Faris al-Khuri's reply, which invoked the Arab League's official backing of Egypt and a prior supporting statement by Quwwatli, was not acceptable; and the idea of sending another emissary (possibly Saudi Arabia's foreign minister Amir Faysal) to "stiffen" Faris al-Khuri's behavior was toyed with.[97]

As it happened, it was decided not to arouse Egyptian suspicions by sending an additional delegate. (The Egyptians had already inquired about the truth of rumors that Jamil Mardam would replace Khuri.) Similarly, it was decided not to make an additional appeal to Faruq.[98] They were, however, able to reach an understanding on a more detailed set of instructions to Faris al-Khuri. Deeply concerned that the upcoming confrontation in the Security Council would adversely affect the Arab cause in Palestine as well as wider regional security interests, Khuri was told to warn the Egyptian delegation head, Prime Minister Nuqrashi, of these dangers and quietly to press for a Security Council resolution calling for the resumption of negotiations.[99]

The instructions proved to be a dead letter, and the fears regarding Faris al-Khuri's conduct proved to be justified. Khuri adopted a blatantly one-sided, pro-Egyptian stance in the debate; this came out both in his conduct of the sessions and in his two addresses to the Council.[100]

The debate ended inconclusively, and Arab and British attention quickly moved to the Palestine question.[101] The unresolved British-Egyptian dispute would continue to fester. The inability of the Arab Asian states first to influence Egypt and then, failing that, to oppose it spoke much for their limitations and for the way they calculated their underlying interests. As was so often the case, frontal opposition was deemed inadvisable, however annoying or disturbing Egyptian actions might be.

THE PALESTINE QUESTION: AUTUMN 1947

The half-measures adopted at the Inshas and Bludan meetings in 1946 had done nothing to stem the rush of events in Palestine. Ten years earlier, the Palestinian Arab revolt against the Zionist presence had challenged Britain's authority and the long-term viability of the Mandate. Now it was the turn of the Zionist movement, spurred on by the urgency of saving the remnants of European Jewry and an outpouring of sympathy among Western public opinion, to press its demands for a Jewish state in Palestine. Throughout 1946, the British government unsuccessfully sought to reconcile the increasingly polarized positions of the Jewish and Arab communities in Palestine, through a scheme offering provincial autonomy within a unitary state. By early 1947, Britain's Foreign Secretary Ernest Bevin "hurled Palestine into the arena of the United Nations," hoping, at least initially, to play for time. The U.N. General Assembly, went the thinking in Whitehall, would not confirm the Zionist demand for the partition of Palestine and the creation of an independent Jewish state, and Britain would then be better placed to secure its strategic interests within a unitary framework.[102] But events would move along a different course.

In May 1947, the eleven-member U.N. Special Committee on Palestine (UNSCOP) was appointed to study the Palestine problem. On August 31, it issued its findings. A majority report recommended the partition of Palestine into independent Jewish and Arab states, linked by an economic union, with the city of Jerusalem and its immediate environs to be internationalized. A minority report recommended a three-year transitional U.N. administration leading to an independent federal government, to be composed of Jewish and Arab states, with Jerusalem the capital. The UNSCOP report triggered a historic British response. On September 26, Britain's colonial secretary announced before the United Nations that Britain would terminate the Palestine Mandate but not impose a solution unacceptable to either side. Given the sense of malaise among the general public in Britain toward Palestine in 1947, it was hardly surprising that most Britons welcomed the decision wholeheartedly.[103]

Whereas the British could now begin the process of washing their collective hands of the whole Palestine imbroglio, the Arab states were now being drawn inexorably into the whirlwind, many against their own better judgment. The upcoming debate on UNSCOP's recommendations in the U.N. General Assembly plunged the Arab states into a frenzy of activity. On September 16 through 19, the Arab League's Political Committee convened in Sofar, Lebanon, to plan a joint response, no easy task given existing inter-Arab rifts. Differences between the Hashimite and non-Hashimite blocs and within the Hashimite camps had already surfaced at the March 1947 League Council session in Cairo.[104] Now, with matters coming to a head, these divisions became even more significant.

As at Bludan a year earlier, Iraq adopted an extremely militant posture. Prime Minister Salih Jabr, who came to power six months earlier, immediately challenged the other Arab representatives at Sofar to implement the Bludan resolutions for economic sanctions, including the cancellation of existing concessions. His tough talk derived from a number of considerations. Domestically, Jabr hoped that militancy on the Palestine question would defuse his pan-Arab critics from among the newly politicized sectors of the population. In inter-Arab terms, he sought to embarrass both the Egyptians and the Saudis. The ideal result would be an appropriate political climate for the successful conclusion of a new Anglo-Iraqi Treaty, replacing the existing treaty of 1930. Doing so would remove the stigma of being subservient to

Britain while retaining the material benefits of the alliance. Jabr was, however, sorely mistaken in his calculations. Growing anti-Zionist sentiment in Iraq fit hand in glove with opposition to continuation of the British-Iraqi relationship in any form. Jabr would pay a dear price for his actions within a few months, when in January 1948 a massive, violent reaction in the streets of Baghdad would render the just-concluded Portsmouth agreement between Britain and Iraq stillborn and force the downfall of his government.[105]

In the meantime, Jabr's efforts at Sofar resulted, predictably, in a number of heated exchanges with the Saudi representative Yusuf Yasin, who under no circumstances would consider Jabr's demands. On the suggestion of Syria's Jamil Mardam, the Political Committee papered over the dispute regarding sanctions by referring it to the upcoming League Council meeting in Aley.[106] On October 4, the Aley Council session passed a resolution proclaiming Arab intentions to implement the Bludan decisions if the UNSCOP partition plan was adopted by the General Assembly. The gap between the resolution and Arab realities, however, was well understood by all sides.[107] Thus, said Transjordan's Samir al-Rifa'i to a British diplomat, the Bludan decisions had been "honorably buried."[108]

Operatively, the Council confirmed the Political Committee's decisions on moral, political, and military assistance to the Palestinian Arabs. The military aspect was to be dealt with by a Military Committee, made up of representatives of Iraq, Syria, Palestine, and Lebanon, and headed by an Iraqi general, Isma'il Safwat. (Transjordan appointed its own delegate in February 1948. Before that, it allowed the Iraqi representative to represent jointly the two Hashimite monarchies.) Significantly, Egypt refused to take part in the military committee's work, although it did agree to share its financial burdens. The committee was charged with mobilizing volunteer Arab forces, the *Jaysh al-Inqadh* (Army of Salvation), to assist Palestinian irregulars. The Council also recommended that "the Arab states should take military precautions on the Palestine frontiers," as well as "facilitate the participation and cooperation" of states not contiguous to Palestine.[109] The Council's decisions gave some comfort to Hajj Amin al-Husayni, who had openly expressed fears over the possible entry of regular Arab armies (i.e., Transjordan and Iraq) into Palestine.[110] At the same time, Egypt's Nuqrashi Pasha took the lead in toning down the mufti's demands for far greater support—this despite King Faruq's own position in favor of the immediate establishment of a Palestine Arab government.[111] The Council's unwillingness to do so was viewed with approval in Amman.

Still, widespread Arab suspicions of Transjordan's intentions regarding Palestine remained. To ease them, Samir al-Rifa'i made bombastic declarations of Transjordan's intent to take over all of Palestine (with Iraq's assistance). In any event, Samir emphasized, his government would act only under the aegis of the League. In reality, 'Abdallah was not even willing, at this juncture, to countenance the presence of Iraqi mobile units on Transjordan's soil.[112] 'Abdallah expressed his actual position to 'Azzam Pasha and Salih Jabr, in Samir's presence, on October 10, in Amman. It was folly, he maintained, to talk of ejecting the Jews from Palestine, thanks to limited Arab capabilities and the force of world opinion. What was necessary was to come to terms with them after, and only after, a British withdrawal, and to restrict them to as small a part of Palestine as possible.[113]

'Abdallah's frankness was a measure of his overall satisfaction with the course of developments. It stood in sharp contrast to the gloomy assessment of the Syrian leadership. Further conflict seemed inevitable, but Arab shortcomings and divisions were considerable. Moreover, the Syrian leadership was utterly opposed to the idea of sanctioning 'Abdallah to be the sole rescuer of Palestine, an aversion matched among other Arabs only by Ibn Sa'ud. Consequently, the Syrians preferred the agreed-on gradualist, indirect approach: aid for the Palestinian Arabs, proper preparations ("can 40 million Arabs afford to take on a fight with the Zionists and fail?"), and continued pressure on 'Abdallah to adhere to his own public endorsements of collective Arab disclaimers against any territorial or political ambitions in Palestine.[114] To demonstrate their resolve vis-à-vis the Zionists, 'Abdallah, and the British, the Syrians demonstratively moved military units up to the border with Palestine in accordance with the League Council's resolution favoring the adoption of military precautions along the Palestine frontier, and called on Lebanon to do the same.

In October and November 1947, as the U.N. debate reached a climax, Nuri al-Sa'id put aside Iraq's previous anti-Saudi posturing in a last-ditch effort to head off the adoption of the partition plan. He proposed to Ibn Saʿud, via the Saudi foreign minister, Amir Faysal, who was heading the Saudi delegation, that the Saudis take the lead in negotiating an Arab-American agreement on a "cantonal" settlement for Palestine. Ibn Saʿud agreed, on the condition that all the Arab delegations at the United Nations fully support him and abide by any agreement he might conclude. Such a commitment was obtained, a rare instance of operative Arab consensus on Palestine (excluding Transjordan, which, conveniently for the Saudis, was not a U.N. member). It was agreed that Faysal and Nuri would approach U.S. Secretary of State George Marshall with their plan, provided that he would wish to see them.[115]

The collective Arab demarche failed to draw a significant U.S. response, however, and the plan was overtaken by events. On November 29, 1947, the U.N. General Assembly partition resolution garnered just over the required two-thirds majority, posing the League members with their most serious collective crisis to date.

AN INTERIM ASSESSMENT

None of the myriad issues and controversies that characterized inter-Arab relations between March 1945 and November 1947 were resolved in a definitive way. Consequently, the new Arab state system's fragile status quo was considerably reinforced. International borders, as well as the overall inter-Arab balance of power, remained unchanged, despite Hashimite ambitions. The "rule of the game" established from 1943 to 1945—namely, Egypt's being able to limit the extent of other Arab states' freedom of action—was buttressed by demonstrations of Egypt's weight on a number of occasions, both inside and outside of the Arab League. The League, as both a symbol of the new framework and a contributing element to it, managed to remain intact, in spite of all the existing divisions and the periodic threats of resignation.

At the same time, however, little progress was made in reconciling the unity tenets of Arab nationalist ideology with the competing reality of Arab particularism. Nowhere was this more evident than in regard to the gathering storm in Palestine. Furthermore, the perceptible weakening of the old sociopolitical order in Egypt, and signs of the same processes elsewhere, made the likelihood of reconciling the competing *qawmiyya* and *wataniyya* tendencies even more remote. Lacking the stability and self-confidence that a well-functioning, mature political system would have promoted, ruling Arab elites in Egypt, Syria, and Iraq were reduced to promoting maximalist pan-Arab positions in foreign policy in order to bolster their positions at home. Add to this volatile mix the particular ambitions and concerns of ʿAbdallah, Ibn Saʿud, Faruq, ʿAbd al-Ilah and Nuri al-Saʿid, respectively, and it is little wonder that the elements within the inter-Arab framework promoting conflict among its members continued to be at least as strong as those elements that promoted cooperation. The fact that the declared, "expressive" ideology of the Arab state system championed solidarity and cooperation, above all, only reinforced and heightened the existing factional tensions.

Ambiguity also marked the relationship between the Arab world and outside powers. Great Britain remained a highly interested party to regional developments, thanks to its direct involvement in both the Egyptian and Palestine questions, its close connections with the Hashimite regimes, and its more general concern with formulating overall regional security arrangements. Furthermore, many local leaders continued to look to Great Britain for backing in their own power struggles. At the same time, its effectiveness in managing and manipulating regional affairs had progressively waned, a reflection of the global processes of decolonization and movements for independence that were beginning to gather strength. Nowhere was this more evident than in Palestine, but it was also true in other Arab states. In Egypt, Britain's status had significantly eroded, while in Iraq, the ruling pro-British elite, although not in any imminent danger, would shortly discover during talks to draw up a new Anglo-Iraqi treaty that intimacy with Britain no longer conferred unlimited domestic political power and in fact could represent a liability among an increasingly mobilized populace. Nor, for that matter, could that intimacy be counted on unabashedly for leverage vis-à-vis Iraq's Arab rivals. Only in Transjordan was the British–local regime connection still cozily secure.

By contrast, the idea of greater U.S. involvement in the region was looked upon favorably from many Arab quarters; for example, the United States' disagreements with Great Britain at the United Nations during the British-Egyptian debate were duly noted and even exploited by Egypt. But Washington's endorsement of the partition plan at the General Assembly served notice to the Arab world of the limitations on what could be expected from the United States.

For their parts, Great Britain and the United States continued to believe that an Arab state system loosely organized under the rubric of the Arab League was preferable to a formal breakup of the League. The League's collapse, they felt, would accentuate Arab polarization and perhaps even lead to the growth of Soviet influence. London and Washington understood, however, that the League had not significantly tempered the more militant aspects of Arab nationalism. On the contrary, it provided a forum for their expression. Moreover, by concentrating on political issues, the League had virtually ignored the promotion of socioeconomic development, upon which, it was believed, the future of the region rested.[116]

On a more theoretical level, the relative proportion of attention devoted by the Arab states to the activities of each other, as opposed to those of the global powers, was significantly greater than during the pre-1945 era. The trend was long-term: The overriding importance of "purely" Arab factors in shaping inter-Arab relations was becoming a lasting feature of the Arab state system.[117]

One of the system's veteran practitioners, Iraq's Tawfiq al-Suwaydi, cogently expressed the mixed feelings among ruling Arab elites engendered by the new reality. "The Arab League," he told an American diplomat, "is as much a truce between [its] leaders as it is the result of the movement for Arab unity for which we older Arab patriots have worked." Still, he continued, the League must be the keystone of their mutual relations, the alternative being general collapse.[118]

3

THE SYSTEM IS TESTED

TENSION AND EXCITEMENT rose steadily throughout the Arab world following the U.N. partition vote. In Palestine, clashes broke out almost immediately between irregular Arab and Jewish forces, inaugurating the "civil war" phase of the first Arab-Israeli war. Organized public opinion in the neighboring Arab states demanded immediate action. Public outcry there stemmed both from genuine distress with the turn of events and from more cynical manipulation by political leaders, particularly in Syria and Iraq. In turn, the hands of Arab decision makers became increasingly tied, boding ill for their capacity to cope effectively with the severe challenge being posed by the Zionist movement. The fundamental tenets of all-Arab solidarity and collective will in the face of challenges to any part of the common Arab patrimony, principles embodied in the Arab League Charter, were now about to be put to their first real test.

Arab prime ministers convened in Cairo from December 8 to 17, 1947, amid the heightened sense of urgency. The participants now believed that bloodshed in Palestine was inevitable and even imperative in order to forestall the implementation of partition. Existing divisions and mutual mistrust over each others' intentions prevented them from developing coherent policies. To gain time, they concurrently appealed to Britain to extend the Mandate, but without effect.[1]

Nonetheless, Arab leaders continued to believe that Britain would not, in the end, withdraw from Palestine, if only because the area would be needed as an alternative military base once British troops were pulled out of Egypt. Their belief was not totally groundless: In September 1947, Britain's general staff informed the cabinet that once an Anglo-Egyptian treaty was concluded, only Palestine would meet Britain's requirements for stationing forces in the region.[2] The cost of remaining in Palestine at a time when British-Egyptian talks were going nowhere rendered the general staff's evaluation irrelevant. The optimism of Arab leaders on this matter would thus cost them dearly.

The main line of inter-Arab division ran, not surprisingly, between the Hashimite and non-Hashimite camps. Their only point of agreement was that clashes with British forces in Palestine must be firmly avoided. The non-Hashimite group favored indirect and intermediate measures to combat the Zionists, emphasizing military assistance to irregular forces, both those within Palestine and volunteers to be raised, equipped, and trained in the Arab world. Even these halfway measures, designed in no small part to convince Great Britain and the United States that partition could not be implemented, were problematic. With an eye to the existing effervescence within Egypt, Nuqrashi Pasha was adamant that no Egyptian volunteers would be permitted to train with anything other than wooden rifles and token equipment.[3] More generally, Nuqrashi's tempered behavior derived from (1) his primary concern with avoiding any actions that might impede the renewal of British-Egyptian negotiations; and (2) his awareness of the Egyptian army's generally unfit state of preparedness. Nuqrashi's cautious, hesitant posture stood in contrast to that of Faruq, who was outspokenly determined to resist partition and openly critical of his prime minister's stand.[4] These differences were replayed in May 1948 at an even more critical juncture.

Although the Egyptian-Saudi-Syrian grouping was not completely of one mind either in their attachments to Palestine or in their commitment to the mufti's leadership, their general policy consensus stood in sharp contrast to the positions of Iraq and Transjordan. At the same time, they sought to avoid overly antagonizing the Hashimites unnecessarily: Witness their lack of insistence at the Cairo meetings on the creation of a Palestinian civil administration in the face of Iraqi and Transjordanian objections.[5] For their parts, Baghdad and Amman stressed that irregular, volunteer forces would not be sufficient and that the entry of regular Arab armies after the British left would be a necessity. Their arguments were bolstered by evaluations of the existing balance of forces made by the head of the just-established Military Committee of the League, Iraqi General Isma'il Safwat.[6] Not coincidentally, it was Iraq and Transjordan that appeared most capable of implementing such a plan. Where they differed, at this stage, was on the extent of the proposed military action.

True to form, the Iraqi leadership continued to posture for its domestic audience, advocating the seizure of as much of Palestine as possible, which would ideally force the Jews to capitulate. According to the Iraqi parliamentary inquiry of the 1948 war, the Iraqi delegation received in December 1947—immediately on the morrow of the Cairo meetings—direct assurances from 'Abdallah that Iraqi support for Transjordan would enable Safwat's recommendations to be implemented without need of additional outside assistance. 'Abdallah's assurance, said the report, led to Salih Jabr's telling the Iraqi Parliament on December 24 that the two Hashimite kingdoms were committed to a joint policy aimed at transforming Palestine into a unitary Arab state in all of Western Palestine.[7]

Jabr was surely overstating himself. In November 1947, 'Abdallah had already somewhat reinforced his previous unwritten understanding with the Zionist leadership about the division of Palestine: the avoidance of military conflict, while the Arab Legion would occupy the parts of Palestine adjacent to Transjordan that had been allocated to the Palestinian Arabs by the United Nations.[8] This was not, of course, revealed to the other Arab states, and subsequent declarations by Transjordanian officials firmly adhered to the declared Arab consensus.[9] Nonetheless, the Transjordanian proposal at the Arab prime ministers' meeting in Cairo did not completely contradict the line being taken with the Jewish Agency in that it advocated halting the advance of regular Arab troops at the frontiers of the projected Jewish state, and only from there carrying on with guerilla activities.[10]

Transjordanian officials were overly optimistic in their accounts of the Cairo meeting. None of the other Arab representatives, said Tawfiq Abu al-Huda, "expressed opposition to the employment of the Arab Legion in Palestine, even if the other Arab states felt themselves precluded by their membership [in] the United Nations from sending in their own regular forces."[11] His optimism was shared by other Transjordanian officials as well: According to one of 'Abdallah's aides, 'Umar al-Dajani, 'Azzam told 'Abdallah that he could secure Egypt's acquiescence to Transjordan's planned seizure of Palestine.¹² Transjordanian confidence was further reinforced by the League's continued rejection of the mufti's entreaties to help him set up some type of civil administration in Palestine.

'ABDALLAH'S PLANS AND BRITAIN

British policy regarding 'Abdallah's plans firmed up only in January and February 1948. On January 11, Britain's Foreign Secretary Ernest Bevin sent a long personal message to 'Abdallah reiterating Britain's intentions to reformulate and improve its overall regional defense arrangements and acknowledging Transjordan's desires to alter, at least cosmetically, their 1946 Treaty of Alliance.¹³ Regarding Palestine, Bevin warned 'Abdallah not to underestimate the crisis that would ensue if Transjordan were to take steps that would isolate it from the other Arab States (i.e., if it took too compromising a posture toward the Jewish Agency) or that would cause the Security Council to consider action against Transjordan (e.g., to blatantly violate the partition plan's boundaries and the U.N. Charter's stipulation against aggression).¹⁴

The fear that 'Abdallah would isolate himself from the Arab world ran deep in Britain's Foreign Office and reappeared on a number of occasions. In the minds of at least some British officials, the best way out of this dilemma was exactly what 'Abdallah had suggested to the League in Cairo in December 1947: the occupation of the Arab sections of Palestine by the regular armies, that is, those of Transjordan and Iraq, and the employment of Arab irregulars against the Jewish areas.¹⁵ Just as 'Abdallah's statements in Cairo did not reflect his actual position, these British musings did not translate into policy. Instead, Britain followed along behind Amman's more cautious approach.

On February 4, 1948, Prime Minister Abu al-Huda explicitly put forth to Bevin Transjordan's plan to occupy the Arab areas of Palestine as laid down in the U.N. partition resolution. The Arab Legion, Abu al-Huda stated in reply to Bevin's question, "would not enter Jewish areas unless the Jews invaded Arab areas." In accordance with Abu al-Huda's own expressed wish, Bevin made no response.¹⁶ For Abu al-Huda, British silence, with its connotation of tacit approval, was apparently the most desired response.

An awareness of the Legion's limitations did not prevent British officials from hoping that the largely uninhabited Negev Desert, most of which had been awarded to the Jewish state by the General Assembly, would wind up in Arab hands. The possibility that Transjordan would not adhere strictly to the partition lines but would achieve at least a corridor across the Negev to Gaza and the Mediterranean was "tempting" to British strategists: It would ensure continuous access between the Suez Canal area and Transjordan and beyond that to British bases in Iraq and to Iraqi and Iranian oil fields. It would have the benefit, according to one British official, of "cutting the Jewish state, and therefore Communist influence, off from the Red Sea."[17] This last comment reflected a not uncommon, albeit mistaken, view held in the Foreign Office that the Zionist movement, having originated in Eastern Europe and possessing a strong collectivist tinge, was both sympathetic and vulnerable to Communist blandishments. Moreover, there was considerable fear that the Soviet Union was infiltrating a large number of agents into the region under the guise of Jewish refugees. Thus, strategic requirements and ideological predilections caused many in the Foreign Office to favor divesting the as yet unborn Jewish state of the Negev. This desire would reappear on a number of occasions throughout the next two years. It seems, however, that in early 1948 Britain was neither pushing Transjordan in this direction nor holding out undue hope that Transjordan would act accordingly.

British fears of an anti-'Abdallah reaction from either the Arabs or the United Nations had not yet dissipated. But the pace of events dictated a positive British stance toward 'Abdallah's plan. General Arab hesitation, with Kirkbride's reports on Transjordan's own determination and on the desirability of such action, apparently reinforced Bevin's own predilection to join an Arab Palestinian rump to Transjordan. It also dovetailed with Great Britain's preference to wash its hands of Palestine and to avoid actively helping to implement partition. Room would thus be left for maintaining and repairing its relationships with the Arab world while waiting for the dust of battle to settle.[18]

THE MUFTI AND THE ARAB LEAGUE

Arab volunteer forces, which infiltrated Palestine during the first months of 1948, and Palestinian Arab irregular troops were both ostensibly under the control of the Arab League's Military Committee. In fact, however, the subject was one of considerable wrangling and maneuvering among Hajj Amin al-Husayni, military commanders in the field, and the committee's members. Before I elaborate, a few more general remarks about the complex relationship between the mufti, his Palestinian Arab opponents, ʿAbdallah, and the rest of the League are in order.

Since the 1930s, relations with the Arab world posed an ongoing dilemma for Palestinian Arabs. Their need for Arab support was acute, but too close an embrace carried the risk of losing their freedom of action. Internal divisions within the Palestinian community complicated matters even further, rendering it especially susceptible to outside blandishments. Palestinian dependence on the Arab states during the Mandate period increased with time, exemplified both by the regionalization of the conflict in 1936 and by the Arab League Charter's special annex on Palestine, which charged the League Council with selecting a Palestinian representative to take part in its work, although not as a full-fledged member. Nonetheless, the Palestinian Arab leadership was hardly passive as the Arab League took up their cause. Moreover, the resonance of the Palestinian question in the domestic politics of Arab states worked to the mufti's advantage. Thus, on a number of occasions, he was able to get the Arab League's backing, whether for strengthening his own internal position, both organizationally and materially, or for his policies, in spite of the fact that he was distrusted and disdained by many Arab leaders.

These complex intertwinings resulted in a number of paradoxes. Hajj Amin's uncompromising position led him repeatedly to demand a total Arab commitment to the Palestinian Arab cause. The only Arab states eager and apparently able to undertake military operations were the mufti's greatest foes: ʿAbdallah, whose backing of opposition Palestinian Arab forces underscored his status as the mufti's chief rival for power in Arab Palestine, and Hashimite Iraq, whose political leadership could not forget Hajj Amin's involvement there during the turmoil of 1941. Moreover, they could not ignore his appeal to pan-Arab nationalist forces in Iraq, rendering the idea of a Palestinian Arab state under his leadership totally unacceptable. Saudi Arabia and Syria were the most eager to block ʿAbdallah and Iraq, and thus looked to Hajj Amin for help. The Saudis, however, were completely unwilling to endanger their relationship with the United States by carrying out the economic boycott stipulated in the Bludan resolutions and had no troops to offer. The Syrians were perhaps the most concerned, both officially and on the popular level, with the pan-Arab aspects of the conflict. As such, they officially backed Hajj Amin at every turn. As the conflict intensified, however, the Syrians began to look in other directions.

Egypt's position was especially complex. Domestic pressures, emanating first and foremost from the Muslim Brotherhood, and Faruq's own aspirations to regional leadership pushed Egypt toward greater involvement.[19] The Egyptian agenda, however, was crowded with other issues. Furthermore, both the government and the armed forces were extremely reluctant to become involved militarily. Consequently, Egyptian policy, and therefore League policy, was supportive of the mufti but not to the extent he desired. When the limitations of this policy became apparent in March and April 1948, Cairo was compelled to reevaluate.[20]

The accelerated maneuverings of all the Arab parties during the first months of 1948 brought many of the ambiguities and complexities of mufti–Arab League relations into the open. In February, Hajj Amin placed a number of demands before the Political Committee, then meeting in Cairo. All of them centered on the extension of his authority. They included the creation of a provisional Palestinian Arab government, which would assume its responsibilities immediately upon the termination of the Mandate; the recognition of the authority of local Arab national committees, which his followers were attempting to set up; the appointment of a Palestinian Arab representative to the League's Military Committee; the granting of a loan to enable the mufti to meet administrative necessities; and the budgeting of money to the Arab Higher Committee for compensation to war victims.[21] The League deflected these demands. Although the non-Hashimite states were not above giving serious consideration to the idea of a provisional Palestinian administration, they preferred not to provoke a crisis at this time with 'Abdallah over the matter.[22] Still, Hajj Amin did not desist from trying to exercise control over the irregular forces fighting in Palestine. His efforts disturbed General Isma'il Safwat, who since December was also formally the commander in chief of the volunteer forces.[23] The mufti, he said, must yield: The soldiers operating in the field must be responsible to the Arab League.[24]

Given the confused and nonunified policies of the Arab states, the lines of authority continued to be blurred.[25] The February League Council session established a special "Palestine Committee" to try to coordinate political and military policies.[26] The mufti was named as one of seven members, along with ʿAzzam Pasha, the Lebanese and Syrian prime ministers, and representatives from Transjordan and Saudi Arabia. Taha al-Hashimi, a veteran Iraqi politician and general, was designated military adviser. The committee exercised no authority, however, and the mufti and his lieutenants continued to act independently. Efforts to mollify him, such as extending the committee's formal recognition to Hajj Amin's nephew, ʿAbd al-Qadir al-Husayni, as commander of the Arab forces in the Jerusalem region, proved worthless.[27] Disagreement between the Arab League's Military Committee and the Arab Higher Committee was rife and repeatedly manifested itself in the field.[28] Overall, although the mufti remained an important symbol of resistance that Arab leaders could not totally ignore, he was increasingly kept at arm's length.

One of the most important manifestations of the mufti's progressive loss of control was the League's appointment of Fawzi al-Qawuqji in October 1947 — on Syria's recommendation and over the mufti's strong objections — to be the field commander of the Arab volunteer forces being dispatched to Palestine.[29] Qawuqji had been active during the 1936–1939 Arab Revolt in Palestine. He also had a deserved reputation as an adventurer, and together with his deputy, Major Adib Shishakli (later strong man of Syria), he often acted on his own, without prior reference to any collective Arab authority. The Syrians were none too confident of his loyalty, despite their considerable assistance in material, men, and finances. Qawuqji testified that his forces were hurriedly ordered by the Damascus-based Military Committee to withdraw and disband on May 15 when the regular Arab armies invaded, due to Syrian fears that ʿAbdallah would absorb his forces and use them eventually to help implement his Greater Syria scheme.[30] The fear of Transjordan winning Qawuqji's allegiance was not totally groundless. Already in February, Kirkbride and part of the leadership in Amman were beginning to think along the same lines.[31]

It was during this period that Transjordan decided not to further hinder the transit of volunteer forces across its territory.[32] Thus, on

March 5, Qawuqji was personally feted by ʿAbdallah before leading an armed unit into Palestine. In reply to Kirkbride's representations, Abu al-Huda stated that it was not possible for Transjordan to persist in its original policy of denying passage because it was already suspected by the other Arab states of having ulterior motives.[33] Transjordan's need not to add fuel to these suspicions was undoubtedly a prime motive in its changed position. In a previous communication, however, Kirkbride conveyed another, less defensive explanation, one tied to Amman's specific plans—the desire to establish contact with these forces so as to preclude any possibility of their clashing with the Arab Legion.[34]

COUNTDOWN TO PARTITION

The atmosphere surrounding the irregular forces was one of general disorganization and competing aims. Moreover, most of the Arab states failed to live up to their commitments to help them.[35] Thanks to initial successes in the field, however, Arab attitudes in the early months of 1948 toward developments in Palestine were characterized by a fair degree of confidence. Concurrently, Arab diplomats suggested to their British counterparts that the Mandate be prolonged.[36] They also again raised various alternatives to partition, such as a unitary state with guarantees for minority rights, a federal or cantonized state, or an international trusteeship. Privately, Arab diplomats hinted at significant concessions on the matter of Jewish immigration, as long as the creation of an independent Jewish state was avoided.[37] On March 19, the temporary U.S. retreat from its support for partition provided further cause for optimism.

The calmness did not last long. Diplomatic soundings remained unfruitful, and the British resolve to quit Palestine on May 14 grew stronger as the date approached. Together with this came a decisive swing of the military pendulum during the month of April in favor of the Jewish Agency's military arm, the Haganah; the defeat of Qawuqji's assault on Kibbutz Mishmar Haʿemek, followed by the capture of Tiberias and Haifa; the temporary relief of the siege of Jerusalem (during which ʿAbd al-Qadir al-Husayni was killed); and at the end of the month, the first assaults on Jaffa and Safed.

On April 10, the Arab League's Political Committee convened in Cairo. In light of the latest military reverses, argued General Safwat, the dispatch of regular armies to Palestine could no longer be postponed. The Transjordanian delegation then declared that the Arab Legion would enter Palestine immediately upon the termination of the Mandate.[38] As expected, the Syrians were especially disturbed by the latest turn of events. According to Jamil Mardam, he and his colleagues lobbied strongly for intervention by Egypt's regular army, in order to put a brake on 'Abdallah's ambitions.[39] Two days later, in the presence of the heads of the Arab delegations, Faruq issued a proclamation that any Arab action in Palestine "must be regarded as a temporary solution devoid of any nature of occupation or partition of Palestine. After liberation, Palestine must be handed over to its own people, who will elect the government it pleases."[40] The statement was unanimously adopted by the Arab League's Political Committee and disseminated to the press. Despite Transjordan's affirmative vote in the Political Committee, the statement was widely understood to be a warning to 'Abdallah.[41]

The Transjordanian reaction to Faruq's declaration was twofold and seemingly contradictory. Officials in Amman publicly praised Faruq's statement, emphasizing that the Arabs of Palestine would enjoy the right to determine their fate once the Arab armies had performed the task of saving Palestine.[42] At the same time, they quickly reiterated their own position, that "Palestine and Transjordan are one, for Palestine is the coast line and Transjordan the hinterland of the same country."[43] On balance, it seems that Transjordanian leaders did not view Faruq's declaration as a serious deterrent to their ambitions in Palestine. Nonetheless, Faruq's declaration was not devoid of impact: It influenced 'Abdallah to shy away from unilateral involvement, ironically at the very moment when the other Arab states were beginning to recognize that the Arab Legion's intervention in Palestine was necessary to forestall defeat. Instead, 'Abdallah moved to legitimize the Legion's activities by placing them within the framework of an all-Arab military action.

This did not mean that he was subordinating the Legion to the rest of the Arab countries. For example, 'Abdallah resisted repeated Arab entreaties either to coordinate the Arab Legion's moves with Qawukji's forces or to move on Palestine, alone or with Iraq, before

May 14.⁴⁴ ʿAbdallah's shying away from unilateral action may have been a case of the king "losing his nerve," in Kirkbride's words.⁴⁵ More likely, however, it had to do with ʿAbdallah's calibrations of his kingdom's place in the Arab system. His previous policies on Palestine and Syria had aroused Arab wrath, and a too openly independent stance now might leave him irreparably exposed to charges of betraying the Arab cause. At the same time, his army was in demand. Thus, he apparently hoped that general Arab military involvement would be of symbolic value, would not seriously hamper his own plans, and would provide them with an important measure of legitimacy.⁴⁶

The collective decision to invade Palestine upon the termination of the Mandate was apparently made, in principle, at the League's Political Committee meeting in Amman on April 24. The operational details needed to be worked out. None were more important than the question of whether Egypt would participate. No Egyptian representative was present at the Amman meeting. Accordingly, Lebanon's prime minister, Riyad al-Sulh, and the Iraqi regent traveled to Cairo to impress upon the Egyptians the necessity for joining in, a poignant commentary on the parameters of the Egyptian-Iraqi rivalry. Behind Iraq's desires for Egyptian participation lay apprehensions regarding Iraq's own military limitations vis-à-vis the Jewish forces. Domestic pressures for forceful action also played a part in the regent's initiative. As for Riyad al-Sulh, it was clear that an all-Arab operation was preferable to a purely Hashimite action that might strengthen their Greater Syria aspirations.⁴⁷ Egyptian responses were mixed. Faruq told the regent that the Egyptian army would indeed participate in the battle.⁴⁸ The Egyptian government, in contrast, still clung to the notion that Egyptian intervention was both undesirable and unlikely.⁴⁹

According to Kirkbride, the joint effort by ʿAbd al-Ilah and Riyad al-Sulh to persuade the Egyptians not to remain aloof was made with the agreement of ʿAbdallah.⁵⁰ This point requires explanation. After all, Faruq posed the main Arab obstacle to ʿAbdallah's territorial ambitions in Palestine. It appears, nonetheless, that ʿAbdallah was not overly disturbed by the prospect of Egyptian involvement, as long as it did not interfere with his own plans. Moreover, ʿAbdallah had no desire at this stage to stand alone in opposition to a budding Arab consensus in favor of Egypt's participation.

What ʿAbdallah did do was press ʿAzzam for the League's full support regarding men, matériel, air support, finances, and the sharing of responsibility for the action in Palestine and for dealing with any international reactions that might ensue.[51] He repeated his requests in a meeting with ʿAzzam in Amman on April 26. Tactically, ʿAbdallah emphasized the negative. He lacked confidence in the rest of the Arab states, he told ʿAzzam, and was therefore reluctant to take the lead in initiating hostilities. On the other hand, how could he agree that Faruq ("the Turk"), Ibn Saʿud ("the brigand"), ʿAbdallah's grandnephew Faysal, and Quwwatli would all rule over their respective lands while he, ʿAbdallah, who had devoted everything for the Arab cause, would rule over only a small piece of poverty-stricken desert? Azzam did not treat ʿAbdallah's comments lightly. Help save Palestine from the enemy, he said, and he would stand by ʿAbdallah's side against the others, if necessary, and crown him king of Palestine and Jordan.[52] One concrete result from the visit was the payment to Transjordan of Egyptian £250,000 from League funds, a first installment of a promised amount of Egyptian £3 million (the balance was never delivered).[53]

During the last week of April military preparations intensified in a number of areas. Iraqi troops began moving into Transjordan (up until then, ʿAbdallah had steadfastly opposed any such move). Concurrently, Egyptian reinforcements were dispatched to al-Arish, and Egyptian naval units reportedly began patrolling the coast of southern Palestine.[54] On April 30, a long-delayed meeting of Arab chiefs of staff, including a representative of the Egyptian general staff, convened in Amman. Their evaluation was that the defeat of the Jewish forces required no less than six fully equipped divisions and five air squadrons and recommended that they be placed under a united Arab command headed by Iraqi general Nur al-Din Mahmud (replacing Ismaʿil Safwat).[55] The Political Committee deemed these requirements impossible to fulfill.

Contrary to widely held perceptions of Arab overconfidence in the coming battle, the mood among Arab leaders was at times sober, even pessimistic, particularly in light of the latest battlefield setbacks. Hope was still expressed that the cease-fire and trusteeship formulas then being explored by the United States at the United Nations could bear fruit, forestall British evacuation, and thus obviate the need for military action.[56] These perceptions and hopes were tempered by a number of other elements: the continued gap between Arab diplomatic soundings and the minimum Arab public position; an acute fear of the retribution (collective and personal, political and physical) that Arab public opinion might inflict on Arab leaders in the aftermath of defeat, or perhaps even worse, of inaction; and a streak of fatalism, perhaps even a certain sense of relief as the day of battle approached — not an unknown phenomenon in the history of warfare by any means.

The actual invasion plans firmed up only during the last days of the Mandate and were shaped by a convergence of short-term interests between Amman and Cairo. Meeting in Damascus from May 11 to 14, the Political Committee of the League appointed Iraq's General Mahmud as overall commander of the combined Arab forces, regular and irregular. General Safwat had resigned some days earlier from his position as commander of the irregulars in protest against the ineffectiveness of his command and particularly against the interference of 'Abdallah.[57] The aim of the plan that Mahmud laid before the Political Committee on May 12

> was to detach the northeastern part of the Jewish state through simultaneous thrusts by four Arab armies. The Syrian and Lebanese armies would move through Safed to Nazareth, and the Transjordanian and Iraqi armies would reach Nazareth via Jenin and Afuleh. In the meantime, the Egyptian army would move towards Tel Aviv, tying down the bulk of the Jewish forces. Once these objectives were achieved, the Arab armies would then be favorably placed to move on Haifa and Tel Aviv.[58]

Neither Mahmud's appointment nor his plan of action suited 'Abdallah. He had previously insisted on the post for himself. One source even states that he had already been awarded it by the Arab chiefs of staff. That 'Abdallah understood this to be the case is confirmed by the protestations of the Jordanian delegate to the Political Committee. On May 13, 'Abdallah successfully demanded that the decision be altered and that he be named overall commander in chief; Mahmud was retained as second in command with operational responsibility. Significantly, the Egyptians agreed to 'Abdallah's request.[59]

'Abdallah then proceeded to alter the invasion plans to bring them into line with his long-standing strategic aims. It was the single occasion in which his commander in chief status was not merely titular.

Instead of focusing on northern Palestine, his forces would, together with the Iraqis, occupy the areas of central Palestine allocated to the Arabs by the United Nations and be in a position to act in Jerusalem, whose fate at that moment hung in the balance. The Syrians were ordered to switch their attack from the center of Palestine's northern border with Lebanon to the southern end of the Sea of Galilee, where they would provide flanking support for the Iraqi and Jordanian forces. Here, too, the Egyptians backed the changes in the plan,[60] in part because they would provide its army with important support on its own right flank as it advanced northward. In addition, Egypt would provide Transjordan with flanking support of its own, via the dispatch of a column of Egyptian-commanded volunteer forces across the northern Negev to the Hebron-Bethlehem area, up to the very outskirts of Jerusalem (they would arrive on May 22).[61] To implement this newly developing coordination between Egypt and Transjordan, Cairo delegated a number of staff officers to Amman.

Although inaccessible Arab archives would presumably clarify matters, there does exist some evidence to support the notion that Transjordan desired the dispatch of Egyptian troops to the Hebron-Bethlehem area. In a subsequent exchange of letters between their two prime ministers in April 1949, both referred to Egypt's having answered 'Abdallah's expressed wish that Egyptian forces participate in the defenses of Jerusalem. 'Abdallah had already mentioned the same point in a message to the Egyptian foreign minister in mid-March 1949, and the Egyptians did not contest it. Although this evidence is not conclusive, it seems to provide further confirmation of a certain measure of understanding between Amman and Cairo in April and May 1948.[62]

The latest turn of events was pleasing to 'Abdallah, who grew more anxious as May 15 approached, particularly because his understanding with the Jewish Agency was overtaken by the events of March and April.[63] Further dispelling his anxiety was the concurrent return from Cairo on May 12 of his foreign minister bearing renewed oral assurances of Egyptian intervention at the end of the Mandate, along with a similar, if vaguer letter from Faruq to 'Abdallah.[64] What remained, from Faruq's end, was to take the steps necessary to overrule continued opposition to committing Egypt's forces to battle by the Egyptian government and its upper military echelons.[65]

Given the subsequent lack of coordination among the Arab armies during even the initial fighting, it would be a mistake to ascribe too much operative value to the later stages of the battle plans. Still, it is worth asking whether their alteration indicates that, despite subsequent charges of betrayal, the rest of the Arab states had agreed to acquiesce to ʿAbdallah's more limited strategic aims. Apparently it did not, at least as far as the Syrians are concerned, even though their compliance with the revisions proved to be a considerable tactical and strategic blunder. One generally reliable Arab source quotes the Syrian chief of staff as stating that the Jordanians had conveyed their intention to move on Tel Aviv in conjunction with the Egyptians.[66] Did the similarity of views between Cairo and Amman during the last weeks before the invasion include an understanding to attack Tel Aviv jointly? Most likely not, although the idea would be referred to periodically during the fighting. Nuqrashi's assurance to the Egyptian commander in the Sinai that the expected war would be more of a political demonstration indicates otherwise.[67] So does Arab Legion Commander Sir John Bagot Glubb's statement that the Egyptian liaison officer in Amman "saw all our operational reports, knew our order of battle and visited our front whenever he wished."[68]

Cairo and Amman continued to have different objectives at this stage, with ʿAbdallah ready to acquiesce to the creation of a Jewish state, and the Egyptians hopeful that the combination of military and political moves would foreclose this possibility. Still, notwithstanding the basic lack of trust between ʿAbdallah and Faruq, frustrating ʿAbdallah's ambitions was not a central motive in Egypt's decision to go to war. Rather, Faruq's own pretensions to grandeur, coupled with the general Arab atmosphere that militated for Egyptian participation, were what governed Egypt's actions. True, Faruq's aspirations required blocking ʿAbdallah at some time or another, but this did not mean that there was an immediate plan to do so. The Transjordanians, for their part, understood that Egyptian involvement carried some risk but thought they were outweighed by more immediate military and political considerations.

Concurrently, Ibn Saʿud was brought into line. The prospects of a Transjordanian-Iraqi move into Palestine had always been anathema to him.[69] Besides, the old mutual suspicions between himself and ʿAbdallah had actually resulted in ʿAbdallah's dispatching a detachment of troops to Aqaba just three months earlier in response to the northern movement of Saudi Arabian Bedouins volunteering for action in Palestine.[70] Now, however, Riyad al-Sulh and Jamil Mardam won Ibn Sa'ud's backing for the joint action being planned.[71] Undoubtedly, that it was not an exclusively Hashimite operation was decisive in winning Ibn Sa'ud's endorsement.

The Syrians were the last to signal their approval. Their loathing and apprehensions of 'Abdallah remained strong, such that Quwwatli opposed, albeit unsuccessfully, his appointment as commander in chief. Furthermore, the revised military plans created significant logistical problems for them, leading Quwwatli to telephone a last-minute plea to 'Abdallah to postpone the invasion.[72] Given the concurrence among Transjordan, Egypt, and Iraq, the Syrians could hardly afford to be left behind, and they withdrew their objections. Thus it was that on May 15, immediately after the British withdrawal from Palestine and the proclamation of the state of Israel, five Arab armies simultaneously moved forward. They were later joined by a token Saudi contingent. In a long cable to the U.N. secretary-general that same day, 'Azzam Pasha justified the Arab states intervention.

> Considering that the security of Palestine is a sacred trust for [the Arab states], and out of anxiousness to check the further deterioration of the prevailing conditions and to prevent the spread of disorder and lawlessness into the neighboring Arab lands, and in order to fill the vacuum created by the termination of the Mandate and the failure to replace it by any legally constituted authority, the Arab Governments . . . by virtue of their responsibility as members of the Arab League which is a regional organization within the meaning of Chapter VIII of the Charter of the United Nations . . . find themselves compelled to intervene for the sole purpose of restoring peace and security and establishing law and order in Palestine. [As soon as this is established and the] sovereign state of Palestine [is able to discharge all of its governmental functions,] the intervention of the Arab states . . . [which was] not inspired by any other motive whatsoever . . . [shall be brought to an end].[73]

WAR AND DIPLOMACY: THE INTER-ARAB SCENE

The invasion of Arab armies marked the end of the civil war phase of the first Arab-Israeli war. The conflict was now primarily an interstate affair, with the new state of Israel trying to consolidate its existence, and the Arab states, nominally under the banner of the Arab League, committed to rolling back the new status quo while simultaneously advancing their individual, particular interests. The difficulties of doing both were soon apparent. Initial Arab reaction to the invasion, both officially and in the press, bordered on the euphoric.[74] After one week of fighting, the Arab armies seemed to have Israeli forces on the defensive. The Egyptians had penetrated well into southern Palestine, and the Arab Legion was in the process of consolidating its hold over part of the Jerusalem area, thus preventing the entire city from falling into Jewish hands. At the same time, Arab leaders were not unaware of the shortcomings that had cropped up. The Syrian, Iraqi, and Lebanese armies were meeting stiff resistance; ammunition, weapon, and supply stores were being depleted; and, perhaps most important, coordination among the various Arab armies was sorely lacking.

On May 19, ʿAbdallah, ʿAbd al-Ilah, Quwwatli, Lebanon's President Khuri, ʿAzzam Pasha, assorted prime ministers, other cabinet ministers and military leaders of Transjordan, Syria, Lebanon, and Iraq, and a representative of the Egyptian general staff gathered in Darʿa, just north of the Syrian-Transjordanian border to assess matters. The Syrians made a conscious attempt to downplay their hostility to ʿAbdallah. Quwwatli and ʿAbdallah publicly embraced, and the Syrian press honored ʿAbdallah as the "Liberator of Palestine."[75] Accompanying (and partly explaining) this public display of unity of Arab ranks was Quwwatli's request that ʿAbdallah press the British to resupply the Syrian army with equipment and ammunition.[76]

A more fundamental reason behind the public show of unity at Darʿa was the desire to pressure ʿAbdallah into dispatching Arab Legion forces to the north, in line with the original plan to advance on Afuleh. ʿAzzam and others made repeated entreaties to this effect, both at Darʿa and at an immediately preceding meeting attended by ʿAbdallah, ʿAzzam, Glubb, Mahmud, and other officers. ʿAbdallah resisted their pleas, insisting that Jerusalem remain the first priority. Once matters were well in hand there, he declared, the Legion's sights would then be set on Tel Aviv, in conjunction with Egyptian and Iraqi forces, and not Afuleh.[77]

After May 15, was ʿAbdallah any more serious about advancing on Tel Aviv than he had been before? All of the evidence indicates that he was not. Kirkbride's reports, Glubb's pessimistic evaluation of the balance of forces, and the decision not to commit the Legion to the defense of Ramleh and Lydda (which fell to Israeli forces during the second round of fighting in July) show that the talk of a second stage of fighting was merely a sop to 'Abdallah's rivals. Furthermore, the fact that the Egyptians were not involved in pressuring 'Abdallah at Dar'a points to the continued existence of at least tacit understanding between Cairo and Amman regarding the limitations on their respective military capabilities. At the very least, it shows Egypt's awareness that 'Abdallah could not be pressured past a certain point. This did not, however, prevent 'Abdallah from subsequently attempting to shift the blame for the fall of Ramleh and Lydda to Egypt because its forces did not advance up the coast to Jaffa as supposedly planned.[78]

An acrimonious exchange at Dar'a between 'Abdallah and Taha al-Hashimi illustrated the other participants' frustration over 'Abdallah's unwillingness to alter his plans. As attested to in 'Abdallah's account to Kirkbride and al-Hashimi's memoirs, the argument was touched off by al-Hashimi's declaration that the Arab armies should be used for military purposes only, not political ones, a reiteration of long-standing Arab suspicions of 'Abdallah's intentions.[79] 'Abdallah's relatively secure position at this juncture was indicated by the fact that the criticism came from al-Hashimi, rather than from his Syrian patrons, and that 'Azzam immediately undertook efforts to mollify 'Abdallah. Nonetheless, suspicions, tension, and perhaps even jealousy toward Transjordan remained considerable. As Kirkbride wrote, the

> fact that all other Arab States were given roles which caused them to invade the Jewish State immediately upon the commencement of hostilities was not entirely accidental, which they have since realized. This realization and the failure of the Lebanese, Syrian [and] Iraqi military efforts make them all the more insistent that the Arab Legion also should advance against the Jewish State.[80]

Despite Arab pressures, however, military realities, political pragmatism, including the fear of being labeled aggressors by the United Nations, and the depletion of supplies led the Arab states to adopt a different course from the one pressed on ʿAbdallah at Darʿa. On June 2, the Arab League Political Committee accepted a May 29 U.N. Security Council resolution calling for a four-week cease-fire, during which time the U.N.-appointed mediator, Count Folke Bernadotte, was to explore the possibilities for a more lasting settlement.[81] Particularly noteworthy was the fact that Egypt aligned itself with the two Hashimite kingdoms in insisting on the cease-fire's acceptance over the initial opposition of Syria, Saudi Arabia, and Lebanon.[82] Transjordan's Tawfiq Abu al-Huda took the lead in rejecting Syria's demands, stating caustically, "I suppose you Syrians want to fight the war in Palestine to the last Transjordanian."[83] For Transjordan, nothing more could be achieved by the war and further fighting could only benefit Israel.[84] Following acceptance of the cease-fire, the Syrian, Lebanese, and Saudi delegates proposed that all Arab states reject any notion of accepting a Jewish state, and that any deviation from this line be considered treasonous. Abu al-Huda's opposition to their obviously anti-Amman thrust, coupled with silence from Egypt, prevented the resolution from being voted on.[85]

Considerable British pressure to accept the truce was exerted in all Arab capitals, including personal representations from Bevin to ʿAbdallah, Faruq, and the Iraqi Regent.[86] As has been seen repeatedly, however, the Middle East was no longer a thoroughly penetrated system in which outside powers could shape events at will. In this case, the confluence of Transjordanian, Egyptian, and Iraqi interests — the need for a respite from the fighting and the desire among some Arab leaders for an imposed solution to the conflict that would preserve a modicum of Arab honor[87] — was what determined, more than British pressure, the collective Arab position.

Faruq's statements to Bernadotte during the consultations over the exact terms of the truce and the provisions for its enforcement illustrated the multiple strands of Egyptian behavior — the militant posturing, the need to cooperate with Transjordan, and the continued suspicions of ʿAbdallah. On the one hand, he stated, the Arabs had nothing to gain from a truce because they would soon conclude the war to their advantage. On the other hand, Faruq was very interested in knowing what ʿAbdallah's attitude to the truce was, indicating that he was not yet prepared to deviate from their common line adopted at the Political Committee. He did, however, warn Bernadotte that he was not sure that 'Abdallah would adhere to his acceptance of Bernadotte's truce implementation proposal.[88]

The first truce went into effect on June 11. The course of the fighting up to that point provides one clue to the state of Transjordanian-Egyptian relations. Amman and Cairo were in similar situations. They had carried the bulk of the Arabs' military burden, taken the greatest risks on the battlefield, and were likely to be the main Israeli targets in any post-truce fighting. Mutual understanding of each other's dilemmas was a necessity. Yet, mutual suspicions continued to be deeply embedded in official thinking. Faruq's wariness was reciprocated by 'Abdallah. In fact, it was precisely at this juncture, during the first truce, that 'Abdallah became more seriously concerned with Egyptian intentions in the Hebron district. Transjordan had appointed a military governor for the area, and now Egypt did so as well. To 'Abdallah, this indicated that the Egyptians were preparing to oppose his plans to consolidate his authority over the areas of Palestine held by his troops. By contrast, Tawfiq Abu al-Huda and Kirkbride more or less accepted the Egyptian denial of having any ulterior motives.[89]

Egypt's dilemma at this stage was this: the Egyptians—apparently Faruq more so than his government—were willing and desired to act in a way that would promote the mufti's aims and obstruct 'Abdallah's. But they were acutely sensitive that a tipping of the scales too far in the mufti's favor might result in a Transjordanian counteraction in the direction of a separate peace with Israel and Transjordan's final and total swallowing of the areas of central Palestine under its control.[90] Overall, Egypt's restraint in promoting anti-'Abdallah, pro-mufti activities seems to indicate that it was conducting an "exploratory" policy—one of testing and probing, but not one in which Egypt entertained exaggerated expectations for success, nor one in which blocking 'Abdallah was the highest priority.

On June 25, 'Abdallah paid a forty-eight-hour visit to Cairo. In his memoirs, he describes the visit in uniformly negative tones. He succeeded neither in securing the return of the ammunition confiscated by the Egyptians from a British ship bound for Transjordan during the third week of May nor in putting into operation his suggestion for a joint Transjordanian-Egyptian-Iraqi thrust to seize all of Jerusalem nor even in arranging his visit to the headquarters of the

Egyptian army in Palestine in his capacity as commander in chief.[91] His comments to British officials at the time, however, refer to the trip's being a "qualified success," and the attendant accounts speak of a visit that was longer on ceremony than substance.[92] One of Faruq's confidants, Edgar Gallad Bey, spoke in a similar vein to the British ambassador in Cairo, directly quoting Faruq that no political matters of any kind were discussed and explaining that ʿAbdallah's travels were designed to promote inter-Arab goodwill "as a background for the promotion of his territorial ambitions in both Palestine and Syria."[93]

Immediately upon his return, ʿAbdallah set off for Riyadh, his first visit to the Arabian Peninsula since his family had been evicted from the Hejaz by Ibn Saʿud in 1925. His meeting with the Saudi monarch, which had been consistently, if discreetly, encouraged by Kirkbride,[94] had even less bearing on the events in Palestine than his Cairo visit. For both leaders, however, the visit had much value. In effect, ʿAbdallah was acknowledging his acceptance of the status quo in the peninsula, no easy task even after twenty-three years. In return, he hoped to bolster his own inter-Arab standing. In all of his accounts of the meetings, ʿAbdallah was unsparing in his praise of Ibn Saʿud, "one of the political geniuses of the Arabs in this day and age."[95] Ibn Saʿud, for his part, emphasized to ʿAbdallah that everything that had been at issue between them was dead and forgotten, a statement that ʿAbdallah took to mean that the Saudi claims to Maʿan and Aqaba and a corridor to Syria would no longer be raised.[96]

If ʿAbdallah thought that his journeys would bring immediate benefits, he was expeditiously disabused of the notion. On July 3, Bernadotte's first set of proposals "to promote a peaceful adjustment of the future situation in Palestine" were rejected in toto, even as a basis for discussion, by the League's Political Committee.[97] The centerpiece of the plan had been the establishment of a Jewish-Arab federal union in all of Mandatory Palestine, including Transjordan. It would have, in effect, put the greater part of Palestine in ʿAbdallah's hands, including all of Jerusalem, and all or much of the Negev.

Officially, Transjordan was a party to the Political Committee's total rejection. Despite the plan's favorable character, ʿAbdallah was unwilling to oppose directly the Arab consensus. On the other hand, it was important for Transjordan that its rejection not be taken as its last word on the matter. Thus, it is not surprising that Bernadotte gained the impression from his followup consultations that the leadership in Amman was disappointed with the collective Arab position.[98]

On July 8, ʿAbdallah received a further warning signal regarding Arab attitudes to his territorial plans. On that day, the League Council approved the Political Committee's recommendation to set up a nine-member "provisional civil administration" for those areas of Palestine under Arab authority, a move the other Arab states had studiously refrained from taking in deference to ʿAbdallah.[99] Tawfiq Abu al-Huda viewed the Council's move as limited in nature and essentially demonstrative, and thus went along with its proclamation.[100] His attitude was consistent with a preference within the Transjordanian civilian elite to try to keep Transjordan within the League consensus as much as possible.[101] ʿAbdallah viewed the Council's decision with more gravity, however, and he redoubled his efforts to consolidate the Legion's authority in the areas of Palestine under its control.[102]

Concurrently, ʿAbdallah suffered an even more serious setback. The League Council rejected the Security Council's request for an indefinite prolongation of the cease-fire, which was due to expire on July 9.[103] ʿAbdallah had strongly opposed the renewal of hostilities, as he was both content with Transjordan's military achievements and concerned with the serious shortage of ammunition facing the Arab Legion. Great Britain had suspended the delivery of military supplies in early June. In opposing further fighting he was backed completely by Britain.[104] At the same time, Bevin and his advisers hesitantly refrained from encouraging ʿAbdallah to unilaterally accept a cease-fire extension and Bernadotte's proposal. ʿAbdallah had raised this possibility with Kirkbride and even expressed his willingness to make peace with Israel if the Arab leaders continued to be unreasonable.[105] Britain's extreme caution and even unwillingness to encourage ʿAbdallah in frontally opposing the collective Arab consensus would repeat itself during the king's subsequent attempts to negotiate a separate political settlement with Israel.

Despite expectations that Nuqrashi would be cooperative regarding the extension of the truce, Tawfiq Abu al-Huda found himself in a minority of one at the Council meeting and acceded to the will of the Arab majority.[106] In doing so, he failed to keep ʿAbdallah informed of developments at the meeting. Upon his return home, the Transjordanian government overruled 'Abdallah's wishes and approved the League's rejection of a cease-fire extension.[107] This is, perhaps, the first example of a phenomenon that would repeatedly impinge on 'Abdallah's actions over the remaining three years of his life—the decline in his absolute control of his country's policies.

Whereas Arab leaders were not unaware of the risks involved, they apparently were at least half-convinced by their explanations to their own publics regarding the first cease-fire; namely, that the Arab armies had been on the verge of victory and the cease-fire's continuation would only further benefit the Jews.[108] Bernadotte interpreted their rejection of the cease-fire in this way: They were still "feeling their oats" and had not yet had enough of the fight knocked out of them.[109] No less central to their rejection of the cease-fire's extension was their concern with Arab public opinion because "a long truce was tantamount to an admission of defeat."[110]

'Abdallah immediately displayed his distress with the turn of events. On July 9, with the fighting already under way, he summoned Bernadotte to an urgent meeting, pressing repeatedly for forceful measures by the Security Council to halt the fighting. The sharply worded Security Council resolution that 'Abdallah urged on Bernadotte, including the expressed threat to impose sanctions on the Arab states if they refused to stop fighting, was passed on July 15. The other Arab states angrily acceded to the indefinite cease-fire, which came into effect on July 18.[111] The ten days of fighting brought about significant Israeli gains: the widening of Tel Aviv's hinterland to the point where it was put out of inland artillery range, the capture of Lydda, Ramleh, and the source of the Jerusalem water supply at Ras al-'Ayn, the widening of the link with Jerusalem, and the capture of large portions of the central Galilee from Qawuqji's forces.

For 'Abdallah, the second cease-fire came none too soon. Despite Israel's gains, the position of the Arab Legion in Palestine had not been seriously impaired. Moreover, with Arab leaders no longer "feeling their oats," 'Abdallah now perceived himself to be less shackled by inter-Arab constraints. The consolidation of his rule in the areas of Palestine under the Legion's control appeared even more attainable. He also hoped that the Security Council would impose a settlement based on recommendations by Bernadotte that were likely to be favorable to Transjordan.[112]

At the same time, Arab public opinion—whether in Iraq, Syria, Egypt or among the Palestinian Arabs, particularly those made homeless during the second round of fighting—was incensed over the latest reverses.[113] Arab governments responded accordingly. Even before the cease-fire, the Iraqi government finely tuned its positions to accord with its volatile political public. Alone among the Arab states, it urged rejection of the Security Council's cease-fire calls, and Prime Minister Muzahim al-Pachachi even recommended that the Arab states withdraw from the United Nations.[114] The regent also engaged in a demonstrative effort to organize an Arab counterattack to retake Lydda and Ramleh before the cease-fire took effect. On this he was opposed even by the Iraqi high command.[115] Within Iraq, the government worked diligently to identify itself with nationalist anger, including the sanctioning of political demonstrations by opposition parties against the Arab League's acquiescence to the cease-fire. The result of these steps was favorable as far as the government was concerned: Press and public approval of government policy was general.[116]

The real pivot of inter-Arab relations in the months following the second cease-fire remained in the Transjordan-Egypt sphere. Their military preeminence in Palestine as compared to the other Arab forces necessarily conferred on them the ability to influence the course of events. Thus, the extent of Transjordanian-Egyptian cooperation, that is, the degree of identity of views or the absence thereof, remained vital in determining both collective Arab policy toward Israel and the fate of the remaining portions of Arab Palestine.

The context in which Egyptian-Transjordanian relations unfolded during the second half of 1948 was five-fold: (1) Explorations for an Arab-Israeli settlement were made by Bernadotte, whose revised recommendations to the U.N. General Assembly were published just after his assassination on September 17 by the dissident Jewish underground group LEHI [Fighters for the Freedom of Israel, commonly known in the West as the Stern gang]. The Bernadotte plan included allotting the Negev to the Arabs, preferably 'Abdallah, and the Galilee to an independent Jewish State. (2) There was a related push in Arab quarters to put forth a Palestinian alternative to Transjordanian aggrandizement. (3) The final two rounds of fighting between Egypt and Israel occurred in late October–early November and in late December 1948–early January 1949. (4) Great Britain repeatedly made efforts to coax Cairo and Amman toward a common position that would dovetail with British strategic interests. (5) Separate explorations with Israel were made by both Egypt and Transjordan for a longer-lasting armistice.[117]

As had been true in earlier months, the Amman-Cairo relationship remained ambiguous. Within Transjordan, the king's views were often at variance with those of his ministers. ʿAbdallah viewed the Egyptian-dominated Arab environment as hostile to his plans. He was particularly exercised by pro-mufti political activities, manifested by demonstrations in Hebron and Bethlehem, and was concerned that the mufti was organizing a "Palestine Army," with the active material and financial assistance of the League.[118] He now believed that an Egyptian withdrawal from the Jerusalem area was essential to his struggle against the mufti.[119] He also hoped for two developments that would allow him to deviate from the Arab consensus. The first was forthright British-U.S. backing, which was to be expressed through the implementation of the forthcoming Bernadotte recommendations.[120] The second was an arrangement with the Israelis. In September 1948, ʿAbdallah lobbied for the readmission of non-mufti backers to Lydda and Ramleh, a step he said would raise his prestige, defeat the intrigues of Nuqrashi and Hajj Amin and deal a blow to the League as a whole, enable him to achieve an Egyptian withdrawal from the vicinity of Jerusalem, and serve as a basis for a five-year arrangement between Israel and Transjordan. That arrangement was to include a population exchange, a solution to the Jewish electric and potash concessions under ʿAbdallah's control, and the granting of possible economic concessions for the Israelis in Transjordan.[121]

By contrast, the views of ʿAbdallah's ministers regarding Transjordanian-Arab relations were more timid and at the same time more sophisticated. This was further evidenced in mid-September following the Arab League's Political Committee declaration of support for the creation of a "Palestinian government," an advance since its call in July for a Palestinian "civil administration." ʿAbdallah viewed the Political Committee's action as a direct challenge to his own authority, and proclaimed his intention to oppose it.[122] His ministers, however, were initially buoyed by the fact that neither Nuqrashi nor the Iraqi delegation favored ʿAzzam's proposal to set up a mufti-led government and a League-funded Palestine Arab Army. They believed the committee's desire for the establishment of a Palestinian government to be provisional only. If the Arabs of Palestine agreed among themselves on the subject of creating an administration, the League would go along, provided that the head of the new Palestine government was acceptable to the Arab state. Concurrently, the idea of a Palestine army was dropped, to Transjordan's satisfaction. Instead, it was agreed that each Arab army operating in Palestine could organize in its area Palestinian volunteer detachments that it would equip and control.[123]

The equanimity of Transjordan's ministers can be explained from at least three angles. On the issue of a Palestinian government, as on so many others, the fear of straying too far from the Arab consensus took priority. Abu al-Huda had always been confident that Transjordan would in the end be able to maintain its control in Arab Palestine, and believed that avoiding an open breach with the other Arab states would allow his country to buy enough time until the consolidation of its rule would be completed.[124] In addition, the fact that the whole notion of a Palestine government had a distinctly unreal quality to it led the ministers to underestimate the impact of the Political Committee's decision, perhaps even to the point of not expecting any steps at implementation. Perhaps the third reason was the most telling. According to a scornful member of ʿAbdallah's royal court, the "pro-Egyptian" orientation of Tawfiq Abu al-Huda and Defense Minister Fawzi al-Mulqi stemmed from their fears for their personal safety in light of Husayni threats.[125]

If Transjordan's ministers did not expect concrete steps toward establishing a Palestinian alternative to ʿAbdallah they were mistaken. Upon the official publication of the decision on September 20, the Arab Higher Committee promptly proclaimed the creation of the "Government of All Palestine," with its seat in Gaza. Ten days later, on September 30, it convened what was designed as the inaugural session of the "Palestine National Council," intended to be the parliamentary branch of the Government of All-Palestine. Hajj Amin was chosen as president of the Council, underscoring the gathering's anti-ʿAbdallah character.

The Egyptian government was extremely annoyed by Hajj Amin's presence in Gaza, all the more so because Nuqrashi believed that he had dissuaded him from attending.[126] Before the gathering adjourned, the mufti was compelled to return to Cairo, accompanied by Egyptian security personnel, with Nuqrashi turning down Hajj Amin's appeal to block the order.[127] Nonetheless, Cairo took the lead in extending diplomatic recognition to the new government. In this it was swiftly followed by all other Arab governments (in disregard of British appeals to do otherwise), except Transjordan.[128]

The reasons behind the swift Arab recognition of the Gaza government were articulated by Lebanon's President Bishara al-Khuri and Prime Minister Riyad al-Sulh to a British diplomat. Arab motives, they said, were threefold. First was a desire to placate Arab public opinion. Second was a determination to safeguard the Arab juridical position, that is, the Palestinian Arab claim to sovereignty over the whole of Palestine; this was directed against both Israel and 'Abdallah. Third, there was the belief that such a government, even if it was a "one-room government," would be the best focal point for continuing resistance to the Jewish state, particularly because the Arab states might not be able to openly carry on the struggle.[129]

Iraqi motivations behind its granting of diplomatic recognition were somewhat different. The regent, for instance, was altogether opposed to the move.[130] The Gaza government, Prime Minister Muzahim al-Pachachi told his unhappy British interlocutor, could not possibly survive for long, and the remaining areas of Palestine would sooner or later have to be annexed by Transjordan alone, or jointly with Egypt. For the moment, the government of all-Palestine served to show that neither the Palestinians nor the Arab states were ready to acknowledge defeat. Eventually, he admitted, there would have to be an acceptance of the Jewish state's existence, but for now it was politically impossible to acknowledge this publicly. To do so, he said, would cause a revolt in Iraq.[131]

Within Transjordan, Tawfiq Abu al-Huda and Defense Minister Fawzi al-Mulqi tried on a number of occasions to convince the king to follow the Arab lead and recognize the Gaza government, but to no avail.[132] 'Abdallah was perturbed by both Iraqi and Egyptian behavior, to the point that he again considered withdrawing from the League. Regarding Iraq, he was initially concerned over a possible shift in orientation. The fact that Pachachi had counseled 'Abdallah to recognize the Gaza government "temporarily" did not sit well with him.[133] Nor did reports that the Iraqis had asked for a million-dollar loan from Egypt: If it were to be granted, he feared, Iraq might tilt into the Egyptian orbit.[134]

Such a tilt contained more direct implications as well. Iraqi army contingents were, in effect, the only military formation left in Transjordan, and 'Abdallah was concerned that they might get out of hand if fighting in Palestine were resumed and went badly for the Arabs.[135]

Iraqi attempts to mollify 'Abdallah were, on the whole, successful. Nonetheless, 'Abdallah remained piqued: One expression of his irritation was his declining to sign an order placing the Arab Legion under the supreme command of the Iraqi commander. This was mandated by a largely meaningless agreement to unify their commands that was concluded on August 4, 1948.

Developments along the southern front in the last quarter of 1948 altered Egyptian and Transjordanian calculations. Egypt suffered significant reverses as a result of an Israeli offensive in the second half of October, including the loss of Beersheba, the cutting off of the Hebron district from Egyptian forces in the Negev, and the entrapment of an entire Egyptian brigade in the Faluja "pocket." In the Galilee Qawuqji's forces were evicted entirely, and in southern Lebanon Israel temporarily occupied a number of villages. A by-product of Arab losses was the almost total collapse of the Government of All-Palestine and a corresponding rise in 'Abdallah's stature among the Palestinian Arabs.[136]

The effects of Egypt's losses on the Cairo-Amman relationship were both manifold and contradictory. During the following months Faruq harped incessantly about Transjordan's failure to come to the aid of Egyptian forces. The Egyptian media, instigated by the palace, branded 'Abdallah a traitor to the Arab cause. One consequence was that palace views against withdrawing from the Negev and thus leaving it clear for 'Abdallah stiffened further.[137]

According to some Arab accounts, the inactivity of the Legion during the last months of 1948 was part of an Israeli-Transjordanian conspiracy.[138] David Ben-Gurion's contemporary account paints a more complex picture. The Israelis understood that Transjordan had no interest in any further combat, something that certainly influenced their decision to attack the Egyptian forces in strength. Ben-Gurion initially believed that the Iraqis would react to the Israeli offensive and possibly drag Transjordan in as well. He quickly modified this view. In a short battle, he wrote, it was possible that neither Iraq nor Transjordan would get involved, nor was it clear that Egypt would even ask them to do so. One week after the offensive began, Ben-Gurion vetoed a plan put forth by Lieutenant-Colonel Moshe Dayan to attack Egyptian forces in Bayt Jalla, south of Jerusalem. Among other reasons, he wanted to avoid involving nearby Arab Legion and Iraqi units after they had been quiescent during the Negev offensive. Ironically, the next day the Israelis overheard an Arab Legion order *not* to go to the aid of Egyptian units in the same areas that were requesting the Legion's assistance following their own violation of the cease-fire.[139]

Nuqrashi did not participate in the anti-'Abdallah campaign of vituperation and recrimination. In fact, at the Arab League Political Committee meeting in Alexandria in mid-November, he rejected 'Azzam Pasha's criticism of the Arab Legion's passivity, stating that it was fully extended and could not be expected to do more. Instead, he requested that the Iraqis help the Egyptian forces at Faluja. Prime Minister Pachachi of Iraq promised to take action, but the Iraqi general staff refused to budge.[140]

Nuqrashi's moderation toward Transjordan was not a one-time exercise. Instead, it indicated a new willingness on both his and Foreign Minister Ahmad Muhammad Khashaba's part to consider an agreement with Transjordan on the disposition of the remainder of Arab Palestine, even if it clashed with Nuqrashi's long-held opposition to territorial aggrandizement. It would be dangerous, said Khashaba Pasha to Harold Beeley of Britain's Foreign Office, for the Arabs to permit the establishment of an independent Arab state in the Arab parts of Palestine. Furthermore, he stated, the Egyptians desired part, but not all, of the Negev for themselves. As to the rest of the Negev, he preferred not to commit himself. He did, however, offer a lengthy exposition on how Egypt should look after her own interests and not seek closer ties with the other Arab countries.[141] On another occasion, Khashaba was more amenable than other Arab representatives to a proposed British resolution at the United Nations that would instruct the U.N.-established Palestine Conciliation Commission (PCC) to proceed on the basis of partition. "The Arabs must recognize," he told Beeley, "that they were not strong enough to give effect to their wishes in Palestine at the present." Only a provisional settlement, as opposed to the fragile truce then prevailing, would enable them to begin strengthening themselves, militarily and otherwise.¹⁴²

Egypt's U.N. ambassador, Mahmud Fawzi Bey, was even more explicit than Khashaba Pasha regarding cooperation with Transjordan. In a conversation with the U.S. ambassador in London, he stated that no real dispute existed between Cairo and Amman regarding the territorial disposition of the remaining parts of Arab Palestine. On the other hand, the claims he advanced for Egypt regarding the Negev were greater than Khashaba's.¹⁴³

On December 1, 'Abdallah injected another factor into an already muddled picture by convening a gathering of Palestinian notables in Jericho for the purpose of legitimizing the extension of his rule to the West Bank. After some hesitation among the participants and much prodding by the palace, the conference proclaimed the union of Palestine and Transjordan and acknowledged 'Abdallah as king of the united country.¹⁴⁴ Official Arab reaction was uniformly negative.¹⁴⁵ Faruq took the lead in publicly rebuking 'Abdallah. The Syrians immediately followed with their own condemnations and speculation was rife regarding possible League sanctions against Transjordan, and even expulsion from the League.¹⁴⁶ At that moment, however, the deeply embedded tendency within the inter-Arab system to shy away from too great a degree of polarization reasserted itself. Within Transjordan, the Council of Ministers, supported by Kirkbride, sharply opposed 'Abdallah's wish to implement the Jericho decision immediately. They very nearly resigned over the matter, but 'Abdallah backed down and accepted a ministerial resolution that merely welcomed the Jericho decision as a step toward Arab unity and promised to adopt measures to secure their implementation as soon as circumstances permitted. As a further sop to Arab sensibilities, the resolution committed Transjordan fully to assist the refugees from Palestine and to secure their return to their homes.¹⁴⁷

As was so frequently the case regarding Transjordanian-Egyptian differences over Palestine, the Iraqis searched for a middle position. On the regent's initiative, Nuri al-Sa'id (who held no public office at the time) led a delegation to Amman on December 15 to urge 'Abdallah to refrain from implementing the Jericho resolutions.¹⁴⁸ Although both the Iraqi prime minister and the foreign minister disclaimed any responsibility for Nuri's mission, they were no less anxious to heal the inter-Arab rifts that had opened up. The Arab states, said Pachachi, should be grateful, not critical, if King ʿAbdallah could achieve any results in Palestine. In any case, Iraq had no intention of voting for Transjordan's expulsion from the League. If it were officially proposed, Pachachi would act to have it shelved.[149] Because expulsion from the League requires a unanimous vote, Iraq's opposition rendered meaningless the threat being made against Transjordan.

Lebanese leaders were also put out by Faruq's hostility, fearing that it would only strengthen the hands of extremists in the region. Some sentiment was also expressed in Beirut for a change in its standing alignment with the League's anti-Hashimite majority. At the same time, President Khuri was anxious that ʿAbdallah take no precipitate action either to implement the Jericho decisions or to conclude an open deal with Israel.[150]

Even ʿAzzam Pasha was now concerned with leaning too hard on ʿAbdallah. Not only would Transjordan's exiting from the League be a vital blow to Arab unity, which ʿAzzam had vigorously promoted throughout his career, but it also might give ʿAbdallah the final push into making a separate deal with Israel.[151] The fact that Transjordan and Israel had agreed on November 30 to a "complete and sincere" cease-fire in the Jerusalem area served as a warning that this could occur.

Egyptian-Transjordanian relations thus continued to fluctuate. Nuqrashi was particularly incensed by two messages from ʿAbdallah. The first claimed that the Palestinian Arabs were with him, whereas the second pledged to act in a constitutional manner regarding Palestine, to keep the other Arab states informed of developments through diplomatic channels, and not to do anything contrary to their will.[152]

When Tawfiq Abu al-Huda expressed his own anger with Nuqrashi's replies, Nuqrashi became conciliatory and hinted at the desire for a personal discussion.[153] Nuqrashi was apparently interested in discussing a series of questions regarding future negotiating strategy with Israel, which he had formulated during his meetings with U.N. acting mediator Ralph Bunche, and on which he had previously requested Abu al-Huda's assistance.[154] This, coupled with a message from a Palestinian journalist in Egypt encouraging Abu al-Huda to go to Egypt to state his case, convinced Abu al-Huda to meet with Nuqrashi.[155] But on the eve of Abu al-Huda's departure, ʿAbdallah sabotaged the trip. On December 16, he sent a message to Sudan's

'Abd al-Rahman al-Mahdi (son of the legendary Sudanese Mahdi and leader of the pro-independence faction in Sudan) congratulating him on his efforts to achieve independence, perhaps the most open challenge ever made by any Arab leader to Egypt's claims of suzerainty over the Sudan. Abu al-Huda had not been privy to the message before its dispatch. Nevertheless, the severely negative reaction in Egypt led him to cancel his trip and even threaten to resign.[156] Subsequent overtures by Abu al-Huda to Nuqrashi were ignored. On December 28, Nuqrashi was assassinated by a member of the Muslim Brotherhood. Abu al-Huda now insisted that any initiative to discuss the Palestine question must now come from the Egyptian side.[157]

None was forthcoming, however, even from those Egyptians more willing than Nuqrashi to countenance a territorial deal with Transjordan. Egyptian officials shied away from dealing with Transjordan directly because 'Abdallah was thought to be ready to negotiate directly with Israel, and too close an association with 'Abdallah would thus taint Egypt.[158] Nor could anyone in Egypt publicly advocate the annexation of part of the Negev to Egypt. As a solution, palace confidant Karim Thabit suggested that 'Abdallah announce that he would refer the Jericho conference resolutions to the Arab League. The League would certainly oppose 'Abdallah's becoming "King of Palestine and Transjordan" but might be induced to agree to certain parts of Palestine being annexed to Transjordan. At the same time, 'Abdallah should negotiate with Faruq, *dans les coulisses*, an arrangement leaving Egyptian forces in a portion of the Negev, including Gaza. Eventually, their occupation would come to be accepted as permanent. All of this, Thabit concluded, should be proposed by 'Abdallah directly to Faruq.[159]

Nothing is more illustrative of how Egyptian thinking was being outpaced by events than Defense Minister Muhammad Haydar Pasha's remarks to Britain's Ambassador Sir Ronald Campbell in the midst of the final Israel campaign against Egyptian forces in late December. The Israelis were now absolutely sure that Transjordan's Arab Legion would not come to Egypt's aid.[160] Haydar made it clear to Campbell that a serious effort to come to an agreement with Amman was vital for the common interests of Great Britain, Egypt, and Transjordan. Egypt could not appear to be seeking agreement with 'Abdallah about dividing up the Negev simply because it was being put on the defensive militarily. The deal he was contemplating, to be achieved through British mediation, awarded Transjordan the stretch of coast north of Gaza, plus the region east and southeast of Beersheba down to Aqaba. Whether or not Transjordan would get a corridor to Gaza and free port facilities there could be worked out. All this was on the condition that Israel's frontier not be drawn further south than the October 14 positions, namely those prior to Israel's October offensive. Finally, Haydar made it clear to Campbell that it would be better not to say anything to Nuqrashi about his ideas.

Haydar was "95 percent sure" that the military emergency posed by Israel's latest offensive could be overcome.[161] By the beginning of January 1949, the Egyptians had been pushed out of Palestine, except for the Gaza area and the Faluja pocket, and on January 13, direct armistice negotiations between Israel and Egypt commenced on the island of Rhodes. For now, at least, the option of real Egyptian-Transjordanian coordination had disappeared.

AN ASSESSMENT

Like no other issue since 1945, the first Arab-Israeli war sorely pointed up the gap between the ideology of all-Arab cooperation and common purpose, and the limitation imposed on its realization by inter-Arab conflicts and particularist, individual policies. Military and political coordination had been desultory, resulting in a colossal failure. A non-Arab state had been established in an area considered to be an integral part of the Arab patrimony. The failure in Palestine would cost Arab regimes dearly in the years ahead, for it catalyzed political opposition among alternative elites and newly mobilized sectors of the population alike.

The defeat also reflected badly on the Arab League as an institution and on ʿAzzam Pasha as secretary-general. Since 1945, ʿAzzam had partially succeeded in staking out an independent role for himself as all-Arab spokesman, notwithstanding that he nearly always identified Arab interests with Egyptian interests. In 1948, he was fully engaged in attempting to coordinate Arab policies and to sell them to the outside world. As developments progressed, his activities became increasingly superfluous. By July 1948, ʿAzzam had lost favor even with his Egyptian patrons, to the point of becoming a scapegoat for Arab failure. Faruq complained to a British diplomat that "the dreams that 'Azzam had put into [my] head of leading the Arab States . . . were empty, and based on nothing but the thin air into which they had vanished."[162]

The ebbs and flows of the Egyptian-Transjordanian relationship during 1948 poignantly illustrate the complexities of the inter-Arab web. As a rule, while the collective Arab interest would have been served by more sustained collaboration, the particularist policies of each generally took priority. Nowhere was this more evident than in their failure to arrive at an agreed-on stand regarding the disposition of the remaining parts of Arab Palestine, especially the Negev. At the same time, their mutual recognition of each other's assets was never far from their policy calculations. The weeks before the British withdrawal provide an apt illustration. The Egyptians knew that without 'Abdallah, the Arab cause was utterly hopeless and thus accepted his military plans; the Transjordanians hoped that Egyptian involvement would legitimize what they intended to do, namely, acquire as much territory as possible. Subsequently, when the Egyptians promoted a Palestinian alternative to 'Abdallah, they did so in a not totally unrestrained fashion. Furthermore, at least part of these efforts were more concerned with the declarative demonstration of fidelity to the cause of Arab Palestine than with actually blocking 'Abdallah.

In addition, the danger of pushing each other too far was always present in Egyptian and Transjordanian minds. For Egypt to ostracize Transjordan or even expel it from the League carried two risks. The first was the possible delegitimization of the inclusive Arab nationalist ideology that all Arab leaders professed. The second, more immediate threat was that Transjordan's expulsion would ironically eliminate the collective Arab restraints blocking Transjordan from making a separate peace with Israel, which was likely to be underwritten by Britain and the United States. Conversely, at least part of the Transjordanian elite was concerned over the widespread disillusionment in Egypt toward Arab affairs at the end of 1948. Too quick an incorporation of the Arab Palestine rump into Transjordan, mused 'Abd al-Mun'im al-Rifa'i, the brother of Foreign Minister Samir al-Rifa'i, might push Egypt to withdraw from Palestine and from the League. In this event, he continued, Transjordan would likely be blamed for undermining Arab unity by creating a situation that Egypt could no longer tolerate.¹⁶³ In other words, Egyptian and Transjordanian leaders were concerned with maintaining the existing, delicate equilibrium among the Arab states and geared their policies accordingly.

Did this include, on Cairo's part, accepting the eclipse of one of the system's weaker, nonstate actors, the Arabs of Palestine? Egypt's unhappiness with the Mufti's involvement in the Gaza government, its restrictions on the latter's activities and its decision not to press for seating the Gaza government at the November 1948 meeting of the Arab League Political Committee all indicate that Cairo's aversion to pushing 'Abdallah to the brink was stronger than its fidelity to the Palestinian Arabs.

Two other points are worth noting. True, the Jewish Agency leadership had maintained fairly continuous contact with Arab statesmen over the preceding years, but Israel's successes on the battlefield now gave it, a non-Arab actor, at least the potential for considerably greater leverage and maneuvering room. What this was to mean was not yet clear. The most optimistic among Israeli diplomats, Eliahu Sasson, actually raised with the Egyptians the possibility of a "Ligue Orientale," which would include Israel and would supersede the Arab League.¹⁶⁴ Despite his interlocutor's openness to the idea, it had no chance of being implemented. Still, on a more concrete level, the parallel soundings between Israel and Egypt and Israel and Transjordan provided at least the potential for new coalition alignments beyond an exclusive Arab framework. In the fall of 1948, all three parties were aware of this potential. 'Abdallah, for example, informed his Israeli interlocutors that he did not mind Israel's negotiations with Egypt, and in fact thought that they would pave the way for an understanding between himself and Israel. At the same time, he was concerned that his interests be safeguarded, particularly in Gaza. Israel's Foreign Minister Moshe Sharett and Prime Minister David Ben-Gurion even more so were concerned that an Israeli-Egyptian settlement permitting Egyptian annexation of the Southern coastal area around Gaza might well bring Israel into conflict with Transjordan and Great Britain.¹⁶⁵

At this stage, contacts among them were outpaced by events. The move by Israel in late December 1948 to pressure Transjordan into concluding a full peace agreement was rebuffed, and when Egypt decided to negotiate for an armistice Israel gave it priority.[166] Efforts to promote a settlement between Israel and its eastern neighbor were resumed in the winter of 1949 and 1950.

Finally, the decline of Britain's ability to shape regional developments continued. The Bernadotte Plan seemed to offer a recovery for British interests, and the British were reasonably hopeful that it could be imposed over Arab and Israeli opposition. This could be done, however, only in conjunction with the United States, a fact that indicates the extent of Britain's decline in hegemony. When the United States waffled, the plan was doomed, and London was reduced to trying to nudge Egypt and Transjordan toward a common policy.[167]

4

UPHEAVAL AND CRISIS

IT DID NOT TAKE LONG for the reality of the collective Arab defeat in Palestine to sink in. The birth of the State of Israel, the first Arab-Israeli war, and the resulting displacement of more than half of the Palestinian Arab population swiftly entered the Arab political lexicon under the heading *al-nakba* (the catastrophe).[1] Intellectuals and more thoughtful political activists engaged in a great deal of self-criticism.[2] For Syria and Egypt, the defeat served as a catalyst for political upheaval. The ruling elite in Iraq was better able to insulate itself from the defeat, thanks mainly to its distance from the front. Its poor performance, however, was added to the list of sins being compiled by radical nationalist elements. In regional terms, the effect was no less profound. From January 1949 to the middle of 1950, the loosely cooperative inter-Arab framework that had emerged in 1945 was plunged into the throes of a systemic crisis that threatened to lead to a significant alteration, even transformation, of inter-Arab relations and in the overall regional balance of power.[3]

Against the background of repeated internal upheavals, Syria's future became a central pivot of inter-Arab rivalry and competition in ways not previously witnessed. The "struggle for Syria" was not, as has been postulated, the only central theme of inter-Arab affairs during the period.[4] In the Arab-Israeli sphere, the relationships between particular and all-Arab interests were repeatedly tested, most profoundly by Jordanian explorations toward a peace settlement with Israel. In a separate but related issue, the disposition of those parts of Palestine remaining in Arab hands was, in turn, a subject of discussion, consensus, and then bitter dispute between Egypt and Jordan, leading to an Egyptian initiative to expel Jordan from the Arab League. Accompanying these two issues was a more general one: the fate of the Arab League, its future role, even its existence.

The nature and extent of Egypt's relationship with the Arab world was again a subject for debate within Egypt, marking another round in a cyclical pattern that has existed from the 1930s until the present day. On the whole, however, Egyptian policy aims did not deviate from previously established lines: promoting and maintaining Egypt's leadership in the region and blocking any challenges to it. When possible, this was to be done through the mechanism of the Arab League. After the debacle in Palestine, however, Egyptian leaders were more sensitive than ever to the need to preserve Egypt's freedom of action and avoid too great a reliance on its Arab neighbors.

With regard to the inter-Arab competition over Syria, Egypt sought to block possible Iraqi gains by supporting anti-Hashimite forces there. Saudi Arabia was a partner to this effort. At an important juncture, Cairo also deemed it vital to employ the Arab League mechanism in pursuit of its aims. In the Arab-Israeli sphere, Egyptian strategies were more complex, particularly as the focus shifted from negotiating armistice agreements to attempts to reach more far-reaching arrangements. As in 1948, Egypt's pursuit of particular interests necessitated considerable tactical flexibility in dealing with Jordan. At times, this entailed extending only a perfunctory nod toward Jordan's concerns. At other times, Egypt was compelled to display considerable understanding. At still other points, Egypt found it necessary to strongly oppose Jordanian initiatives. Throughout, Egypt kept an ever-watchful eye on Jordan's activities.

The policy aims of Iraq were more limited. Notwithstanding differences within the Iraqi hierarchy, they were consistent with previous goals. Iraq still held pretensions to Fertile Crescent leadership and desired to lessen the influence of the Arab League framework, in general, and 'Azzam Pasha, in particular. Two factors distinguished this particular period from previous years. The first was Iraq's unilateral military withdrawal from Palestine, marking a major deemphasis of Iraqi involvement in Arab-Israeli issues. The second was the internal fragmentation of the Syrian polity, creating new possibilities for Iraq and intensified competition with Egypt and Saudi Arabia.

Iraq's strategy in Syria was to promote pro-Hashimite tendencies, although there were differences within Iraq regarding the degree of initiative to be taken. To block the involvement of other Arab states, Iraq occasionally sought understanding with Egypt on the Syrian question, as opposed to frontal confrontation. Such an approach was reminiscent of Nuri al-Sa'id's overtures to Nahhas Pasha in 1943. It also jibed with a more general tendency within part of the Iraqi political establishment (not including the regent) to view Egypt's participation in Arab affairs as vital.[5]

Jordan's attention, like Iraq's, was directed primarily toward a single set of issues. Jordan's foremost priority at this juncture, however, was to consolidate its position in Palestine, although 'Abdallah never gave up aspiring for a Greater Syria.[6] The inter-Arab aspects of Jordan's strategies in the Arab-Israeli sphere mirrored those of Egypt, with the pursuit of particularist interests being conducted with considerable tactical flexibility. An additional factor, in Jordan's case, was the decline in 'Abdallah's absolute authority and the concomitant increase in influence of Jordan's civilian politicians. During the first half of 1950, the interaction between Jordanian internal dynamics and Egyptian-led Arab pressure on Jordan was decisive in preventing 'Abdallah's bold initiative toward Israel from bearing fruit. Nonetheless, 'Abdallah was able to buck Arab pressure and consolidate his hold over the remaining portions of Arab Palestine. Saudi Arabia, Syria, and Lebanon were in similar situations because their ability to shape regional events was limited. Saudi Arabia's weakness impelled it to seek Western assistance in pursuit of its regional goals. The Saudis remained obsessed with Hashimite ambitions toward Syria and liberally employed financial largesse, their single weapon in combatting Hashimite activities there.[7] In the Arab-Israeli sphere, the Saudis consistently entreated for an imposed British-U.S. solution.

Lebanon's vulnerability was suggested by its efforts in early 1949 to achieve cooperation between Great Britain and the Arab states in general and Syria in particular. The Syrians also gave hints of working in the same direction.[8] The thrust of Quwwatli's policy, however, was to search for Arab backing to bolster Syria against Israel and 'Abdallah. Thus, he sought to establish closer ties with Iraq and Egypt. Quwwatli also emphasized the importance of Egyptian involvement in Arab affairs.[9] Elsewhere, Quwwatli apparently lent support to a plot inspired by Hajj Amin al-Husayni to kill 'Abdallah, a plan that was frustrated by the Transjordanians at the end of March 1949.[10] Whatever leverage Syria had in regional affairs was decisively weakened by Quwwatli's overthrow on March 30, 1949, and the resultant instability in Syrian political life.

ARAB-ISRAELI NEGOTIATIONS, ROUND 1

The central question on the inter-Arab agenda at the beginning of 1949 was how, or even whether, to formulate a collective Arab formula for political dealings with Israel, either in the framework of the upcoming armistice talks on the island of Rhodes or through the Palestine Conciliation Commission (PCC), which was due shortly to begin explorations for a permanent settlement. The British strongly favored it, believing that a common position among the three principal Arab states—Egypt, Transjordan, and Iraq—offered the best hope for reaching a settlement in which the Arabs could acquiesce.[11] Moreover, a common position might still make possible the redrawing of frontiers so as to make Egypt and Transjordan limitrophe in the Negev, something that British officials desired. Thus, notwithstanding the lack of progress during the preceding months in effecting a common position between Cairo and Amman, the British renewed their efforts. This time they sought to include the Iraqis, hoping that they would help bring Egyptian and Transjordanian positions closer.

Nuri al-Sa'id's agenda was not commensurate with British entreaties, however, for his primary concern was to avoid being saddled with part of the blame for the Arab defeat in Palestine. Moreover, the entire thrust of his policies was in the demonstrative realm, geared to shoring up his position internally and regionally. In any case, Iraq's leverage on Egypt and Transjordan was limited.

Shortly after the conclusion of the last round of Egyptian-Israeli fighting in January 1949, Nuri formulated a four-point plan designed to serve as the basis of PCC-based negotiations for an Arab-Israeli settlement. The plan's features were as follows. First, all of Jerusalem would come under Palestinian Arab rule (although in practice Nuri was not antagonistic toward 'Abdallah's ambitions there), with freedom of worship guaranteed. Second, Israel's frontiers would be guaranteed by the United Nations, and also by Great Britain and the United States, if need be, and Israel's armed forces were to be disbanded, except for police. Third, all Arab refugees would be allowed to return to their homes or receive compensation if they so desired. Failure to do so, he warned, would bring about the mass expulsion of Iraqi Jewry to Palestine. Fourth, the port of Haifa and the terminal of the Anglo-Iraqi Oil Company pipeline would be placed under international control.[12]

The purely demonstrative nature of the Iraqi posture was never more in evidence. None of the conditions had the remotest chance of being accepted, even as a basis for discussion by Israel, a point not lost on other Arab leaders. 'Abdallah, for one, characterized them as conditions that might be imposed by victors but did not jibe with the existing realities, and he intentionally kept the document (in his waistcoat pocket, no less) from his ministers.[13] Hand in hand with Nuri's declarative posturing came a firm disinclination to be associated in any way with the armistice talks, so as to give the Iraqis "the chance of withdrawal from Palestine without incurring the odium of recognizing Arab defeat."[14] At the same time, the Iraqis continued to give private assurances that they would not object to any settlement reached by the others.[15] They assented to whatever armistice arrangements Transjordan could obtain, which would also cover the Iraqi front in Palestine, and they allowed Transjordan to set up a civil administration in the areas occupied by the Iraqi army, on the condition that the Transjordanians give it no publicity.[16] Nuri's final gesture was to propose sending the Egyptians a mobile column in the event that fighting resumed on their front. Subsequent Egyptian inquiries to verify Iraqi intentions if the cease-fire were to break down drew an evasive response.[17]

The Transjordanian and Egyptian leaderships were not particularly keen on developing a common stance. They went along with British-inspired contacts mainly to satisfy Britain, but they made sure to avoid having their hands tied. They were more geared to pursuing their own separate talks with Israel, although here, too, there were differences. The Egyptians were especially concerned lest Transjordan be first to conclude an agreement with Israel, which would expose Egyptian forces to further Israeli military pressure. From a historical perspective, Egypt's unwillingness either to coordinate positions at Rhodes or to concert directly with ʿAbdallah was similar to Anwar al-Sadat's behavior at Camp David thirty years later vis-à-vis King Husayn of Jordan on both policy and personal levels. ʿAbdallah, for his part, was impatient to get on with a peace settlement and confident that he could do so without being hindered by the other Arab states.[18] The main beneficiaries of all this, as Britain's Foreign Office noted, were the Israelis, although Israel's own efforts to manipulate Arab positions through tendentious propaganda, bribes, and so on, were desultory and had little impact.[19]

ʿAbdallah's deep mistrust of the Egyptians was evidenced in his attitude toward the future status of the Gaza area. If Egypt were to be given Gaza, ʿAbdallah told the Israelis, it would mean that Arab extremists such as the mufti would be handed a base from which to foment trouble throughout the region.[20] At one point, he told his interlocutors that if Gaza could not be obtained for Jordan, then even Israeli rule was preferable to that of Egypt. The Israeli response was to try to explain that some Egyptian presence in Gaza would be unavoidable until a final settlement was achieved. At the same time, Israeli negotiators conveyed Ben-Gurion's understanding of Transjordan's need for an outlet to the Mediterranean.[21] But at this stage Israel was not giving serious thought to ʿAbdallah's requests. Although they initially demanded an Egyptian withdrawal from Gaza, Israeli policymakers did not countenance a possible transfer of the region to Transjordan in the event of Egyptian compliance.[22] As it happened, Egypt stood firm and although Israel's chief negotiator, Walter Eytan, voiced concern to the Egyptians that Israel's conceding to continued Egyptian control in Gaza might jeopardize the chances of agreement with Transjordan, Israel's overall satisfaction with the terms of the Egyptian-Israeli armistice took priority.[23]

Similarly, the Egyptians were firm in opposing any mention of Transjordan in their armistice agreement.[24] Moreover, they asked the Israelis to limit their talks with Transjordan to military issues. Following a number of meetings with Egyptian officials, Eliahu Sasson, Israel's seasoned Arabist, concluded that although Egypt desired to forestall formal annexation moves by ʿAbdallah, it did not believe that an independent Palestinian Arab state was a viable option. Gaza, by contrast, already had a special status in Egyptian eyes. Its ultimate future, Sasson was informed, would best be determined by a referendum among the inhabitants. His Egyptian interlocutors were definitely not in favor of turning the Gaza area over to ʿAbdallah.[25]

In spite of British prodding, Egyptian-Transjordanian soundings during January and February 1949 were inconclusive. Once the Egyptian-Israeli armistice talks neared successful conclusion, however, the atmosphere between Egypt and Transjordan began to warm up. On the eve of the armistice agreement (signed on February 24, 1949), Cairo conveyed to Amman a more forthright willingness to concert positions regarding the next stage of talks with Israel. Moreover, Egypt's Prime Minister ʿAbd al-Hadi was sympathetic to Transjordan's aspirations in Jerusalem. He also stated that Arab rule in the Negev was the important thing, not whether it was in Transjordanian or Egyptian hands.[26] The Transjordanians, as well as Sir Alec Kirkbride, were encouraged, and Tawfiq Abu al-Huda cabled instructions to his minister in Cairo to suggest a meeting between the former and an Egyptian cabinet minister. Unexplainably, the initial set of messages never arrived.[27]

In the meantime, the relatively low priority that Egypt and Transjordan accorded the Negev and the overall lack of a common negotiating stance made it that much easier for Israel to implement its own strategies. In mid-February, as its negotiations with Egypt neared completion, Israel decided to stall during the talks with Transjordan and instead urge Bunche to concentrate on the discussions with Lebanon. The breathing space this was to provide would permit the carrying out of "Operation ʿUvda."[28] Events went according to plan. The operation was successfully carried out between March 6–10. Israel established a presence on the shores of the Gulf of Aqaba and was consequently better able to press its claim for retention of the entire Negev.

Just as in the previous December, the pace of events again outran Egyptian official thinking. On March 7, in the midst of "Operation ʿUvda," Egypt's Foreign Minister Khashaba reiterated to the British ambassador his government's long-standing views regarding the Negev. Great Britain, he said, should take the lead in bringing about a common Egyptian-Transjordanian stand regarding the disposition of the area south of the projected Israeli frontier, especially because Egypt could not concert with ʿAbdallah directly (backtracking from his prime minister's recent conciliatory expressions). He was too "versatile," Khashaba declared, forever changing his mind, and therefore making it impossible to know what his objectives were. As for the Israeli frontier, that was a question for ʿAbdallah alone. Whatever he could obtain would be satisfactory for Egypt. This actually implied a preference for a Transjordanian "buffer" area between Egypt and Israel. Similarly, in regard to the rest of Arab Palestine, Egypt would be glad to see Transjordan receive all of it because Egypt had no ambitions or desires there. His recognition of the existing situation was something that had been absent from Egyptian official thinking in previous months.[29]

ʿAbdallah was not overly disturbed by Israel's advances in the Negev. He had received prior notification of Israel's plan in general terms,[30] and in any case, was more concerned with wrapping up the Transjordanian-Israeli armistice talks. At this stage, his Arab policies were focused on two areas: easing tension with Egypt, and achieving the replacement of Iraqi troops in Palestine with his own forces. On March 14, ʿAbdallah dispatched a long message to Khashaba Pasha. Motivated by his desire "to find out the true reasons" for Egyptian hostility to Transjordan, he laid forth what Kirkbride termed a "reasonabl[y] uncontroversial" version of the Palestine war, and particularly the conduct of the Arab Legion. If Khashaba was really interested in removing the existing suspicions, ʿAbdallah wrote, Amman awaited his reply. ʿAbdallah closed the message by noting that he had desired to write to Faruq directly but was prevented from doing so by Faruq's failure to reply to a previous message. Moreover, he added, "it has come to my knowledge that His Majesty is surrounded by slanderers from Syria, the Lebanon, and Haj Amin." According to Khashaba, an additional communiqué from ʿAbdallah had spoken favorably of Egyptian needs with respect to Palestine and of Egypt's central role in preserving the Arab League. In response, Khashaba then dispatched his own friendly message to Abu al-Huda (who claimed Khashaba as a personal friend). These exchanges made Abu al-Huda determined to use the opportunity of their upcoming participation in a meeting in Beirut between Arab states' representatives and the PCC to work for a reconciliation with Egypt.[31] The accounts of the Abu al-Huda–Khashaba meeting conflict, although both were pleased by the meeting itself. According to Abu al-Huda, Khashaba told him frankly that all that Egypt wanted was the Gaza-[Rafah] area with possibly some of the hill country to the south (this for reasons of prestige and by way of compensation to justify public opinion for the heavy sacrifices made by Egypt during the Palestine campaign) and that Egypt was not interested in the rest of the Negev or in Beersheba, which were matters for settlement between Israel and Transjordan.[32]

To Kirkbride, Abu al-Huda added that Egypt was intent on retaining Gaza but would provide every possible facility there for trade to and from Transjordan if Transjordan could secure access to it across Israel.[33]

On this point, Khashaba's account was in general agreement. His version of what he told Abu al-Huda regarding Egypt's territorial ambitions was far different, however, and contradicted what he told Campbell only two weeks earlier. Now Khashaba reiterated that Egypt desired the acquisition of the Negev south of a line running from Gaza and Beersheba to the Dead Sea.[34] According to him, Abu al-Huda also made appropriate overtures regarding the needs of Egypt as the leading country in the Arab League.[35] The most likely explanation for the discrepancy between the two accounts is that Khashaba was referring to Egypt's optimal position in case an Israeli withdrawal could be achieved through the PCC while Abu al-Huda expressed what he undertook to be Egypt's fallback position in the absence of an overall political settlement.

The warming between Cairo and Amman[36] allowed the two countries to overcome what could have been a serious source of friction: the deterioration in relations between the Egyptian units and the Arab Legion forces in the Hebron-Bethlehem area. The Egyptian units consisted mostly of Muslim Brotherhood volunteers with regular Egyptian officers and numbered approximately one thousand soldiers. The Arab Legion forces numbered approximately three thousand. Tension between the groups had been generated mainly by the anti-Transjordanian activities of local Egyptian commanders. With the imminent conclusion of the Transjordanian-Israeli armistice at the end of March 1949, their disagreements now came to a head. Cairo received reports, apparently untrue, that the Legion was preparing to evict the Egyptian forces.[37] Either concurrently or in response, the

Egyptian military governor in Hebron received a coded message from Cairo, probably from the palace, "instructing him to make arrangements for a plebescite, on the results of which Egyptian policy regarding their continued occupation of the Hebron area would be based."[38] The breaking point came on March 31, when a hostile mob stirred by the Egyptians stoned senior Transjordanian officials visiting Hebron. The Legion promptly imposed a curfew, and the following day, on the direct orders of ʿAbdallah, seized all Egyptian communications, an act that included sealing their radio station and cutting their telephone wire. Egyptian troops confined themselves to their billets in defensive positions.[39]

The affair did not deteriorate further, as neither government had an interest in allowing things to get out of hand. The trust that had developed between officials of the two governments made it easier to treat the episode with equanimity. So did the fact that Abu al-Huda and his colleagues had never been overly disturbed by the Egyptian presence.[40] Their position was bolstered by Egypt's commitment to withdraw its troops, as indicated in an exchange of letters accompanying the Egyptian-Israeli armistice agreement.

On April 4, the Jordanian-Israeli armistice agreement was signed. The price that ʿAbdallah paid for Israel's agreeing to the takeover of Iraqi positions by the Arab Legion was a modification of the military lines in Israel's favor, involving some 400 square kilometers along its narrow waist and the Wadi ʿAra section connecting the coast with the Jezreel Valley. This area encompassed a score of Arab villages whose total population was approximately thirty-five thousand. Iraq's determination to unilaterally withdraw its force before the armistice placed Jordan in an untenable position.[41] ʿAbdallah had earlier been led by Sasson to believe that no adjustments would be demanded by Israel, proving that either Sasson was being disingenuous or, more likely, that others in the Israeli hierarchy carried greater weight.[42] The concession would forever be held up by militant Arab nationalists as a betrayal of the Arab cause.

The concessions had no effect on the course of Egyptian-Jordanian relations. In mid-April, Tawfiq Abu al-Huda paid a week-long visit to Cairo to firm up the series of tacit understandings that had evolved over the previous week. His discussions with Prime Minister ʿAbd al-Hadi resulted in the joint drafting of an exchange of letters covering a number of the points raised. Most important, from the Egyptian view, was Abu al-Huda's firm assurance that the Jordanian-Israeli armistice agreement contained "no other agreement or secret supplement . . . deal[t] with military affairs only and stipulate[d] that it will not in any way affect the final settlement of the Palestine case."[43]

Also addressed was ʿAbd al-Hadi's expressed concern that a withdrawal of Egyptian forces from the Bethlehem-Hebron area would result in the loss of territory to Israel in the same manner that had occurred in the Iraqi sector. Abu al-Huda repeated Jordan's defense of the territorial adjustments, stressing that they had been balanced by changes in Jordan's favor in the Hebron area.[44] (This was true only on paper, with a fig leaf added to the armistice agreement for Jordan's benefit.[45]) As for the territory to be vacated by Egyptians, Abu al-Huda's letter stated that it "[would] be maintained by the Jordanian Arab Legion in the interest of the Arabs which, in accordance with the permanent armistice agreement concluded between us and the Jews, is territory entirely for the Arabs, with no right whatsoever for the Jews in it."[46] On this point, ʿAbd al-Hadi wanted the reference to be to territory belonging to the "Arabs of Palestine." Abu al-Huda refused, stating that Jordan intended to keep those parts of Palestine that its forces had occupied. After some argument, he got his way.

As a sop to the Egyptians, Abu al-Huda agreed that his government would continue to work in cooperation with Egypt and other states "for a final just settlement of the Palestinian case," a commitment that was "received with satisfaction" by ʿAbd al-Hadi. The Egyptian government was also pleased by Jordan's assurance that "the military and administrative position of the Egyptian army" [in Gaza], as fixed by the Egyptian-Israeli armistice agreement, would "continue to be respected" by Amman. Finally, Abu al-Huda remembered "with deep appreciation and thanks" the "valuable aid" that Egyptian forces had extended since May 1948, in response to ʿAbdallah's expressed desire (noted earlier), for the protection of the south of Jerusalem.[47]

During their talks, ʿAbd al-Hadi also reiterated to Abu al-Huda Egypt's intention to retain Gaza but promised to support Jordan in securing access to the coast. If Jordan was not able to secure a port of its own, he stated, then it would receive all transit facilities it required, either in Gaza or elsewhere in Egyptian territory. He regretted that Great Britain had failed to prevent Israel from establishing a presence on the Gulf of Aqaba, and suggested that Jordan and Egypt should combine in pressing Britain to dislodge the Israelis and that Ibn Saʿud should be moved to use his influence with the United States toward the same end. If this were to prove successful, he concluded, then Jordan was welcome to any recovered part of the Negev. Neither this discussion nor their cautious exchanges regarding the concurrent upheaval in Syria was mentioned in their exchange of letters.

The results of Abu al-Huda's visit gave him cause for considerable satisfaction. The previously hostile atmosphere had dissipated; the tone of the Egyptian press toward Jordan had improved noticeably; and the relations between the two governments, if not their two kings, were on a more solid footing. More specifically, the talks helped achieve a considerable measure of understanding over the future status of the portions of Palestine remaining in their respective hands—a point crucial to Jordan. One year later, when relations reached their nadir, Abu al-Huda would accuse the Egyptians of reneging on this understanding.

More generally, the modicum of Egyptian-Jordanian understanding dovetailed nicely with overall trends in the Arab-Israeli sphere. The separate and consecutive armistice agreements between Israel and Egypt, Lebanon, Jordan, and Syria, respectively (the last signed on June 20), were explicitly designed "to facilitate the transition . . . to permanent peace" and to "remain in force until a peaceful settlement between the Parties [was] achieved."[48] Israel's leadership was at least momentarily optimistic that things were moving in the right direction. During April and May 1949, the peace overtures of Syria's new strongman, Husni al-Zaʿim, although probably not constituting a real opportunity for a quick breakthrough, did confirm to Israeli leaders their perception that time was indeed on their side.[49] Inter-Arab relations appeared to be less of an obstacle to an Arab-Israeli peace settlement than previously.

EGYPT, IRAQ, AND THE ARAB LEAGUE

Throughout the first months of 1949, Cairo had pursued its interests without reference to the Arab League. In fact, Egypt's entrance into separate armistice negotiations with Israel, its resistance to British and Arab suggestions for the inclusion of other Arab states in the negotiations, and the officially-inspired attacks on the Arab League by the Egyptian press had raised apprehensions within the other Arab states as to Egypt's future orientation toward the rest of the Arab world.[50] The Syrians were especially fearful that Egypt's acceptance of armistice talks might free Israeli troops for activity on their front[51] (mirroring Egypt's own concerns with respect to the Transjordanian-Israeli talks). Syria's general apprehensions over a possible Egyptian withdrawal from Arab affairs were shared by individual members of the Hashimite governments as well, although not to 'Abdallah, the Regent, or Nuri.

From the International Relations perspective, Egypt's behavior called into question the durability of a number of specific attributes of the fledgling Arab state system. Its insistence on separate negotiations at Rhodes hinted at a challenge to an existing, if implicit "rule" of the system—no separate moves toward a modus vivendi with Israel. (This rule was to be made explicit in the spring of 1950, ironically at Egypt's behest.) More generally, an Egyptian withdrawal from active involvement in Arab affairs would have radically altered the system's power distribution.

As it happened, however, Egypt's policy did not extend to the point of allowing the League to die.[52] This was already evidenced in March 1949, when Egypt chose to use the League as an instrument to attack Iraq. The occasion was the absence of Iraq's representative at the opening sessions of the Arab League Council meeting in Cairo on March 17. In response and apparently on Faruq's instructions, the Egyptian press, led by *al-Misri*, mounted a frontal campaign against Iraq's alleged denigration of the League and its aspirations in Syria.[53]

Iraqi explanations notwithstanding, it was likely that the sudden departure of Iraq's representative from Cairo on the eve of the meeting had been deliberate.[54] Behind the timing, said the British ambassador to Iraq, Sir Henry Mack, was Nuri al-Sa'id's fear that "the League might get involved in discussions of the Palestine situation which might be embarrassing to Iraq" (i.e., the imminent withdrawal of Iraqi troops from Palestine).[55] Adding fuel to the fire, Nuri al-Sa'id's newly installed government now chose to mount a frontal assault on

Nuri's long-standing bête noire, 'Azzam Pasha, and his conduct of Arab League affairs.

The first step came with Foreign Minister Fadil al-Jamali's memorandum to the Egyptian Ministry of Foreign Affairs and to all Arab Legations in Cairo, informing them that Iraq would have no further contact with the existing League Secretariat due to its failure to have maintained payments to Arab irregulars serving under the Iraqi command in Palestine.[56] One month later, in a May 3 speech to the Iraqi Chamber of Deputies, Jamali mounted an unprecedented public attack on 'Azzam. His accusations were numerous. By virtue of internal regulations that 'Azzam prepared in December 1945, and having consciously ignored alternative Iraqi proposals, 'Azzam came to

> control and dominate the policy of the League, [and thus act] as an independent head of State [or Government], supreme over the Foreign Ministers of the Arab States. [This was] the root of all evil, the reason for the confusion and the embarrassment, and one of the sources of disagreement among the States of the League themselves. This has made the League a problem in . . . inter-Arab relations which, before the existence of the League, were extremely close and sincere.

Jamali then elaborated on 'Azzam's alleged failure to maintain funding of Arab volunteers under Iraqi command, comparing it unfavorably to the continued funding of the Syrian-based Yarmuk Army irregulars (Qawuqji's Army of Salvation in an earlier incarnation). Henceforth, he declared, Iraq would divert its Arab League contributions directly to the volunteers under its own command. Finally, Jamali announced that Iraq was intent on altering the League's internal regulations in order to redefine and limit the power of the Secretary-General.[57]

On May 14, 'Azzam handed his reply to the Iraqi chargé d'affaires in Cairo, asking also that it be sent to the president of the Iraqi Chamber of Deputies, read to the Chamber, and broadcast to the public. In it, 'Azzam completely rejected Jamali's charges. He declared that his powers were less than those of secretary-generals in other international organizations. Regarding charges that he had acted independently, 'Azzam insisted that he had "not taken any measure, allowed any action or assumed any functions except what was unanimously decided upon by the Council of the League." Jamali's allegations regarding the lack of payments to Iraqi-commanded volunteers, ʿAzzam claimed, were untrue. Nor, he said, was his continuing limited funding of the Yarmuk Army tantamount in any way to his siding with Syria against Iraq. Finally, ʿAzzam countered, it was the Iraqi government that had not paid its dues to cover the secretariat-general's expenses during the previous two years and still owed over £200,000 for Palestine relief.[58]

For Iraq, ʿAzzam served as a convenient lightning rod, even a scapegoat, for its own frustrations and embarrassments. The intensity and public nature of the Iraqi attack were indicative of and a contributing factor to a state of affairs that ʿAzzam's spirited defense could not hide. The fact of the matter was that the prestige of the collective body that he personified had declined sharply over the previous eighteen months.

THE STRUGGLE FOR SYRIA: THE SYRIAN COUPS OF 1949

Inter-Arab strains stemming from the Arab-Israeli conflict had cooled down considerably by the spring of 1949 in the wake of Israel's armistice agreements with Egypt, Lebanon, and Jordan. This did not, however, presage greater inter-Arab calm. Syria's internal weakness confined the country to a peripheral role in the events of 1948. This same weakness now resulted in Syria becoming the focus for increased inter-Arab tensions, thanks to the bloodless overthrow of Syria's President Shukri al-Quwwatli on March 30, 1949, by the Army Chief of Staff, Colonel Husni al-Zaʿim. Zaʿim and his supporters were motivated by a combination of factors: high-minded national goals, defense of the Syrian army from charges of corruption and ridicule, preservation of the salary levels of Syria officers, and perhaps even Zaʿim's personal need to forestall accusations of corruption.[59] The British were aware of Zaʿim's intentions;[60] the Americans actively supported them. Central Intelligence Agency (CIA) operatives and Zaʿim were on intimate terms, so much so that Miles Copeland claimed over twenty years ago that the CIA had masterminded the entire operation. Indeed, Assistant Military Attaché Stephen Meade had an unusually close relationship with Za'im throughout his brief rule. More recently, however, Copeland acknowledged that the CIA contribution was minor and that "it was Husni's show all the way."[61]

By contrast, the coup caught Arab leaders by surprise. Patrick Seale provided a vivid description of Arab concerns. "The question on everyone's lips," he wrote, was: "Who is backing Za'im? Which way will he turn?"[62] 'Abdallah quickly assured a nervous Ibn Sa'ud that he had not been involved in the coup and had no intention of interfering. For all of his obsessions, the Jordanian monarch was under no illusions that the coup provided any immediate opening for realizing his aspirations for Greater Syria. Nonetheless, he was hopeful that quiet assurances of support and goodwill would bring Za'im to look favorably on the scheme.[63] The Egyptians, for their part, were apprehensive regarding the coup's possible regional implications and the example it might provide for dissident elements at home. Accordingly, Egyptian newspapers were prevented for three days from making anything more than vague references to events in Syria. Editorially, the censors were a bit more lenient. Stability, declared the government organ *al-Asas*, was what the Arab peoples needed in order to preserve their independence and social and economic progress. "Nothing could be more foolish," therefore, than violent upheavals.[64]

Some of Iraq's leaders held similar apprehensions. The regent, for example, feared that the coup might have a contagious effect on the Iraqi army, particularly in view of its expected resentment at the withdrawal from Palestine.[65]

Still, Iraqi leaders also recognized that the coup provided them with new opportunities. Consequently, on April 1, they sent to Damascus Iraq's newly appointed minister to Lebanon, Jamil Baban, and 'Awni al-Khalidi, the Iraqi representative to the Palestine Conciliation Commission meetings in Beirut, in order to meet Za'im and important Syrian politicians. By the end of their week-long stay, they were convinced that Za'im was neither responsible nor stable and therefore could not be considered an appropriate partner for advancing Iraqi interests. They also were warned by Faris al-Khuri, president of the now-dissolved Chamber of Deputies and thus the symbol of Syria's endangered constitutional system, that Iraq should not oppose Za'im by force. The two envoys found other Syrian public figures more eager to cooperate with Iraq in actively opposing Za'im. Baban and Khalidi strongly urged Nuri al-Sa'id to exploit the opportunity to the fullest. Initial steps would involve financing supporters and creating a clandestine radio station to send a message of opposition to Za'im and unity with Iraq. Their ideal outcome was an Iraqi military intervention to depose Za'im, followed by the establishment of a Syro-Iraqi union whose guiding format would be "two states, one crown." All of this could be conveniently justified, they said, by reference to the threat to Syria posed by Israel.[66]

The regent was initially enthusiastic, but Nuri al-Sa'id was not inclined to take undue risks.[67] He was particularly concerned with possible outside reaction to a military move, whether by the U.N. Security Council, France, or Turkey. British urging for caution focused on Israel, with its ambassador to Baghdad warning Nuri that Iraqi military moves would likely provoke Israel into action, either on the West Bank (the territory gained by Jordan in the 1948 war) or against Syria.[68] He was however encouraged by reports of widespread Syrian dissatisfaction with Za'im and was willing to strengthen this tendency with Iraqi funds. In the Arab arena, Nuri attempted to reassure Egypt that ongoing Iraqi contacts in Syria were only preliminary ones. At the same time, the Iraqi Foreign Ministry warned Cairo against interference by any "irresponsible circles" in the Arab League (i.e., Arab League Secretary-General 'Azzam Pasha). On this point, the Iraqis received assurances from Egyptian Prime Minister 'Abd al-Hadi.[69]

On April 9, there came a new development: Husni al-Za'im proposed that Syria and Iraq conclude a defensive military agreement as soon as possible (he believed it could be done within a month).[70] Desirous of probing Za'im's intentions while keeping his options open, Nuri promptly sent an Iraqi military delegation to Damascus.

At the root of Za'im's overtures to Iraq were two factors: the desire to strengthen his hand in the forthcoming armistice negotiations with Israel and his acute need to obtain diplomatic recognition for his regime in order to legitimize his takeover. The tactical nature of his overtures to Iraq was aptly illustrated on April 12, the day the Iraqi military delegation arrived, when Za'im dispatched two representatives to Saudi Arabia to meet with Ibn Sa'ud. The causes of the revolution in Syria, they told him, were purely internal, and no change was intended in Syria's constitution or its international position. Thus, they requested the immediate granting of de facto recognition. The version of Ibn Sa'ud's reply obtained by the British ambassador in Jidda was extremely cautious and noncommittal. Until he had some satisfactory evidence of a firmly established government, no recognition was possible. Ibn Sa'ud also expressed concern for the personal welfare of Quwwatli (who had long-standing business and personal ties with the Saudis).[71]

In addition, the Iraqi representative in Jidda reported that Ibn Sa'ud and Egypt made recognition conditional on the absence of a Syrian tilt toward Iraq. Concerned, the Iraqi Foreign Ministry instructed its Damascus legation to ask what Za'im's position would be if Saudi Arabia or Egypt were to object to Iraq's granting military or economic assistance to Syria. On the following day, April 13, a Syrian delegation arrived in Baghdad with the text of a draft bilateral agreement for a unified military command in wartime, joint planning, the exchange of military missions and a commitment to "immediately . . . join in any hostilities originating in Jewish aggression."[72] They also brought suggestions for economic agreements, including a customs union and joint development of the Euphrates.[73] Nuri prevaricated: Constitutional life, he said, must first be restored in Syria before any agreement could be concluded. Furthermore, a military agreement would be dependent on a clear and specific Syrian foreign policy. In addition, Iraq was treaty-bound to consult with Great Britain regarding any proposed military agreement. As for the "Zionist danger," Nuri pledged assistance by the Iraqi army to Syria even without a formal military agreement if it was attacked. Regarding the nonmilitary aspects of cooperation, the Syrians could, he said, refer to his 1946 proposals for an Iraqi-Syrian alliance and express their views about what should be added or discarded.[74]

Nuri also inquired about the nature of the Syrian mission to Ibn Sa'ud. The reply he received was that it dealt with previous Saudi inquiries regarding Quwwatli. The Syrians also brought a request for two Iraqi brigades to be stationed on the Syria-Israel frontier in order to defend Syria against Israel. On this, Nuri's rebuff was unequivocal: The Iraqi army, he said, had not been withdrawn from Palestine only to be placed in a combat situation at another point. He did agree that Iraqi forces would remain near Mafraq (in Jordan, near the Syrian border) to be available in the event of an Israeli attack on Syria. Their presence was a double-edged sword: The troops could also be made available to move against Za'im.[75]

Nuri's hesitations toward the Syrian mission's suggestions to forge closer ties were actually part of a two-pronged tactical approach formulated during the preceding hectic days. Skeptical of Za'im's underlying intentions, he nevertheless hoped to induce him to restore constitutional procedures, which, in turn, would set in motion a process that would ultimately lead to Syria's opting for union. The key to this process was Iraq's cultivation of as many Syrian politicians as possible. Ideally, this would result in the Syrian Chamber of Deputies' inviting Iraq to intervene for the purpose of achieving union. At the very least, it would allow Nuri to keep his fingers in the Syrian pie while awaiting further developments. Finally, Nuri's emphasis on the restoration of constitutional life in Syria as a precondition for developing closer ties stemmed from his profound concern that legitimization of Za'im's actions might affect the Iraqi military.

At this point, Nuri decided to make a closer inspection. On April 16, he headed a top-level delegation to Damascus on what his foreign minister, Fadil al-Jamali, described as an "exploratory" visit.[76] Before meeting with Za'im, Nuri contacted Faris al-Khuri. The latter's belief—that Iraq ought not to oppose Za'im by force—had not changed in the two weeks since his previous meetings with Baban and Khalidi. Nuri emphasized to Khuri the necessity of working for closer cooperation between Syria and Iraq, and the need to ignore Saudi and Egyptian objections. He reaffirmed, moreover, that the initiative for this must come from within Syria and not from Iraq.[77]

After a brief tête-à-tête with Za'im in a side chamber (in which Nuri is said to have used threatening language), the two leaders exchanged formal statements in the presence of both countries' delegations.[78] Speaking first, Nuri sidestepped the recognition issue, stating disingenuously that Syria's independence and sovereignty and the Syrian people's satisfaction with their new administration made formal recognition by other states unnecessary. Regarding Syrian proposals for military cooperation, Nuri reiterated what he had told the visiting Syrian delegation three days earlier. In any case, what was preferable in a world of "quick, rapid and dangerous developments" was a wider collective defense pact to cover most, if not all, of the Middle Eastern countries.

As for nonmilitary forms of cooperation, Nuri again referred to his 1946 discussion with Syria's prime minister, the late Sa'dallah al-Jabiri. Since then, he continued, the conditions Jabiri and Quwwatli had said were needed for their implementation—assuagement of Saudi and Egyptian objections—had not been prepared. Hence, if Iraq were now to come forward with a suggestion or opinion "she might be accused of ulterior motives. Therefore, it might be better for us to wait for the time being as regards the active steps, and wait also until our sister [Syria] seized an opportunity to ask us to undertake some action or to study a plan on this subject."[79]

Za'im did not repeat his request for a defense agreement. Syria no longer feared "Jewish aggression," he said, for Syria was now receiving sufficient arms shipments from France, giving Za'im greater confidence in his ability to chart an independent course.[80] The only thing Syria might need from Iraq in the event of war, Za'im stated, would be its air force. As for Nuri's proposals to Jabiri, Za'im admitted ignorance. In any case, "friendship and brotherhood" and cooperation in combating communism ought to be the guiding principles in foreign policy matters. He also referred to the strategic need to build a railway across the Syrian Desert between Homs, Palmyra, and Dayr al-Zur—for the defense of Syria and Iraq and Turkey as well—if it were to participate in a regional defense scheme. Ironically, in 1946, Nuri had tried to encourage closer ties between Syria and Turkey. What was different now, of course, was that it would not take place under Iraq's protective wing.[81]

Before Nuri left Damascus, he met with a number of Syrian personalities, including 'Adil and Nabih al-'Azma (of Quwwatli's National party) and the venerable former President Hashim al-Atasi, to report on his talks with Za'im. He emphasized that the ball was in the court of those Syrians interested in forging closer ties with Iraq and willing to mobilize Syrian public opinion toward that end. Without their initiative, Nuri reiterated, Iraq could not take any action.[82]

Nuri had correctly assessed that a significant number of Syrian politicians from the National and People's parties and independents all favored some kind of "Iraqi option" (if only to counteract Za'im's growing monopolization of Syrian political life). Nuri's suggestion that Syrian political leaders issue a declaration inviting Iraqi intervention was too risky for the Syrians. Similarly, Edmond Homsey, a prominent banker and former Syrian minister, and ten others considered presenting Za'im with a declaration in favor of union. The idea was dropped because its promoters thought that it would result in their imprisonment. The most that could be expected, Homsey told a British diplomat, was that if Iraq intervened, he and his friends would publicly come forward. Finally, he stressed the urgency of the situation. Action was imperative before the proposed elections, which would undoubtedly confirm Za'im's position and further strengthen his hold on the army. Ironically, Homsey was subsequently named by Za'im as ambassador to Great Britain.[83]

During these hectic weeks, Nuri counted on the Syrian civilian politicians to lead the way. As a result, Nuri was reluctant to take decisive action toward a merger, while the option of turning Za'im into an ally had already been discarded.

Still, Nuri miscalculated Za'im's speed in embracing the Egyptians. On April 18, 'Azzam Pasha flew to Damascus to meet Za'im. 'Azzam was of two minds regarding Syria. Any attempt by the Hashimites to shake the regional status quo, he believed, would only lead to trouble, and possibly to Syria's becoming another Spain, a reference to outside involvement in the Spanish civil war. On the other hand, he was not enamored with Za'im's methods and, like his old rival Nuri, urged Za'im to restore constitutional procedures.[84]

Three days later, Za'im paid a secret visit to Faruq at Inshas, sealing the alliance with Egypt. It may have been sweetened by Faruq's personal loan of between two and four million Egyptian pounds. In return, Za'im symbolically proclaimed Faruq to be king of Syria, with Za'im as his viceroy in Damascus. The two leaders also agreed to take steps toward a Syrian-Egyptian merger *(indimaj)*, but this was quickly blocked by the Egyptian government. Nonetheless, both the palace and the government agreed that Egyptian interests were preserved. Egypt had bided its time while Iraqi-Syrian contacts ran their course and then stepped in to shore up its regional preeminence. This pattern would repeat itself in the fall of 1949.[85]

In light of these developments, Ibn Sa'ud concluded that the assurances given him by Za'im's envoys were genuine. Thus, on April 23, he extended formal diplomatic recognition to Za'im's government and pressed the United States and Great Britain to do likewise. Failure to do so, they were told, might lend encouragement to Iraqi designs on Syria. Within a few days, London and Washington extended recognition as well, although not necessarily as a result of Ibn Sa'ud's advice.[86] Za'im's maneuverings thus gave sharper definition to the Arab world's basic Hashimite/anti-Hashimite division.

When Za'im placed himself in the anti-Hashimite embrace of

Egypt and Saudi Arabia, he inaugurated a period of attempted consolidation of power at home and more self-confidence, even brazenness, toward his Hashimite and Lebanese neighbors. The Syrian press (and Za'im himself) heaped scorn on 'Abdallah, in the process emphasizing Syria's traditional position that Jordan was part of the Syrian motherland and could rejoin it when it so desired. In addition, Za'im concentrated military units along the Syrian-Jordanian border and threatened to close the frontier crossings in "retaliation" for fictitious Jordanian military movements. To add insult to injury, the aide de camp of Arab Legion Commander Bagot Glubb was arrested in Damascus in late May, held incommunicado for a number of days, and subjected to repeated interrogation and electric shock torture. Whether this was done with Za'im's personal knowledge, or, alternatively, by Syrian army officers acting on their own is not known.[87]

Toward the Iraqis, Za'im initially acted to reduce tension. Ideally, the moderation of Iraqi-Syrian friction would lessen the Iraqi propensity for engaging in penetration (i.e., by cultivating a Syrian opposition to Za'im) and forestall any further deterioration in relations that might lead to Iraqi military intervention. Thus, the Iraqis were told that Syria was willing to work for closer economic ties and even an economic union that would include Lebanon, on the condition that the regional status quo would be the basis of their bilateral relations. Concurrently, Za'im suspended the publication of the independent Damascus daily *al-Nidal*, following its publication of a censored tribute to Iraq's King Faysal II on the occasion of his fourteenth birthday. The author of the tribute, the veteran Syrian politician of various shades, Munir al-'Ajlani, was imprisoned.[88]

Damascus also engaged in a time-honored Arab political method for shoring up a government's position at home and abroad: seeking to mediate between two other disputants, in this case Iraq and Egypt, following the acrimonious exchanges between Iraq's Foreign Minister Jamali and 'Azzam Pasha. For his part, Jamali directed soothing words toward Syria.

> Iraq recognizes the independence and sovereignty of Syria; the form of the regime is a matter which concerns the Syrians themselves. ... Yes, we seek unity, and we want unity with any Arab state, but we do not want to impose that on any country. Union

with any territory must spring from the free desires for union of
the people of that territory.⁸⁹

Nonetheless, the Iraqis were willing to pursue a contrary line in secret. One member of the Syrian delegation then visiting Iraq, Asad Tlas, was approached by the Iraqis with a proposal to liquidate Zaʿim. His positive response apparently resulted in a substantial sum of money being placed at his disposal.⁹⁰

The Iraqi-Syrian thaw proved extremely short-lived, and by the end of May 1949, Iraqi-Syrian animosity was again out in the open. Now, instead of Syria mediating between Iraq and Egypt, Iraq sought Egyptian assistance to block Zaʿim's forthcoming election, on June 25, to the presidency of the republic and an accompanying four-part referendum to define and consolidate his powers.

On June 13, Nuri sent former Prime Minister Muzahim al-Pachachi, known among Iraqi leaders for his pro-Egyptian orientation, to Cairo to persuade the Egyptian government not to recognize the impending Syrian election and referendum.⁹¹ Concurrently, Nuri asked Lebanon's Prime Minister Riyad al-Sulh to endeavor to persuade Zaʿim to cancel the referendum and help bring the Egyptians into line.⁹²

The Iraqi initiative fell on deaf ears, and Cairo wasted no time informing Damascus of the Iraqi demarche. Zaʿim's response was swift: on June 15, the Syrian press carried banner headlines announcing alleged Iraqi troop concentrations of five thousand men along the Iraqi-Syrian frontier at al-Qaʾim.⁹³ As a countermeasure, Zaʿim announced that he was sending roughly the same number of troops to the area, including armored cars, artillery, and air support. In the political sphere, Zaʿim, Ibn Saʿud, and the Egyptian government all quickly requested that Great Britain and the United States restrain Nuri.⁹⁴ To the French minister in Damascus, Zaʿim also expressed the hope that France would intervene with the British and Americans to ensure their recognition of the election results.⁹⁵

The Iraqis strongly denied the presence of troops in the border region and suggested to the Syrian chargé d'affaires in Baghdad that he go anywhere in Iraq to verify their denial. On June 18, Zaʿim privately acknowledged that there were at that moment no Iraqi troops in the border region but claimed they had just been withdrawn. In any case, he intended to leave his own force, which numbered closer to five hundred than five thousand, in place until after the referendum.⁹⁶

Concurrently, the Iraqis stepped up their financial incentives and encouraged anti-Zaʻim political initiatives among various Syrian figures in the political mainstream and minority communities alike. Their Syrian interlocutors suggested a number of anti-Zaʻim actions, all in order to forestall Zaʻim's June 25 election.⁹⁷

All of Iraq's efforts came to naught. Zaʻim carried out his unopposed election and referendum. Arab reactions were predictable. Egypt and Saudi Arabia sent congratulatory missions to Damascus.⁹⁸ The Saudis promised a $6 million loan. Egypt's friendliness was reciprocated by a goodwill visit to Cairo by newly appointed Syrian Prime Minister Muhsin al-Barazi, from July 7 to 9, 1949.

In contrast, Iraq temporarily withdrew its minister from Damascus (ostensibly for consultations) to avoid having to congratulate Zaʻim on his election.⁹⁹ His subsequent return failed to bring any thaw, and the remaining six weeks of Zaʻim's rule were characterized by mutual vitriolic press attacks (occasionally involving Jordan as well) and continued Iraqi contacts with opposition groups in Syria. Cognizant of the latter, Zaʻim was convinced that Iraqi-inspired assassination plots were afloat. Confirmation, including the names of persons allegedly involved and the sums of money offered to them by Iraq, were provided by Prime Minister Barazi to the French legation in Damascus during the second week of August. As a result, the Iraqi minister to Damascus was declared persona non grata.¹⁰⁰

The complex interplay in Syria between domestic, bilateral, regional, and international factors intensified with the bloody overthrow of Zaʻim's regime on August 14, 1949, by army officers led by Colonel Sami al-Hinnawi. In terms of inter-Arab relations, Syria's second coup d'état in four and one-half months reopened the question of Syria's place in the inter-Arab network. As Zaʻim had suspected, Iraq was involved in encouraging the coup's plotters. Nonetheless, its importance was secondary. Although some Iraqi officers had suggested a coup to their Syrian counterparts, the main initiatives for overthrowing Zaʻim came from within Syria.¹⁰¹ The Iraqi response, in fact, was only lukewarm. In late July, Nuri was informed by the Iraqi minister in Damascus, Ibrahim ʻAkif al-ʻAlusi, that Hinnawi, Colonel Asad Tlas (Hinnawi's brother-in-law), and Zaʻim's defense minister, ʻAbdallah ʻAtfa, were planning to assassinate Zaʻim on August 10 or 11. Furthermore, they were requesting that Iraqi military forces be moved into position along the Syrian border to raise the threat of intervention in support of the coup, and even the feigning of air battles. Together, they hoped these actions would spur the dissolved Syrian Parliament to reconvene and thus restore its authority. Nuri rejected the request.

He did, however, encourage them to go forward with their plans and strongly urged Hinnawi to return to constitutional life as soon after the coup as possible.[102] At one point, Hinnawi asked the Iraqi government if it could print leaflets and distribute them from the air just before the coup. Nuri agreed to the first part of the request but refused the second.[103] Hinnawi or Tlas may also have requested refuge in Baghdad in the event of failure. According to Fadil al-Jamali, Nuri did not believe that they actually intended to carry out their plans. Consequently, Nuri was caught by surprise when the coup actually occurred.[104]

Hinnawi also apparently provided advance knowledge of the coup to ʿAbdallah, who was merely an interested and satisfied observer. At the same time, the very success of the coup made him apprehensive about Iraqi ambitions, another indication of the enduring nature of intra-Hashimite competition.[105]

It is not surprising that neither Faruq nor Ibn Saʿud was pleased by the Hinnawi coup. The fact that Zaʾim's prime minister, Muhsin al-Barazi, had been murdered along with Zaʾim was a particular blow. Barazi made many personal contacts and friendships in Egypt during his tenure there as Syria's minister. Faruq immediately declared a three-day mourning period, a gesture whose significance was not modified by subsequent Egyptian comment that it was an automatic courtesy required by protocol on the death of any chief of state.[106] Overall reaction in Egypt to the coup was mixed. The motivation was understood to be mainly domestic and even personal.[107] At the same time, the coup also engendered considerable disgust with Arab affairs.[108] This did not, however, translate into a meaningful reassessment of Egypt's policies. Faruq and the newly installed prime minister, Husayn Sirri Pasha, continued to be concerned with the coup's regional implications. Previously, Sirri had not been counted among those Egyptian politicians strongly oriented toward involvement in Arab affairs. But once he assumed the prime ministership, his actions fell more or less into line with those of his predecessors. Thus, on August 22, Sirri made strong representations to the American chargé d'affaires in Cairo that Syria was being threatened by Iraq and Jordan, and that the U.S. government should declare itself opposed to any attempt against Syrian independence. Toward the Syrians, Egypt asked the new prime minister, Hashim al-Atasi, to refrain from working for closer ties with Iraq, even though it was permitted under ARTICLE 9 of the League Charter.[109]

Ibn Saʿud, for his part, had no personal ties with the Zaʿim regime comparable to those that he had with Quwwatli. His sole concern was that the coup not shift Syria's regional orientation. To bolster the status quo, Ibn Saʿud insisted on going ahead with negotiations for the loan previously promised to Syria. In doing so, he overruled the advice of a number of his counselors that the Saudi government's own precarious financial state militated against the loan. Another group with influence in the palace, namely Ibn Saʿud's coterie of foreign-born advisers—Yusuf Yasin (born in Syria), Fuʾad Hamza (a Lebanese Druse), and Hafiz Wahba (Egyptian by birth)—was jubilant over Zaʿim's downfall. This may also have helped to placate Ibn Saʿud's initial wariness.[110]

Iraq, by contrast, hoped that the coup provided a new opportunity for closer ties with Syria. Baghdad was particularly pleased by the swift establishment of Atasi's civilian caretaker government, which included a number of People's party leaders who had previously advocated closer ties with Iraq. Nuri's concern for acting along constitutional lines was once again paramount. Thus, as before, he believed that it was incumbent on the Syrians to make the first move. Furthermore, the process could only be pursued gradually. The new Syrian government needed to consolidate its own authority and neutralize elements in the Syrian army opposed to closer ties with Iraq. Moreover, a gradualist approach initiated by legitimate Syrian authorities would protect Iraq from Egyptian and Saudi charges of machinations.

Nuri's gradualist approach has led some scholars to conclude that Nuri was only paying lip-service to unity, in order to create "an engrossing foreign diversion" for the Iraqi regent, ʿAbd al-Ilah.[111] This seems overstated. True, the regent advocated an even more activist Iraqi policy, motivated, unquestionably, by the fact that he might well benefit from the unification of Syria and Iraq under one crown.[112] Nonetheless, the available evidence suggests that, for all of Nuri's "changing moods" regarding what course to adopt, his desire for closer ties with Syria was quite genuine.[113]

Among other perceived virtues of the gradualist approach was that it would give Iraq time to defuse opposition in Egypt. Consequently, on August 22, Nuri al-Sa'id met with Egypt's prime minister, Husayn Sirri Pasha, in Alexandria. Responding to Sirri's insistence on maintaining Syria's independence, Nuri reiterated that his government saw no contradiction between agreements to deepen bilateral military, economic, and financial ties and each side's continued independence. He cited a number of examples: the Iraqi-Saudi Treaty of Friendship and Arab Brotherhood of 1936, various Syrian-Lebanese agreements, and the British Commonwealth. He also referred to Iraq's support for the unity of Egypt and Sudan. For the Iraqis, their own advocacy of Fertile Crescent unity was no less legitimate than Egyptian aspirations for Nile Valley unity. In any case, Nuri assured Sirri, Iraq would not contemplate intervention in Syria without a request from legally constituted Syrian authorities.

According to Nuri's account of the meeting, Sirri Pasha was reassured by what he heard. He also told Nuri that it was Faruq who was the main advocate in Egypt of a more active, Arab-oriented foreign policy, that is, one that would challenge Iraqi aspirations in the Fertile Crescent.[114] The two prime ministers issued separate statements indicating that they had reached a measure of understanding on Syria's future.[115] This was, however, not the case. The Iraqis could only hope that the process of building closer relations between Syria and Iraq would reach a point where Egyptian opposition would not matter.

Much depended on the Syrians. For Foreign Minister Nazim al-Qudsi and others in the new provisional government, a federation was the answer to Syria's internal and external troubles. Qudsi was not at all clear how this might be done but was convinced that an Iraqi-imposed federation would be bitterly opposed in Syria and have no chance of success. Instead, like Nuri, he strongly favored using voluntary, constitutional means. This could begin by including a demand for federation in the constitution that the Constituent Assembly (scheduled to be elected in November) would be called upon to draft.

Regarding the Syrian army, Qudsi asked Great Britain to cultivate closer ties with key elements there to combat the alleged intrigues of Egypt, Saudi Arabia, France, and the United States.

To support his claims of Egyptian intrigue, he cited conversations with Syrian army officers that were conducted by Faruq's special representative in Damascus, Colonel Muhammad Yusuf, behind the back of the Syrian government.[116] At the same time, Qudsi also sought to reassure Egypt that closer Syria-Iraqi ties would not be an anti-Egyptian act.[117]

In the beginning of September, Iraq's special envoy, Ahmad Mukhtar Baban, met Nazim al-Qudsi in Damascus. Previously, the Syrians had requested advice on whether their desire for union with Iraq should be expressed publicly by the provisional government or only later by a newly elected parliament. Such a statement, replied Baban, should most definitely not be issued by the current provisional government, because of its caretaker, therefore shaky, status.[118] At the same time, the two governments began secret discussions regarding steps toward a federation.[119]

By the end of the month, each side put forth a draft proposal. The Syrian draft provided for a federation under the crown of Iraq's young King Faysal II, who would be represented in Damascus by a Syrian viceroy (and not 'Abd al-Ilah, as the latter had hoped). The proposal also called for the election of a Federal Council that would draft a constitution and a Federal Parliament, composed of equal numbers of Syrian and Iraqi deputies, which would sit one-half of the year in Damascus and one-half in Baghdad. The king would nominate a prime minister who, in turn, would chose a cabinet. Foreign affairs, defense, and economic matters would be in the hands of the federal government. The Iraqi proposal was for a looser confederation under the Iraqi crown while maintaining independence and freedom for each side. In effect, the Iraqi proposal followed Nuri's earlier "commonwealth" suggestion: Syria's status would be similar to that of a British dominion.[120]

Their lack of agreement on the federation's particulars did not deter them from agreeing, on September 17, to a preliminary implementation plan. The first stage would involve formal consultations with Great Britain and the United States. The Syrians would then examine the proposed federation's effect on their financial and economic relations with Lebanon, including their bilateral customs union. This would be followed by talks between Iraq and Britain on how their own treaty relations would be affected. Finally, a union proposal would be submitted to both parliaments (the new Syrian Parliament was scheduled to meet on November 20). Once the idea had been accepted in principle, joint committees would prepare the details and draft the constitution to be submitted again to both parliaments. Elections would then have to be held there, and the new parliament would have to ratify again the new constitution by a two-thirds vote. The whole process was envisaged as taking eight months.[121]

In their ongoing discussion with British officials, Nuri and Qudsi at first downplayed the problems created by the Anglo-Iraqi Treaty for the prospective federation. It was, in fact, an important stumbling block. The application of the treaty to Syria, with the possible establishment of British military facilities there, was anathema for many Syrians, particularly in the army. One way around this, Qudsi suggested, was to water down the application of the Anglo-Iraqi Treaty to Syria. The British ambassador in Iraq, Sir Henry Mack, understood this to mean that the Syrians would receive protection, arms, and training facilities, without having to grant bases to Great Britain, in exchange only for promises of consultation in foreign policy and for the granting of facilities in the event or imminence of war. Nor would Syria be obligated to recruit British military experts for their army, as the Anglo-Iraqi Treaty stipulated.[122] Alternatively, Nuri and Qudsi advised an arrangement in which previous international obligations by each country would remain in force and the new federal government would be legally responsible for these previous obligations. It would then be possible for the federation to draw up a new accord along the line of the stillborn Portsmouth Treaty of January 1948.[123] But British policymakers desired further clarifications.[124] Lacking a definitive statement of support from Great Britain, Qudsi could not convince opponents within Syria that it would result in a degree of foreign domination and a loss of independence.[125]

Instead, the Syrians suggested an immediate military alliance with Iraq, pending the conclusion of the federation, to make the plan acceptable to at least part of their factionalized army. The Iraqi military mission in Syria would be expanded from six to about forty instructors.[126] For the Syrian army, the proposal was a double-edged sword. It would benefit from improved equipment, training, and finances. At the same time, an enlarged Iraqi presence would serve as a check on any anti-unionist tendencies. Nuri suggested that the alliance take the form of Syria's accession to the 1936 Iraqi-Saudi treaty. The Syrians noted that this would permit Iraq to intervene militarily, upon the Syrian government's request, to suppress disturbances or disorders in line with ARTICLE 5 (3) of the treaty, a point they were unwilling to make explicit. They thus preferred to conclude a new, separate treaty, which Nuri shied away from, fearing criticism in the Arab world.[127]

It was clear by mid-October 1949 that no immediate breakthrough was in sight and that further developments would have to await the outcome of the Syrian elections in early November. In the meantime, the Syrian-Iraqi moves began to draw fire from other parties in the region, particularly after the National party, in an electoral ploy, reversed on September 29 its long-standing opposition to Syrian-Iraqi unity. Although an assessment of French involvement in mustering anti-union forces in Syria, both in the army and in the civilian sectors, must await the opening of the French archives, French opposition to the entire process was clear.[128] In the Arab arena, Jordan was the first country to express overt opposition.[129] The Saudis channeled money to anti-unionists in Damascus and offered financial and commercial inducements to the Syrian government.[130]

At this point, Egypt added its weight to the anti-union forces. The occasion was a regularly scheduled Arab League Council meeting in Cairo, beginning on October 17. During the previous months, the League had been moribund. Suddenly, it became the renewed focal point for inter-Arab activity, thanks to the developments in Syria.

Egypt had already served notice of its intent by effusively welcoming Syria's former President Shukri al-Quwwatli to Cairo from his Parisian exile in early October, and may have even given him funds to finance anti-Iraqi officers.[131] On October 10, Egypt appointed a heavyweight delegation, headed by the prime minister, to the upcoming League Council meeting.[132] Other League members followed suit, transforming a low-level meeting into a major inter-Arab gathering.

The prospect of a Syrian-Iraqi federation was not directly addressed by the Council, although the Political Committee did take up the matter upon Egypt's insistence and over the objections of Nazim al-Qudsi, who insisted that the matter was an internal Syrian affair.[133] More striking were the indirect methods that Iraq, Syria, and Egypt all used to advance their positions. Nuri adopted a diversionary tactic at the Council's opening session by renewing his long-standing call for the reorganization of the secretariat and the diminution of ʿAzzam's responsibilities.[134] He also succeeded in moving the matter to the top of the Council's agenda, but his efforts were unfruitful. Egypt grabbed the spotlight by proposing an inclusive collective security pact designed to forestall the Syrian-Iraqi federation by offering the Syrians a wider framework for safeguarding their security.[135]

The idea may have originated in the palace, in another of Faruq's periodic assertions of authority in the Arab arena.[136] Or, the genesis may have been more complex. "Secret sources" informed the British embassy in Cairo that the suggestion for a collective security pact was first made by Nazim al-Qudsi to Faruq's press counselor, Karim Thabit, "not however with the intention that it should be adopted, but rather in the expectation that Egypt would refuse to be drawn"; the Syrians would then be able to argue that there existed no alternative to forging closer ties with Iraq.[137] The fact that Qudsi had floated a similar strategy six weeks earlier lends some credence to this version.[138] If it is in fact true, then Qudsi miscalculated badly.

In any case, the Egyptians lobbied intensively between October 18 and 21 to mobilize support for the proposal. The Saudis (and probably the Yemenis) were amenable; the Lebanese prime minister fell into line after some prodding from his Maronite president. Nazim al-Qudsi, trapped, perhaps, by his own machinations, was also willing to comply, as long as it was not a substitute for closer ties with Iraq and a general Arab "confederation."[139] The Jordanians remained aloof, so as not to antagonize either Egypt or Iraq. Their own opposition to the Syrian-Iraqi federation plans made them amenable to the Egyptian proposal, and ʿAbdallah's priorities at that juncture were elsewhere. A peace agreement with Israel and the final absorption of those parts of Palestine under Jordan's control would be greatly facilitated by quiet in the inter-Arab arena. By October 22, the Iraqis had been outmaneuvered and Sirri Pasha formally introduced the collective security proposal, "in accordance with the desire of His Majesty the King." It was then referred to the Political Committee for study.

The rudimentary nature of the proposal became apparent in the Political Committee's deliberations when the Egyptians produced a rough sketch of the scheme. Consequently, the League Council could only agree on setting up a special committee to discuss the project further. It would meet periodically during the following weeks.

Neither the content nor the slow pace of the committee's discussions were to Iraq's liking. Iraqi officials correctly understood that the Egyptians would prolong the discussions until after the Syrian elections, but there was little they could do to speed things up.[140] The Syrians made their own desultory efforts to advance matters. Officially, they proposed that the committee create, in principle, an all-Arab federation of states.[141] Unofficially, the Syrian delegate, ʿAdnan al-Atasi (son of the prime minister), alarmed the Egyptians by advocating that the military obligations in any collective security pact apply only to states with common frontiers.[142] On November 26, the committee adjourned, minus the Iraqi delegate, Yusuf al-Gaylani, who had already been ordered home by Nuri al-Saʿid.[143] It had agreed to submit a draft proposal to Arab governments for comment and to refer specific questions to teams of military and economic experts.[144]

By November 1949, the prospect for speedy adoption of an Iraqi-Syrian federation had weakened, thanks to the lack of progress in Syrian-Iraqi contacts and the mobilization of opposition inside and outside of Syria. The Syrian elections for a Constituent Assembly in mid-November did little to reverse this trend. The People's party, the strongest historic advocate of closer ties with Iraq, did emerge with the largest number of seats in the new Assembly but it had by no means received a mandate for action. The National party's boycott of the elections had partially delegitimized them, important elements in the army remained opposed to the federation scheme, and the People's party leadership was unsure of what course to adopt.

During this period, those Syrians most in favor of an explicit link with Iraq were bitter toward Iraq's failure to pursue a more activist policy. Indeed the Iraqis were not totally passive. As anti-unionist force increased their intrigues, so did Baghdad. For example, a sum of £10,000 sterling was transmitted to Asad Tlas to ensure the election of appropriate candidates in the Jazira region. As the new assembly's inaugural session neared, the Iraqis sent special emissaries to Damascus to supplement their minister's efforts in cultivating pro-

Iraqi forces. The response, however, was less favorable than it had been during the previous months.[145]

Within Iraq, Regent ʿAbd al-Ilah apparently decided to use the opportunity of a cabinet reshuffle to promote the unity cause. He had been advised on various occasions that Nuri al-Saʿid's presence in the government was an obstacle owing to the mistrust it engendered in Syria and elsewhere. Consequently, the regent backed the formation on December 10 of a government headed by ʿAli Jawdat and excluding Nuri entirely.[146] Swift-moving events in Syria rendered this meaningless, and the new cabinet would cause him considerable displeasure during its brief life-span.

On December 17, Syria's new Constituent Assembly approved the text of the oath of office to be taken by the head of state and the assembly members. In a rare display of decisiveness, the advocates of closer ties with Iraq succeeded in having the oath omit a pledge to preserve the republican regime and include a pledge to "work for the realization of the unity of the Arab states." The effect on the army's anti-Iraqi forces was immediate. In fact, General Hinnawi had been warned by the Iraqis that a plot was being hatched, but he failed to take the necessary steps in time.[147] During the night of December 18 and 19, Colonel Adib Shishakli arrested Hinnawi and a number of his supporters in the army, and Colonel Tlas went into hiding in the Iraqi legation. Although civilian politicians were not touched at this stage, notice had been served that the Syrian army was now the ultimate arbiter of political life.[148]

As is usually the case in military coups, the motives were a mixture of national and personal factors. For example, junior officers feared a loss of position and influence in an expanded, mostly British-equipped and British-trained Syro-Iraqi army. Ideologically, Shishakli had been an adherent to the principles of the Syrian-centered *Parti Populaire Syrien*.[149] This was consistent with his support of a union with Iraq, but only if Syria was the dominant partner and under a republican regime.[150]

Jordanian, Saudi, and Egyptian leaders were all concerned about the latest Syrian upheaval and its long-term domestic and regional implications. Initially, they were again excessively worried about a possible Iraqi military intervention. Egypt's Prime Minister Sirri Pasha was also uneasy with the ever-growing influence of Syrian army officers, who in his view were entirely ignorant of politics and devoid of statesmanship.[151] Still, neither the Saudis nor the Egyptians could deny that, for the moment, events in Syria had again tilted in their favor. This feeling was most clearly expressed in an Egyptian, pro-palace newspaper editorial entitled "The Oath of Treason Was Not Taken."[152] Ironically, the same oath was taken without alteration by Hashim al-Atasi on January 7, 1950, upon his ascension to the presidency.[153]

At the end of January 1950, a brief episode occurred that marked an appropriate conclusion to the preceding months of hectic maneuvering within and around the Syrian polity: an ill-fated effort by Iraqi Deputy Prime Minister and Foreign Minister Muzahim al-Pachachi and Minister of Culture Najib al-Rawi to put Egyptian-Iraqi relations on a new footing. Known for their advocacy of better ties with Egypt, Pachachi and Rawi hoped that the new Wafd government in Egypt would be less antagonistic towards a gradualist unity approach in which Egypt would be consulted at every stage. The Iraqis also hoped that improved ties would provide a counterweight to Saudi Arabia, the real obstacle in their view, to unity with Syria. According to 'Ali Jawdat's memoirs, the regent had agreed to his insistence on improving ties with Cairo as a condition for his assuming office. The regent had not, however, intended them to go as far as they did. Without prior consultation with the cabinet, they reached a tentative "hands off Syria" agreement with the new Egyptian foreign minister, Muhammad Salah al-Din, on January 30, 1950. The agreement committed both governments to

> (1) [refrain for five years] from intervention, either direct or indirect, in Syrian internal affairs and from any agitation and encouragement which might be considered as intervention; and (2) [promote] the stabilization of conditions in Syria on a sound constitutional basis in conformity with the wishes of the Syrian people.

An annex to the agreement stipulated that the "agitation or encouragement" referred to in the first article of the agreement included, inter alia, the Greater Syria and Fertile Crescent schemes.[154]

The Egyptians had been skeptical whether the agreement would be acceptable in Baghdad, and rightly so. When Pachachi and Rawi returned home, the agreement was immediately disavowed by the regent, with Nuri al-Sa'id's encouragement. Having become dissatisfied with 'Ali Jawdat's minority government, he now found the moment appropriate to compel its resignation.[155]

AN ASSESSMENT

Syria's internal political order and its ability to project even a minimal amount of power were irreparably damaged by the succession of military coups. In addition, the overthrow of Syria's veteran nationalist regime and the military's ever-deepening involvement in Syrian political life was an example followed during the next decade in Egypt and Iraq. Finally, internal Syrian politics became intimately bound up with inter-Arab rivalries. Nonetheless, Syria's standing within the inter-Arab framework at the beginning of 1950 was the same as it had been one year earlier. The inter-Arab system of checks and balances had triumphed over Iraqi Hashimite revisionist aspirations. But Syria was kept within the Egyptian-Saudi fold; the dominant "cooperation" model of inter-Arab relations was perpetuated; and the Hashimite-sponsored, geographically based "unity," or "federative," model again failed to be consummated. Moreover, the basic nature of the system, one of loosely structured, fluid alliances existing in a state of uneasy equilibrium, remained unchanged.

This came about thanks to a number of interlocking factors. Nuri al-Sa'id's desire for closer ties with Syria was genuine. Syrian domestic and regional considerations militated against swift action or undue risk, outweighing the demands of the regent, 'Abd al-Ilah.[156] Although not averse to covert backing for pro-Iraqi elements in Syria, Nuri insisted that any aboveboard initiatives come first from the Syrians, and through legitimate constitutional channels. Nuri's concern with restoring constitutional life to Syria was motivated by two concerns: the need to defuse the expected opposition within Syria and the Arab world to closer Syrian-Iraqi ties, and the fear of possible spillover effects of the Syrian army's involvement in politics on the Iraqi armed forces.

Regarding Egypt, Nuri consistently sought to avoid a frontal confrontation over the Syrian question. His efforts alternatively to cajole, mollify, and consult Egyptian officials, all the while chafing under Egypt's dominance of the Arab League and testing the degree of Egypt's commitment to the affairs of the Fertile Crescent had been features of his foreign policy since the early 1940s. Aware of the voices in Egypt calling for a reassessment of Egypt's involvement following the debacle in Palestine, Nuri may well have hoped in 1949 that the Egyptians had had enough. In this he was disappointed, as he had been so many times before. Both the Egyptians and the Saudis actively sought to block Iraq. Their penetration of the Syrian polity helped to fragment Syrian political life, making it impossible for a coherent and effective pro-Iraqi grouping to emerge. The Egyptians also revived the Arab League mechanism at the appropriate moment to offer Syria a viable alternative to alignment with Iraq. As for the regent's Hashimite cousins in Jordan, they were of no help. On the contrary, ʿAbdallah was steadfastly opposed to Iraq's Syrian ambitions. Thus, by December 1949, the combination of inter-Arab and internal Syrian dynamics had effectively prevented Iraqi hopes from coming to fruition. All that remained was for Adib Shishaskli to provide the coup de grâce.

Any assessment of the events in Syria must also refer to the role of factors external to the Arab system. French opposition to closer Syrian-Iraqi ties was expressed through encouragement of Zaʿim and later of anti-Hinnawi elements in the Syrian army. The absence of British and U.S. encouragement for a federation was also important in shoring up the status quo. Britain's strictly neutral posture did not prevent Iraq from exploring the possibilities of closer ties with Syria. But repeated cautioning by British officials against military intervention and London's reluctance to risk altering the Anglo-Iraqi Treaty militated against Iraqi and Syrian decisiveness. In addition, there was the Israeli factor. Israel repeatedly made known its strong opposition, on strategic grounds, to a Syrian-Iraqi amalgamation, to the point where the U.S. State Department felt it necessary to warn against any Israeli attempt to intervene.[157] Indirectly, too, the Israeli factor was a consideration, as illustrated by Jordanian and British fears that chaos in Syria would eventually bring about an Israeli move against the Jordanian-held areas of the former Palestine Mandate. Thus, directly and indirectly, Israel played a balancing role, contributing further to the reinforcement of the regional status quo.

There can be no doubt that Arab leaders were acutely concerned with the struggle for regional hegemony being waged in Syria between Egypt and Iraq during the 1940s and 1950s. The hectic events of 1949 were the first round of this competition. As Leonard Binder stipulates, the "struggle for Syria" may well have been only one aspect of a very complex pattern of struggle that characterized the international politics of the entire region. Nonetheless, the significance of what Seale terms the "two-way traffic in and out of Syria" was a central component in the evolving Arab state system.[158]

ISRAEL, JORDAN, AND THE WEST BANK

Just as the challenge to the inter-Arab status quo posed by the upheavals in Syria receded, another one appeared. The catalyst was twofold. The first was ʿAbdallah's negotiations with Israel for a far-reaching political arrangement, which culminated on February 24, 1950, in the initialing of a draft agreement of principles for a five-year nonaggression pact and provisions for the renewal of economic and commercial ties severed at the end of the British Mandate. The second was Jordan's concurrent move to complete the incorporation of the hilly areas of central Palestine already under its control. The result, in inter-Arab terms, was the collapse of the fragile Jordanian-Egyptian understanding that had been built up over the previous months, accompanied by a prolonged rift between Jordan and the other Arab states, which threatened to split the Arab League wide open.

The crisis was slow in developing. For months after the modicum of understanding achieved by the Egyptian and Jordanian prime ministers in April 1949, Jordan and Egypt took care not to antagonize one another too openly. Together with the other Arab states, they were involved in collective Arab-Israeli negotiations in Lausanne under the auspices of the Palestine Conciliation Commission. ʿAbdallah was extremely, and rightly, pessimistic that the joint Arab stand at the PCC-sponsored discussions could bring results. Thus, he continued to prefer direct bilateral talks with Israel in order to deal with the issues leftover from Rhodes.[159] Jordanian-Israeli contacts were, in fact, already resumed in mid-April and shifted into high gear toward the end of the year.

Throughout 1949, Egypt's attitude toward Jordan's bilateral probings with Israel and its planned incorporation of the West Bank was one of equanimity, if not quite approval. One indication of this was Egypt's bowing to Jordanian insistence that Palestinian Arab representatives be excluded from both the Arab League Council and Political Committee sessions in October 1949.[160] Concurrently, the incumbent Egyptian prime minister, Husayn Sirri Pasha, reiterated to Tawfiq Abu al-Huda what Ibrahim ʿAbd al-Hadi had told Abu al-Huda earlier, that there was no alternative to the union of Jordan and the West Bank. Sirri was likewise to have said that Gaza would have to be retained by Egypt for reasons of internal politics; but if Jordan ever obtained access to that port, Egypt would give it all possible trade facilities. On Sirri's suggestion, the two prime ministers agreed in principle that it would be desirable to conclude a "secret treaty" with regard to the future of any areas of Palestine that remained in Arab possession or that might be restored to the Arabs, along the following lines:

> (a) such areas of which the frontier ran with Israel and one Arab State should be annexed by that Arab State,
> (b) such areas whose frontiers ran with Israel and more than one Arab State should be divided between those Arab States, the division being made in the light of strategic and economic considerations with due regard being paid to the wishes of the Arab inhabitants, [and]
> (c) any such areas which constituted enclaves in Israel would be administered by the nearest Arab State.

The two prime ministers agreed to obtain the assent of their respective monarchs and then to meet again.[161] ʿAbdallah quickly gave his, for it dovetailed with both the principle of a negotiated settlement and the reality of Jordanian control of the West Bank.[162] Whether Sirri ever raised the issue with Faruq is not known. Sirri was soon out of office, and the matter was not discussed again.

Sirri's position was not the only one current in upper Egyptian echelons. His willingness to countenance Jordanian territorial gains contrasted with the position taken earlier by Muhammad ʿAbd al-Munʿim Mustafa, Egypt's delegate to the Lausanne meetings, in his talks with Israel's Eliahu Sasson.[163] At one point, ʿAbd al-Munʿim spoke of creating a territorial barrier between Israel and Egypt in the northern Negev, which would serve a dual purpose: allow the resettling of a large proportion of Palestinian Arab refugees, and make more tangible the idea of an independent Palestinian Arab state, a preferred alternative, in his mind, to 'Abdallah's expansionist plans. This may have been an optimal position. Nonetheless, the Egyptian interlocutor perhaps thought it would appeal to the Israelis, particularly in the context of solving the refugee question. Underlying Egypt's stand at Lausanne was a belief, later acknowledged by 'Abd al-Mun'im, that time was on its side, and that Israel, being in greater need of a stable and final settlement, would eventually be compelled to bow to international pressure and make concessions in the Negev and on matters relating to Palestinian Arab refugees.[164]

In any case, by the time of the Sirri-Abu al-Huda meeting in late October, the possibilities of a PCC-inspired settlement had receded. Thus, as far as the Jordanians were concerned, Sirri's statements to Abu al-Huda and Egypt's reluctance to push the issue of Palestinian representation in the League were acknowledgments of the existing reality.

Concurrently, on October 28, the Israeli government informed the Conciliation Commission that it preferred to negotiate with each Arab state separately and would no longer send a representative to its meetings. Israel's sporadic contacts with the Jordanians quickly turned into more sustained negotiations.[165]

The Egyptians were aware of these developments but did not yet move to block them. For Egypt, the issue was not the principle of negotiations per se but their content. For example, Colonel Isma'il Shirin (formerly a senior official in the presidency of the Council of Ministers, a member of Egypt's Rhodes delegation, and most importantly, Faruq's brother-in-law) was not pleased by what he knew of the Jordanian-Israeli talks. He feared that 'Abdallah might accede to Israel's remaining on the Aqaba coast and thus asked Britain to restrain Jordan. The crucial point, in his view, was that Jordan and Egypt obtain a common land frontier that would provide Egypt direct access to the eastern half of the Arab world. As for Egypt's own territorial needs, Shirin stressed that negotiations for a peace settlement, which he said he sincerely favored, could only be achieved by an Israeli agreement, guaranteed by Great Britain or the United States, to withdraw from the Red Sea coast, preferably to the southern tip of the Dead Sea. Egypt would then seek to retain the Gaza Strip and draw a frontier through Beersheba to the point of Israel's withdrawal. On the basis of these long-standing Egyptian conditions, he was confident of finding a solution for the refugee problem and for Jordan's desire for a Mediterranean outlet.[166]

In light of Shirin's overtures, the British Foreign Office weighed the option of again trying to promote a closer association of Egypt and Jordan, either in joint or simultaneous negotiations. In contrast to its policy of the previous year, it now concluded that "there would be a danger of their double-crossing each other." Thus, went Foreign Office reasoning, it would be better for Egypt not to start its own talks unless the Jordanian-Israeli discussions either reached a deadlock or showed signs of a successful conclusion.[167] Nor was the Foreign Office at all willing to countenance a British "guarantee" of any future Israeli dispositions.[168]

In talks with their Israeli interlocutors, the Jordanians initially pressed for a common frontier with Egypt, linking it to their demand for an outlet to the Mediterranean.[169] For Israel, however, the Negev was nonnegotiable. Moreover, the absence of meaningful Jordanian-Egyptian coordination, along with the lack of clarity regarding Egypt's ultimate intentions for the Negev (creation of a Palestinian buffer state, division with Jordan, or annexation), further ruled out possible Israeli calibration of its positions in the negotiations with Jordan according to Egypt's needs. What Israel did accede to was the principle of a narrow corridor from Hebron to the coastal region in the Gaza-Majdal [Ashkelon] area, a point that the Jordanians insisted was vital materially and for their standing in the Arab world. Disagreement remained on the corridor's width, exit point, and exact juridical status. These outstanding matters were important enough to call into question one historian's characterization of Israel's agreement in principle to a corridor as a "major breakthrough" later scuttled by recalcitrant military officials.[170]

By mid-February 1950, Great Britain's ambassador to Jordan, Sir Alec S. Kirkbride, reported that obtaining access to the sea seemed to have lost importance for the Jordanians and that they might well agree to drop it entirely in return for the recovery of land ceded to Israel in the Jenin area in the armistice agreement.[171] Indeed, when

'Abdallah stepped in a week later to break the negotiating deadlock, the draft agreement of principles that he imposed on his ministers went even further: no territorial adjustments were to be made at this stage; and the various outstanding matters, such as the corridor, refugees, and Jerusalem, were to be taken up by special joint committees.[172]

Whereas the Egyptian press virulently attacked the impending Jordanian-Israeli agreement from the beginning, the Egyptian government did not fully take the offensive against it until mid-March. Although a number of explanations have been offered for the delay, the most likely one is that it simply took a few weeks for the Egyptian authorities, divided as they were between the Wafd government and the palace, to digest the terms of the Jordanian-Israeli draft agreement, conclude that it was inimical to Egypt's interests, and decide on a response.[173]

Egypt's basic policy line had already been laid out during early February 1950 at the Cairo conference of Egyptian chiefs of mission in Arab states: (1) the rejection of a separate peace with Israel while maintaining the armistice indefinitely, (2) the continuation of the boycott on Israeli products and not recognizing Israeli passports or visas, and (3) the forbidding of transit of oil tankers via Suez to the Haifa refinery before the lifting of the Iraqi embargo on oil to Haifa.[174] Consequently, at a meeting in Geneva Muhammad 'Abd al-Mun'im Mustafa repeated to Israeli officials Egypt's satisfaction with the status quo, as long as Israel was unwilling to countenance territorial concessions in the Negev. He did express some interest in further discussions of a possible interim nonaggression agreement that would be more than the armistice but less than formal peace. Given his government's impending condemnation of a similar Israeli-Jordanian arrangement, the Egyptian's comments are more than a bit ironic, and lend substance to existing American doubts about 'Abd al-Mun'im's authority to conduct direct talks with Israel.[175]

In the meantime, Jordan's civilian leadership was far more sensitive than 'Abdallah to Arab attitudes and thus strongly resistant to 'Abdallah's bold diplomatic strokes. On February 26, the Council of Ministers approved the draft agreement of principles initialed at 'Abdallah's insistence two days earlier, but with revisions designed to forestall the expected accusation that Jordan was concluding a separate peace. The revisions included linking the new agreement to the armistice agreement by calling it an "appendix" and omitting specific reference to either the renewing of economic links or the duration of the agreement.[176]

Receiving Israel's revised, more detailed draft proposal on February 28 increased the civilian politicians' nervousness.[177] Then, on March 2, an attempt by ʿAbdallah to force the issue of reopening trade with Israel precipitated a government crisis, fanned by the three recently coopted Palestinian members of the Council of Ministers. Tawfiq Abu al-Huda resigned the premiership, ostensibly because of ill health, and Samir al-Rifaʿi agreed to form a new Council after Saʿid al-Mufti, the outgoing minister of the interior, declined to do so. Rifaʿi obtained the agreement of five members of the old Council to join him. The combination of anti-Jordanian attacks in the Syrian and Egyptian media and rumors within Jordan that Abu al-Huda's resignation was provoked by ʿAbdallah's desire to give in to Israeli demands resulted in the five outgoing ministers retracting their agreement to join Rifaʿi's cabinet. In the end, the crisis was resolved by Abu al-Huda's withdrawal of his resignation on the condition that no further negotiations with Israel take place until after the upcoming parliamentary elections, when he personally would no longer be involved in government.[178]

Thus, on March 7, a short meeting between Jordanian and Israeli officials resulted in the adjournment of the talks until after the April elections. During the meetings, Defense Minister Fawzi al-Mulqi read a *note verbale* stating that his government had accepted ʿAbdallah's plan as a basis for a settlement and expressed the hope that the talks would resume at the earliest possible moment, to be "animated by [the] same spirit and objectives as in [the] conferences to date."[179]

ʿAbdallah remained determined to press on with the talks once the elections and the incorporation of the West Bank were concluded. For his part, Abu al-Huda went out of his way to reiterate to the U.S. ambassador in Amman that his only criticism of ʿAbdallah was in regard to the timing of the negotiations. He also claimed that he was recommending that Jordan attempt to persuade the other Arab governments at the upcoming Arab League Council meeting that it was compelled to negotiate a settlement with Israel because of its special geographic and economic situation.[180] He apparently did not do so, however, and events took a different course.

On the eve of the March League Council meeting, a new round of anti-'Abdallah virulence was touched off by the publication in the Cairo press of secret documents supplied by former Arab Legion Colonel 'Abdallah al-Tall detailing wartime Jordanian-Israeli contacts, many of which he had been involved in personally.[181] The Egyptian government also took a number of substantial anti-Jordanian actions. The first was to insist on inviting the head of the Government of All-Palestine, Ahmad Hilmi Pasha, to attend the Council sessions, an affront to 'Abdallah.[182] Even more seriously, it began threatening to have Jordan expelled from the League.

The Jordanians attempted to deflate Egypt's offensive by declining to send an official delegation from Amman to the Council meeting. Only its minister in Cairo, Jamal Tuqan, was present for the opening sessions. On March 28, the Jordanian government issued an official communiqué that denounced the League's invitation to Hilmi Pasha but ignored the furor stirred by its negotiations with Israel. Instead, it concentrated on Egyptian behavior, which, claimed the statement, ran contrary to what had been agreed on between Jordan and successive Egyptian governments between the latter part of 1948 until the end of 1949, "when it was agreed in principle on the fate of the two Arab sections of Palestine, the Eastern and the Southwestern, on cooperation to secure a corridor to connect these sections and even with regard to the use of the port of Gaza."

As has already been shown, there was substance to the Jordanian claim even if it fell short of a hard and fast agreement. These same principles, the Jordanian government's statement claimed, had also been found acceptable by Syria, Lebanon, and Iraq. For Jordan to acquiesce in the new state of affairs would lead to "restlessness and agitation" in the West Bank and cause "anger and alarm amongst the brethren who have linked their fate and destiny with those of this Kingdom and who have insisted that they are of it and that it is theirs." Therefore, concluded the statement, it was sufficient for its minister in Cairo to represent Jordan at the Council meetings, with the caveat that "he should avoid discussing unacceptable subjects but participate in talks on other matters."[183]

By leaving room for continued participation in League affairs and by not raising the subject of its talks with Israel, Amman helped trigger the collective Arab "mechanism" of mediation, which militated against irreparable splits. Concurrently, the Egyptians signaled their desire to tone down their expulsion threat and the mediators—this time Iraqi Prime Minister Tawfiq al-Suwaydi, the Regent ʿAbd al-Ilah, and Lebanese President Camille Chamoun—moved into action. Concerned with the future of the Hashimite House, particularly in view of the venomous attacks in the Egyptian press, the regent urged ʿAbdallah to "seek help and light from the serious opinions of the sincere men" in his kingdom, that is, move in the direction of constitutional monarchy and, by implication, not push for a peace with Israel against his ministers' will.[184] Suwaydi tried to persuade the League members to modify their attitudes toward Jordan, to prevent any vote in the Council on Jordan's expulsion, and to block the subject of the West Bank's annexation from even being discussed. At the same time, Suwaydi reiterated his support for the principle of the League, declaring, for example, that Iraq would support an economic boycott of any Arab state negotiating with Israel, even Jordan.[185] According to another Iraqi delegate in Cairo, Suwaydi deliberately took the lead in the initial attacks on Jordan in order to establish a better atmosphere between Iraq and Egypt, Saudi Arabia, and Syria. This was contrary to his government's instructions to keep a low profile. Having shown the anti-ʿAbdallah Arab majority that Iraq's heart was in the right place, Suwaydi was able to carry out his mediation efforts.[186] Chamoun also entered the mediating picture, at ʿAbdallah's request.[187]

As a result of these contacts, Egypt's Prime Minister Nahhas Pasha dispatched a letter to ʿAbdallah on March 30 asking him to reconsider his decision not to send a delegation to Cairo and accept a proposed League resolution barring any Arab state from making a separate peace with Israel without the League's consent, with expulsion the penalty for violation. On his decision regarding the Cairo delegation, ʿAbdallah and his ministers were unanimous that no development had occurred to warrant a change in their decision. Regarding the proposed League resolution, the king feared that accepting it would preclude Jordan from ever making peace with Israel. By contrast, his ministers argued that continued Jordanian opposition at this juncture would only give rise to further Arab attacks, thus hindering the prospects of smooth elections on both banks of the Jordan. As for future peace moves, they stated, Jordan could always notify the League of its intentions and leave the onus of breaking up the League to the others. The present circumstances, they told 'Abdallah, proved that the other League members were reluctant to adopt extreme, irreversible measures. On 'Abdallah's request, Kirkbride added his voice to those of 'Abdallah's ministers: The completion of the elections and the declaration of union by the new Parliament, he said, was the first priority. "Once the union [was] effected, Jordan would be in a stronger position both as regards Israel and the Arab League."[188]

'Abdallah accepted this reasoning.[189] Thus, on April 1, 1950, the Arab League Council unanimously passed a resolution forbidding any member from negotiating for, or concluding "a separate peace or any political, military or economic agreement with Israel." The resolution was somewhat ambiguous regarding penalties for violation. It referred to immediate expulsion, in line with ARTICLE 18 of the Charter, which necessitates a separate, unanimous expulsion decision, not counting the state considered to be in violation of its obligations. It then charged the Political Committee to propose appropriate measures against the offender.[190] On April 13, the Council unanimously approved a supplementary resolution fleshing out the Political Committee's role and the exact penalties to be imposed. The Committee would be charged with investigating whether there had been a violation of the April 1 resolution. Its decision would be binding if four member states agreed on it—a deviation from the Charter. Not only would a violator be expelled from the League, the remaining members were obligated to undertake a number of concrete steps: (1) sever political and consular relations with the offending state, (2) close any common frontiers, and suspend economic, commercial and financial relations with it, and (3) prohibit all financial relations or commercial exchanges, direct or indirect, with the subjects of that state.[191] The basic message was clear. A separate peace agreement with Israel was an unacceptable violation of fundamental collective Arab tenets.

Jordan's Jamal Tuqan was now charged with trying to prevent any discussion by the League of Jordan's imminent annexation of the West Bank.[192] The April 11 elections for a new, united Jordanian Parliament galvanized the League to search for some way to avoid de jure recognition of Jordan's action while recognizing, de facto, its administration of the area.[193] That same day, Egypt's Foreign Minister Salah al-Din requested Britain to intervene with Jordan to forestall outright annexation.[194] On April 13, the League Council reaffirmed the Political Committee's resolution of April 12, 1948, that the entry of Arab armies into Palestine was only a temporary measure and that final political arrangements would be subject to the will of the inhabitants. In addition, the Council declared that any member state violating the resolution would be considered as having broken the obligations it had assumed under the Charter, a reference to both the pledges of cooperation contained in ARTICLE 2 and the commitments to Palestinian rights embodied in the Special Annex relating to Palestine. In the event of violation, the Political Committee would then meet to consider operative steps.[195]

The Iraqi delegation, having lobbied for the mildest possible League action, was again quite satisfied with the outcome and claimed partial credit that the Council had not directly and specifically condemned the impending annexation.[196] Privately, Iraq's Prime Minister Suwaydi appealed to the British to restrain ʿAbdallah from going ahead.[197] Jordan's Tuqan was less pleased. He believed, nonetheless, that the resolution's failure to specify precise penalties for a violation, as had been done regarding the conclusion of a separate peace with Israel, probably meant that the League did not take the annexation as seriously.[198]

Originally, the formal act of unification of the East and West banks was scheduled to take place sometime after May 1, when the new Parliament was due to open. The dates of both actions were pushed forward in reaction to the heightened collective Arab pressure against the annexation. As soon as the elections were over, said Kirkbride, strenuous efforts were initiated "by the Saudi and Egyptian Legations in Amman, and by hostile Palestinain organizations in Lebanon and Syria (working under the covert encouragement of the Syrian Government and probably that of the Lebanese Premier also) to influence the Palestinian deputies and senators and ministers against the proposed Union. The means used were persuasion, money and threats."[199]

The Israelis were also active. The government's official stand was that the annexation was "unilateral" and did not in any way determine the final status of the area. While conveying this to the Jordanians via "HaYogev" (a code word for ʿAbd al-Ghani al-Karmi who, as a Royal Court official acted as a liaison between ʿAbdallah and the

Israelis and received a retainer from Israel), Israel made it clear that their opposition could be modified by the conclusion of a Jordanian-Israeli agreement.[200]

On April 24, the newly elected Jordanian Parliament opened. Its representatives were equally divided between the West and East banks. That same day, after desultory maneuvers by some Palestinian delegates to block the inevitable, Parliament proclaimed the "complete unity of the eastern and western banks of the Jordan and their merging into one state" under the Hashimite crown, this in accordance with the "right of self-determination" and in view of the two Banks' "national, natural and geographic unity, as well as the necessities of their common interests and vital capacities." In a sop to Jordan's critics, the resolution also reaffirmed Jordan's intention to "preserve all the rights of the Arabs in Palestine . . . without prejudice to the final settlement of the just cause (of Palestine) and within the framework of national aspirations, Arab co-operation and international justice."[201] The resolution was immediately ratified by 'Abdallah, and took effect that same day.

In essence, 'Abdallah had thrown down the gauntlet to the League, and particularly Egypt. The next few weeks were marked by acrimonious exchanges between Amman and Cairo and by new measures against Jordan in the League. In the Jordanian Parliament, Tawfiq Abu al-Huda elaborated on the Council of Ministers' March 28 communiqué and his own statements to the press that Egypt had previously agreed in principle to the extension of Jordanian rule over the West Bank. In particular, he cited his meeting with Sirri Pasha in October 1949, where Sirri had proposed a secret agreement to be put in force in the appropriate circumstances. He also cited statements to the same effect made by Egyptian representatives to British officials, causing no small amount of embarrassment in British diplomatic circles.[202] For their part, Egyptian former Prime Ministers 'Abd al-Hadi Pasha and Sirri Pasha and former Foreign Minister Khashaba Pasha all denied Abu al-Huda's contentions.[203] In fact, they had all previously expressed equanimity with the reality of Jordan's rule on the West Bank, and had even seen it as possibly commensurate with Egyptian interests. What they, the palace, and all Egyptian governments had shrunk back from was giving it a formal legal basis, for fear that it would imply the liquidation of the central emotional motif of Arab nationalism, the cause of Palestine, and the formal acceptance of its partition.[204]

Once again, the Egyptians turned to the Arab League mechanism to restrain Jordan's actions, or at least adapt them to all-Arab exigencies. The Political Committee convened on May 10 to discuss the issue. Although a fuller understanding requires the opening of Egyptian archives, it appears that, as on previous occasions, the palace was advocating a tougher line than the government.[205] Prime Minister Nahhas Pasha was initially inclined to search for a formula that would satisfy the Political Committee that Jordan's actions had not violated the League Council's April 13 resolution and therefore did not warrant punitive measures.[206] After a few days of acrimonious exchanges with Jordan's Foreign Minister Shurayki, Nahhas, with the encouragement of Syria's Prime Minister Khalid al-'Azm, proposed that the Jordanian government declare the annexation of the West Bank to be the imposition of a trusteeship and therefore provisional, pending a final settlement.[207] Iraq's Tawfiq al-Suwaydi urged the regent to pressure 'Abdallah to accept it. At the same time, he left no doubt in Cairo that Iraq would not go along with a vote for Jordan's expulsion if it failed to comply.[208] The Jordanian delegation referred the proposal to Amman. Apart from vague assurances that the annexation would not prejudice a final settlement, the Jordanians would not budge. 'Abdallah instructed his delegation in Cairo to reject the trusteeship formula. At the same time, it was told to declare that Jordan had no desire to leave the League and would therefore not withdraw from it in anticipation of a hostile decision. If Jordan were to be expelled from the League, said 'Abdallah, the responsibility for the consequences would rest upon those who had prompted it.[209]

Despite Jordan's determination, the Egyptians decided to push through a resolution, on the night of May 15, that the annexation was indeed a violation of the April 13 resolution and that the Committee was thus recommending to the League Council that Jordan be expelled from the organization.[210] The Iraqi and Yemeni delegates abstained from the expulsion portion of the resolution and initiated the postponement of the next Council meeting until June 12.[211]

Notwithstanding the resolution's maximalist, uncompromising nature, the whole proceeding possessed an unreal quality. Nahhas knew beforehand that, thanks to Iraq, the recommendation for ex-

pulsion would not win the unanimous approval needed under ARTI-
CLE 18 of the Charter and therefore would possess neither operative
nor legal value. The decision to go ahead anyway, therefore, must be
understood on two levels. One was that of the murky world of internal Egyptian politics. Either Nahhas adopted a maximalist stand to
bolster his position vis-à-vis the palace or he simply bowed to palace
pressure. The other level was purely inter-Arab. The resolution emphasized Egypt's ideological purity and leadership, and was a more
forceful attempt somehow to modify Jordan's action and preserve a
collective Arab consensus on the issue.

The four weeks between the Political Committee's adjournment
and the Council's reconvening were taken up by numerous Arab efforts
to bridge the gap between Jordan and Egypt. Their goal was to avoid
a final decision to expel Jordan and to prevent an anti-Hashimite
walkout from the League by Egypt. The latter possibility, however
remote, caused genuine consternation in Iraq and Syria.[212] Ibn Sa'ud
urged 'Abdallah to accept the League's position on trusteeship, because
it would "release the Arabs from this embarrassment on the one hand,
and on the other hand the situation of Your Majesty will remain just
the same—what is in your hand will still be in your hand."[213]

In an effort to get Britain to intervene with 'Abdallah, Khalid
al-'Azm made the same point. "All the Arab leaders knew full well
that eastern Palestine would in fact from now on always remain part
of Jordan and were resigned to this. 'Abdallah's position was therefore
perfectly secure and he could make the statement without any qualms
about the future. But public opinion in the Middle East demanded
such a statement even if it meant nothing."[214]

For their part, Iraq's Salih Jabr, interior minister and strongman
of the Iraqi cabinet, and Lebanon's prime minister, Riyad al-Sulh, suggested that the Arab states accept the status quo in the West Bank
until such time as the whole of Palestine was freed and restored to
its Arab inhabitants, when the future status of the country could be
reconsidered. 'Abdallah's immediate reaction was sarcastic, remark-
ing to Kirkbride that the day the Arab League conquered Israel he
would not only place the West Bank of the kingdom at its disposition
but the East Bank as well.[215] The Jordanians told the Iraqis that they
were inclined to accept their compromise formula if the Egyptians
would as well.[216] Already on May 28, Jordan's Council of Ministers

had attempted to demonstrate some flexibility. Although declaring that the matter of the union was "settled and not open to further discussion," it also referred to the second part of the Unity Act, namely that the union was "in accordance with the aims of the Arab cause and without prejudice to the Palestinian case."[217]

The Iraqi-Lebanese formula was too vague for the Egyptians. Aware of their opposition, the Jordanians chose not to send a delegate to the June 12 Council meeting. What emerged was a stalemate and a backing away from an irreversible rupture. The Egyptians chose not to follow through on their expulsion threat. Instead, they pushed through a resolution calling on Jordan to declare that

> the annexation of a part of Palestine [had been] only an expediency dictated by factual necessities, and that Jordan [would] preserve that part as a trust pending the final settlement of the Palestine problem when the other parts shall have been liberated and restored to their pre-aggression status, and that it [would] accept our unanimous decision made by the other member states of the League, thereby realizing the objectives aimed at by the Arab States in their previous resolutions tending to preserve the entity of Palestine.[218]

Jordan's response was to be taken up by the October Council session.

In Iraq, there was general satisfaction that the expulsion question had been relegated to the indefinite future.[219] Iraqi leaders immediately renewed their efforts to win Jordanian acceptance of the League's trusteeship formula, both directly and indirectly. The regent and Salih Jabr visited Amman at the end of June, while Prime Minister Suwaydi again urged the British to apply pressure on ʿAbdallah.[220] In Amman, the regent and Jabr met firm resistance. The trusteeship formula, they were told, was too dangerous. The League would always demand an account from Jordan and might vary at any time the provision that Jordanian rule would continue until all of Palestine was liberated. Only the earlier, vaguer Iraqi formula was acceptable.[221] Suwaydi's entreaties were similarly unsuccessful.

There matters stood. Despite Iraqi fears of the consequences of continued Jordanian obstinacy, the October League Council meeting did not take up the issue and the entire matter faded away. The single remnant of the controversy was that no Arab state ever officially recognized the annexation. It would take the June 1967 War to reopen the Arab debate on the status of the West Bank.

AN ASSESSMENT

Just as the expulsion threat faded away, so did the prospect of real progress toward a Jordanian-Israeli settlement, even though ʿAbdallah had fully intended that the negotiations be resumed immediately after the annexation of the West Bank. On the night of April 25, 1950, he told Israel's Reuven Shiloah, a veteran specialist in Arab affairs, that he was hopeful that negotiations could begin in two weeks time.[222] ʿAbdallah, however, had become a prisoner of the situation he helped to create.[223] Older and weaker, he was no longer able to impose his absolute authority on a governing elite that was looking over its shoulder at the newly expanded, half-Palestinian Parliament and the other Arab states. Having successfully defied the Arab League on the annexation issue, Jordan's veteran politicians were in no mood to enter into another, more explosive struggle. In their view, it was now up to others, whether it be Lebanon, Egypt, the PCC or the United Nations to take the lead.[224] This was not, as some writers have implied, a simple trade-off between Jordan and the League, that is, the acceptance of the annexation in return for no further moves toward a peace agreement.[225] The dynamics were subtle: On the Jordanian side, apart from reluctance, there was also a feeling that a peace treaty was not as pressing a necessity as it had been. Jordan's hold on the West Bank was not only official but also more secure, thanks to Britain's prompt extension of the Anglo-Jordanian Treaty to cover the area. Subsequently, the Tri-Partite Declaration by the United States, Great Britain, and France on May 31, 1950, with its guarantees of the existing armistice lines, gave a further boost to the regional status quo.

From the Egyptian standpoint, the actual expulsion of Jordan from the League raised the paradoxical but distinct possibility that the collective Arab limitations on Jordan's behavior would be removed, thus pushing Jordan into Israel's arms. ʿAzzam Pasha, who still regarded himself as the keeper of the all-Arab flame, had always warned against such a possibility. As long as Jordan could be restrained from going too far toward Israel, Cairo would refrain from breaking up the League over the West Bank's annexation.

Consequently, this last phase of the nearly eighteen-month-long systemic crisis gradually came to an end. Regional and domestic political fluctuations had not resulted in radical transformation. Rather, the regional status quo, in terms of territory, alliance configurations, and the balance of power was more or less retained, with one exception: the West Bank's incorporation into the Hashimite Kingdom of Jordan, and the prolonged eclipse of the Palestinian Arabs as a political force.

Concurrently, the status quo was further reinforced by two additional events. The first was the signing of the Tri-Partite Declaration, which had originally been conceived by Great Britain to bolster Jordan's hold on the West Bank, but expanded into a U.S.-British-French effort to strengthen the overall regional status quo and to address the region from the perspective of Western defense needs. The second was the signing by five Arab states on June 17, 1950, of the long-discussed collective security pact, officially called the Treaty of Joint Defense and Economic Cooperation. (Iraq withheld its approval, pending clarifications; Jordan's delegation was not present.)

On the theoretical level, the crisis had been a political-diplomatic one, less "severe" than the military crises that so often resulted in disequilibrium and irreversible changes in the international system. Historically, it was a period of critical importance. The collective Arab framework had emerged both stronger and weaker: stronger, in the sense that certain challenges had been rebuffed, existing patterns of interaction reinforced, and the overall structure of the system left intact; weaker, in that the internecine struggles had contributed to the decline and delegitimization of both the Arab League as an instrument for promoting the collective Arab agenda and a number of individual Arab regimes.

5

SOLIDIFICATION AND TRANSITION, 1950–1954

THE ARAB-ISRAELI CONFLICT and the status of Syria remained subjects of attention and contention on the collective Arab agenda during the early 1950s, although not to the same degree as during the previous two years. Inter-Arab politics did not, however, lack in turbulence. The latest issue crowding its way onto center stage was the question of how to respond, individually and collectively, to British and U.S. schemes for regional defense. The problem was not a new one. For some time, Great Britain had desired to put its relations with the Arab states on a new footing in order to reinforce both its own standing and overall regional security against a possible Soviet threat. It had been prevented from doing so, in no small measure, by the failure to implement the Bevin-Sidqi draft agreement of October 1946 on the future of Britain's Suez Canal base and on the Sudan, and by Iraq's immediate repudiation in January 1948, under public pressure, of the newly signed Portsmouth Treaty, which had been designed to replace the Anglo-Iraqi Treaty of 1930. Meanwhile, from the Arab side, official solidarity with Egypt in its conflict with Britain masked considerable frustration with what they perceived to be Egypt's rigidity. Attempting to get around the deadlock, leaders such as Nuri al-Sa'id and Riyad al-Sulh floated the concept of an Arab collective security pact during early 1948. This would, they hoped, somehow serve as a framework for collective Arab-Western relations and thus bypass the British-Egyptian impasse by providing a substitute for an unachievable Anglo-Egyptian treaty.[1] Nothing had come of their idea, and when the collective security pact became a central part of the all-Arab agenda in the fall of 1949, it was in the context of Egyptian efforts to block Iraqi ascendancy in Syria.

Subsequent to the signing of the Joint Defense Pact in June 1950 some of the original thinking behind its conception again surfaced, albeit for contradictory reasons. For Iraq, a "package" formula linking the Arab Joint Defense Pact to a solution to the British-Egyptian dispute and Western regional defense schemes held considerable merit.[2] For Baghdad it offered yet another chance to try to break out of its subordinate, "junior" status opposite Cairo. Egypt, on the other hand, desired to bring Iraq and Jordan into the fold (neither had subscribed to the original agreement) in order to consolidate further the inter-Arab status quo under its leadership. To this end, it was willing to tolerate concessions to Iraq regarding the exact terms of the pact, and to view with equanimity the idea of the pact serving as a basis for future relations with the West. This was only the case so long as it did not interfere with its fundamental position vis-à-vis Great Britain or threaten to alter the regional balance of power.

In the middle stood some of the veteran Syrian civilian politicians, particularly Prime Minister Nazim al-Qudsi, who tried to bridge the Iraqi and Egyptian positions in order to ease the inter-Arab competition over Syria. In part, this entailed reassuring each side that Syria could withstand the embrace of the other. It also involved exploring new formulas regarding both the existing Joint Defense Pact, and Arab-Western relations. Qudsi's view was that all the Arab states should federate, sign an alliance with Turkey, and abandon any pretence of neutralism in favor of close ties with the West.[3] As he recognized, however, even to begin moving in this direction was a formidable task, given existing inter-Arab rivalries, Qudsi's circumscribed power in the fractured Syrian polity, and the general "neutralist" climate there.[4]

As for the Western powers, the emphasis in the May 31, 1950, Tri-Partite Declaration on the need of the local actors to play their part in "the defense of the area as a whole" indicated their primary concern. Less than one month later, on June 27, war broke out in Korea. In this new phase of the no longer purely "cold" war, the Middle East theater, although far from the battlefront, assumed an even larger importance for Western strategic planners. In the minds of many, the likelihood of a combined Soviet land thrust via the Caucasus and air strike against Egypt had now increased considerably. One former U.S.

diplomat described the feeling. "There was really a definite fear of hostilities, of an active Russian occupation of the Middle East physically, and you could practically hear the Russian boots clumping down over hot desert sands."[5]

Thus, it was from 1950 to 1952 that the Western powers' defense proposals, British-Egyptian negotiations, and inter-Arab contacts on finalizing the Joint Defense Pact became intertwined more closely. The meager results were certainly not commensurate with the effort. Nazim al-Qudsi's first attempt at inter-Arab mediation came during his visit to Baghdad in the second half of November 1950. Qudsi brought with him the idea of adding the constitution of the North Atlantic Treaty Organization (NATO) to the Arab Joint Defense Pact in order to ensure equality and collective responsibility among the signers. He also pressed Nuri to agree to an Egyptian commander-in-chief, to be chosen by all of the Arab defense ministers. Nuri's response was negative on both counts. As presently constituted, said Nuri, the pact appeared to be directed only against Israel. If it was to remain so, then Iraq would confine itself to aiding its neighbors that bordered on Israel (Syria and Jordan). As for the subject of the commander-in-chief, Baghdad had alternative ideas, tabled in a draft amendment to the pact. Either the commander-in-chief must be an Iraqi, if the fighting were within Iraq's territory or on its frontiers, or the commander-in-chief should be the senior commander of the largest contributing country or he should be chosen on his merits. Details aside, it was Iraq's continued reluctance to accept an Egyptian-dominated organization that determined the tenor of Nuri's response.[6] Qudsi left Baghdad unsatisfied and critical of Nuri for becoming, like all Arab politicians trained in the old Turkish school, so obsessed by formulas that he lost sight of the objects in view.[7]

Two weeks later, Qudsi brought his ideas to Cairo, but he made little headway. The Egyptians remained preoccupied with their bilateral negotiations with Great Britain. Although not directly urging a continued British presence in the Canal Zone, Qudsi did express the hope that the British-Egyptian talks would bear fruit. This was a necessary preliminary, he believed, to attaining inter-Arab defense collaboration and to blocking communism. Over optimistically, Qudsi claimed that Faruq, Nahhas, and Interior Minister Fu'ad Siraj al-Din were all terrified of the potential for a Communist threat from within

Egypt and outside and were thus searching for formulas that would enable the British to retain some presence in the Canal Zone.⁸

Arab-Western relations and the future of the Joint Defense Pact dominated the combined meetings in Cairo of the Arab League Political Committee and Council, from January 23 to February 2. The energy expended indicated the continued value that Arab leaders attached to the League as an institution. On the other hand, the proceedings did little to reverse the cynicism and scorn for the League that now dominated the Arab media.⁹

As was his wont, Nuri al-Sa'id came to Cairo with a comprehensive scheme of his own. The idea, as he had already clarified to Qudsi, was to modify the existing Joint Defense Pact so as not only to strengthen its military aspects but also to change its scope from that of defense against Israel to that of defense against any aggression (in accordance with the U.N. Charter's ARTICLES 51 and 52 on promoting regional defense, and the recent U.N. resolution entitled "Uniting for Peace," directed at the Korean War). Any nation interested in the defense of the Middle East, and not just from among the Arab states, would be eligible to adhere to the new pact. (He had in mind Great Britain, Turkey, and Greece, but not, of course, Israel.) One of the stipulations was that existing bilateral defense treaties would not be affected for the next two years, during which time it would become clear whether war would come to the region. After the end of 1952, existing treaties would have to be modified as far as they were incompatible with the terms of the new pact.¹⁰

Under these terms, Nuri explained to Egypt's Foreign Minister Muhammad Salah al-Din, British evacuation of Egyptian soil and a handing over of its military bases was required no later than December 1952. In a further sweetener to Egypt, Nuri suggested that British-Egyptian negotiations be conducted on the basis of linkage between the evacuation and Sudan issues, with the latter to be settled on the basis of unity under the Egyptian Crown, with Sudan receiving dominion status.¹¹

Nuri's private meeting with Salah al-Din was part of his strategy of prior consultation with Egypt and Great Britain. If the general line was agreeable to both, he would then present it to the rest of the League. Not surprisingly, however, the specifics of Nuri's plan regarding Egypt were deemed completely unacceptable by Great Britain. Thus, Nuri was compelled to address the issues of Arab-Western relations, regional defense, and the Arab Joint Defense Pact in a piecemeal fashion.

On January 23, at the Political Committee's third meeting, Nuri introduced a long resolution declaring the Arab states' "attachment to the principles" of "supporting all measures adopted by the UN"; their intention of "withholding assistance from any state against which the UN adopts a repressive measure"; and their pledge to "carry out faithfully" all "measures adopted by the UN in pursuit of international peace and security." The sweeping nature of the resolution was designed to nail down an Arab-Western alignment both on the Korean issue and, more importantly, against any future Soviet threat. As a sop to Arab nationalist sensitivities and criticisms, the resolution concluded with an implied linkage between Arab support for the West and Western military and economic aid to the Arab world.

The final resolution adopted by the League Council was considerably watered-down, thanks to Egyptian efforts in the Political Committee discussions. Although it referred to the Arab states' faith in U.N. principles, it placed much greater emphasis on the importance of peaceful negotiations as the means to end international disputes. Moreover, in language specifically calibrated to Egypt's needs, it asserted that U.N. principles could not be implemented "if the big powers persist in intervening . . . in the domestic affairs of small nations." The Arab states, it continued, "cannot discharge their international obligation under the UN Charter unless they obtain their full national [*wataniyya*] rights or settle their national [*qawmiyya*] cases in accordance with the principles of freedom, justice and equality."[12]

Putting the best face on things, the Iraqis insisted privately that adherence to the modified resolution still indirectly committed the Arab states to oppose Soviet aggression.[13] Nuri was still far from achieving a Western-Arab military alignment, but he remained intent on nailing down an amended Joint Defense Pact that would serve as a basis for future Arab-Western defense cooperation. By this time, obtaining the agreement had become more important to Nuri than the substance of the alterations to the original pact. As a result, a divergence emerged between Iraq and its Hashimite ally, Jordan. Jordan continued to refuse to sign the pact in lieu of modifications.[14] The Iraqis, in contrast, were sufficiently satisfied by the League's adoption of its own proposal, embodied in the form of a supplementary protocol, to establish a Military Advisory Committee composed of the chiefs of staff of the Arab armies, to advise the previously established Permanent Military Committee. Thus, on February 2, Nuri affixed his signature to the pact, leaving Jordan as the only major League state in open opposition (Yemeni reservations, expressed the previous year, were deemed insignificant).

The Iraqis were not happy about Jordan's continued refusal to sign the pact, ascribing it to 'Abdallah's pique over the others' refusal to recognize his incorporation of parts of western Palestine into Jordan. Nonetheless, they told the United States, Jordan could be counted on fully in the event of a real test to the agreement.[15] Shortly afterward, 'Abdallah confirmed to the United States that they could in fact count on him in the event of a Soviet attack.[16]

Despite Iraq's accession to the agreement, Nuri harbored no illusions that the pact as it stood could be an effective instrument either against Israel or in the broader global context. In fact, within a few months, in a speech to the Iraqi Senate, Nuri openly ridiculed its value.[17] What was important at this juncture, however, was Iraq's adherence to the pact under face-saving terms. Having achieved a mild declaration of affinity with the United Nations, and a collective security pact that he hoped would serve in the future as a link to Western defense plans, Nuri departed Cairo having at least established two modest building blocks for his overall scheme.

That the Joint Defense Pact was considered of little practical value was further illustrated by the slowness of its actualization. Legally, it required the ratification of four states before taking effect. By mid-summer 1951, only Syria and Egypt had done so. In early 1952, however, the post-'Abdallah Jordanian government decided, as part of its general fence-mending policies, to drop Jordan's previous objections, and signed and ratified the agreement. Jordan's accession to the pact cleared the way for Iraqi ratification. Thus, on August 23, 1952, over two years since the pact was first approved by the League Council, it formally took effect. The Saudis had by this time also ratified it; the Lebanese ratification came shortly afterward, in October 1952; and Yemen's came a year later.[18]

On paper, the organizational mechanism established by the pact looked impressive. The Joint Defense Council, composed of Arab foreign and defense ministers stood at the top. The ongoing body was to be a Permanent Military Committee (PMC) and appropriate subcommittees, staffed by officers of the member states. It was charged with (1) drawing up contingency military plans, (2) making proposals for the organization of forces, including the fixing of the minimum necessary forces for each state (but not with fixing contributions to an all-Arab army), (3) the enhancement of efficiency in maintenance and training, (4) the exchange of training and study missions, (5) coordinating the exploitation of their common, natural, industrial, and agricultural resources in time of war, and (6) examining facilities and other mutual aid to be provided in war time. In between, as the Iraqis had demanded, stood an Advisory Council of Chiefs of Staff, charged with supervising the PMC's work and submitting it to the Joint Defense Council.[19]

It was not until the summer and fall of 1953 that the organization actually began to operate, owing primarily to the reluctance of Egypt's new military government to divert its attention from consolidating its rule.[20] Earlier Arab chiefs of staff, minus Yemen, and with a Jordanian officer deputizing for Glubb Pasha, met in Bludan in June 1951, in the aftermath of Syrian-Israeli clashes in the Huleh Valley, albeit with no effect. The 1951 gathering and the first series of meetings of the PMC and the Chiefs of Staff Advisory Council, and those that would come subsequently, had little to show for their work.[21] Despite all the debates, discussions, and tactical maneuvers that preceded it, the agreement quickly became a dead letter. Thirty years later, the Iraqis would repeatedly and unsuccessfully evoke it in their war with Iran.[22]

However active Nuri al-Sa'id was during 1950 and 1951 in pushing for closer Arab-Western ties, it was Egypt's position that continued to be decisive on both Arab-Western and inter-Arab matters. This fundamental inter-Arab "rule" was reasserted in October 1951. After nineteen months of intermittent negotiations with Britain over the future of its canal base and the Sudan, Egypt unilaterally abrogated the 1936 Anglo-Egyptian Treaty, and proclaimed Faruq "King of Egypt and the Sudan." The timing was finely calculated. Announced by Prime Minister Nahhas Pasha on October 8, the move was made to counter the imminent publication of a multilateral approach to bypass the Anglo-Egyptian impasse. This came on October 14, with a Four-Power proposal—by Great Britain, the United States, France, and Turkey—for the creation of an Allied Middle East Command (MEC) to defend the area against outside aggression. The Command was to be headquartered in Egypt, with Egypt being offered the status of "founder member."[23] Simultaneously, a quadripartite approach was made to the other Arab states explaining the purpose of the MEC and expressing the hope that they would agree to be associated with it in some as yet undefined way. Following Egypt's unequivocal rejection of the proposal, the four powers amplified their offer to the other Arab states, inviting individual association with the command, "on the basis of equality," through a "Middle East Defense Liaison Organization" intended to link the MEC with those countries "ready to join in the defense of this area." Requests for military assistance in the form of arms, equipment, and training would "be filled . . . to the extent possible following the coordination of such requests through the MEC." At the same time, this was not to be understood as a scrapping of the Tri-Partite Declaration's commitment to maintain a military balance between the Arab states and Israel.[24]

The Arab League Political Committee was quick to endorse Egypt's abrogation of the Anglo-Egyptian treaty and to affirm the members' support for "immediate evacuation (by Britain) and permanent unity of the Nile Valley under the Egyptian Crown."[25] The other Arab states did not succumb to Egyptian pressure, applied during the U.N. General Assembly gathering in Paris, to line up behind the Egyptians in supporting the rejection of the MEC.[26] Without exception, their leaders were both intrigued by the Western proposals and disturbed by Egypt's negative stance and also with Cairo's failure even to consult with them before its rejection.[27] Their desires to break the impasse were intensified by the crisis atmosphere in the Canal Zone, which held out the specter of full-scale disorder and large-scale British military action. At the same time, the ever-present constraints of anti-Western public opinion, particularly in Syria, but also in Iraq and Jordan, dictated circumspection.

Given Syria's extremely fragile internal situation, it was not surprising that the Four-Power proposals and Egypt's actions became the focus of contention there. On the demonstrative level, the Syrian Parliament declared unanimously its support for Egypt's "historic decision" to abrogate the 1936 Treaty.[28] One month later, people of nearly all shades of Syrian political opinion participated in a well-organized march of solidarity with Egypt through the streets of Damascus.[29] Nazim al-Qudsi's participation, despite his consistent advocacy of closer ties with the West, indicated the extent to which public support for Egypt was deemed politically necessary.

At the same time, the conspicuous absence of Prime Minister Hasan al-Hakim and his forbidding the participation of any cabinet member, emphasized the deep divisions in Syrian politics over the issue.[30] Throughout this period, Hakim was the Syrian figure most consistently critical of the extreme anti-Western nationalist and pro-Egyptian tenor of the public debate in Syria. In statements to the press, he declared that he would not be influenced in the conduct of Syrian foreign policy by "street politics." These, he said, had been responsible for King Faysal I's downfall in 1920, and the loss of Alexandretta and Palestine. Although Hakim desired to see Egypt's aspirations fulfilled, he believed that Egypt's rejection of the Four-Power proposal had been hasty, and ought not have been done without prior consultation with the other Arab states. The Western defense proposals, he told his interviewers, would help prevent Israeli expansion. They would also mean increased economic and military aid to the Arabs.[31]

Shortly afterward, the People's party, using Hakim's pro-Western orientation as an excuse, withdrew its parliamentary support from Hakim, thus forcing his resignation. Nazim al-Qudsi was a tacit party to the maneuver. Nonetheless, despite his acquiescence to Hakim's ouster and his own public backing for Egypt, Qudsi's views were at variance with the accusations of subservience being hurled by his party against Hakim.[32] Taken in toto, Qudsi's contradictory actions provide evidence of a "double message" style that was an almost standard feature of Syrian political life.

Eventually, the People's party was able to form a broad-based government under Ma'ruf al-Dawalibi, known for both his ties with the Syrian Muslim Brotherhood and his avowed "neutralist," anti-Western views. Twenty-four hours later, he too was removed, this time by Shishakli, who now assumed more direct control. Shishakli's own views on ties with the West were far more similar to those of Qudsi and Hakim than to those of Dawalibi.[33] In some ways, Shishakli was even more desirous of an alliance with the West, sensing the benefits for the Syrian military.[34] At the same time, the general anti-Western outlook of Arab ideological movements during the 1950s could not have failed to influence Shishakli to some degree, given that he himself was a product of these movements. In any case, Shishakli never made a serious move during the next two years to get out in front of Egypt and align himself openly with the Western defense proposals. Rather, he draped himself, if tardily, with the banner of Arabism.[35]

Within Egypt, neither Nahhas Pasha nor the palace were euphoric about the turn of events. On the contrary, they understood the dangers inherent in Egypt's slide toward extra-parliamentary extremism and initiated overtures to Great Britain for renewed negotiations.[36]

For Nuri al-Sa'id, the combination of Egyptian anxiety and his own predilection toward an alliance with the West led him to undertake another round of diplomacy. Once again, Nuri sought to enhance Iraq's status, not through a direct clash with Egypt, but through displaying to Egypt his good intentions. This entailed both a mediation mission between Egypt and Britain and a more general search for new formulas on Arab-Western ties.

Nuri's soundings with senior Egyptian officials elicited a number of suggestions to break the British-Egyptian impasse.[37] None of them bore fruit. The general Egyptian tendency was to look for a bilateral solution with Britain while shying away from any multilateral approach. This was completely at variance with the Four-Power proposals. The divergence of priorities within the upper Egyptian echelons also militated against success. Faruq was mainly interested in being recognized as king of the Sudan. If this were to come about, he would then be prepared to accept all of Great Britain's views on defense matters. Moreover, he was disturbed over the behavior of the Wafd government since the treaty abrogation and desired to replace it immediately. For Egyptian governmental officials, British evacuation from the Canal Zone was of greater priority, although they acknowledged that Faruq's obsession with the Sudan had to be satisfied. As for defense arrangements, Interior Minister Siraj al-Din was sympathetic to one of Nuri's previous ideas, basing them on the Arab Joint Defense Pact, to which Great Britain and other interested states could accede through a special protocol.[38]

Apart from periodic suggestions by some British officials to link the MEC symbolically with the Joint Defense Pact, London remained unreceptive to Nuri's idea. As one British Foreign Office official pointed out, the idea of MEC sponsors associating themselves with the Arab Collective Security pact was "a complete reversal of roles." More specific objections were: (1) The Arab states would never be capable of resisting the Soviets, even with generous military aid; (2) The MEC would not be able to cooperate effectively with such an unwieldy and contentious grouping; (3) Demands for arms would be exorbitant and constantly made under the threat of a loss of collaboration; and (4) Israel remained the pact's main objective, not the Soviet Union.[39]

Britain's rejection was not too heavy a blow for Nuri al-Sa'id because he had never been exclusively wedded to the idea anyway. Concurrently, he and 'Abd al-Ilah also entertained varied notions. One was an Iraqi-Saudi arrangement for the defense of the Persian Gulf, which might also involve non-Arab Pakistan. The real purpose of his proposal, he said, was to draw Saudi Arabia out of the Egyptian fold.[40] Another was to establish a "Council for the Organization of Mutual Defense" in which Israel might even be made a member. A third, even more farfetched notion was to replace Egypt with Great Britain as a member of the Arab Joint Defense Pact in the event that Egypt remained intransigent in its negotiations with Britain.[41]

The impreciseness of Nuri's suggestions was often belittled by British officials. Nonetheless, they varied on the tactical level only. Strategically, Nuri continued to search for a formula that would enhance Iraq's strength in the Fertile Crescent by means of its links with the West. On the inter-Arab level, he continued to oscillate, as he had since 1943, between currying Egyptian favor and seeking alternatives to the Egyptian-dominated League that he held in contempt.

London's lack of interest in linking the MEC to the Joint Defense Pact, its expressed determination to go forward with the MEC, and Egypt's inability to renew the diplomatic momentum all led Nuri al-Sa'id to a more forthright assertion of Iraqi interests. In his February 1952 talks with British officials, including the commander of Britain's Middle East forces, General Sir Brian Robertson, Nuri asked that Iraq be brought into any discussions on Middle East defense on an equal footing with Egypt. Its right to equal status, he stated, stemmed from the bases and facilities that Iraq would be expected to offer. Nuri also again expressed interest in developing defense links between the Arab states and Turkey and Pakistan, respectively, in what would essentially be a divorcing of the Joint Defense Pact from the Arab League framework.[42] Robertson and the Joint Chiefs of Staff thought that Nuri had a strong case, militarily and politically, for equal treatment.

But the British Foreign Office view predominated. Nuri was informed that Egypt's supreme strategic value could not be compared with Iraq's. Consequently, the first priority for Great Britain was to renew negotiations with Egypt on its participation in the MEC, and to avoid saying anything that might jeopardize the talks. If the negotiations were successful, then Iraq's status in the MEC could be discussed by the founder members, with Britain promising to "spare no efforts" in getting the best terms possible.[43]

No progress was achieved with Egypt in the following months, and British and U.S. officials lowered their sights. They now contemplated a more limited, planning-oriented Middle East Defence Organization (MEDO; the name was deemed more palatable than "Command"), to be based in Cyprus. These plans, too, came to naught, and were placed on hold until the British-Egyptian impasse could be resolved. All of Nuri's efforts to alter Iraq's global and regional relations foundered on the rock of Egypt's regional primacy. As a U.S. government interagency intelligence assessment concluded in March 1952, Egypt's participation in even a planning-oriented MEDO would come about only after a settlement of the British-Egyptian controversy, and on terms acceptable to Egypt. The Arab states, stated the assessment, would then follow Egypt's lead, motivated chiefly by the promise of arms and economic aid.[44]

Events have a way of outrunning policy plans. The overthrow of Faruq and the consolidation of power by the Free Officers Movement altered the calculus. British-Egyptian negotiation resumed shortly after the July 1952 coup. An agreement on the Sudan was signed on February 12, 1953, and agreements on the evacuation of British troops from the Canal were signed on July 27 and October 19, 1954. Concurrently, U.S. officials cultivated a special relationship with the new Egyptian leadership, and the question of U.S. military and economic aid became central in both Cairo and Washington.[45] Inexorably, the United States was supplanting Great Britain as the Western power primarily responsible for the defense of the area and the management of intraregional affairs, although the final blow to British supremacy would not be delivered until 1956 with the Suez debacle.

By mid-1954, the idea of an inclusive MEDO had been replaced by John Foster Dulles's "Northern Tier" strategy. Despite the developments of the previous two years, the conclusion of the March 1952 assessment remained salient. "Over the longer term, an effective Middle East defense organization would require an improvement in Arab-Israeli relations, a lessening of the hostility of Arab nationalists to cooperation with the West, and the inducing of Arab states to give primary emphasis to the defense of the area against Soviet aggression."[46] As Nuri al-Sa'id was to discover unpleasantly in 1955, the combination of inter-Arab rivalries and the genuine anti-Western, pro-neutralist sentiment that predominated among wide sections of the Arab public would continue to take priority over the defense of the area against the Soviets and cooperation with the West.

SYRIA AND ITS ARAB NEIGHBORS

The Shishakli coup in December 1949 was a milestone in the post-World War II inter-Arab competition over Syria. Henceforth, up until the crisis of 1957 that resulted in Syria's embrace of Egypt and the establishment of the United Arab Republic (UAR), Syria's position vis-à-vis existing inter-Arab alignments was not challenged seriously. This was noteworthy, given the continuous instability in Syrian politics, in which the country's regional and global orientations were major subjects of contention. The period between Shishakli's first coup and his final removal from power in March 1954 can be divided into two phases, before and after his assumption of direct control in December 1951.

The initial Shishakli coup did not by any means provide Syria with full insulation from outside influences and machinations. On the contrary, uncovered during the following year were anti-regime intrigues from both the Hashimite and the anti-Hashimite Arab camps. Ironically, these multiple challenges provided added impetus to the efforts of Nazim al-Qudsi, who served as prime minister between June 1950 and March 1951, to forge a precarious middle path between the two competing Arab camps.

Whereas the Iraqis, having had their fingers burned in 1949, adopted a relatively low profile during 1950, it was now Jordan's turn to become caught up in a web of intrigue against the existing order in Syria. A glimpse into Jordanian activities was afforded by the arrest, on the night of September 25 and 26, 1950, of a number of Syrian army officers, the most important of them being Lieutenant Colonel Bahij al-Kallas, who was designated to be Syria's military attache in Washington, and Munir al-ʿAjlani, an independent, pro-Hashimite parliamentary deputy, on charges of conspiring to overthrow the government.

Their prime Jordanian contact, in terms of encouragement and financing, was Shaykh Muhammad Amin al-Shanqiti, the minister of education and close confidant to ʿAbdallah.[47] In addition, ʿAbdallah met with some of the participants several times.[48] Befitting a plot whose participants were variously motivated by a conglomeration of political, ideological, personal, organizational, and communal factors, the exact linkage that the participants envisaged between Jordan and a new Syrian regime remained vague. Nonetheless, the mere possibility of closer ties was sufficient for ʿAbdallah.[49] Thus, once the initial overtures from the Syrian side were received, his support was practically inevitable. It did, however, expressly exclude committing units of the Arab Legion in support of the plotters.[50]

The conspiracy was amateurish, quickly penetrated and exposed by Syrian army's Deuxième Bureau. But the conspirators' trial, which began on December 17, 1950, revealed the Deuxième Bureau's actions as agent provocateur to be so pervasive as to hopelessly confuse the proceedings. The army's leaders, Shishakli and Akram Hawrani, therefore concluded that a speedy end to the trial and leniency toward the defendants was the best way to safeguard their own position against military and civilian rivals. Thus, on January 28, 1951, seven of the ten accused, including ʿAjlani and Kallas, were acquitted. (The fact that a brother of Kallas's was a close friend of Akram Hawrani may also have been a factor in his acquittal.) The others, two civilians and one officer, received light prison sentences.[51]

The conclusion drawn by at least some Syrian politicians, including Prime Minister Qudsi, was that the best way to deal with Jordanian intrigues was to establish formal diplomatic relations with Amman.[52] Such a step, the pro-Jordanian Cabinet Minister Hasan al-Hakim told the Syrian Cabinet, would be in Syria's interests, as it would mean a formal recognition of Syria's independence by Jordan.[53]

Despite various overtures during the next half-year by leaders from both sides, nothing came of the idea, and the two governments exchanged recriminations and accusations over who was to blame.[54] The issue was rendered less acute with 'Abdallah's assassination in July 1951. Nonetheless, although 'Abdallah's passing marked the formal end of irredentist expressions from Jordan toward Syria, it was not until August 1954 that the two sides formally opened legations in each others' capitals.

Antiregime intrigues in Syria during 1950 involved non-Hashimite Arab actors as well. On October 12, an unsuccessful assassination attempt was made on Colonel Shishakli while he was being driven in his car near Damascus. Arrests of the four men who had attacked the car and nineteen other conspirators were made almost immediately. The formal indictment, released on November 11, revealed the existence of a multinational organization, *Kata'ib al-Fida' al-'Arabi*,[55] dedicated to violent, "patriotic" actions against Western, Jewish, "traitorous" Hashimite, and other such Arab targets.

Paradoxically, this radical, revolutionary group (which included Dr. George Habash, subsequent leader of *al-Qawmiyyun al-'Arab* and still later head of the Popular Front for the Liberation of Palestine) was aided by ultraconservative Saudi Arabia. At this juncture, the Saudis distrusted Shishakli and were uneasy about his ability to withstand pressures from the pro-Hashimite forces within and outside of Syria. They preferred a known quantity and traditional ally, the exiled President Shukri al-Quwwatli, and hoped that Shishakli's downfall, however achieved, would lead to Quwwatli's comeback.

The conduit for Saudi funding was Nash'at al-Ard, the brother of King Ibn Sa'ud's personal physician. A further sign of a Saudi hand was the involvement of the followers of Amir Fawaz Sha'lan, chief of the Ruwallah tribe and relative by marriage to Ibn Sa'ud. The disburser of the Saudi financial largesse was Dr. Amin Ruwayha, president of the Syrian Doctors Organization, supporter of Shukri al-Quwwatli and friend of Ibn Sa'ud. His own motivation was at least partly fear. Following the August 1950 murder of Shishakli's rival and his own close friend, Air Force Commander Muhammad Nasir (Deuxième Bureau Chief and Shishakli ally, Major Ibrahim al-Husayni was subsequently acquitted of the murder charges), Ruwayha believed that he was next on Shishakli's hit list.[56] Another Quwwatli supporter was former Defense Minister Ahmad al-Sharabati. The group was led by Husayn Tawfiq, who escaped from an Egyptian prison where he was being held on charges of murdering the Egyptian Finance Minister Amin 'Uthman in 1946 (a murder in which Anwar al-Sadat was also involved).[57] Ironically, Tawfiq had been recruited in 1947 to the Syrian Deuxième Bureau by Sharabati, on the recommendation of King Faruq.[58] Thus, his presence in the group, along with other Egyptians, pointed to possible sanction from Egyptian official circles. Egyptian officials nevertheless strenuously denied to Nazim al-Qudsi that Egypt intended actively to support Quwwatli's return to power.[59]

The official indictment of the group was handed down by the Military Prosecutor, without prior consultation with Qudsi's cabinet, on November 11, 1950.[60] It came while Qudsi was in Riyadh as part of a swing through Arab capitals. Accompanied by Shishakli's ally, Defense Minister Fawzi Silu, Qudsi had intended to present the Saudis with the evidence of their agents' wrongdoing, but in a quieter fashion.[61] The bluntness of the prosecutor's indictment preempted him. The embarrassment he was caused was apparently intentional. In both its timing and its explicit accusations against Saudi Arabia, the indictment can be understood as an effort by Shishakli to weaken Qudsi, another example of the interplay between Syrian domestic politics and its foreign relations. For their part, the Saudis were annoyed at the public insult and insisted that false evidence had been given to unjustly accuse the group.

Qudsi tried hard not to exacerbate matters further, explaining to the Saudis that the wording and timing of the indictment had not been authorized. He did not, however, retract the accusation and expressed the hope that the Saudi actions would not be repeated. In any case, Qudsi told Ibn Sa'ud, there were no real obstacles to closer Syrian-Saudi ties. The problem, he said, was that dynastic rivalries in the Arab world had produced a band of professional agitators working for their personal profit. For its part, Syria had no intention of being victimized by their intrigues but would remain independent and an advocate of all-Arab solidarity. In response to Ibn Sa'ud's questioning, Qudsi promised that he would convey exactly the same message to the Iraqis the following week. The Saudis were sufficiently buoyed by Qudsi's position that they undertook to pay the second installment of their $6-million loan to Syria, made in 1949.[62]

The dénouement to the affair was the postponement of Ruwayha's trial in February 1951, on grounds of ill-health, followed by his release, together with Ahmad al-Sharabati and Nash'at al-Ard, in June 1951. The latter two had already received lenient sentences of twenty-eight months and five years imprisonment, respectively. According to Ruwayha, the releases came as a direct result of Saudi and Egyptian ministrations, including Saudi threats to close their Legation.[63] In addition, the four men who had received death sentences had them commuted; and the final session of the military court reversed its previous finding in declaring that the aims and principles of *Kata'ib al-Fida' al-'Arabi* were consistent with the spirit of the Syrian Constitution and therefore were not criminal or evil![64] With the trial now satisfactorily disposed of, Saudi-Syrian relations returned to normal in the summer of 1951 when Colonel Shishakli collected the outstanding $4 million of the Saudi loan during his visit to Ibn Sa'ud.

Thus, as in the trials of the pro-Hashimite conspirators and of the Deuxième Bureau head accused of murdering Shishakli's rival, Syria's judicial process remained highly subject to the vicissitudes within the increasingly fractured Syrian polity and to wider regional influence.

One of Nazim al-Qudsi's prime objectives in his tour of Arab capitals during November and December 1950 was to compose Saudi-Hashimite differences. Another was to nudge Arab leaders toward an agreed-on formula for cooperation with the Western powers, which in the process would solve the Anglo-Egyptian dispute.[65] Qudsi made little progress toward either of his objectives. He did, however, remain acutely conscious of the need to protect Syria from competing Arab influences. He was no less concerned with Syria's security posture vis-à-vis Israel and mindful of the deteriorating international situation. At the Arab League Political Committee meeting in Cairo from January 23 to February 2, 1951, Qudsi presented a twenty-two-point proposal to fashion among all the Arab states a "unification in foreign policy, in the national defense forces, in economics and in the basic (public) utilities." His proposal could be actualized, he declared, in one of three ways: either a union into a single "Arab United States" (the "supreme ideal of every Arab"), a "less effective" federation (*ittihad*) of states, or—"the weakest" of the three possibilities—a "confederation" format.

Qudsi's analysis of the international situation and the collective Arab weakness was trenchant and his criticism of the Arab League withering. The League, he declared, had

> frustrated the hopes of the Arabs. It [had] been prodigal in display and words, and sparing in results and accomplishments.... The individual Arab [had] not felt its existence because it [had] not provide[d] for any of his needs or revive[d] in him any hope for evolution and progress.... Accordingly, either the League should disintegrate in the eyes of the nation, if it is to continue in its argumentations, commentaries, adjournments and references to committees and governments; or else, it should be rejuvenated if it is to adopt whatever will bring confidence to (Arab) public opinion.[66]

In view of the cool reception Qudsi received in other Arab capitals, it is unlikely that he had much hope of his proposal's being adopted. In fact, speculation in anti-Western and anti-Iraqi circles within Syria was that Qudsi was consciously attempting to use the Arab League's expected inaction to gain a freer hand to forge closer ties with Iraq. The most authoritative work on this period takes essentially the same view.[67] This appears too Machiavellian, however, for Qudsi was under no illusions about the internal and external constraints under which he was operating. Rather, the proposal fell more within his effort to insulate Syria from outside pressures and his "gradualist" approach to the question of Arab unity, as well as his need to put his views on record. In the fall of 1949, when conditions were more ripe for federation with Iraq, Qudsi favored a cautious approach. Qudsi strenuously denied the accusations being leveled against him, and stressed that his proposal remained open to modification. In any case, it was not Syria's intention to leave the League if his plan was rejected.[68]

Despite the misgivings of Qudsi's domestic rivals regarding his motives, the power of a unity proposal was such that it was received favorably nearly all across the Syrian political spectrum. As expected too, the other Arab states responded tepidly. The proposal was effectively shelved on February 2, when the Arab League Council's last meeting created a seven-member commission, chaired by Egypt's foreign minister, to study the plan, confirming, ironically, Qudsi's description of the League's "argumentations, commentaries, adjournments and references to committees."

One month later, on March 10, 1951, Qudsi was out of office, following irreconcilable differences with Shishakli. Although these centered on internal issues, Shishakli was also very critical of two aspects of Qudsi's foreign policy. The first was Qudsi's advocacy of a revised Arab collective security pact that he feared would lead to the Syrian army's subordination to a foreign command. The second was Syria's association with the Arab League's recent protest over France's actions in Morocco, something that Shishakli feared might result in the suspension of French arms deliveries.[69] Qudsi and other People's party leaders believed that the French had actually instigated the crisis, both out of anger at Syria's support of Moroccan nationalists in their struggle for independence from France and out of suspicion that Qudsi's federation plan was merely a veiled revival of the Fertile Crescent scheme.[70] Confirmation of this will have to wait for the opening of the French archives.

Iraq's low profile throughout this highly fluid, unstable period in Syrian politics did not indicate disinterest. Rather, it stemmed from its failures during the previous year. Initially, the Iraqis were somewhat downcast. Qudsi's assumption of the premiership in June 1950 gave them renewed, albeit cautious encouragement. Baghdad's political establishment understood well Qudsi's own "gradualist" leanings regarding a Syrian-Iraqi union and the constraints under which all Syrian governments were operating.[71] If they needed any further reminder, it came with Qudsi's fall from power nine months later.

The military clashes between Syria and Israel in April 1951 over the disputed demilitarized zone in the Huleh Valley, which included the employment of the Israeli air force against Syrian positions, provided Iraq with a welcome opportunity to demonstrate its fidelity to all-Arab concerns. Responding to Syrian Prime Minister Khalid al-'Azm's urgent request for military aid, Iraq speedily dispatched a twelve-plane air squadron, six 40-millimeter antiaircraft guns, and a small number of troops to be deployed in the defense of Damascus.[72]

Their presence had more symbolic than practical significance. Nonetheless, it drew wide reaction. Although the Syrian public applauded, Iraq's Arab neighbors were less pleased. The Jordanians were unpleasantly surprised and also thought the timing unwise, as the Syrian-Israeli dispute was then being discussed in the U.N. Security Council.[73] Of greater inter-Arab significance was Egypt's unhappiness and embarrassment, which outweighed Egypt's concern with the actual Syrian-Israeli clashes.[74]

Egypt was at this time in one of its "low profile" periods vis-à-vis regional affairs. Nonetheless, Egyptian officials were anxious to avoid appearing less vigilant in defending Arab rights than their traditional rivals in Baghdad. They even considered dispatching units of their own to Syria to maintain the balance of influence there.[75] This possibility was exactly the kind of "snowball" effect that Britain and the United States had been afraid of and had worked to head off. British efforts to dissuade Nuri al-Sa'id succeeded only in scaling down the number of planes sent by Iraq and in incurring Syrian displeasure.[76] Shortly afterward, the potential for escalation of tension passed, and Iraqi units were quietly withdrawn. The incident did serve, however, to indicate Syria's continued centrality in inter-Arab disputes and the ever-present potential for overlapping and linkage between the Arab-Israeli and inter-Arab issue clusters.

Iraqi equanimity with the situation in Syria evaporated on November 29, 1951, with Shishakli's final dismantling of Syria's civilian governmental structure. Once again, Baghdad found itself at a disadvantage. On December 3, Shishakli launched a blistering attack against the People's party, including an accusation that it wanted to bring Syria under a foreign—that is, Hashimite—crown, accompanied by criticism of Iraq's treaty commitments with Great Britain.[77] The scenario was a familiar one, harking back to Shishakli's initial coup in December 1949.

The Iraqi response, too, had an air of *déjà vu* about it. Its concern and actions in many ways paralleled those of two years earlier, when the upheavals in Syrian political life began. As in the Za'im and the first Shishakli coups, the Iraqis contemplated the possibility of active intervention, either military or political. Once again, their thinking was partly bound up with the concerns of Iraqi domestic politics. Nuri al-Sa'id was again subjected to charges of "do-nothingism" from Salih Jabr's camp as well as from more extreme nationalist groups, and felt compelled to respond.[78] Moreover, the regent's own long-held inclination toward an "activist" policy also had to be taken into account. Thus, as on previous occasions, the course Nuri adopted was a middle one that tread delicately among competing factors and impulses.[79]

Intervention would be seriously entertained if one of the deposed but still legitimate authorities in Syria—the president, the short-lived Dawalibi government, or the Chamber of Deputies—requested it. In that event, Nuri intended to approach Shishakli to try to resolve the crisis with the hope that the threat of force in the background would be sufficient. Even if force was to be employed, he assured the British ambassador to Baghdad, it would be solely in order to reestablish constitutional government in Syria and not for the purpose of achieving any form of annexation or union. In any case, he said, Iraq would not use force without having obtained the concurrence of Ibn Sa'ud (a most implausible eventuality).[80]

Within days, it was clear that support for the People's party in Syria had dissipated and that there was consequently little likelihood of a credible invitation for Iraqi intervention from anyone in Syria. Thus, by the time British and U.S. representations were made in regard to the Tri-Partite Declaration's forbidding the use of force to solve disputes, Nuri no longer entertained the notion. Still, he took care to dispute the applicability of the Declaration, stating that it applied only to the frontiers with Israel and it did not cover the use of force by one state at the request of legitimate authorities in another.[81]

The only avenue left for Nuri was to try to mobilize Arab and non-Arab countries to withhold diplomatic recognition of the new regime in Syria.[82] His efforts were based not solely on considerations of power politics. Again, as was made evident in previous Syrian upheavals, Iraq's leaders had a genuine concern with maintaining the superstructure of constitutional civilian government. Nuri and the rest of the Iraqi political establishment were well aware of the legitimacy that they derived from such a framework. Furthermore, the fear of elements in the Iraqi (and also Jordanian) military's taking up the example of intervention in political life put forth by their Syrian counterparts deepened with each episode.[83] Thus, it was incumbent upon Nuri to try to isolate and thus delegitimize Shishakli as much as possible.

To counter Nuri's diplomacy, Shishakli dispatched two of his trusted colonels to Cairo, Riyadh, and Amman, and with good effect.

Within weeks, Nuri's attempts to deny diplomatic recognition to Shishakli were proven a failure; the Western Powers, Saudi Arabia, and Lebanon all recognized the new regime. The Saudis had gruffly rejected Iraqi overtures with the comment that it was Iraqi intrigues that had led to Syria's sorry state.[84] Jordan, for its part, viewed the matter as purely a Syrian domestic issue in which the role of recognition did not arise.[85] The only solace Iraq could take was that the Egyptians also remained guarded, partly because they shared some of Nuri's dislike of the intrusion of the military in politics and partly because of their uncertainty over Shishakli's position toward the proposed Middle East Command.[86]

Given the established facts, Nuri moved quickly to minimize the damage. His government, he told Shishakli's envoys on December 22, would make no trouble for the present Syrian regime. It would, however, continue to withhold formal diplomatic recognition.[87] For the next twelve months, the state of Iraqi-Syrian relations was anomalous, although not at all unique in inter-Arab relations. Despite the lack of diplomatic recognition, the two countries' legations in each other's capitals continued to function.

In mid-July 1952, at a "break-the-ice" luncheon with Shishakli in Shtura, Lebanon, Nuri repeated his insistence on the restoration of parliamentary life in Syria as a sine qua non for recognition.[88] The meeting, initiated by Nuri, was an encouraging sign for Shishakli. So was Iraq's Foreign Minister Fadil al-Jamali's effort to normalize the personal position of the Syrian minister to Baghdad.[89] In addition, Iraq withdrew its candidacy for the U.N. Trusteeship Council in favor of Syria, a decision made during the September Arab League Council meeting.[90] Finally, on December 3, 1952, Iraq made the requisite gesture; an Iraqi military delegation attended ceremonies marking the first anniversary of Syria's new National Day. Later that day, the Iraqi minister in Damascus joined the rest of the diplomatic corps in congratulating Syria's official chief of state, Shishakli's right-hand man General Fawzi Silu. For the Syrian government, Iraq's attendance constituted the long-denied recognition.[91]

Ironically, Iraq's gesture did not remove Syrian-Iraqi relations from its previous vicissitudes. With Faysal II reaching maturity in 1953, 'Abd al-Ilah lost his status as regent, although he continued to dominate palace politics until the regime's overthrow in 1958. Once

Faysal married and produced an heir, ʿAbd al-Ilah would lose his status as crown prince as well. Thus, his motivation to intrigue in Syria in search of a position for himself increased. Moreover, the timing seemed propitious: the death of Ibn Saʿud in November 1953 and the ascension of his son, the less forceful Saʿud, held out promise that Riyadh might not be as effective in blocking Baghdad as it had been previously.[92]

The next bout of tension came in April 1953. Shishakli discovered that Iraqi officials, particularly the regent, were giving financial and material backing to a Baghdad-based group of former Syrian officers and politicians. That group, in turn, intrigued with frontier tribes and disseminated anti-Shishakli propaganda. Representations to Iraqi authorities to curb their activities were only partially successful. Thus, even though the Syrian government did not feel threatened by the self-styled "Free Syria Command," it served as another source of suspicion in Syrian-Iraqi relations.[93] Inevitably, then, when Shishakli began losing his grip on the reins of power in early 1954, the Iraqis were immediately blamed.[94] Despite its intrigues, contingency planning, and diplomatic initiatives, including the tabling of yet another federation plan by Prime Minister Fadil al-Jamali at the Arab League Political Committee Meeting in January 1954, Iraq's involvement in Shishakli's overthrow on February 25, 1954, appears to have been less than it was even in the coup against Husni Zaʿim.[95] What was most similar about the two coups was the satisfaction they engendered in Iraq.

For its part, the Egyptian leadership, while having been no great supporter of Shishakli, was also suspicious of an Iraqi hand, particularly because the lines of inter-Arab conflict over the Baghdad Pact were already being drawn.[96] The Saudis saw the change as a potential threat as well and resumed their own machinations within Syria, including substantial disbursements of financial largesse.[97] This, too, was a familiar pattern.

THE ARAB-ISRAELI CONFLICT ON LOW BURNER

As an inter-Arab issue, the Arab-Israeli conflict had low saliency during the first part of the 1950s, largely because of its static nature.[98]

The overall parameters had been laid down during 1949 and 1950: separate armistice agreements, the act of Jordan annexing the West Bank, and collective Arab rejection of a separate peace between Jordan and Israel. Bilateral, back-channel contacts between Israel and Egypt and Jordan and Syria during the first half of the 1950s, failed to produce any diplomatic breakthroughs.[99] The Arab position during these years was summed up by ʿAzzam Pasha: Until Israel was ready to make concessions regarding Arab refugees and territory, in line with U.N. resolutions, there was no advantage in changing the present situation, which, logically, had much to be said for it from the Arab point of view.[100] Thus, no major rifts between any of the Arab states derived from Arab-Israeli issues. Conversely, common strategies toward actively solving the numerous, still-festering issues that together comprised the conflict were minimal.

In inter-Arab terms, Jordan derived its major satisfaction during this period from the other Arab states' de facto acceptance of its incorporation of the West Bank. Publicly, no Arab state ever recognized the move, and only Lebanon continued to maintain a consulate in Jordanian Jerusalem (up until 1948, the others had maintained consulates in the city). Privately, even Egyptian officials admitted to their Jordanian counterparts that the setting up of the now-moribund Government of All-Palestine as a competitor to Jordan had been an error and that Jordan's incorporation of the West Bank had been the best solution under the circumstances.[101]

Consequently, Jordan's relations with Egypt, which had reached their nadir between March and June 1950, improved slowly over the next few years. Although Egypt acquiesced in the annexation, it could be especially sanguine about having restrained Jordan from advancing toward a separate peace with Israel. These restraints were reinforced from within Jordan, for ʿAbdallah's grip on the reins of power was weakening unmistakably.[102] This had already been portended by ʿAbdallah's failure in the spring of 1950 to impose his will on recalcitrant ministers to support the draft nonaggression pact with Israel. It became ever more apparent in the remaining year of his life, helped along by both his own physical weakening and the expansion of Jordan's Parliament to include generally more critical West Bank Palestinians.[103] Thus, despite ʿAbdallah's own continued efforts to achieve a negotiated settlement or even a resolution of problems within the framework of the existing armistice agreement, Jordan's policies were increasingly in harmony with the collective Arab consensus.

'Abdallah's assassination in July 1951 further accented this trend. At the same time, it did not bring an end to Jordanian-Israeli contacts. Their extent and their limitations were demonstrated in the spring of 1952. The two sides may have been close to concluding a draft agreement on the division of the demilitarized zone in the Latrun area. Prime Minister Tawfiq Abu al-Huda of Jordan denied considering such a possibility after rumors were spread in neighboring Arab states, especially in the Syrian media, about his intentions.[104] Ironically, Adib al-Shishakli pursued a similar arrangement for the Syrian-Israeli demilitarized zones that would help serve to remove the Arab-Israeli conflict from the Syrian political agenda. To this end, secret high-level talks between Israeli and Syrian officials were held from October 1952 to May 1953. But, like the Israeli-Jordanian discussions, these also foundered on the unwillingness of both sides to overcome the existing gaps by making substantive concessions.[105]

The armistice agreement with Israel and Egypt's successful restraint of Jordan allowed Egypt to turn its attention to its dispute with Britain. As had been the case from 1946 to 1947, Egyptian leaders at times explored ways to solve both the Anglo-Egyptian and Arab-Israeli conflicts through a single formula. Occasionally, this necessitated bringing Jordan into the picture. The "Gaza Plan" was an idea periodically floated in Egyptian and British circles. It envisaged the transfer of all or part of Britain's Suez base to the Gaza area, as part of a combined British-Egyptian settlement and an Egyptian-Israeli peace agreement. In British eyes, Gaza was unfeasible as the location for its Middle East forces. In addition, Egypt's insistence on total evacuation of Suez and its reluctance to countenance an accompanying peace agreement with Israel cast cold water on the notion of linking British-Egyptian and Arab-Israeli agreements.[106] Still, during at least one stage in the latter part of 1951, there is evidence that Egypt was exploring with Jordan the possibility of transferring Gaza to its control.[107]

Further details await the opening of Arab archives, but a number of points can be surmised. Egypt's decision to consider the idea, after earlier ignoring a similar Jordanian inquiry, obviously derived from the crisis atmosphere of October 1951. Egyptian officials apparently hoped that the transfer of Gaza to Jordan might provide a way out of their impasse with Britain. An added benefit was that it would rid them of the burden of administering and caring for a poverty-stricken area swollen with Palestinian Arab refugees.[108] Finally, Egyptian officials could not have failed to understand that Jordan's agreement to assume control of the Gaza Strip would have undoubtedly been dependent on the establishment of a land link with the rest of its territory, providing Jordan with its desired outlet to the Mediterranean.[109] This in turn would have necessitated Israeli agreement, most likely as part of a Jordanian-Israeli settlement.

Nothing came of these explorations, mainly because of the gap between British and Egyptian positions. They nonetheless indicate that in late 1951 some Egyptian officials were at least willing to consider paying the price of an Arab-Israeli settlement and further Jordanian territorial aggrandizement in return for a favorable resolution to Egypt's crisis with Britain. As for what-might-have-beens, a common Jordanian-Egyptian position may have made the British more amenable to the whole notion. But the limits to Egyptian-Jordanian cooperation were set by Jordan's need not to antagonize its British benefactor by adopting an overtly pro-Egyptian position, as well as the existing degree of mutual mistrust between Cairo and Amman.[110] Cairo's unwillingness to extradite 'Abdallah al-Tall and a co-conspirator, both convicted in absentia for plotting 'Abdallah's assassination, did not improve matters either. Thus, just as during the 1948 war and its aftermath, the establishment of real strategic cooperation between Egypt and Jordan on Arab-Israeli issues remained elusive.[111]

As for the Arab-Israeli conflict, Iraq's demonstrative show of support for the Syrian regime during the Syrian-Israeli clashes in the Huleh Valley in April 1951 touched off a new round of inter-Arab tensions. By contrast, Israel's large-scale military action against Jordanian forces in the border village of Qibya on the night of October 14, 1953, and the resulting large number of civilian casualties produced a genuine wave of anger throughout the Arab world and a swift show of Arab solidarity from Arab governments. Responding to an urgent call from Jordan's Prime Minister Fawzi al-Mulqi, whose government was in serious danger of falling because of the Arab Legion's failure to defend against the Israeli attack, the Arab League Political Committee convened from October 21 to 24, 1953 in Amman.

The meetings, which included a visit to Qibya, resulted in pledges of a four-fold increase of a previous Arab League allocation to strengthen Jordan's National Guard units in frontier villages, from 500,000 to 2 million dinars. Moreover, the pledges were not just of declarative value. Iraq's Prime Minister Fadil al-Jamali had brought with him 150,000 dinars for the expressed purpose of assisting the Jordanians, as well as a special check for 10,000 dinars from young King Faysal II, which he gave directly to Qibya's notables. The Saudi minister to Amman came to the meetings with a check for 85,000 dinars. The Egyptians followed with a grant of Egyptian £195,000 as part of a promised £500,000. Other decisions by the Political Committee included the apportionment to border villages of 100,000 dinars from Arab League funds left over from the 1948 war and the rebuilding of Qibya at the League's expense. The frontline states pledged to reinforce their armies along the frontiers with Israel, while other Arab states would station troops at points nearest to Jordan's frontier to be ready to come to assistance in case of a serious Israeli attack.[112] In practice, the last point applied only to Iraq. Some months later, the Jordanians and Iraqis decided against the actual stationing of Iraqi troops in Jordan.[113]

The temporary show of solidarity sparked by the Qibya raid did not, however, translate into sustained backing for Jordan. The decisions involving troop movements to the border areas were not implemented. Within six months, the funds allocated to Jordan by the League were exhausted, forcing the disbandment of at least one full-time National Guard regiment.[114]

Egypt's behavior at this point deserves comment. The first signs of its greater involvement in Arab-Israeli issues were exemplified by its financial grant to Jordan and by the concurrent convening of the Joint Defense Pact's constituent bodies. They did not yet mark Egypt's decisive shift toward a more militant leadership. This would not begin until one year later, in the fall of 1954, with more sustained financial and political backing of Jordan, high level talks, and the invoking of the Joint Defense Pact. In late 1953, the eyes of Egypt's military rulers were still focused on ensuring British evacuation. They were also not averse to examining privately options for negotiation with Israel. Nonetheless, the swiftness of the Arab response to the escalation of tension along the Jordanian-Israeli border was a reminder that existing inter-Arab divisions did not automatically preclude displays of collective solidarity in the Arab-Israeli sphere, and that the *nakba* of 1948 was not a closed chapter, either for Arab public opinion or for Arab governements.[115]

BETWEEN TWO ERAS

The end of what can loosely be characterized as the "dynastic phase" of inter-Arab politics occurred in the first part of the 1950s. The death or removal, in turn, of ʿAbdallah, Faruq, and Ibn Saʿud, and to a lesser extent, the decline in ʿAbu al-Ilah's official status after Faysal II reached maturity (in 1953), meant that the interpersonal jealousies, rivalries, and suspicions that had built up over the previous decades were now much less of a determining factor in inter-Arab relations. Quite naturally, moreover, the successors to these veteran Arab statesmen had to devote much of their energies to legitimizing and consolidating their own authority. As a result, inter-Arab politics were initially conducted in somewhat lower tones and without the edge of hysteria that had marked system-wide dynamics in previous years.

In other ways, however, the passing of the old guard in Arab politics militated against the status quo. In Egypt and Syria, the changes were not merely of individuals, but occurred on the societal level as a whole. In one of his more lucid and penetrating discourses, ʿAzzam described the process of radicalization underway in the region and warned the British of its long-term consequences for the existing sociopolitical order in the Arab world and for Arab relations with the rest of the world. The views of the new generation being turned out by schools and universities in the Middle East, he stated, were violent, bound up with frustration and in need of being worked out. They might give vent to movements "against the Pashas or the King" (Faruq), as well as against the British or other foreigners.[116] As has been shown, these dynamics were already dominating the responses in Egypt and Syria to Western efforts to form a regional defense organization, as well as contributing further to an uncompromising line on the Arab-Israeli conflict. In a few short years, ʿAbd al-Nasir and radical political movements in the Fertile Crescent would tap these somewhat inchoate feelings in fashioning a more militant, anti-Western brand of Arab nationalism.

Regarding the Egyptian-Iraqi competition for regional leadership, which had provided one of the central themes of inter-Arab affairs since the mid-1940s, not much changed during the early 1950s. Despite its periodic aloofness from wider Arab affairs, Egypt was still able to block challenges to its own position, as demonstrated by the inability of the other Arab states to act favorably on Western defense proposals. Moreover, the settling in 1953 and 1954 of Egypt's dispute with Great Britain would not lead to greater Egyptian equanimity toward Iraq's desires for closer ties with the West. For all of Iraq's probings, neither it nor any other Arab states was yet willing to buck Egyptian veto power. At the same time, this was also a period of accumulating Iraqi frustrations, a factor that helps explain Iraq's subsequent decision in 1954 and 1955, profound in inter-Arab terms, to test the limits of Egypt's veto power by adhering to the Baghdad Pact.

One of the ironies of the years immediately preceding the Nasirist, "integral unity" era was the scorn and even dismissiveness that greeted the various Arab unity proposals being tendered. Such was the fate of Nazim al-Qudsi's federation scheme of February 1951 and of Fadil al-Jamali's proposal of January 1954. The succession crisis in Jordan during 1951 and 1952 briefly raised hopes in Baghdad for an Iraqi-dominated Hashimite union, but these too were dashed.[117] With regard to the notion of unity, the change, if any, was one of degree only. Arab leaders and interest groups were even more jealous of their separate, sovereign rights and perhaps less in need of paying ritual homage to the chimera of Arab unity. The concept of even partial, geographically based unity suffered a further blow when Egypt conceded in February 1953 that Sudan's right to self-determination outweighed Cairo's historical insistence on a single political framework to reflect the natural "unity of the Nile Valley." This further reinforcement of the status quo did not, however, signify the final triumph of state nationalism over the ideology of Arab unity. The inability of the existing regimes to provide real solutions for their increasingly mobilized populations would shortly open the way for a more massbased, populist brand of Arab nationalism.

As for the Arab League, by the early 1950s its effectiveness was being roundly scorned in official Arab circles and in the Arab media. Accordingly, its meetings attracted far less interest than previously, with Arab governments usually deigning to send only second- or third-rank representatives. At the same time, it was not rendered totally irrelevant. The League remained a forum that was deemed useful for mobilizing Arab support in times of crisis, as was demonstrated by Jordan after the Qibya raid. Similarly, the Joint Defense Pact, which was nonfunctional from the beginning, would still be deemed useful by Egypt in 1954 as a tool to assert its regional leadership.

The Arab state system was also expanding. The League had always expressed an interest in developments in North Africa, and it quickened during the early 1950s. Involvement in the affairs of the Persian Gulf principalities was still a few years off, although the British were cognizant of its eventuality, especially in regard to Kuwait.[118] The first official expansion came in an area long of interest to ʿAzzam: on March 28, 1953, Libya was formally admitted to League membership. Ironically, ʿAzzam was not at all pleased with the developments that had led to Libyan independence and the assumption of power by the Sanusis. Despite being immediately subjected to Egyptian pressures, Libya would remain in what was to become the conservative Arab camp until Muʿammar al-Qadhdhafi's ascension in 1969.[119]

The periodization of history, although analytically handy, often gives the appearance of arbitrariness. Nonetheless, the year 1954 seems to be the most appropriate point to conclude the study of the Arab state system's formative years, for a number of events occurred that, together, precipitated a new era in inter-Arab relations. First, Jamal ʿAbd al-Nasir emerged as the strongman of Egypt's ruling Revolutionary Command Council. Concurrently, Egypt and Great Britain concluded an agreement providing for Britain's full evacuation from Suez within two years and the right of Sudan to self-determination and independence. Second, the overthrow of Syria's Colonel Adib Shishakli in February, 1954 and the return of civilian government there reopened the question of Syria's future status in the region and marked the beginning of Syria's slide in the mid-1950s towards fragmentation, a development arrested only by the Baʿth party's embrace of ʿAbd al-Nasir in February 1958 and the establishment of the United Arab Republic. Finally, for the first time since his reluctant acquiescence to an Egyptian-dominated Arab system in 1945, Nuri al-Saʿid adopted in 1954 and 1955 a non-Arab-centered regional and global orientation, embodied in the Baghdad Pact. Together, these events set the stage for ʿAbd al-Nasir's emergence as the supreme all-Arab figure, espousing a more fervently populist style of Arab nationalism that went over the heads of Arab leaders to appeal to their increasingly socially mobilized populations, a nationalism that was also intimately linked with Egyptian power and specific Egyptian interests. The cumulative result was that the inter-Arab "temperature" was raised to the boiling point.

CONCLUSION

THE LOOSENING OF TIES that bound Arab governments to Great Britain and France up until the end of World War II conferred a historic opportunity upon ruling Arab elites. They could now reverse, if they so desired, the post-World War I trends that Arab nationalists angrily viewed as the balkanization of the Arab world. The task was enormous. Leaders' visions of what the common good (Arab solidarity) ought to be were inseparable from practical considerations of *raison d'état* and *raison d'individu*. The Iraqis dreamed of being an Arab Prussia. 'Abdallah sought to escape from his desert principality, for it did not befit his status as the legitimate heir to the Great Arab Revolt. The Syrians wanted closer Arab ties to help them in their struggle against the French and in line with Syria's historical role as "the beating heart of Arabism," but not at the price of Hashimite dominance. Egypt, the latecomer to Arab politics, wanted to prevent the emergence of a strong Arab competitor in the Fertile Crescent. Ibn Sa'ud saw the Hashimite threat everywhere. None possessed the capabilities by themselves either to impose their will or to stand apart. Consequently, the foundation of the Arab League institutionalized Arab divisions as much as it served to promote Arab solidarity.

No significant strengthening of links between ruling Arab elites occurred during the first decade after World War II, neither in the political, military, economic, nor cultural spheres. In lieu of interlocking sets of interests that would bind the elites in different countries together, the chances for giving greater content to their common ideology of Arabism were remote.

Instead, what crystallized was a system that was state-centric, marked by high levels of both conflict and cooperation, with no one state possessing sufficient capabilities either to triumph decisively over its rivals or to ignore them altogether. The system's modus operandi was the fashioning of loosely structured, shifting coalitions derived from temporarily shared interests. Coalitions evolved over time against the backdrop of the end of the Palestine Mandate and the resulting conflict with Israel, the "struggle for Syria," the question of security and political relations with the Western powers, and the need to define the role of the Arab League. Nonetheless, the equilibrium of the system as a whole tended to be maintained. Like the collective ideology of Arabism to which all states subscribed, the coalition framework imposed restraints on the policies of individual states. These were frequently tested during the late 1940s and early 1950s, causing innumerable bouts of inter-Arab tension. The ensuing conflicts were nearly always contained. Irreversible schisms were avoided, sometimes by design, sometimes as the outcome of what seemed to be almost a built-in mechanism of inter-Arab checks and balances.

Thus, no radical systemic transformations occurred during the first, formative decade of the Arab state system, and at least some of the factors that in 1945 had militated against the regional status quo had fallen by the wayside or were rendered less salient. Hashimite designs on Syria were rebuffed; the Egyptian-led Arab majority was compelled to acquiesce to Jordan's territorial aggrandizement in Palestine; Jordan was restrained from making a separate peace with Israel by a combination of domestic and inter-Arab pressures; and Iraq's efforts to forge a collective security system linked with the Western powers were blocked. Only once was the division into rival Arab coalitions temporarily superseded by a grand coalition against Israel in 1948. The ensuing dismal results owed much to the persistence of inter-Arab divisions among ostensible allies. Israel was able, despite its status as both outsider and foe to the Arab system, to form links with Jordan to their mutual benefit, albeit with important limitations. Overall, however, the proposition by one historian that Israel has not just been a focus for Arab divisions but has made a significant contribution to them by actively meddling in Arab politics, beginning with Husni al-Za'im's coup, seems off base.[1]

Egyptian behavior warrants mention in a wider context as well.

Despite all of the changes of government in Egypt between 1944 and 1954, the colossal Egyptian-led Arab failure in Palestine, and periodic signs of Egyptian frustration with Arab affairs, Egypt's Arab policies exhibited remarkable continuity with Nahhas Pasha's original initiative in 1943. Once the decision had been made to assert a preeminent role in Arab affairs, there was no going back. Egypt periodically mobilized Arab support during the late 1940s for its own particularist interests in the Sudan and against Great Britain. At the same time, it was extremely reluctant to concede that any other Arab state had a similar right to pursue its own particularist policies, whether in regard to the issue of regional defense, Palestine, or Fertile Crescent politics. It also reserved the right temporarily to adopt a lower profile in regional affairs, as events warranted. This continuity would presist throughout the 'Abd al-Nasir years and even beyond. Ironically, Egypt's centrality for the Arab world vis-à-vis non-Arab regional and global actors and the accompanying fear of the consequences of a possible Egyptian withdrawal from Arab affairs was recognized at various times even in countries whose freedom of action stood to be circumscribed by Egyptian assertiveness, a dilemma that has never been fully resolved. Clearly, this recognition was related to the role that Arab nationalist sentiment played in the domestic politics of Arab states. Thus, Egypt's importance was grudgingly acknowledged even in Iraq, the only other Arab country with serious pretensions to regional leadership during these years. At the same time, both Nuri al-Sa'id and 'Abd al-Ilah chafed at Iraq's junior standing and sought incessantly to alter it, occasionally by cajoling Egypt, but more often by intriguing in Syria (and Jordan as well), denigrating 'Azzam and the League, promoting regional defense schemes, and seeking help from the outside, usually Britain, but also the United States and even Turkey. Ultimately, however, Iraq's limited capabilities, combined with Nuri's extremely cautious nature, prevented their efforts from bearing fruit.

Whereas inter-Arab relations continued to be characterized by ambiguities, fluid alliances, and an uneasy equilibrium that militated against definitive outcomes, the status of the Arab League, intended by its founders to serve as the forum for collective Arab action and as the symbol and repository of Arab hopes, was irreparably eroded. Instead of serving as a forum to fashion and implement the collective Arab will, it became a symbol of collective Arab impotence, "a sack into which seven heads were thrust . . . and with remarkable haste," in 'Abdallah's derisory language.[2] Hence, by the early 1950s it was largely relegated to the sidelines.

This decline was epitomized by the fate of 'Azzam Pasha. On September 10, 1952, he was forced by Egypt's new military rulers to resign from the post of Arab League secretary-general, which he had held since its inception.[3] 'Azzam's fading into irrelevance went hand-in-hand with the cynicism engendered among wide sections of the Arab public by the League's activities. Undoubtedly, this helped prepare the ground for 'Abd al-Nasir's challenge to the inter-Arab status quo via a more militantly populist pan-Arab ideology. As a corollary, the League's decline into irrelevance left the Arab world without a credible, high-level collective forum for many years. It was only in 1964 that one reemerged, on 'Abd al-Nasir's initiative—the ad hoc Arab Summit Conference, which did not belong to the League framework (it has since been coopted as a League institution).

One of the most obvious, yet nevertheless striking features of inter-Arab politics during the system's formative years was the insignificance of the economic dimension. Neither the cooperative nor the conflictual aspects of inter-Arab affairs had their roots in the economic sphere. Rather, the prevailing state of Arab economies complemented and reinforced the predominant particularist tendencies in the Arab world.

The low level of economic development and accompanying problems of health, widespread illiteracy, limited technological education, and poor infrastructure among the Arab states undoubtedly militated against the forging of closer economic ties.[4] With the exception of Saudi Arabia, Arab economies were primarily agricultural, producing a mixture of subsistence and cash crops, and involving the bulk of the population, despite the process of urbanization already underway. Even in Lebanon, where the service and manufacturing sectors were rapidly expanding, the agricultural sector produced more of the national income than any other and engaged nearly one-half of the population.[5] Moreover, the efforts of Arab leaders to promote development, however sluggish and uneven, further increased the competitive nature of their economies, as Arab governments guarded their particular interests in the economic sphere as jealously as they did in the political realm. The same industries were founded: "textiles, cement, sugar refining, vegetable oils, glass, matches, soap, etc., with the result that the region now contains several small and inefficient factories producing the same goods."[6]

Arab economies during the 1940s lacked what a prominent Arab economist terms the "institutional framework for Arab economic complementarity" as well as the necessary actions emanating from the private sector.[7] In the final analysis, however, what was missing was not institutions but an economic justification for them. To be sure, one could develop all kinds of possible models illustrating the benefits of economic integration,[8] or point to a degree of complementarity between Egypt and the other Arab countries.[9] Still, in terms of political economy, there existed neither sufficient mutual need nor a strong enough economic center to take even beginning steps toward integration.

Ironically, the only examples of genuine Arab economic integration were those imposed by foreigners—the Ottomans, the Middle East Supply Center, and the French mandated Syrian-Lebanese Customs union.[10] By the end of 1951, there was almost nothing left of Arab economic integration. Prewar patterns had been restored, except for a relatively high level of imports from the United States, and intraregional trade was at a "very low level."[11] No subsequent progress was made in effecting closer inter-Arab trade relations by extending preferential treatment within the prevailing quantitative and tariff frameworks.[12] Moreover, the value of intraregional trade among the Fertile Crescent countries and between them and Egypt had decreased in proportional and absolute terms. The reasons were at least threefold: (1) the breakup between 1948 and 1950 of the Syrian-Lebanese Custom Union, a framework that had been retained from the Mandate albeit without a strong institutional machinery and without any joint sense of direction;[13] (2) the loss of Palestine, which had been an important component in the Middle East Supply Center's activities; and (3) substantial increase in trade with countries outside the region.[14]

The Arab League periodically addressed this sorry state of affairs but with almost no effect. The economic clauses of the Arab League's Charter and the 1950 Treaty of Joint Defense and Economic Cooperation remained more of a wish list than a blueprint for action. Subsequent League recommendations regarding the unification of members' currencies, the establishment of a preferential trading area among member states with the ultimate objective of creating an Arab common market, and the strengthening of transportation and communication links were acted upon only partially or not at all. On the bilateral level, numerous agreements were concluded during the first part of the 1950s. They had only a very limited effect on the size and structure of inter-Arab trade for a number of reasons. Exemptions from customs duties were applied mainly to agricultural commodities, which had either already been exempt or subject to negligible tariffs. Virtually all of the agreements were only for one year's duration, which tended to discourage private entrepreneurs. Annexes to the agreements often contained lists of goods that were not covered by the agreements. Moreover, the agreements were usually silent on the matters of exemptions from import licenses, and quantitative and foreign exchange restrictions. Lastly, the agreements were liable to be ignored once the political relations among the signatories became strained, a not infrequent occurrence.[15]

Finally, a few comments from the perspective of elite attitudes and behavior may shed additional light on the period under study. Of the five central "players" in the inter-Arab game during the first decade of the Arab League's existence, only Jordan and Saudi Arabia continued to be governed during subsequent years by the same political elites. The *ancien régime* in Egypt was overthrown by the Free Officers Coup in 1952. Repeated upheavals in Syria between 1949 and 1966 irreparably eroded the strengths of the traditional, land-owning elite, which had led Syria into independence, and a more heterogeneous counter-elite, which was seeking to undermine the exclusive power of the older political brokers. Ultimately, they were both swept away by a third elite, whose core came from lower socioeconomic groups to whom secondary education had only recently become available.[16] In Iraq, the erosion of the old elite's power occurred more slowly than in Syria. Nonetheless, by the early 1950s, it was clear that what British officials called the "old gang" would face increasing challenges in the years ahead. As it happened, the ruling oligarchy was overthrown in a bloody coup d'état in July 1958. Internally, the coup inaugurated a long period of domestic instability, limiting Iraq's ability to play the geopolitical role it had conferred upon itself since the 1930s.

The attitudes of Arab ruling elites toward Arab nationalist ideology were inextricably bound up with concern for both maintaining their own preeminence at home and advancing their statuses in the region as a whole. For the promoters of unity—Hashimite Iraq and Jordan—it could be realized only under their respective, separate auspices. For the others, it was an ideal to be paid lip service, but otherwise prevented. Solidarity and fidelity to a common Arab cause were more limited, and thus useful concepts for the governing elites. Indeed, in the words of one historian, Arab nationalism in the hands of Syria's urban notable political leadership was not a revolutionary ideology aimed at overturning existing political hierarchies. Rather, it was a tool to consolidate their own positions at the apex of Syrian society during the Mandate and after independence. Moreover, as early as the mid- and late 1930s, they rejected Arab unity as their principal political goal.[17]

By contrast, full-fledged Arab nationalists during the 1930s and 1940s were most often agents of opposition and dissent. As time went on, a more strident, militant brand of pan-Arabism became the banner brandished by newly emerging groups challenging the socioeconomic and political status quos. Given the prevailing low level of state legitimacy, the rising counterelites from among the middle and lower classes had a fertile ground on which to operate. Their ability to mobilize people behind a more stridently anti-Zionist and anti-Western brand of Arab nationalism placed severe policy constraints on the authorities. The collective Arab defeat in 1948 further catalyzed their activities, particularly within the military, pointing as it did to the impotency of the Arab League and its constituent parts. The horizons of the ascending elites seemed wider than those of the old notable classes. Unity as a remedy for the ailments of the Arab body politic seemed more urgent than ever. For the rising class of officer politicians that would come to dominate Arab political life over the ensuing decades, the point of departure of their radicalism was their "awareness of the backwardness of Arab countries," militarily, economically, and socially.[18] The ground for Arab political transformation and consolidation had not been adequately prepared during the previous decade and thus the new ruling elites would confront many of the same difficulties as their despised predecessors. The consolidation of the inter-Arab system of checks and balances among independent states during the first decade after World War II contributed heavily to inhibiting their efforts to implement their vision.

NOTES
SOURCES CITED
INDEX

NOTES

INTRODUCTION

1. P. J. Vatikiotis, *Arab and Regional Politics in the Middle East* (London: Croom Helm, 1984), 115.

2. Ghassan Salame, "Inter-Arab Politics: A Return to Geography," in *The Middle East: Ten Years after Camp David*, ed. William B. Quandt (Washington, D.C.: Brookings Institution, 1988), 319–53.

3. Alan Richards and John Waterbury, *A Political Economy of the Middle East* (Boulder, Colo.: Westview, 1990), 430–31. Gad G. Gilbar, *Calcalat Hamizrah Hatikhon Be'et Hahadasha* (Tel Aviv: Defense Ministry Publishing House, 1990), 207–10.

4. Clement Henry Moore, "On Theory and Practice among Arabs," *World Politics* 24, no. 1 (1971): 106–26. See also Leonard Binder's explanation regarding the lack of any meaningful application of Arab nationalist ideology to everyday life. (Binder, *The Ideological Revolution in the Middle East* [New York: Wiley, 1964], 92.)

1. GENESIS

1. Ilya Harik, "The Origins of the Arab State System," in *The Foundations of the Arab State*, ed. Ghassan Salame (London: Croom Helm, 1987), 21–22, 24.

2. For a brief summary of the literature, see C. Ernest Dawn, "The Formation of Pan-Arab Ideology in the Inter-War Years," *International Journal of Middle East Studies* 20, no. 1 (1988): 85–86n. The most recent work is *The Origins of Arab Nationalism*, ed. Rashid Khalidi, Lisa Anderson, Muhammad Muslih, Reeva S. Simon (New York: Columbia Univ. Press, 1991).

3. Ernest Gellner, *Nations and Nationalism* (Ithaca, N.Y.: Cornell Univ. Press, 1983), 41.

4. Sylvia Haim, "Islam and the Theory of Arab Nationalism," in *The Middle East in Transition*, ed. Walter Lacquer (London: Routledge and Kegan Paul, 1958), 280–307.

5. Sylvia Haim, *Arab Nationalism: An Anthology*, 2d ed. (Berkeley: Univ. of

California Press, 1976, 42–54; Bassam Tibi, *Arab Nationalism: A Critical Inquiry* (London: Macmillan, 1981), passim.

6. Dawn, "Formation of Pan-Arab Ideology," 82.

7. For Sati' al-Husri's anger and lament during the 1950s over the way things turned out, see Ghassan Salame, "Integration in the Arab World: The Institutional Framework," in *The Politics of Arab Integration*, ed. Giacomo Luciani and Ghassan Salame (London: Croom Helm, 1987), 27.

8. Harik, 44.

9. Gabriel Ben-Dor, *State and Conflict in the Middle East* (New York: Praeger, 1983).

10. Theoretical works dealing with the Middle East regional subsystem include: Leonard Binder, "The Middle East as a Subordinate International System," *World Politics* 10, no. 3 (1958): 408–29; Yair Evron, *The Middle East: Nations, Superpowers and Wars* (London: Elek, 1973); Yair Evron and Yaacov Bar Simantov, "Coalitions in the Arab World," *Jerusalem Journal of International Relations* 1, no. 2 (1975): 71–107; Gabriel Ben-Dor, "Inter-Arab Relations and the Arab-Israeli Conflict," *Jerusalem Journal of International Relations* 1, no. 4 (1976): 70–96; Tareq Y. Ismael, "The Middle East: A Subordinate System in Global Politics," in *The Middle East in World Politics*, ed. Tareq Y. Ismael (Syracuse: Syracuse Univ. Press, 1974), 240–56; Louis Cantori and Steven Spiegel, *International Politics of Regions* (Englewood Cliffs, N.J.: Prentice-Hall, 1970).

11. Itamar Rabinovich, "Inter-Arab Relations Foreshadowed: The Question of the Syrian Throne in the 1920's and 1930's," in *Festschrift in Honor of Dr. George S. Wise*, ed. Hayyim Ben-Shahar et al. (Tel Aviv: Tel Aviv Univ., 1981), 237–50.

12. For Iraq's developing regional outlook, see Elie Kedourie, "The Kingdom of Iraq, a Retrospect," in *The Chatham House Version and Other Middle Eastern Studies*, ed. Elie Kedourie (London: Weidenfeld and Nicholson, 1970), 271–72; Yehoshua Porath, *In Search of Arab Unity, 1930–1945* (London: Frank Cass, 1986), 1–57. For contrasting views on the varying ideological and political trends in Egypt during the interwar years, see Nadav Safran, *Egypt in Search of Political Community* (Cambridge, Mass.: Harvard Univ. Press, 1961); Ralph M. Coury, "Who 'Invented' Egyptian Arab Nationalism?," *International Journal of Middle East Studies* 14, nos. 3–4 (1982): 249–81, 419–34. James Jankowski, "The Egyptian Wafd and Arab Nationalism, 1918–1944," in *Nationalism and International Politics in the Middle East: Essays in Honour of Elie Kedourie*, ed. Edward Ingram (London: Frank Cass, 1988), 164–86; Israel Gershoni and James Jankowski, *Egypt, Islam and the Arabs* (New York: Oxford Univ. Press, 1987), and Israel Gershoni, *The Emergence of Pan-Arabism in Egypt* (Tel Aviv: Shiloah Institute, Tel Aviv Univ., 1981).

13. Yehoshua Porath, "Agada 'Umetzi'ut Betahalikh Hakamat Haliga Ha'aravit," *Zmanim*, no. 5 (1981): 36. For a different interpretation of the genesis of the 1936 treaty crediting Ibn Sa'ud with being its initiator, see Ahmad Gomaa, *Foundation of the League of Arab States* (London: Longman, 1977), 7.

14. Nuri's move stemmed from his own political troubles with the Baqr Sidqi-Sulayman-King Ghazi leadership in Iraq. (Porath, "Nuri al-Sa'id's Arab Unity Programme," *Middle Eastern Studies* 20, no. 4 (1984): 80–81.

15. For a sampling of the literature on this issue, see J. C. Hurewitz, *The Strug-*

gle for Palestine (New York: Shoecken, 1976); Elie Kedourie, "Great Britain and Palestine: The Turning Point," in *Islam and the Modern World,* ed. Elie Kedourie (London: Mansell, 1980), 93–170; Yehoshua Porath, *The Palestine Arab National Movement,* vol. 2, *1929–1939: From Riots to Rebellion* (London: Frank Cass, 1977); Barry Rubin, *The Arab States and the Palestine Conflict* (Syracuse: Syracuse Univ. Press, 1981); Yosef Nevo, *'Abdallah Ve'araviyey Eretz Yisrael* (Tel Aviv: Shiloah Institute, Tel Aviv Univ., 1975); Michael J. Cohen, "Origins of the Arab States' Involvement in Palestine," *Middle Eastern Studies* 19, no. 2 (1983): 244–52.

16. For a sampling of Egyptian attitudes, see Sylvia Haim, "The Palestine Problem in *al-Manar,*" and James Jankowski, "Zionism and the Jews in Egyptian National Opinion, 1900–1939," in *Egypt and Palestine,* ed. Amnon Cohen and Gabriel Baer (Jerusalem: Ben Zvi Institute, 1984), 299–313, 314–31. For Syrian views, see Phillip Khoury, *Syria under the French Mandate* (Cambridge: Cambridge Univ. Press, 1987), 513–34.

17. Elie Kedourie, "The Arab-Israeli Conflict," in *Arabic Political Memoirs,* ed. Elie Kedourie (London: Frank Cass, 1974), 224; Hurewitz, *Struggle for Palestine,* 194.

18. For an account of British Foreign Office thinking along these lines, see William Roger Louis, *The British Empire in the Middle East 1945–1951* (Oxford: Oxford Univ. Press, 1984), 129.

19. A contemporary U.S. intelligence view regarded Great Britain as the prime string puller in these matters. (Office of Strategic Services [OSS], R&A, no. 1754, "Notes and Comments on Arab Federation and Arab Unity, Covering August to December 1943.")

20. Elie Kedourie, "Pan-Arabism and British Policy," in *The Chatham House Version,* 213–35.

21. For the more recent scholarship, based on newly opened archival sources, see Porath, *Search,* and Gomaa. For a review of the historiographical process, see Israel Gershoni, "The Arab League as an Arab Enterprise," *Jerusalem Quarterly,* no. 40 (1986): 88–101.

22. Jordan, Royal Jordanian Court, *al-Kitab al-Urduni al-Abyad* (Amman: Royal Jordanian Court, 1947), 19–20; Nevo, *'Abdallah,* 25n. 67. For an account of the ideological underpinnings of 'Abdallah's effort, see Israel Gershoni, "Hale'om Ha'aravi, Beyt Hashim, VeSuriya Hagedola Bikhtavav shel 'Abdallah," *Hamizrah Hehadash* 25, nos. 1–2, 3 (1975): 1–26, 161–83.

23. For an account of 'Abdallah's efforts up until 1945, see Yehoshua Porath, "Abdallah's Greater Syria Programme," *Middle Eastern Studies* 20, no. 2 (1984): 172–89.

24. Porath, *Search,* pp. 186–87.

25. For the text of the relevant portions, see George Kirk, *The Middle East in the War* (London: Oxford Univ. Press, 1953), 334.

26. Nuri al-Sa'id had been pressing London for some time to make such a declaration to help shore up his own position vis-à-vis the pro-Axis "Golden Square." (Porath, "Agada 'Umetzi'ut," 39). This was notwithstanding a brief, albeit unfruitful, flirtation with the Axis powers in 1940. (Majid Khadduri, "General Nuri's Flirtations with the Axis Powers," *Middle East Journal* 6, no. 3 (1962): 328–36.)

27. Porath, *Search,* 192–93. Porath does not subscribe to the explanation put forth by Michael J. Cohen ("A Note on the Mansion House Speech, May 1941," *Asian and African Studies* 2, no. 3 [1977]: 375–86) that Eden's speech was made primarily

as a propaganda counter to Berlin in the wake of Britain's crushing of Rashid 'Ali (Porath, *Search*, 353n. 176. Rather, in his view, Eden had acted hurriedly to counter Winston Churchill's proposal for an Arab federation that would have room for an independent Jewish state in *all* of Western Palestine (*Search*, 247–49).

28. Porath, "Abdallah's Programme," 182–83; Porath, "Nuri al-Sa'id's Programme," 89–91.

29. The inclusion of the Palestine question in a comprehensive plan for the postwar regional system, in essence the "killing of two birds with one stone," appealed to many British officials, beginning with Churchill. Churchill, however, was far more generous than Nuri to the Zionists (Gabriel Cohen, *Churchill Veshe'elat Eretz Yisrael*, (Jerusalem: Ben-Zvi Institute, 1976), passim: and Porath, *Search*, 58–148). For the text of the relevant material in Nuri's memorandum, see Muhammad Khalil, ed., *The Arab States and the Arab League* (Beirut: Khayats, 1962) 2:9–12; P. J. Vatikiotis, *The History of Egypt*, 2d. ed. (London: Weidenfeld and Nicholson, 1980), pp. 347–49.

30. Porath, *Search*, 258. For the broader motivations and content of the Wafd's emerging Arabism, see James Jankowski, "Egyptian Wafd," 164–86.

31. Porath, *Search*, 257.

32. Kirk, pg. 336; Porath, *Search*, 255–56.

33. Gomaa, 155–57.

34. The phrasing is Porath's (*Search*, 54).

35. Gomaa, 160–61.

36. The idea of two Arab blocs—one of countries east of Suez led by Iraq and the other of North African countries led by Egypt—was put forward in 1943 by a Cairo newspaper and was indicative of at least one current of thought among Cairo political circles. (OSS, R&A, no. 1754, "Notes and Comments," 9.)

37. Gomaa, 166n. 2.

38. Ibid.

39. R&A, no. 1754, "Notes and Comments," 6.

40. One writer characterizes Nuri as the archetype of "realistic" Arab military politicians. (Majid Khadduri, *Arab Contemporaries* [Baltimore: Johns Hopkins Univ. Press, 1973], 19–42.)

41. 'Abdallah's instructions to Tawfiq Abu al-Huda before the talks were clear on both these issues.

> The Amir of Transjordan supports with all his powers the efforts of Egypt and Iraq, and insists that Egypt and Iraq *should work for the unity or federation of Syria before any other federation* [author's emphasis]. [Any wider Arab federation would] not be durable unless the Syrian territories—Greater Syria—are either united or federated. If the sovereignty of these territories remains incomplete under foreign mandates, or if [they remain] locally disunited, their conformity [in policy] with Egypt and Iraq will be so weak and inconsistent that they will be unable to carry out their obligations in this respect.

As for Egypt, it was "one of the leading Arab countries . . . and has (with us) ancient relations and national bonds which (we) cannot disown, God forbid. The Arab countries, therefore, welcome with all their might unity with this dear state" ("unity", [*wahda*], did not mean more than a policy of coordination). Regarding the Yemen and Saudi Arabia (the latter still referred to by ʿAbdallah as "Najd and Hejaz," in an obvious unwillingness to accept the legitimacy of Ibn Saʿud's rule there, ʿAbdallah did not see them as likely candidates for the budding Arab framework, although he did recommend that "they should be kept informed of what is taking place." (Jordan, *al-Kitab al Urduni al-Ayad*, 101–3, translated by Khalil, 2: 16–18.)

42. Porath, *Search*, 261.
43. Gomaa, 172–79; Porath, *Search*, 262.
44. Porath, *Search*, 262–63.
45. Gomaa, 183; Itamar Rabinovich, *The War for Lebanon* (Ithaca, N.Y.: Cornell Univ. Press, 1984), 24–25.
46. Porath, "Nuri al-Saʿid's Programme," 94.
47. ʿAbdallah was also angry with Nuri for "trespassing" into Palestine, following his attempts to reorganize the Palestinian Arab leadership and his meetings with officials of the Jewish Agency. (Mary C. Wilson, *King Abdullah, Britain and the Making of Jordan* [Cambridge: Cambridge Univ. Press, 1987], 144.)
48. Gomaa, p. 194.
49. For the differences of opinion in 1944 among British officials on the movement for Arab unity, see Porath, *Search*, 296–98; Gomaa, 225.
50. For a translation of the *proces verbal* of most of the sessions, see FO 371/45235, Killearn to Eden, Dec. 22, 1944. For a summary of the meetings, including those sessions not included in the above, see Gomaa, 217–25; and Porath, *Search*, 277–87. For the debate on whether the recognition of Lebanon's independence was conditional on Lebanon's continuing to present an "Arab face" as embodied in its National Pact of 1943, see Gomaa, 227–28, and Fayez Sayegh, *Arab Unity, Hope or Fulfillment?* (New York: Devin-Adair, 1958), 128n. For the text of the Protocol, see Khalil, 2:53–56.
51. According to ʿAzzam, however, the Protocol was tainted by its association with Nahhas and Nuri, making the proposed Arab League, in his words, Britain's "illegitimate new-born child." ʿAzzam, of course, was not a disinterested observer, but a political rival to both Nahhas and Nuri (ʿAbd al-Rahman ʿAzzam, "Dhikrayat al-Amin al-ʿAm Lijamiʿat al-Duwal al-ʿArabiyya ʿAzzam Pasha," *al-Usbuʿ al-ʿArabi* [Jan. 31, 1972]).
52. Porath, *Search*, 287, 288.
53. For a comment on the French translation of the Pact, which circumscribes the Council's powers on this issue even more, see Gomaa, 297n. For the discussions leading to the Pact's signing, see Porath, *Search*, 284–90.
54. Nuri's first frontal challenge to Cairo's dominance of the system came only ten years later, with the creation of the Baghdad Pact.
55. Gomaa, 262–63.
56. Porath, *In Search*, pg. 289.
57. For a point-by-point comparison on this issue, see Sayegh, 126–29.
58. For the text of the Charter, see Khalil, 2:56–61.
59. Albert Hourani, "Ottoman Reform and the Politics of Notables," in *The Beginnings of Modernization in the Middle East*, ed. William R. Polk and Richard L. Chambers (Chicago: Univ. of Chicago Press, 1968), 41–68.

60. Albert Hourani, *The Emergence of the Modern Middle East* (London: Macmillan, 1981), 18.

61. Gabriel Ben-Dor, "Stateness and Ideology in Contemporary Middle East Politics," *Jerusalem Journal of International Relations* 9, no. 3 (1987): 21.

62. Clifford Geertz, *The Interpretation of Cultures* (New York: Basic, 1973), 269–70.

63. Charles Issawi, *An Economic History of the Middle East and North Africa* (New York: Columbia Univ. Press, 1982) 41–43.

64. Alfred G. Mursey, *An Arab Common Market: A Study in Inter-Arab Trade Relations. 1920–1967* (New York: Praeger, 1969), 11–22.

65. Issawi, *Economic History,* 161; Mursey, 30–39.

2. THE FORMATIVE YEARS, 1945–1947

1. Sir Edward Spears, *Fulfillment of a Mission: The Spears Mission to Syria and Lebanon, 1941–44* (London: Cooper, 1977); Yosef Olmert, "British Policy Towards the Levant States, 1940–1945" (Ph.D. diss., Univ. of London, 1983); Asher Susser, "Western Power Rivalry and Its Interaction with Local Politics in the Levant, 1941–1946" (Ph.D. diss., Tel Aviv Univ., 1986).

2. RG59/890D.01, Tuck to Secretary of State, Cairo tel. nos. A-265 and DCG-1149, May 22, 31, 1945.

3. For an account of Egyptian Prime Minister Nuqrashi Pasha's representation to the French, see Tuck to Secretary of State, May 31, 1945; for ʿAzzam's public condemnation of France's "imperialistic, colonial state of mind," see Tuck to Secretary of State, May 22, 1945. For a sampling of the entire spectrum of the Baghdad press, featuring condemnations of the French and calls for Arab League action, see RG59/890D.01, enclosure no. 3 to dispatch no. 743 from American Legation, Baghdad, May 25, 1945.

4. Susser, 674–78.

5. This cautious statement of support by British Minister of State Law came in response to a parliamentary question put forth by Sir Edward Spears about what steps were being carried out to fulfill Eden's May 1941 pledge. (Great Britain, *Parliamentary Debates [Hansard], House of Commons* 410, no. 7 [1945]: 1885.)

6. Scheduled before Britain's intervention, the meeting was called at the request of Syria and Lebanon under the terms of Article 6 of the Charter, "should aggression . . . against a member state of the League take place or be . . . threatened"; the Council would then determine "by unanimous assent . . . the appropriate measures to check this aggression." (Khalil, 2:58.)

7. FO 371, 68366/E13328, "The Activities of the Arab League from Its Formation in March, 1945 to 15th May, 1948," Research Department, Foreign Office, Sept. 30, 1948.

8. For an account of British deliberations on whether officially to correspond with the League Secretariat (prompted by ʿAzzam's initiative on the matter), the querying of Arab governments' attitudes, and their qualified affirmative responses, see FO 371, 52315/8954 "Correspondence with the Arab League," P. Garran, Sept. 4, 1946.

9. "If he had our frontiers," said Prime Minister Hamdi al-Pachachi, "he would talk differently." (FO 371, 52312/E261, Stonehewer-Bird to Foreign Office, Baghdad tel. no. 16, Jan. 5, 1946.)

10. RG59/890.B.00, Moose to Secretary of State, Baghdad tel. no. 474, Dec. 6, 1945. The immediate cause for Nuri's unhappiness was the draft regulations governing the functioning of the secretariat-general that ʿAzzam had submitted to the Council for approval. By first boycotting the Council session and then raising objections, Nuri was successful in having the proposal deferred to committee and effectively shelved. (ALC Protocols, 2d meeting, sess. 11–13, Dec. 2, 5, 12, 1945, 167–202.)

11. FO 371, 45241/E9518, Stonehewer-Bird to Foreign Office, Baghdad tel. no. 929, Dec. 5, 1945. Nuri later blamed the British Embassy in Baghdad for exerting pressure on the Iraqi Regent and Pachachi to prevent Iraq's departure. (FO 371, 61523/E1372, Stonehewer-Bird to Foreign Office, Baghdad tel. no. 122, Feb. 10, 1947.) In fact, it appears that opposition within the Iraqi political establishment was the determining factor in shelving Nuri's idea. (FO 371, 52426/E957, Cunningham to Secretary of State for the Colonies, Transjordan tel. no. 20A Feb. 6, 1946.) The British Foreign Office was divided on how much initiative to take in patching up Arab differences. The dominant view remained that of preferring the continuation of the Arab League's tenuous unity over a definitive split. (FO 371, 5242/E1032, FO to Beirut, no. 113, Feb. 8, 1946; FO 371, 52426/E926, J. Thyme Henderson "Minute," Mar. 14, 1946.)

12. On Nov. 30, 1945, the conservative Baghdad newspaper *al-Zaman* published a letter from ʿAbdallah on the desirability of Arab unity, which could, he said, be advanced initially by an Iraqi-Transjordanian union. (RG59/890B.00, Moose to Secretary of State, Baghdad dispatch no. 981, Dec. 3, 1945.)

13. Walid Khalidi, "The Arab Perspective," in *The End of the Palestine Mandate*, ed. William Roger Louis and Robert W. Stookey (Austin: Univ. of Texas Press, 1986), 110.

14. The joint statement issued at the close of their meeting on Jan. 24 contained an explicit reiteration by Ibn Saʿud of his commitment to the Arab League. It also attempted in a general way to exert influence on the upcoming Anglo-American Commission Report on Palestine, and on the British-Egyptian dispute. (RG59/890B.00, Tuck to Secretary of State, Cairo dispatch. no. 1288 and enclosure, Jan. 24, 1946.)

15. RG84/800A, American Legation Damascus, Confidential Correspondence 1949, box 680, Sands to Secretary of State, Jidda dispatch no. 204, Feb. 7, 1946.

16. FO 371, 52426/E926, Henderson "Minute," Mar. 14, 1946.

17. Majid Khadduri, *Independent Iraq* (London: Oxford Univ. Press, 1951), 262.

18. RG59/890G.00, Moose to Secretary of State, Baghdad Dispatch no. A-53, Feb. 28, 1946, "Political Review—Iraq—February 1946"; Khadduri, *Independent Iraq,* 262–63.

19. For an account of the annexation, see Khoury, 494–514. Witness the storm aroused in June 1946 by young King Faysal's departure from Turkey via the port of Hatay (Alexandretta), the alleged remarks by the now former Premier Pachachi that Alexandretta was "Syria's problem," and the subsequent newspaper attack against him emanating from one of his political opponents, Jamil al-Midfaʿi. (RG59/890G.00, Moose to Secretary of State, Baghdad tel. no. 1294, and enclosure, June 15, 1946.)

20. Khadduri, *Independent Iraq*, 262–63.

21. The Baghdad newspaper *Istiqlal* published the minutes on Oct. 5, 1946. Their authenticity was vouched for by Iraq's foreign minister, Fadil al-Jamali. (RG59/790D.90G, Schoenrich to Secretary of State, Baghdad dispatch no. 1467 and enclosure, Oct. 22, 1946.)

22. For an account of the anniversary reception hosted by ʿAzzam, see FO 371, 52312/E2678, Campbell to Foreign Office, Cairo tel. no. 538, Mar. 23, 1946.

23. FO 371, 52313/E2877, Campbell to Foreign Office, Cairo Saving tel. no. 125, Mar. 26, 1946, and enclosure, *Le Journal d'Egypte*, Mar. 25, 1946; 52313/E3219, Campbell to Bevin, Cairo dispatch no. 453, Apr. 2, 1946.

24. RG59/890B.00, "Review of Arab League's First Year," enclosure to Tuck to Secretary of State, Cairo dispatch no. 1441, Mar. 29, 1946.

25. For critical remarks in Egyptian and Syrian newspapers, see *al-Ahram*, Apr. 3, 1946; quoted by *Haboker*, Apr. 4, 1946; *Barada*, quoted by Jewish Telegraphic Agency News, Apr. 4, 1946 (Shwadran Collection, Transjordan, 1946–1947, file no. 8.1).

26. *New York Times*, Apr. 3; *Haboker*, Apr. 4, 1946 (Shwadran Collection, file no. 8.1); ALC Protocols, 3d meeting, 1st sess., Mar. 25, 1946, 7–8.

27. FO 371, 52314/E5250, Campbell to Foreign Office, Cairo tel. no. 1047, June 8, 1946, and enclosure, "Conversation with Nuri Pasha Saʿid," I. N. Clayton, May 28, 1946. On the other hand, Shukri al-Quwwatli claimed privately to the United States that Syria had actually done more than was called for in acknowledging ʿAbdallah's ascension in status, especially because no one from the Syrian government had been invited to come from Damascus to attend the ceremonies. He also noted that the Syrian Consul in Jerusalem officially attended and conveyed, as instructed, his government's congratulations (RG84/800A, American Legation, Damascus, Confidential Correspondence 1946, box no. 2, Mattison to Secretary of State, Damascus dispatch no. A-71, May 25, 1946). See also Wilson, 149.

28. FO 371, 52426/E3161, Campbell to Foreign Office, Cairo tel. no. 621, Apr. 5, 1946.

29. FO 371, 52314/E5250, "Conversation with Nuri Pasha Saʿid," I. N. Clayton, May 28, 1946, enclosure to Campbell to Foreign Office, June 8, 1946.

30. This section of the memoirs was completed in early 1944. ʿAbdallah bin-Husayn, *Mudhakkirati* (Jerusalem: Matbaʿat Bayt al-Muqaddas, 1945), 245. Attempting to smooth things out, ʿAbdallah denied that their publication indicated any intention to cause renewed conflict between the Hashimites and Saudis (*Filastin*, n.d., quoted by *Haboker*, Apr. 5, 1946, Shwadran file, no. 8.1). ʿAbdallah's anti-Saudi remark was deleted from a later volume that was purported to be a complete collection (ʿAbdallah bin-Husayn, *al-Athar al-Kamila lil-Malik ʿAbdallah bin-Husayn* [Beirut: al-Dar al-Muttahida lil-Nashr n.d.]).

31. E.g., the advice, in an "indiscreet" moment, of the Saudi foreign minister to ARAMCO that it should wait to build a projected Trans-Arabian pipeline with a terminal point at Aqaba until it could be included entirely within the Saudi frontier (the line was never built). (RG84/Damascus, 1946, vol. 2, American Legation in Jidda to Department of State, Mar. 10, 1946).

32. The first manifestation of this effort was the Arab collective response to

President Truman's proposal to British Prime Minister Atlee on Aug. 31, 1945, to admit 100,000 Jewish refugees into Palestine. *FRUS,* 1945, Chargé in Egypt (Lyon) to the Secretary of State, Nov. 14, 1945, 817–19.

33. *FRUS,* 1946, Cairo dispatch no. 1382, Mar. 4, 1946, 82n. 11.

34. Muhammad Husayn Haykal, *Mudhakkirat Fi al-Siyasa al-Misriyya* (Cairo: Matba'at Misr Sharika Musahima Misriyya, 1977), 2: 325; Hasan Yusuf, *al-Qasr wa Dawrahu Fi al-Siyasa al-Misriyya, 1922–1952: Mudhakkirat Hasan Yusuf* (Cairo: Markaz al-Dirasat al-Siyasiyya wal-Istratijiyya bi al-Ahram, 1982), 202.

35. It was first suggested in the fall of 1945, apparently by 'Azzam Pasha and like-minded Egyptian pan-Arabists. It was vigorously opposed at the time by Lebanon's Bishara al-Khuri (Wahid al-Dali, *Asrar al-Jami'at al-'Arabiyya wa-'Abdal-Rahman 'Azzam* [Cairo: Matabi' Ruz al-Yusuf, 1982], 143–44).

36. Saudi officials later claimed that the arrangement had emanated from Cairo, following Faruq's invitation to Ibn Sa'ud to attend the meeting that "so pointedly assumed his inability to attend . . . that it would have been almost indelicate for Ibn Sa'ud to accept in person." (FO 371, 53303/E2784, Grafftey-Smith to Foreign Office, Jidda Saving tel. no. 65, June 18, 1946). A further indication of the nature and limitations of Saudi-Egyptian relations was provided by Amir Sa'ud's disparaging remarks to a British official about Faruq's emotional outbursts; these were pointedly made out of the earshot of Yusuf Yasin, described in Grafftey-Smith's dispatch as Faruq's "instrument" in the Saudi hierarchy (Grafftey-Smith to Foreign Office, June 3, 1946).

37. Avraham Sela, "She'elat Eretz Yisrael Bema'arekhet Habeyn- 'Aravit Mehakamat Haliga Ha'aravit 'Ad Pelishat Tzva'ot 'Arav Le'eretz Yisrael, 1945–1948 (Ph.d. diss., Hebrew Univ., 1986), 125–26.

38. Faruq's move was, in a way, a precursor to the institution of an official Arab summit conference in 1964 by Jamal 'Abd al-Nasir as the supreme Arab decision-making body, superseding the by now largely emasculated League Council. The same link with the League Secretariat was also maintained.

39. Summary translation issued on May 30 through Arab League Secretary-General. (FO 371, 52313/E5024, D.O. tel. no. 561, June 1, 1946.) A general statement of sympathy with Egyptian aspirations had already been expressed on behalf of the Council members by the chairman of the Dec. 1945 Council session, Syria's Jamil Mardam. (*Le Progres Égyptien,* Dec. 15, 1945, enclosure to FO 371, 45241/E10219, Killearn to Bevin, Cairo tel. no. 1688, Dec. 18, 1945.) The Mar. 1946 Council session passed a short resolution conferring blanket support of "Egypt's national demands" [*matalibuha al-qawmiyya*] and of "the withdrawal of British forces from Egyptian territory at an early date." (Resolution no. 25, ALC Protocols, Mar. 25, 1946.)

40. "Report of a Meeting with His Majesty King 'Abdallah on June 1, 1946," Cunningham Papers, VI/2/3, St. Anthony's College. Ibn Sa'ud's statement was said to have been made during his Jan. 1946 visit to Cairo. (*Al-Misri,* Jan. 21, 1946, quoted in RG59/890B.00, Tuck to Secretary of State, Cairo tel. no. 1288, Jan. 24, 1946.)

41. FO 371, 52313/E5049, Clayton to Smart, May 29, 1946 (enclosure to Campbell to Foreign Office, Cairo tel. no. 984, May 30, 1946).

42. The Saudis told the British that they had been surprised by Egypt's action; on the other hand, they may have stressed their surprise in order not to appear at odds

with one of their two main benefactors. Amir Saʻud also related that the summit participants had been unpleasantly surprised to receive a multi-subject agenda just before the first meeting, including in it the issues of the future status of Libya and the development of the Yemen, all without prior notice. (FO 371, 52313/E5155, Grafftey-Smith to Foreign Office, Jidda tel. no. 219, June 3, 1946.)

43. Nuri's attachment to the delegation brought about Tawfiq al-Suwaydi's resignation from the premiership. (Sela, "She'elat Eretz Yisrael," 126n. 61; FO 371, 52313/E5049, Clayton to Smart, May 29, 1946.

44. ʻAbdallah's account was transmitted to the High Commissioner for Palestine from Glubb. (FO 371, 53302/J2677, Cunningham to Secretary of State for the Colonies, Jerusalem dispatch no. 810, June 5, 1946.)

45. Clayton to Smart, May 29, 1946.

46. For the Foreign Office's opposition to any ʻAbdallah venture in this regard, see FO 371, 5302/J2677, Scrivener (Foreign Office) to Smith (Colonial Office), June 21, 1946. Kirkbride, although doubtful about the outcome, did not discourage ʻAbdallah in his planned inquiry to Sidqi on the concessions Egypt might be willing to make. (FO 371, 53304/E2942, Kirkbride to Foreign Office, Amman tel. no. 390, June 21, 1946).

47. RG59/890B.00, enclosure no. 2 to Tuck to Secretary of State, Cairo dispatch no. 1610, June 8, 1946. FO 371, 52313/E5155, Grafftey-Smith to Foreign Office, June 3, 1946.

48. Nevo, ʻAbdallah, 27–60; Avraham Sela, *Mimagaʻim Lemasa ʻUmatan* (Tel Aviv: Dayan Center, Tel Aviv Univ., 1985), 11; Avi Shlaim, *Collusion Across the Jordan* (Oxford: Oxford Univ. Press, 1987), 87–88.

49. Jon Kimche and David Kimche, *Both Sides of the Hill* (London: Secker and Warburg, 1960), 49; Rubin, 154–55; FO 371, 2314/E615, Grafftey-Smith to Foreign Office, Jidda tel. no. 237, June 16, 1946.

50. Nevo, ʻAbdallah, 31–32.

51. Kimche and Kimche, 52.

52. Rubin, 15. For the text of the "secret" resolutions, see Khalil, 2: 517–18.

53. For the effect of this lobbying on the Syrian delegation, see Clayton's conversation with Quwwatli and Prime Minister Jabiri, FO 371, 53302/J2711, Shone to Foreign Office, Beirut tel. no. 527, June 14, 1946.

54. FO 371, 52314/E5462, Shone to Foreign Office, Beirut tel. no. 528, June 14, 1946.

55. FO 371, 53304/J2939, Campbell to Foreign Office, Cairo tel. no. 232, June 29, 1946.

56. FO 371, 52315/E6259, Kirkbride to Wikeley, Amman dispatch no. S/621/41, July 9, 1946.

57. Bruce Maddy-Weitzman, "Jordan and Iraq: Efforts at Intra-Hashimite Unity," *Middle Eastern Studies* 26, no. 1 (1990): 65.

58. RG59/890i.001, Pinkerton to Secretary of State, Jerusalem tel. no. 281, July 11, 1946.

59. For a report by the British Consul in Aleppo on the outspoken backing of ʻAbdallah's Greater Syria scheme by the Greek Catholic Archbishop in Aleppo, see FO 371, 61492/E2529, Vaughan-Russell, memorandum, Aleppo, Feb. 27, 1947; for a sum-

mary of attitudes within the different sectors of Syrian society to ʿAbdallah's plan, see FO 371, 61497/E9137, "The Greater Syria Movement," Research Department, Foreign Office, Jan. 10, 1948, 10–13.

60. FO 371, 68403/E300, Broadmead to Bevin, Damascus dispatch no. 156, Dec. 22, 1947; 68403/E2001, Amman Chancery to Eastern Department, dispatch no. S/963/47, Jan. 5, 1948.

61. Most prominent in this campaign was *Barada*, ed. Munir al-Raʾis. (RG59/890D.9111, Mattison to Secretary of State, Damascus dispatch nos. 1071 and A-287, Oct. 23, 29, 1946.)

62. FO 371, 61497/E9137, "The Greater Syria Movement," 9.

63. Jordan, *al-Kitab al-Urduni al-Abyad*, 233–36 (trans. in Khalil, 2: 21–23).

64. *Palestine and the Middle East*, Jan. 1947 (Shwadran, file no. 8.1). For accounts of the angry response in the Lebanese Parliament, see RG59/890B.00, Kuniholm to Secretary of State, Beirut via Navy tel. no. 6477, Dec. 1, 1946.

65. ALC Protocols, 4th meeting, 5th sess., Nov. 26, 1946, 79–90.

66. RG59/890B.00, Tuck to Secretary of State, Cairo Dispatch no. 2057, Dec. 14, 1946.

67. Jordan, *al-Kitab al-Urduni al-Abyad*, 266; trans. in Majid Khadduri, "The Scheme of Fertile Crescent Unity," in *The Near East and the Great Powers*, ed. Richard N. Frye (Cambridge, Mass.: Harvard Univ. Press, 1951), 149.

68. RG59/890D.00, "Royal Message from Abdullah Ibn al-Hussein," enclosure no. 1 to Patterson to Secretary of State, Cairo dispatch no. 2838, Aug. 21, 1947. ʿAbdallah's call came in the wake of general elections in Syria, which indicated an erosion of support for the Quwwatli government. Wilson, *King Abdullah*, 158–59.)

69. RG59/890D.00, enclosure to Childs to Secretary of State, Jidda dispatch no. 351, Aug. 26, 1947.

70. FO 371, 61497/E8993, Kirkbride "Minute," Sept. 9, 1947; 61497/E9327, Pirie-Gordon to Garran from Amman, Sept. 25, 1947.

71. Jordan, *al-Kitab al-Urduni al-Abyad*, 3–4.

72. "Ramadan Manifesto," 17 Ramadan 1366/Aug. 4, 1947, trans. contained in RG59/890D.00, Memminger to Secretary of State, Damascus tel. no. 266, Aug. 28, 1947.

73. Quwwatli speech of September 15, 1947, contained in RG59/890D.001, enclosure no. 1, Hinton to Department of State, Damascus dispatch no. 775, Sept. 22, 1947.

74. For a different view, see Daniel Pipes, *Greater Syria* (New York: Oxford Univ. Press, 1990).

75. Saudi Arabian Government Official Notice no. 104, *Umm al-Qura*, supplementary issue no. 1173, Aug. 31, 1947, trans. contained in RG59/890D.00, enclosure no. 1, Bailey to Secretary of State, Jidda Dispatch no. 361, Sept. 8, 1947.

76. See *FRUS*, 1947, "Interest of the United States in Proposals by Transjordan for a Greater Syria," 738–59, and RG59/890D.00, Bailey to Secretary of State, Jidda dispatch no. 364, Sept. 18, 1947.

77. Mardam statement on Aug. 25, 1947, contained in RG59/890D.00, Memminger to Secretary of State, Damascus tel. no. 268, Aug. 29, 1947.

78. RG59/890D.00, Memminger to Secretary of State, Damascus airgram no. A-336, Sept. 8, 1947. Egyptian propaganda also linked Great Britain to this alleged Zionist-'Abdallah strategy. (FO 371, 61496/E8613, Busk to Bevin, Baghdad dispatch no. 324, Sept. 9, 1947.)

79. FO 371, 61497/E8901, Pirie-Gordon to Garran, from Amman, Sept. 18, 1947.

80. FO 371, 61497/E8993, Kirkbride "Minute," Sept. 9, 1947; FO 371, 6197/E9327, Pirie-Gordon to Garran, from Amman, Sept. 25, 1947.

81. Stephen M. Walt, *The Formation of Alliances* (Ithaca, N.Y.: Cornell Univ. Press, 1987).

82. Khalidi, 115–16.

83. For the text of the treaty, see Khalil, 2: 226–28.

84. FO 371, 61497/E9137, "The Greater Syria Movement," 16.

85. FO 371, 61495/E7966, Busk to British Legation, Amman, Baghdad tel. no. 55, Aug. 27, 1947; RG59/890D.00, Patterson to Secretary of State, Cairo tel. no. 1070, Sept. 3, 1947.

86. A number of Iraqi leaders had previously expressed their disapproval of the regent's alleged pro-'Abdallah, pro-Greater Syria leanings (*FRUS*, 1947, Ambassador in Iraq [Wadsworth] to the Secretary of State, June 18, 1947, 749–50; FO 371, 61496/E8570, Pirie-Gordon to British Legation, Baghdad, Amman tel. no. 49, Sept. 15, 1947).

87. A less than completely reliable Arab source detailed the continued ill-feeling on all sides, which manifested itself during a state dinner given by 'Abdallah for the Arab League Council delegates on Oct. 13, 1947. (*Barada*, reported in RG59/890B.00, Memminger to Secretary of State, Damascus dispatch no. A-390, Oct. 18, 1947.)

88. For a thorough official British account, including the text of the draft agreement, see FO 371, 62962/J520/12/16, "Anglo-Egyptian Treaty Negotiations, 1945–1947."

89. Eran Lerman, "The Egyptian Question, 1942–1947" (Ph.D. diss., Univ. of London, 1982), 460. Faruq's personal appearance in Parliament that day was widely understood as a signal of his personal support for Nuqrashi (*FRUS*, 1947, "The Ambassador in Egypt (Tuck) to the Secretary of State," Jan. 28, 1947, 762–63).

90. The alleged equivocation by Nuri al-Sa'id on support for the Egyptian position on the Sudan was vehemently pounced on in early Feb. 1947 by a number of Cairo dailies, despite an official Iraqi denial of any such intent. (RG9/890D.00, Tuck to Secretary of State, Cairo tel. no. 2215, Feb. 11, 1947, and enclosures, *Akhbar al-Yawm*, Feb. 8, 1947, and *al-Ahram*, Feb. 11, 1947.)

91. FO 371, 661523/E1372, Stonehewer-Bird to Foreign Office, Baghdad tel. no. 122, Feb. 11, 1947; RG59/890B.00, Tuck to Secretary of State, Cairo dispatch no. 2270, Feb. 27, 1947.

92. Lerman, 473–75; RG84/800A, American Legation, Damascus, Confidential Correspondence, 1947, box 680, Moose to Morrison, Feb. 27, 1947.

93. RG59/890B.00, "Recent Developments in the Current Session of the Arab League Council," Tuck to Secretary of State and enclosures, Cairo dispatch no. 2371, Mar. 25, 1947; RG59/890B.00, Tuck to Secretary of State, Cairo dispatch no. 2369, Mar. 24, 1947, and enclosure no. 1, "Memorandum of Conversation Between Dr. Fadil Jamali (foreign minister of Iraq) and Phillip W. Ireland (first secretary of embassy)"; Lerman, 477; ALC Protocols, 6th meeting, 3d sess., March 23, 1947, 60–65. According to

Tuck's dispatches, the uproar created by Ramadan occurred during the Mar. 23 Council session. The resolution, which the Council received for consideration already included the word "absolute" (*mutlaq*), however, and according to the Protocols of the Council session, the matter was not debated further. Therefore, either the uproar must have taken place in the last of the preparatory discussions of the Political Committee, or the episode was not included in the text of the Protocols. Also at issue was the resolution's endorsement of "everlasting" (*da'ima*) unity: Hafiz Ramadan was again prominent, arguing successfully before the Council that the word should remain in the resolution.

94. FO 371, 61525/E5111, Stonehewer-Bird to Foreign Office, Baghdad tel. no. 540, June 13, 1947 (although Iraq's Foreign Minister Jamali did apparently make an abortive, "private" overture to Nuqrashi: FO 371, 61526/E5817, Foreign Office to Damascus, tel. no. 349, July 7, 1947).

95. Fu'ad Hamza, the Saudi participant, was markedly more pro-British than Saudi Deputy Foreign Minister Yusuf Yasin, and his realistic and moderate attitude was deemed "most helpful" by Lebanon's Foreign Minister Hamid Franjiyya. (FO 371, 61527/E6555, Houstoun-Boswell to Foreign Office, Beirut tel. no. 548, July 22, 1947.)

96. FO 371, 61527/E6284, Houstoun-Boswell to Foreign Office, Beirut tel. no. 523, July 14, 1947.

97. Houstoun-Boswell to Foreign Office, July 22, 1947.

98. FO 371, 61528/E6558, Houstoun-Boswell to Foreign Office, Beirut tel. no. 568, July 26, 1947.

99. FO 371, 61528/E6833, Houstoun-Boswell to Foreign Office, Beirut tel. no. 571, July 28, 1947.

100. Lerman, 522–23, 533–34.

101. Fabunmi, L. A., *The Sudan in Anglo-Egyptian Relations* (London: Longmans, Green, 1960), 47–64.

102. Louis, 456–63.

103. Ibid.

104. Iraq and Transjordan expressed reservations with a proposed resolution proclaiming the League's intention to defend Arab rights over Palestine in the United Nations. Iraq opposed going to the United Nations without a prior understanding with Great Britain and the United States that would guarantee an independent Palestine with an Arab majority. Failing that, the Iraqis stressed the need to implement the "secret" aspects of the Bludan resolutions. Transjordan's Samir al-Rifa'i, while diassociating Transjordan from Iraq's unwillingness to go to the United Nations, expressed his country's desire to reserve its "freedom of independent action" in light of its special relationship, politically, economically and socially, with Palestine. (ALC Protocols, 6th meeting, 3d and 4th sess., Mar. 23–24, 1947, 49–60, 67–79.) Concurrently, Samir told the Egyptians that the Western powers were unreliable and that the forthcoming UNSCOP efforts would be ineffective. Only concerted and practical actions by the Arab states, he said, could save Palestine for the Arabs (ISA, 02376, 367/2, Transjordan Prime Minister to Egyptian Consul-General in Jerusalem, Mar. 15, 1947).

105. Michael Eppel, "The Iraqi Domestic Scene and Its Bearing on the Question of Palestine, 1947," *Asian and African Studies* 24, no. 1 (1990): 58–69.

106. RG59/890B.00, Memminger to Secretary of State, Damascus dispatch no. 783, Sept. 26, 1947.

107. See letter from high Syrian official, possibly Shukri al-Quwwatli, to Faris al-Khuri on the morrow of the Council meeting, elaborating on the underlying Arab divisions that impeded effective joint military and economic moves. The letter was intercepted by Zionist intelligence and then in turn by British intelligence and then passed on to the United States. (RG59/890B.00, Memminger to Secretary of State, Damascus dispatch no. 85, Dec. 5, 1947.)

108. FO 371, 61530/E9551, Houstoun-Boswell to Foreign Office, Beirut tel. no. 740, Dec. 12, 1947.

109. FO 371, 68366/E13328, "The Activities of the Arab League," 5.

110. Muhammad Amin al-Husayni, *Haqa'iq 'An Qadayat Filastin*, 21, cited by Zvi Elpeleg, *Falastin 'Atzma'it Besvakh Hayerivut Habeyn- 'Aravit, 1946–1948* (Tel Aviv: Shiloah Institute, 1982), 10.

111. RG59/890B.00, Damascus dispatch no. 783, Memminger to Secretary of State, Sept. 26, 1947; Thomas Mayer, "Egypt's 1948 Invasion of Palestine," *Middle Eastern Studies* 22, no. 1 (1986): 31.

112. Yoav Gelber, "The Negotiations Between the Jewish Agency and Transjordan, 1946–1948," *Studies in Zionism* 6, no. 1 (1985): 59–60.

113. FO 816/89, Kirkbride to Foreign Office, Amman tel. no. 302, Oct. 11, 1947 (thanks to Ilan Pappé for providing me with this document). Kirkbride very much doubted 'Abdallah's claim that his visitors had concurred with his views (Gelber).

114. RG59/890B.00, Memminger to Secretary of State, Damascus dispatch no. 85, Dec. 5, 1947.

115. *FRUS*, 1947, Wadsworth to Acting U.S. Representative at United Nations (Johnson), Oct. 21, 1947, 1192–94.

116. *FRUS*, 1947, "Statement by the United States and the United Kingdom Groups," "Problem: The Arab League" [undated], 606–7.

117. Evron and Bar Simantov, "Coalitions," 72.

118. RG84/350, box 680, Wadsworth to Secretary of State, Baghdad tel. no. 800, June 13, 1947.

3. THE SYSTEM IS TESTED

1. al-Dali, 232.

2. 'Azzam, Feb. 7, 1972; Gabriel Cohen, "Mediniyut Britanya 'Erev Milhemet Ha'atzma'ut," in *Hayinu Keholmim*, ed. Yehuda Wallach (Ramat Gan, Israel: Massada, 1985), 121–28, 171–72.

3. RG59/890B.00, "Developments at Meeting of Arab League," Dec. 8–17, 1947, Tuck to Secretary of State, and enclosure, Cairo tel. no. 3106, Dec. 20, 1947.

4. E.g., *FRUS*, 1947, Ambassador in Egypt (Tuck) to Secretary of State, Dec. 3, 1947, 1295–97; see also RG59/890B.00, Tuck to Secretary of State, Dec. 20, 1947.

5. Zvi Elpeleg, *Hamufti Hagadol* (Tel Aviv: Defense Ministry Publishing House, 1989), 88–89.

6. For Safwat's reports and activities during the winter of 1947 and 1948, see

Hashimite Kingdom of Iraq, *Me'ahorey Haparagod: Va'ada Parlimentarit 'Iraqit 'al Hamilhama Beyisrael*, Shmuel Segev, trans. (Tel Aviv: Ma'arakhot, 1954), 66–103.

7. Ibid., 20–22.

8. Shlaim, *Collusion*, 105–21; Uri Bar-Josef, *The Best of Enemies: Israel and Transjordan in the War of 1948* (London: Frank Cass, 1987), 8–12; Gelber, 62–65; Alec S. Kirkbride, *From the Wings* (London: Frank Cass, 1976), 4–5; Sela, *Mimaga'im Lemasa 'Umatan*, 14–26.

9. Bar-Josef, 25–26.

10. RG59/890B.00, Tuck to Secretary of State, Dec. 20, 1947; FO 371, 68364/E31, "Note on the Proceedings of the Meeting of the Arab Premiers in Cairo, December 8th to 17th 1947."

11. FO 371, 68403/E1877, Beeley (Eastern Department) to Bromley (Washington Embassy), Jan. 20, 1948.

12. FO 371, 68364/E306, Jan. 7, 1948.

13. For an admission that these alterations were primarily intended by both sides for demonstrative purposes, see ibid.

14. FO 371, 68367/E12264, FO tel. no. 12 to Amman, Jan. 10, 1948.

15. FO 371, 68403/E1877, Beeley to Bromley, Jan. 20, 1948.

16. FO 371, 68366/E1916, "Conversation with the Transjordan Prime Minister," Bevin to Kirkbride, Foreign Office dispatch no. 19, Feb. 9, 1948.

17. FO 371, 68367/E2163 and E2696, Foreign Office "Minute," Feb. 13, 1948.

18. Louis, *The British Empire*, 464–77; Alan Bullock, *Ernest Bevin, Foreign Secretary, 1945–1951* (London: Heinemann, 1983), 476–78, 564–65.

19. A demonstrative example of this trend was Faruq's granting of asylum to Hajj Amin al-Husayni when he escaped from France in 1946. The Egyptian government, by contrast, was not happy with the move and refused to grant the mufti official status as a political refugee. (Yusuf, *al-Qasr*, 202.)

20. For more on the attitudes of the Arab states toward the mufti, see Rubin, 266.

21. Iraq, *Me'ahorey Haparagod*, 59.

22. Yosef Nevo, "The Arabs of Palestine 1947–48: Military and Political Activity," *Middle Eastern Studies* 23, no. 1 (1987): 22.

23. For the text of Safwat's complaint, see Iraq, *Me'ahorey Haparagod*, 83–85.

24. Taha al-Hashimi, *Mudhakkirat Taha al-Hashimi*, ed. Khaldun Sati' al-Husri (Beirut: Dar al-Tali'a, 1978) 2: 194. For an account of one of the mufti's subsequent steps to assert his authority, see Elpeleg *Falastin 'Atzma'it*, 13–14.

25. One example of this was the dispatch to Palestine of a detachment of Iraqi volunteers without prior notification to League authorities. (al-Hashimi, 197.)

26. For the text of the resolutions defining its authority, see Iraq, *Me'ahorey Haparagod*, 80–82.

27. RG59/890D.00, American Embassy, Damascus, to Secretary of State, tel. no. 80, Feb. 6, 1948; Ya'acov Shim'oni, "Ha'aravim Likrat Milhemet Yisrael-'Arav, 1945–1948," *Hamizrah Hehadash* 12, no. 3 (1962): 208; Iraq, *Me'ahorey Haparagod*, 83–85.

28. Nevo, "Arabs of Palestine."

29. For the views of Musa al-'Alami on Syria's own aspirations in Palestine, see

FO 371, 68367/E2137, Kirkbride to Foreign Office, Amman tel. no. 82, Feb. 12, 1948. For the mufti's opposition to Qawuqji, see Elpeleg, *Hamufti Hagadol*, 87.

30. Fawzi al-Qawuqji, "Memoirs, 1948, Part I," *Journal of Palestine Studies* 1, no. 4 (1972): 27–58.

31. FO 371, 68367/E2163, Kirkbride to Foreign Office, Amman tel. no. 90, Feb. 14, 1948.

32. This decision was reportedly conveyed during the visit to Damascus by the Legion's chief of staff, 'Abd al-Qadir al-Jundi, in late Jan. or early Feb. 1948. (FO 371, 68369/E3806, Cunningham to Secretary of State for Colonies, Palestine tel. no. 691, Mar. 18, 1948.)

33. FO 371, 68369/E4381, Kirkbride to Foreign Office, Amman tel. no. 210, Apr. 7, 1948.

34. FO 371, 68369/E3729, Kirkbride to Foreign Office, Amman tel. no. 172, Mar. 20, 1948.

35. Sela, "She'elat Eretz Yisrael," 468–69.

36. E.g., 'Azzam's remarks to Sheringham (Britain's vice counsul in Jerusalem) on Feb. 16, 1948. (FO 371, 68381/E2618, Sheringham to Burrows, Cairo (BMEO) dispatch no. 31/43/1, Feb. 17, 1948.) The desire for Britain to stay on, said Britain's ambassador to Egypt, Sir Ronald Campbell, to Egyptian Foreign Minister Khashaba Pasha, was ironic to say the least: "while the British were on the stage, everybody else was in the audience, and often throwing things at the actors, while at the same time applauding the idea that they should go on with the play" (FO 371, 68370/E5234, Campbell to Bevin, Cairo tel. no. 100, Apr. 17, 1948).

37. *FRUS*, 1948, Memorandum by Mr. Samuel K. C. Kopper to United States Representative at the United Nations (Austin), Mar. 14, 1948, 723–25.

38. Kimche and Kimche, 107; FO 816/117, Kirkbride to Secretary of State, Foreign Office, Amman tel. no. 225, Apr. 13, 1948.

39. Khalidi, 128.

40. FO 371, 68370/E4735, Campbell to Foreign Office, Cairo tel. no. 459, Apr. 14, 1948.

41. al-Hashimi, 213. It should be noted, however, that the resolution was formally confirmed by the League Council only two years later (see chap. 4).

42. Nevo, *'Abdallah*, 68.

43. Rubin, 198.

44. al-Hashimi, 214; FO 371, 68372/E5998, Kirkbride to Foreign Office, Amman tel. no. 300, May 8, 1948.

45. FO 371, 68370/E5159, Kirkbride to Foreign Office, Amman tel. no. 49, Apr. 25, 1948.

46. For Tawfiq Abu al-Huda's earlier thoughts along these lines, see Kirkbride to Secretary of State, Apr. 13, 1948.

47. Sela, "She'elat Eretz Yisrael," 55.

48. al-Hashimi, 217–18; *FRUS*, 1948, Ambassador in Egypt (Tuck) to Secretary of State, Apr. 26, 1948, 862–63.

49. E.g., Foreign Minister Khashaba Pasha, in conversation with British ambassador, FO 371, 68370/E5299, Campbell to Foreign Office, Cairo tel. no. 517, Apr. 26, 1948.

50. FO 371, 68370/E5159, Kirkbride to Foreign Office, Amman tel. no. 249, Apr. 25, 1948.
51. FO 371, 68852/E5068, Kirkbride to Foreign Office, Amman tel. no. 237, Apr. 21, 1948.
52. al-Dali, 233.
53. Kirkbride, 24.
54. *FRUS*, 1948, Ambassador in Egypt (Tuck) to Secretary of State, Apr. 28, 1948, 871–72.
55. 'Arif al-'Arif, *al-Nakba* (Sidon: Manshurat al-Maktaba al-'Asriyya, 1956) 1: 283–84.
56. E.g., Egyptian and Saudi officials, in conversation with U.S. ambassador to United Nations, *FRUS*, 1948, United States Representative at United Nations (Austin) to Secretary of State, May 3, 1948, 886–89; Secretary of State (Marshall) to Ambassador to United Kingdom (Douglas), May 5, 1948, 915–16; Egyptian Foreign Minister, in conversation with British ambassador, FO 371, 68371/E5603, Campbell to Foreign Office, Cairo tel. no. 544, May 2, 1948; Lebanese Foreign Minister, in conversation with British ambassador, FO 371, 68371/E5614, Houstoun-Boswell to Foreign Office, Beirut tel. no. 320, May 2, 1948.
57. al-'Arif, 1: 108n.
58. Shlaim, *Collusion*, 199–201.
59. al-Hashimi, 217, 219; al-Dali, 233. Egypt's agreement is correctly noted by Dan Schueftan (*Optzia Yardenit* [Tel Aviv; Hakibbutz Hameuhad, 1987], 61n. 37). He speculates that the representative of Egypt's chief of staff in Amman was perhaps not aware of the political significance of his agreement. On the other hand, his action makes more sense if Faruq was, as suggested here (see n. 62), acquiescing at this stage to 'Abdallah's maneuvers in order to protect his own forces and perhaps to achieve a foothold in Hebron.
60. al-'Arif, 2: 288–89; Kimche and Kimche, 151. 'Arif writes that it was Glubb who altered the plans; the Kimches, on the other hand, state that 'Abdallah did not even consult Glubb. Glubb claims that "we were in ignorance of the strength or intentions" of the Syrian and Lebanese armies, although Egyptian and Iraqi intentions were known; in other words, he denies the exisence of *any* overall plan. (Sir John Bagot Glubb, *A Soldier with the Arabs* [New York: Harper and Brothers, 1957], 105).
61. Iraq, *Me'ahorey Haparagod*, 149–50; Kimche and Kimche, 164–65; Kedourie, "Pan-Arabism," 230–32. 'Arif states that a decision to dispatch Egyptian forces to the Hebron-Bethlehem area was included in the original invasion plans (al-'Arif, 2: 342).
62. Letters exchanged between Tawfiq Abu al-Huda and Ibrahim 'Abd al-Hadi, Apr. 17, 1949, published in the government organ *al-Asas*, Cairo, Mar. 29, 1950, text of exchange contained in enclosures to FO 371, 81932/E1071/158. 'Abdallah's letter is contained in FO 371, 75532/E3735, enclosure to Amman Chancery to Eastern Department, no. S.143.49, Mar. 16, 1949. A Haganah intelligence estimate one week before the invasion expected such Egyptian-Transjordanian coordination. (Elhanan Oren, "Matarot Vetotsa'ot Bemilhemet Ha'atzma'ut," *Ma'arakhot*, nos. 279–80 [1981]: 17. A nongovernmental Egyptian source states that they were sent in response to requests from the local residents themselves. (Kamal Isma'il al-Sharif, "Ha'ahim Hamuslimim

Bemilhemet Palastina," in *Be'eyney Ha'oyev,* trans. and ed. Shmuel Segev, [Tel Aviv: Ma'arakhot, 1954], 86.) For Nevo's comment on the latter, see *'Abdallah* 104n. 3.

63. For accounts of Golda Meyerson's meeting on May 11 with a "worried" and "distraught" 'Abdallah, see Gelber, 81–82, and Shlaim, *Collusion,* 205–14. Much has been written about the extent of the understanding between 'Abdallah and the Jewish Agency. For a penetrating historigraphical critique, which emphasizes that the policies of both sides in 1948 were governed primarily by the numerous and complex military and political considerations, and not by a prior grand strategic understanding, see Sela, "Israel, Transjordan and the 1948 War: Myth, Historiography and Reality," *Middle Eastern Studies* 28, no. 4 (1992): 623–88.

64. FO 371, 68372/E6177, Kirkbride to Foreign Office, Amman tel. no. 317, May 12, 1948.

65. Mayer.

66. al-Hashimi, 221.

67. Kimche and Kimche, 14.

68. Glubb, 94.

69. FO 371, 68369/E3366, Trott to Foreign Office, Jidda tel. no. 105, Mar. 11, 1948.

70. FO 371, 68367/E2185, Kirkbride to Foreign Office, Amman tel. no. 86, Feb. 13, 1948. General Safwat declined their services, as they were thought to more likely engage in the plundering of Arab villages than in helping to fight the Jews. (FO 371, 68367/E2251, Kirkbride to Foreign Office, Amman tel. no. 95, Feb. 16, 1948).

71. FO 371, 68372/E6131, Mack to Foreign Office, Baghdad tel. no. 510, May 11, 1948. A few days earlier, 'Abdallah and Ibn Sa'ud exchanged, at the former's initiative, generally worded telegrams regarding the upcoming clash. (FO 371, 68373/E6400, Trott to Foreign Office, Jidda tel. no. 202, May 16, 1948).

72. 'Abd al-Latif al-Yunis, *Shuqri al-Quwwatli, Ta'rikh Umma Fi Hayat Rajul* (Cairo: Dar al-Ma'arif, 1959), 170; al-Hashimi, 221; 'Abdallah Bin Husayn (Abdallah, King of Jordan), *My Memoirs Completed, "Al-Takmilah"* (London: Longman, 1978), 20–21; Kimche and Kimche, 153.

73. John Norton Moore, ed., *The Arab-Israeli Conflict* (Princeton: Princeton Univ. Press, 1974), 3: 352–57.

74. FO 371, 68373/E6405, Campbell to Foreign Office, Cairo tel. no. 641, May 17, 1948; 68373/E6692, Houstoun-Boswell to Foreign Office, Beirut tel. no. 366, May 20, 1948; RG59/890D.00, Memminger to Secretary of State, Damascus airgram no. A-227, "Syria, Monthly Political Review, May 1948," May 31, 1948.

75. "Syria, Monthly Review," May 31, 1948; and RG59/890D.00, Memminger to Secretary of State, Damascus tel. no. 305, May 21, 1948.

76. 'Abdallah replied that they should make the request themselves, adding that it came oddly from one who had organized opposition to British treaties with Iraq and Transjordan. (FO 371, 68373/E6769, Kirkbride to Foreign Office, Amman tel. no. 372, May 22, 1948.)

77. al-Hashimi, 223; 'Abdallah al-Tall, *Karithat Falastin* (Cairo: Dar al-Qalam, 1959), 191; al-'Arif, 2: 344. An authorized Jordanian history of the Arab Legion also stipulates that an Egyptian-Transjordanian linkup for the purpose of conquering Tel

Aviv had been agreed upon (Syed Ali el-Edroos, *The Hashimite Arab Army, 1908–1979* [Amman: Amman Publishing Committee, 1980], 245).

78. ʿAbdallah, *Memoirs*, 21. Kirkbride had already suggested to the Foreign Office (and presumably to the Transjordanians), that a failure by Egypt to continue its advance would make it possible for Transjordan to plead an inability to continue their own advance. (FO 371, 68373/E6897, Kirkbride to Foreign Office, Amman tel. no. 370, May 22, 1948.

79. al-Hashimi, 224; FO 371, 68373/E6769, Kirkbride to Foreign Office, Amman tel. no. 372, May 22, 1948.

80. FO 371, 68373/E6897, Kirkbride to Foreign Office, Amman tel. no. 379, May 22, 1948.

81. For the texts of the Security Council resolution and the Arab reply, see Khalil, 2:561–63.

82. *FRUS*, 1948, Chargé in Egypt (Patterson) to Secretary of State, June 15, 1948, 1114–15.

83. Ibid.

84. *FRUS*, 1948, Vice Counsul at Jerusalem (Burdett) to Secretary of State, June 8, 1948, 1105–06.

85. *FRUS*, 1948, 1086 (editorial note).

86. *FRUS*, 1948, Ambassador in the United Kingdom (Douglas) to Secretary of State, and 1040-41n. 1.

87. E.g., remarks to this effect made by the Iraqi regent. (FO 371, 68373/6722, Mack to Foreign Office, Baghdad tel. no. 562, May 22, 1948.)

88. Sune O. Persson, *Mediation and Assassination: Count Bernadotte's Mission to Palestine in 1948* (London: Ithaca, 1979) 130–31.

89. FO 371, 68374/E8236, Kirkbride to Foreign Office, Saving tel. no. 3, June 16, 1948.

90. Elpeleg, *Falastin ʿAtzmaʾit*, 24.

91. ʿAbdallah, *Memoirs*, 22. One historian states that Egypt's confiscation of the Transjordan-bound ammunition was done mainly as a result of Egyptian anger toward Britain's failure to resupply them. (Ilan Pappé, *Britain and the Arab-Israeli Conflict, 1948–1951* [London: Macmillan, 1988], 35.) The Egyptian move seems at odds with Kirkbride's concurrent report that Egypt was supplying Transjordan (with what he did not specify). (FO 371, 68373/E6819, Kirkbride to Foreign Office, Amman tel. no. 379, May 24, 1948.)

92. FO 371, 68457/E8993, Kirkbride to Burrows, June 26, 1948; 68457/E8930, Mack to Foreign Office, Baghdad tel. no. 731, July 2, 1948; 68457/E9054, Campbell to Bevin, Cairo tel. no. 340, July 1, 1948.

93. FO 371, 68457/E9810, Campbell to Bevin, Cairo tel. no. 366, July 14, 1948.

94. FO 371, 68770/E8297, Kirkbride to Foreign Office, Amman tel. no. 493, June 17, 1948.

95. ʿAbdallah, *Memoirs*, 50–51.

96. FO 371, 68857/E9629, Kirkbride to Bevin, Amman dispatch no. 38, July 6, 1948. The possibility of ʿAbdallah mediating Saudi-Iraqi tensions was also discussed, particularly those problems connected to the administration of the Saudi-Iraqi frontier, and

the status of former Iraqi Prime Minister Rashid 'Ali, whose nationalist, pro-Axis government had been removed in 1941 and the Hashimite monarchy restored by the British. The Saudis had granted him asylum two years earlier and kept him in reserve as a possible card to be played against Iraq, but he was apparently wearing out his welcome. 'Abdallah gave conflicting accounts to British representatives on whether he had expressed his willingness to take 'Ali off the Saudis' hands (FO 371, 68457/E8930, Mack to Foreign Office, Baghdad tel. no. 751, July 2, 1948, and Kirkbride to Bevin, July 6, 1948). As it happened, 'Ali remained in Saudi Arabia for a number of years afterward.

97. Bernadotte's appointment, and terms of reference, had been laid down by U.N. General Assembly Resolution 186(S-2), adopted on May 14, 1948. (John Norton Moore, 346-7).

98. For text of the suggestions and the responses of the parties, see Persson, 144-50.

99. For the text of the decision, released on July 10 by 'Azzam, see Khalil, 2:566-68.

100. For indications to this effect, see Elpeleg, *Falastin 'Atzma'it,* 27-28; Pappé, *Britain and the Arab-Israeli Conflict,* 82.

101. For Abu al-Huda's previously expressed concerns along this line, see FO 371, 68374/E7209, Kirkbride to Foreign Office, Amman tel. no. 417, May 29, 1948.

102. Elpeleg, *Falastin 'Atzma'it,* 28.

103. For the text of the two memoranda submitted to Bernadotte and the Security Council rejecting the ceasefire, see Khalil, 2:563-65.

104. FO 371, 68375/E9168, Foreign Office to Amman, tel. no. 641, July 6, 1948.

105. *FRUS,* 1948, Ambassador in the United Kingdom (Douglas) to Secretary of State, July 9, 1948, 1203-5; FO 371, 68375/E9169, Kirkbride to Foreign Office, Amman tel. no. 538, July 7, 1948.

106. Shlaim, *Collusion,* 261.

107. Muhammad Faysal 'Abd al-Mun'im, *Asrar: 1948* (Cairo: Maktabat al-Qahira al-Haditha, 1968), 416-18.

108. For comments to this effect emanating from Baghdad press, see RG59/890G.00, Wadsworth to Secretary of State, Baghdad tel. no. 417, July 1, 1948.

109. *FRUS,* 1948, Chargé in Egypt (Patterson) to Secretary of State, July 7, 1948, 1196.

110. Ilan Pappé, "British Foreign Policy Towards the Middle East, 1948-1951: Britain and the Arab-Israeli Conflict" (Ph.D. diss., Oxford Univ., 1984), 73.

111. For the text of the Arab reply to the Security Council resolution, see ibid, 569-72.

112. *FRUS,* 1948, Mr. Wells Stabler to Secretary of State, Amman, July 25, 1948, 1237-38.

113. Benny Morris, *The Birth of the Palestinian Refugee Problem, 1947-1949* (Cambridge: Cambridge Univ. Press, 1987), 197-213. The Transjordanian monarch was reportedly referred to in Baghdad coffee houses as "Rabbi Abdallah" (RG59/890G.00, Wadsworth to Secretary of State, Baghdad tel. no. 460, July 29, 1948.)

114. RG9/890G.00, Wadsworth to Secretary of State, Baghdad tel. no. 453, July 24, 1948.

115. al-Hashimi, 231–32.
116. RG9/890G.00, Wadsworth to Secretary of State, July 29, 1948.
117. Dissatisfaction with Bernadotte's proposals was widespread. For ʿAzzam's reaction, see *FRUS*, 1948, Ambassador to Egypt (Griffis) to Acting Secretary of State, 422–23. For the Saudi reaction, see *FRUS*, 1948, "Memorandum of Conversation," by Henry S. Villard of the Advisory Staff of the United States Delegation to the General Assembly, 1416. The Syrians saw the Bernadotte Plan as giving ʿAbdallah the opportunity to realize his lifelong ambitions of expanding his territory (RG59/890B.00, Griffis to Secretary of State, Cairo tel. no. 85, Oct. 5, 1948, and enclosure, "Memorandum of Conversation Between Syrian Foreign Minister Muhsin Barazi and First Secretary of Cairo Embassy, Phillip W. Ireland"). Suspicions were also current in Syria that Great Britain was angling for Transjordan's expansion, with an eye eventually to include Syria as well (FO 371, 68861/E11760, Dundas to Foreign Office, Damascus tel. no. 464, Sept. 7, 1948). Unlike in July, when Bernadotte's first set of recommendations were intended to serve as a basis for discussion among the parties, the new set of proposals was envisaged as the basis for an imposed settlement (Saadia Touval, *The Peace Brokers* [Princeton: Princeton Univ. Press, 1982], 38–39).
118. RG59/890i.00, Stabler to Secretary of State, Amman tel. no. 47, Sept. 3, 1948.
119. *DFPI*, vol. 1, no. 522, Shertok to Sasson, Sept. 19, 1948, p. 611.
120. FO 371, 68861/E11809, Kirkbride to Foreign Office, Amman tel. no. 707, Sept. 8, 1948.
121. *DFPI*, Shertok to Sasson, Sept. 19, 1948. The negative Israeli reaction to the idea of permitting a partial return to Lydda and Ramleh can be found in the same document, and also in a previous communiqué (*DFPI*, vol. 1, no. 499, 516–17, Shertok to Sasson, Sept. 9, 1948. For the overall Israeli position regarding the refugees during this period, see Benny Morris, "The Crystallization of Israeli Policy Against a Return of the Arab Refugees: April–December 1948," *Studies in Zionism* 6, no. 1 (1985): 85–118.
122. Nevo, ʿ*Abdallah*, 99–101.
123. FO 371, 68366/E12098, Kirkbride to Foreign Office, no. 720, Sept. 15, 1948.
124. FO 371, 68374/E7209, Kirkbride to Foreign Office, Amman tel. no. 417, May 29, 1948.
125. *DFPI*, vol. 2, no. 126, 161–63, Sasson to Shimʿoni, Nov. 10, 1948.
126. FO 371, 68642/E12703, Chapman-Andrews to Foreign Office, Cairo tel. no. 1358, Sept. 29, 1948.
127. Elpeleg, *Falastin ʿAtzamaʾit*, 32–33; al-Hashimi, 241–42.
128. FO 371, 68861/E12835, Foreign Office to Cairo, no. 1672, Oct. 2, 1948.
129. FO 371, 68376/E12392, Evans to Foreign Office, Beirut tel. no. 688, Sept. 21, 1948.
130. al-Hashimi, 242; FO 371, 68643/E13348, Mack to Foreign Office, Baghdad tel. no. 1023, Oct. 13, 1948.
131. Chapman-Andrews to Foreign Office, Oct. 6, 1948.
132. Sasson to Shimʿoni, Nov. 10, 1948.
133. FO 371, 68642/E13253, Kirkbride to Foreign Office, Amman tel. no. 800, Oct. 12, 1948.

134. RG59/890B.00, Stabler to Secretary of State, Amman tel. no. 74, Oct. 3, 1948.

135. FO 371, 68862/E12925, Kirkbride to Foreign Office, Amman tel. no. 775 Oct. 4, 1948.

136. FO 371, 68643/E14087, Acting British Consul, Jerusalem, to Foreign Office, no. 578, Oct. 29, 1948.

137. FO 371, 68644/E15734, Campbell to Foreign Office, Cairo tel. no. 1717, Dec. 11, 1948.

138. An analysis of Arab views on this matter in the fall of 1948 can be found in Pappé, *Britain and the Arab-Israeli Conflict*, 169.

139. David Ben-Gurion, *Yoman Hamilhama*, ed. Gershon Rivlin and Elhanan Oren (Tel Aviv: Defense Ministry Publishing House, 1982) 3:736–37, 760–61, 766.

140. FO 371, 68366/E14672, Kirkbride to Foreign Office, Amman tel. no. 883, Nov. 13, 1948.

141. FO 371, 68643/E14735, Beeley (U.K. delegation to U.N. General Assembly, Paris) to Burrows (Eastern Department), Nov. 11, 1948.

142. FO 371, 68599/E15142, U.K. delegation to U.N. General Assembly, Paris, to Foreign Office, no. 537, Nov. 25, 1948.

143. *FRUS*, 1948, 1625–27.

144. Nevo, *'Abdallah*, 112–16.

145. Pappé, *Britain and the Arab-Israeli Conflict*, 93–94; A. Haydar Hassan Abidi, *Jordan—A Political Study, 1948–1957* (London: Asia, 1965), 55–56.

146. RG59/890D.00, Keeley to Secretary of State, Damascus tel. no. A-389, Dec. 15, 1948. For Transjordan's queries about what Iraq's position would be on an expulsion resolution, see FO 371, 68644/E16342, Amman Chancery to Eastern Department, Dec. 22, 1948.

147. FO 371, 68643/E15690, Kirkbride to Foreign Office, Amman tel. no. 938, Dec. 9, 1948.

148. FO 371, 68644/E15904, Mack to Foreign Office, Baghdad tel. no. 1184, Dec. 15, 1948.

149. FO 371, 68644/E16231, Mack to Foreign Office, Baghdad tel. no. 1201, Dec. 23, 1948.

150. FO 371, 68644/E16097 and E16136, Houstoun-Boswell to Foreign Office, Beirut tel. nos. 966 and 972, Dec. 18 and 21, 1948.

151. RG59/890B.00, Patterson to Secretary of State, Cairo tel. no. 171, Dec. 14, 1948; Cairo Embassy to Secretary of State, tel. no. A-999, Dec. 16, 1948.

152. FO 371, 68664/E16005, Campbell to Foreign Office, Cairo tel. no. 1745, Dec. 17, 1948.

153. FO 371, 68644/E1592, Kirkbride to Foreign Office, Amman tel. no. 954, Dec. 15, 1948.

154. Nuqrashi's message ended with the reiteration that Egypt had no territorial ambitions in Palestine and would leave its future to be decided by its inhabitants. (FO 371, 68643/E15730, Kirkbride to Foreign Office, Amman tel. no. 941, Dec. 9, 1948.)

155. Kirkbride to Foreign Office, Dec. 15, 1948.

156. RG59/890i.00, Stabler to Secretary of State, Amman tel. no. 161, Dec. 17, 1948.
157. FO 371, 68644/E16339, Kirkbride to Foreign Office, Amman tel. no. 981, Dec. 29, 1948.
158. FO 371, 68644/E16260, Campbell to Foreign Office, Cairo tel. no. 1786, Dec. 27, 1948.
159. FO 371, 68664/E16005, Campbell to Foreign Office, Dec. 17, 1948.
160. *DFPI*, vol. 3, no. 181, "Telephone Conversation: E-Sasson–A. al-Tall (Jerusalem, Dec. 13, 1948)," 331–33.
161. FO 371, 68644/E16260, Campbell to Foreign Office, Dec. 27, 1948.
162. Campbell to Wright, July 26, 1948, cited in Louis, 145.
163. RG59/890B.00, Stabler to Secretary of State, Amman tel. no. 1, Jan. 1, 1949.
164. *DFPI*, vol. 2, no. 8, Sharett to Eytan, Oct. 5, 1948, 21–29.
165. *DFPI*, vol. 2, no. 118, Sharett to Eytan, Nov. 9, 1948, 155; no. 8, Sharett to Eytan, Oct. 5, 1948, 21–29; no. 17, Ben-Gurion to Sharett, Oct. 8, 1948, 44; Ben-Gurion, 739–40.
166. FO 371, 68644/E16384, Kirkbride to Foreign Office, Amman tel. no. 982, Dec. 29, 1948.
167. Louis, 547–63.

4. UPHEAVAL AND CRISIS

1. Qustantin Zurayq, *Ma'na al-Nakba* (Beirut: Dar al-'Ilm lil-Malayim, 1948), (English trans. by R. Bayly Winder, *The Meaning of the Disaster* [Beirut: Khayat's College Book Cooperative, 1956]); al-'Arif, passim.
2. Musa Alami, "The Lesson of Palestine," *Middle East Journal*, 3, no. 4 (1949): 373–405; Zurayq, passim.
3. Michael Brecher and Hemda Ben-Yehuda, "System and Crisis in International Politics," *Review of International Studies* 11 (1985): 17–36.
4. Patrick Seale, *The Struggle for Syria* (London: Oxford Univ. Press, 1965).
5. One illustration of this came in Jan. 1949, when a number of Iraqi personalities, including Jamil Midfa'i, General Safwat, and Fadil al-Jamali were somewhat successful in softening the bitterness in Egyptian political circles toward the rest of the Arab world and in promoting the notion of strengthening the League. (al-Hashimi, 256–59; FO 371, 75331/E2039, Mack to Foreign Office, Baghdad tel. no. 137, Feb. 11, 1949.)
6. 'Abdallah's renewed promotion of his scheme in early 1949 caused much unease with both Shuqri al-Quwwatli and Ibn Sa'ud (RG59/890D.00, Childs to Secretary of State, Jidda tel. no. 88, Feb. 3, 1949; FO 371, 75077/E1726, Trott to Foreign Office, Jidda tel. no. 28, Feb. 5, 1949).
7. According to Ibn Sa'ud, a meeting in early Feb. 1949 between the Iraqi regent and 'Abdallah had dealt with "practical procedures through which they can take over the Syrian government and install a President in the event their press propaganda fails." The plan was to be carried out, he said, after the annexation of the Arab areas

of Palestine to Transjordan (RG59/890B.00, Childs to Secretary of State, Jidda tel. no. 100, Feb. 9, 1949).

8. FO 371, 75330/E38, Trott to Foreign Office, Jidda tel. no. 13, Dec. 30, 1948; 53305/E356, Houstoun-Boswell to Foreign Office, Beirut tel. no. 11, Jan. 7, 1948; 53305/E381, Broadmead to Foreign Office, Damascus tel. no. 6, Jan. 10, 1948.

9. FO 371, 75077/E1152, Broadmead to Bevin, Damascus tel. no. 7, Jan. 18, 1949. Not all Syrian officials considered the situation to be so dire. For the views of Education Minister (and former foreign minister and future prime minister) Muhsin al-Barazi, see RG59/790i.00, "Memorandum of Interview," Jan. 26, 1949, enclosure to Keeley to Secretary of State, Jan. 27, 1949.

10. RG59/890i.00, Stabler to Secretary of State, Amman tel. no. 32, Apr. 22, 1949.

11. FO 371, 75530/E713, Foreign Office to Baghdad, tel. no. 62, Jan. 12, 1949.

12. FO 371, 75330/E1111, Note by Sir H. Mack, Jan. 19, 1949; 75336/E1011, Mack to Foreign Office, Baghdad tel. no. 76, Jan. 20, 1949. Nuri noted that many of the Arab refugees would be likely to find work in the Haifa area under his plan.

13. FO 371, 75331/E1360, Kirkbride to Foreign Office, Amman tel. no. 61, Jan. 27, 1949; 75331/E1430, Kirkbride to Foreign Office, Amman tel. no. 64, Jan. 31, 1949.

14. FO 371, 75330/E813, Mack to Foreign Office, Baghdad tel. no. 59, Jan. 17, 1949.

15. FO 371, 75330/E717, Mack to Foreign Office, Baghdad tel. no. 52, Jan. 15, 1949.

16. FO 371, 75331/E1360, Kirkbride to Foreign Office, Amman tel. no. 61, Jan. 27, 1949; 75331/E1709, Kirkbride to Foreign Office, Amman tel. no. 72, Feb. 4, 1949.

17. FO 371, 75330/E813, Mack to Foreign Office, Jan. 17, 1949; 75330/E1084, Trevelyan to Foreign Office, Baghdad tel. no. 83, Jan. 22, 1949; 75331/E1712, Trevelyan to Foreign Office, Baghdad tel. no. 111, Feb. 4, 1949.

18. FO 371, 75337/E1482, Kirkbride to Foreign Office, Amman tel. no. 66, Jan. 31, 1949.

19. Israel's tactics varied. Lebanon's prime minister reported that Israel was trying to persuade his government that Britain was the greatest danger to the Middle East because it was behind 'Abdallah's Greater Syria plans (FO 371, 75539/E3924, Houstoun-Boswell to Foreign Office, Mar. 4, 1949). In Mar. 1949, Israel planted a number of articles in Lebanese and Syrian newspapers whose theme was that Israeli-Transjordanian negotiations on the future of the Greater Syria plan were about to commence—this in order to pressure the Syrians into armistice negotiations (*DFPI*, vol. 3, no. 246, Sasson to Eytan, Mar. 22, 1949, 464–67). As for financial assistance, one Syrian National party leader reported that Israel had tendered a huge sum of money—Egyptian £100,000—to the editor of Egypt's *Akhbar al-Yawm* (al-Hashimi, 261). The enormity of the sum can be discounted; the possibility of some form of monetary transfer cannot.

20. FO 371, 75335/E873, Kirkbride to Foreign Office, Amman tel. no. 41, Jan. 18, 1949.

21. *DFPI*, vol. 3, no. 186, Sasson to Sharett, Feb. 1, 1949, 344–47.

22. *DFPI*, vol. 3, no. 27, Eytan to Ben-Gurion, Sharett, and Dori, Jan. 18, 1949, 37; and Sharett's reply, no. 34, Sharett to Eytan, Jan. 19, 1949, 48.

23. *DFPI*, vol. 3, no. 99, "Meeting of the Delegations of Israel and Egypt," Feb. 5, 1949, 193–94.

24. *DFPI*, vol. 3, no. 118, Sasson to Sharett, Feb. 9, 1949, 221–22.

25. *DFPI*, vol. 3, no. 154, Sasson to Sharett, Feb. 2, 1949, 271–73.

26. FO 371, E75338/E2487, Kirkbride to Foreign Office, Amman tel. no. 97, Feb. 23, 1949.

27. FO 371, 75331/E2617, Campbell to Foreign Office, Cairo tel. no. 308, Feb. 25, 1949; 75331/E2667, Kirkbride to Foreign Office, Amman tel. no. 107, Feb. 28, 1949; 75331/E3053, Campbell to Foreign Office, Cairo tel. no. 354, Mar. 7, 1949.

28. *DFPI*, vol. 3, no. 141, Eytan to Sharett, Feb. 17, 1949, 254–56; and no. 191, Sharett to Eytan and Sasson, Feb. 15, 1949, 353–54.

29. Campbell held out no hope for Khashaba that the British government would take on the role of mediator. (FO 371, 75332/E3476, Campbell to Bevin, no. 152, Mar. 12, 1949).

30. British officials, for their part, were less sanguine about Israel's advance, owing especially to their anxiety about the safety of the British contingent in Aqaba (Pappé, *Britain and the Arab-Israeli Conflict*, 178–79). Bevin also suspected Egypt of complicity, perhaps rightly so, because the head of the Egyptian military delegation to the armistice talks understood that the nonextension of the reduced forces zone to the triangle east of the Beersheba-Eilat line was directed against Transjordan. (FO 371, 75331/E3053, Foreign Office to Amman, no. 21, Mar. 11, 1949; Israeli General Yigael Yadin, quoted in *al-Asas*, Mar. 29, 1950, enclosure to FO 371, 81932/E1071/58, Campbell to Eastern Department, no. 1062/156/50, Mar. 29, 1950).

31. FO 371, 75332/E3529, Pirie-Gordon to Foreign Office, Amman tel. no. 160, Mar. 15, 1949; 75332/E3735, enclosure to Amman Chancery to Eastern Department, no. S.143/49, Mar. 16, 1949; 75332/E3584, Campbell to Foreign Office, Cairo tel. no. 407, Mar. 16, 1949.

32. FO 371, 75332/E4004, Houstoun-Boswell to Foreign Office, Beirut tel. no. 173, Mar. 25, 1949.

33. FO 371, 75332/E4708, Kirkbride to Burrows, S.1/49, Apr. 4, 1949.

34. FO 371, 75332/E4150, Campbell to Foreign Office, Cairo tel. no. 474, Mar. 29, 1949.

35. FO 371, 75332/E4282, Campbell to Foreign Office, Cairo tel. no. 67, Mar. 31, 1949.

36. These were symbolized by 'Abdallah's tendering a "high decoration" to Khashaba; Khashaba sought Faruq's permission to accept, but the outcome is not known (Ibid).

37. FO 371, 75332/E4133, Pirie-Gordon to Foreign Office, Amman tel. no. 193, Mar. 29, 1949; FO 371, 75332/E4005, Campbell to Foreign Office, Cairo tel. no. 469, Mar. 28, 1949.

38. FO 371, 75332/E4251, Dow to Foreign Office, Jerusalem tel. no. 259, Mar. 31, 1949.

39. FO 371, 75332/E4284, Dow to Foreign Office, Jerusalem tel. no. 267, Apr. 2, 1949; 75332/E4328, Dow to Foreign Office, Jerusalem tel. no. 268, Apr. 4, 1949.

40. *DFPI*, vol. 3, no. 147, Eytan to Sharett, Feb. 21, 1949, 261–65, and exchange of letters between Eytan and Ralph Bunche, 703–21.

41. 'Abdallah al-Tall ascribed Iraq's haste to well-planted Israeli rumors of an imminent attack on Iraqi forces (al-Tall, 526–27).

42. *DFPI*, vol. 3, no. 181, Sasson–al-Tall conversation, Dec. 13, 1948, 331–33; no. 186, Sasson to Sharett, Feb. 1, 1949, 344–47; no. 248, Eytan to Sharett, Mar. 23–24, 1949, 468–72.

43. For the text of the letters exchanged on Apr. 17, 1949, between Abu al-Huda and ʿAbd al-Hadi, see *al-Asas*, Mar. 29, 1950, enclosure to FO 371, 81932/E1071/58, Campbell to Eastern Department, no. 1062/156/50, Mar. 29, 1950. Accounts of the discussions are also contained in FO 371, 75332/E5395, Kirkbride to Bevin, dispatch no. 26, Apr. 21, 1949; and 75332/E5395, Campbell to Foreign Office, Cairo tel. no. 530, Apr. 23, 1949.

44. "The lines have been brought into accordance with military positions ... always provided that this should not lead to any harm to the inhabitants of the territories affected by the change, and that no Jewish forces should enter the villages therein" (*al-Asas*, Mar. 29, 1950).

45. Shlaim, *Collusion*, 420–22.

46. *al-Asas*, Mar. 29, 1950.

47. Ibid.

48. For the texts of the armistice agreements, see John Norton Moore, 3: 380–414.

49. The best analysis of this fascinating episode can be found in Itamar Rabinovich, *The Road Not Taken* (New York: Oxford Univ. Press, 1991), 65–110.

50. FO 371, 75337/E1883, Campbell to Foreign Office, Cairo tel. no. 209, Feb. 8, 1949; al-Hashimi, 256.

51. FO 371, 53305/E381, Broadmead to Foreign Office, Damascus tel. no. 6, Jan. 9, 1949.

52. Campbell to Foreign Office, Feb. 8, 1949.

53. RG59/783.90G, Patterson to Secretary of State, Cairo tel. no. A-359, Mar. 25, 1949; FO 371, 75077/E3631, Campbell to Foreign Office, Cairo tel. no. 422, Mar. 19, 1949.

54. Patterson to Secretary of State, Mar. 25, 1949.

55. FO 371, E75138/E4236, Mack to Campbell, no. 416/1/49, Mar. 21, 1949.

56. FO 371 75074/E [unnumbered], Baghdad Embassy to Eastern Department, no. 100/18/49, Apr. 11, 1949.

57. Khalil, 2: 61–64. On Aug. 8, *al-Ahram* published what was purported to be the text of Iraq's proposal for amending the League's internal regulations governing League activities, and specifically the functioning of the secretariat-general (FO 371, 75075/E10217, enclosure to British Embassy, Alexandria, to Eastern Department, no. 553/48/49, Aug. 14, 1949).

58. Khalil, 2: 65–72.

59. Seale, 36–46; Khalid al-ʿAzm, *Mudhakkirat Khalid al-ʿAzm* (Beirut: Dar al-Muttahida lil-Nashr, 1973), 2: 181–93; Nadhir Fansa, *Ayyam Husni al-Za ʿim* (Beirut: Dar al-Afaq al-Jadida, 1982), 18.

60. FO 371, 75529/E4071 and E4072, Broadmead to Foreign Office, Damascus tel. nos. 110 and 111, Mar. 28, 1949; Foreign Office to Damascus, no. 195, Mar. 30, 1949.

61. RG84/350/2 (Syrian Politics), box 681, Keeley to Secretary of State, Damascus dispatch no. 137 and enclosure, June 9, 1949; Miles Copeland, *The Game of Nations* (London: Weidenfeld and Nicholson, 1969), 48–54; Copeland, *The Game Player:*

The Confessions of the CIA's Original Political Operative (London: Aurum, 1989), 94–95; Douglas Little, "Cold War and Covert Action: The United States and Syria, 1945–1958," *Middle East Journal* 44, no. 1 (1990): 55–57. My thanks to Itamar Rabinovich for clarifying the nature of the continuing Meade-Za'im relationship.

62. Seale, 46.

63. RG59/890D.00, Stabler to Secretary of State, Amman tel. no. 147, Apr. 4, 1949; FO 371, 75529/E4201, Pirie-Gordon to Foreign Office, Amman tel. no. 201, Mar. 31, 1949.

64. RG59/890D.00, citation contained in Patterson to Secretary of State, Cairo tel. no. A-384, Apr. 2, 1949.

65. FO 371, 75550/E4248, Mack to Foreign Office, Baghdad tel. no. 303, Mar. 31, 1949.

66. al-Hashimi, 266–68, 281; FO 371, 75530/E4605, Mack to Foreign Office, Baghdad tel. no. 328, Apr. 9, 1949.

67. al-Hashimi, 270; FO 371, 75550, Mack to Foreign Office, Baghdad tel. no. 331, Apr. 9, 1949.

68. FO 371, 75550/E4605, E4606, and E6617, Mack to Foreign Office, Baghdad tel. nos. 328, 331, Apr. 9, 1949, and no. 482, May 26, 1949; al-Hashimi, 274.

69. FO 371, 75551/E8974, trans. of *al-Misri*, June 6, 1949, of what it purports to be secret Iraqi documents, contained in enclosure to Cairo Embassy to Eastern Department, no. 40/288/49, July 15, 1949. The documents appear to be authentic; they closely parallel the official Iraqi report on the events in Syria, which forms the basis of Seale's account. See also Fansa, 110.

70. al-Hashimi, 268; Seale, 50.

71. FO 371, 75532/E4743, Trott to Foreign Office, Jidda tel. no. 79, Apr. 12, 1949.

72. *al-Misri*, June 6, 1949. Saudi Arabia's and Egypt's condition for recognition of the new Syrian government was confirmed in the subsequent account of Syria's Khalid al-'Azm (al- 'Azm, 204).

73. FO 371, 75550/E4828, Mack to Foreign Office Baghdad tel. no. 348, Apr. 15, 1949.

74. *al-Misri*, June 6, 1949.

75. FO 371, 75550/E4889, Mack to Foreign Office, Baghdad tel. no. 353, Apr. 18, 1949; *al-Misri*, June 6, 1949. Fansa, 112.

76. FO 371, 75550/E4832, Mack to Foreign Office, Baghdad tel. no. 350, Apr. 16, 1949. For the text of the 1936 Iraqi-Saudi treaty, see 'Abd al-Razzaq al-Hasani, *Ta'rikh al-Wizarat al-'Iraqiyya* (Sidon: Matba'at al-Irfan, 1940), 4:171–74.

77. *al-Misri*, June 6, 1949.

78. Seale, 55–56.

79. *al-Misri*, June 6, 1949.

80. Seale, 52–54.

81. *al-Misri*, June 6, 1949.

82. Ibid.

83. FO 371, 75532/E4820, Houstoun-Boswell to Foreign Office, Beirut tel. no. 223, Apr. 14, 1949; 75550/E5097, Houstoun-Boswell to Foreign Office, Beirut tel. no. 238, Apr. 22, 1949.

84. al-Hashimi, 276–77; FO 371, 75534/E5091, Houstoun-Boswell to Foreign Office, Beirut tel. no. 233, Apr. 21, 1949.

85. RG59/783.90D, Patterson to Secretary of State, Cairo dispatch no. 694, July 13, 1949 (information supplied by *London Times* correspondent, former Brigadier General Quilliam); Yusuf, 208–9. For details of Zaʻim's visit to Faruq, see Seale, 56, and Yusuf, 208–9. ʻAdil Arslan, who at one point served as Zaʻim's foreign minister, stated that the trip was made without the knowledge of the Syrian government (DOS, enclosure to Ankara to Department of State, no. 493 [n.d.]).

86. RG59/890D.00, Childs to Secretary of State, Jidda, tel. nos. 291 and 302, Apr. 20 and 26, 1949; FO 371, 75534/E5101, Trott to Foreign Office, Jidda tel. no. 91, Apr. 23, 1949. Ibn Saʻud was not completely pleased with the accompanying British statement that recognition should not be considered proof that it was either in favor or opposed to any particular political arrangements, whether federal or nonfederal. The Iraqis, by contrast, were quite satisfied that Britain had included this clarification in its statement (RG59/890D.00, Childs to Secretary of State, Jidda tel. no. 312, Apr. 30, 1949; FO 371, 75534/E51551, Mack to Foreign Office, Baghdad tel. no. 372, Apr. 23, 1949).

87. RG59/890D.00, Keeley to Secretary of State, Damascus tel. nos. A-121, A-249, A-124, and A-143, Apr. 27, 27, 29, and May 17, 1949; FO 371, 75535, Kirkbride to Foreign Office, Amman tel. no. 240, Apr. 27, 1949; 75536/E5378, Broadmead to Foreign Office, Damascus tel. no. 218, Apr. 28, 1949; ʻAdil Arslan, in installment no. 4 of *al-Hayat*, Aug. 1949, translation in RG59/890D.00, enclosure to dispatch no. 227, American Legation, Damascus, to Secretary of State, Sept. 20, 1949; FO 371, 75283/E7467, Glubb to Kirkbride, ALC/56, June 4, 1949, and his ADC's statement.

88. RG84/350/2 (Syrian Politics), box 681, Keeley to Secretary of State, Damascus tel. no. A-134, May 11, 1949; RG59/890D.918, R. P. Davies to State Department, Damascus dispatch no. 111, May 12, 1949.

89. FO 371, 75550/E6127, Mack to Foreign Office, Baghdad tel. no. 442, May 14, 1949.

90. RG59/890D.003, American Legation, Damascus to Department of State, dispatch 223, Dec. 21, 1949.

91. Similar overtures were made to Great Britain and the United States. Nuri also floated a trial balloon regarding possible military moves in order to gauge the British reaction (FO 371, 75550/E6617, Mack to Foreign Office, Baghdad tel. no. 482, May 26, 1949).

92. FO 371, 75551/E7434, Houstoun-Boswell to Foreign Office, Beirut tel. no. 385, June 18, 1949.

93. FO 371, 75551/E7302, Broadmead to Foreign Office, Damascus tel. no. 326, June 15, 1949.

94. FO 371, 75551/E3792, Foreign Office to H.M. Ambassador, Paris, Inward tel. no. 815, June 16, 1949.

95. FO 371, 75551/E7431, Harvey to Foreign Office, Paris tel. no. 668, June 18, 1949.

96. FO 371, 75542/E7436, Broadmead to Foreign Office, Damascus tel. no. 344, June 18, 1949; 75551/E7702, Mack to Foreign Office, Baghdad tel. no. 571, June 22,

1949; RG59/890B.00, Crocker to Secretary of State, Baghdad tel. no. 355, June 21, 1949.

97. On Syrian appeals for Iraqi intervention, see FO 371, 75550/E6617, Mack to Foreign Office, Baghdad tel. no. 482, May 26, 1949; on an Iraqi overture to involve Syria's ʿAlawi community in some type of projected military operation, see FO 371, 75550/E7165, Broadmead to Foreign Office, Damascus tel. no. 318, June 10, 1949; on an effort by the Iraqi minister in Syria, ʿAlusi, to persuade the independent politician Muhsin al-Barazi (recently relieved of his position as governor of Aleppo and a future prime minister) to lead an anti-Zaʾim movement, see FO 371, 75550/E7165, Broadmead to Foreign Office, Damascus tel. no. 320, June 11, 1949; on the Iraqi regent's support for a possible Baghdad-based Syrian government-in-exile, see FO 371, 75550/E7116, Mack to Foreign Office, Baghdad tel. no. 524, June 9, 1949; on a request for Iraqi help in setting up a provisional government, see FO 371, 75551/E7212, Mack to Foreign Office, Baghdad tel. no. 539, June 12, 1949.

98. FO 371, 75338/E8386, Broadmead to Bevin, Damascus dispatch no. 88, July 2, 1949.

99. FO 371, 75059/E8659, British Embassy, Baghdad to Eastern Department (218/152/49), July 8, 1949.

100. For a survey of these exchanges in the press, see RG59/890D.9111, Keeley to Secretary of State, Damascus tel. no. A-219, July 25, 1949; Davies to Secretary of State, Damascus tel. no. A-230, Aug. 5, 1949; 890D.00, American Legation, Damascus to Division of Near Eastern Affairs, and enclosures, Aug. 10, 1949. On Zaʾim's references to Iraqi assassination plots, see FO 371, 75539/E10311, British military attaché, Damascus, to War Office, Aug. 10, 1949; RG84/350/3 (Syrian Politics), box 681, "Memorandum to Charge d'Affaires of Conversation between Zaʾim and Major Stephen J. Meade, assistant military attaché," Aug. 11, 1949; see also RG59/890D.00, Burdett to Secretary of State, Jerusalem tel. no. 541, Aug. 30, 1949; FO 371, 75542/E9917, Trevelyan to Foreign Office, Baghdad tel. no. 714, Aug. 15, 1949.

101. RG59/890D.00, Harrison to Secretary of State, Damascus tel. no. 518, Sept. 1, 1949.

102. al-Hashimi, 279.

103. FO 371, 75538/E10027, Foreign Office to Baghdad, no. 788, Aug. 15, 1949.

104. Harrison to Secretary of State, Sept. 1, 1949; FO 371, 75539/E715, Trevelyan to Foreign Office, Baghdad tel. no. 715, Aug. 17, 1949.

105. FO 371, 75542/E9869, Pirie-Gordon to Foreign Office, Amman tel. no. 422, Aug. 14, 1949; Stabler to Secretary of State, Aug. 14, 1949.

106. RG59/890D.00, Patterson to Secretary of State, Cairo tel. no. 771, Aug. 16, 1948.

107. Interview with Hasan Yusuf (acting chief of the Royal Cabinet), RG59/890D.00, Patterson to Secretary of State, Cairo tel. no. 776, Aug. 17, 1949.

108. FO 371, 75542/E10013, Chapman-Andrews to Foreign Office, Alexandria tel. no. 109, Aug. 16, 1949.

109. al-Hashimi, 281; RG59/890D.00, Patterson to Secretary of State, Cairo tel. nos. 785 and 830, Aug. 22, Sept. 4, 1949.

110. FO 371, 75542/E10188, Scott-Fox to Foreign Office, Jidda tel. no. 272, Aug. 21, 1949; 75543/E10823, Scott-Fox to Foreign Office, Jidda tel. no. 294, Sept. 5, 1949;

RG59/890D.00, Hill to Secretary of State, Jidda tel. no. 487, Aug. 18, 1949; Eilts to Secretary of State, Jidda tel. no. 499, Aug. 22, 1949.

111. Seale, 82–83; Phoebe Marr, *The Modern History of Iraq* (Boulder, Colo.: Westview, 1985), 109.

112. For a description of the regent's high expectations governing his stopover in Damascus on Oct. 5, see Seale, 78; for his sympathy with the more activist posture being advocated by Taha al-Hashimi, see al-Hashimi, 283–84; for the differences between the regent and Nuri, see Reeva S. Simon, "The Hashemite 'Conspiracy': Hashemite Unity Attempts, 1921–1958," *International Journal of Middle East Studies* 5 (1974): 314–27.

113. Waldemar J. Gallman, *Iraq under General Nuri* (Baltimore: Johns Hopkins Univ. Press, 1964), 159–64. The book covers the period from 1954 to 1958 only, but the description of Nuri's concern with Syria seems apt for the preceding years as well.

114. al-Hashimi, 282–83.

115. RG59/890D.00, enclosures to American Embassy, Baghdad dispatch no. 308, Aug. 30, 1949.

116. FO 371, 75552/E10713 "Record of Conversation with Nazim Bey Qudsi, Syrian Minister for Foreign Affairs," M. C. G. Man, Damascus, Aug. 28, 1949.

117. FO 371, 75540/E10825, Man to Foreign Office, Damascus tel. no. 498, Sept. 4, 1949.

118. FO 371, 75552/E10826, Trevelyan to Foreign Office, Baghdad tel. no. 769, Sept. 5, 1949.

119. FO 371, 75552/E11326, Man to Foreign Office, Damascus tel. no. 517, Sept. 17, 1949.

120. FO 371, 75552/E11670, Man to Foreign Office, Damascus tel. no. 530, Sept. 25, 1949; 75552/E12008, Broadmead to Foreign Office, Damascus tel. no. 548, Oct. 3, 1949.

121. FO 371, 75552/E11783, Trevelyan to Foreign Office, Baghdad tel. no. 845A, Sept. 28, 1949.

122. FO 371, 75553/E12143, Mack to Foreign Office, Baghdad tel. no. 874, Oct. 8, 1949.

123. FO 371, 75553/E12089, Broadmead to Foreign Office, Damascus tel. no. 551, Oct. 5, 1949; 75554/E12754, "Syrian-Iraqi Federation and the Anglo-Iraqi Treaty," B. D. B. Burrows, Oct. 8, 1949.

124. FO 371, 75553/E12444, J. E. Chadwick, Oct. 20, 1949.

125. FO 371, 75555/E12946, Campbell to Foreign Office, Cairo tel. no. 1143, Oct. 26, 1949.

126. FO 371, 75553/E12254, Mack to Foreign Office, Baghdad tel. no. 875, Oct. 10, 1949.

127. FO 371, 75553/E12443, Mack to Foreign Office, Baghdad tel. no. 888, Oct. 14, 1949; 75554/E12649, Broadmead to Foreign Office, Damascus tel. no. 577, Oct. 19, 1949; 75555/E13173, Mack to Foreign Office, Baghdad tel. no. 947, Oct. 31, 1949; 75555/E13453, Mack to Foreign Office, Baghdad tel. no. 965, Nov. 8, 1949.

128. FO 371, 75553/E12138, Franks to Foreign Office, Washington tel. no. 4830,

Oct. 7, 1949; RG59/790D.90G, "Memorandum of Conversation—Closer Relations between Syria and Iraq," Dec. 12, 1949; al-Hashimi, 295; Seale, 81.

129. ʿAbdallah and his ministers were like-minded in their opposition to a Syrian-Iraqi union, although not for the same reasons. The king's motivations were personal and dynastic. His ministers were convinced that the union would be unworkable, and that its eventual breakup would lead to chaos in Syria, which would draw Jordan in as well. This in turn, went the scenario, would provide Israel with an opportunity to move against the Jordanian-held areas of Palestine. (FO 371, 75553/E12316, Kirkbride to Foreign Office, Amman tel. no. 513, Oct. 11, 1949.)

130. Seale, 47n; al-Hashimi, 282; RG59/890D.00, Bruce to Secretary of State, Paris tel. no. 4414, Oct. 21, 1949; RG84/350/4 (Syrian Politics), box 681, Keeley to Secretary of State, Damascus tel. no. A-342, Dec. 28, 1949.

131. FO 371, 75555/E12954, Campbell to Foreign Office, Cairo tel. no. 1138, Oct. 25, 1949.

132. FO 371, 75076/E12322, Campbell to Foreign Office, Cairo tel. no. 1041A, Oct. 11, 1949.

133. "Dhikrayat al-Amin al-ʿAm Lijamiʿat al-Duwal al-ʿArabiyya ʿAzzam Pasha," al-Usbuʿ al-ʿArabi, Feb. 7, 1972.

134. These had been formally submitted to the League at the beginning of August (RG59/890B.00, Patterson to Secretary of State, Cairo tel. no. A-848, Aug. 8, 1949). For the official text of Nuri's proposals in Oct. 1949, see RG59/890B.00, enclosure to American Embassy, Cairo, to Secretary of State, dispatch no. 932, Oct. 21, 1949.

135. Nazim al-Qudsi was distressed by what he termed Nuri's "sabotage." By pushing his reorganization proposal, Nuri gave the impression that he was deeply hostile to the League and even desirous of its breakup. This, according to Qudsi, aroused animosity in the League and spoiled the atmosphere for sober reflection on any other project with which Nuri was associated. (FO 371, 75555/E12946, Campbell to Foreign Office, Cairo tel. no. 1143, Oct. 26, 1949.) For ʿAzzam's expressions of satisfaction with the way things turned out, see RG59/890B.00, "Memorandum of Conversation," enclosure no. 1 to Cairo dispatch no. 961, Oct. 29, 1949.

136. FO 371, 75080/E13402, Campbell to Foreign Office, Cairo Saving tel. no. 164, Nov. 5, 1949; 75080/E13391, British Embassy, Cairo, to African Department, no. 1150/14/490, Nov. 10, 1949.

137. FO 371, 75076/E14607, "Memorandum on the Proceedings of the 11th Regular Session of the Council of the Arab League held at Cairo from 17th to 31st of October 1949," enclosure to Troutbeck to Bevin, dispatch no. 42/31/8/354, Nov. 22, 1949.

138. FO 371, 75540/E10825, Man to Foreign Office, Damascus tel. no. 498, Sept. 4, 1949.

139. RG59/890B.00, "Memorandum of Conversation between Nazim al-Qudsi and Phillip W. Ireland," enclosure to Caffery to Secretary of State, Cairo dispatch no. 959, Oct. 29, 1949. As a whole, the Syrian delegation was divided over the Egyptian proposal. (RG59/890B.00, Caffery to Secretary of State, Cairo tel. no. A-1126, Oct. 24, 1949.)

140. FO 371, 75080/E15092, Foreign Office Minutes (L. G. Thirkell, Jan. 5, 1950),

and Mack to Atlee, Baghdad Confidential no. 236 (1082/16/49), Dec. 13, 1949, and enclosure; RG59/890B.00, Caffery to Secretary of State, Cairo tel. no. A-1253, Nov. 19, 1949.

141. An unofficial text of the Syrian proposal was published in the Damascus newspaper *al-Sha'b* on Dec. 7, 1949. A translation of the text is contained in enclosure to RG59/890B.20, American Legation, Damascus, to Secretary of State, dispatch no. 267, Dec. 9, 1949.

142. RG59/890B.00, Caffery to Secretary of State, Cairo tel. no. 1263, Nov. 21, 1949.

143. FO 371, 75080/E15092, Mack to Atlee, Baghdad dispatch no. 238, Dec. 13, 1949.

144. For the text of the draft, which was based on the Egyptian proposal but was also intended to satisfy the Iraqis (by establishing a Permanent Military Committee) and the Lebanese (by including references to economic development and cooperation), see RG59/890B.20, enclosure to Caffery to Secretary of State, Cairo dispatch no. 1090, Dec. 8, 1949; for the text of the adjournment communiqué, see RG59/890B.20, Howard to Secretary of State, Cairo tel. no. A-1294, Nov. 29, 1949.

145. al-Hashimi, 299–301.

146. Seale, 83. On the other hand, Egyptian Prime Minister Sirri Pasha felt that with Nuri's absence, the movement in Iraq for unity would lose some of its impetus (RG59/890G.002, Caffery to Secretary of State, Cairo tel. no. A-1224, Nov. 15, 1949).

147. ISA, 2408/20/Aleph (159/404/Aleph), "Yedi'ot Lenatziguyot Yisrael, 50: Hahafikha Hashlishit Vetotza'oteha, Tasbir no. 2"; *Barada,* Dec. 20, 1949 enclosure to RG59/890D.00, Davies to Secretary of State, Damascus dispatch 273, Dec. 21, 1949.

148. RG59/890D.00, Keeley to Secretary of State, Damascus tel. 721, Dec. 19, 1949; Seale, 84–86; Khadduri, "Scheme of Fertile Crescent Unity," 163–67.

149. For background on the *PPS,* see Daniel Pipes, "Radical Politics and the Syrian Social Nationalist Party," *International Journal of Middle East Studies* 20, no. 3 (1988): 303–24.

150. FO 371, 75541/E14465, Harmar (British military attaché) to Hewitt (War Office), Nov. 29, 1949.

151. FO 371, 75544/E15275, Campbell to Foreign Office, Dec. 28, 1949.

152. Text is contained in RG59/890D.00, Caffery to Secretary of State, Cairo tel. no. A-1365, Dec. 20, 1949.

153. RG59/783.00, Keeley to Secretary of State Damascus tel. no. 17, Jan. 9, 1950.

154. FO 371, 82409/EQ1017/8, enclosure to Mack to Bevin, no. 37, Feb. 13, 1950.

155. Detailed accounts of internal Iraqi goings-on can be found in 82407/EQ1016/2, Mack to Wright, no. 1018/1/50, Jan. 9, 1950, and 82409/EQ1017/8, Mack to Bevin, no. 37, Feb. 13, 1950; see also 'Ali Jawdat, *Dhikrayat, 1900–1958* (Beirut: Matba'at al-Wafa', 1967), 275–85.

156. Seale seems to argue that a swift Iraqi move in April would have been able to establish a fait accompli without drawing a counter-response, thanks to initial Egyptian hesitations over their own role in the Arab framework (Seale, 57).

157. RG59/783.00, Department of State to Tel Aviv, no. 15, Jan. 17, 1950; FO 371, 82790/EY1022/10, Frank to Foreign Office, Washington tel. no. 176, Jan. 17, 1950.

158. Leonard Binder, "The Tragedy of Syria," review article, *World Politics* 19, no. 3 (1967): 521–49; Seale, 3.

159. *FRUS*, 1949, Chargé in Transjordan (Stabler) to Secretary of State, Apr. 13, 1949, 916–17.

160. FO 371, 75076/E13646, Kirkbride to Burrows, Amman dispatch no. S.152/49, Nov. 7, 1949.

161. FO 371, 75076/E13672, Kirkbride to Burrows, Amman dispatch no. S.152/49, Nov. 7, 1949.

162. FO 371, 75333/E14277, Kirkbride to Burrows, Amman dispatch no. S.152/49, Nov. 17, 1949.

163. For reports on these meetings, see Eliahu Sasson's letters from Lausanne to Moshe Sharett, *Yedi'ot Aharonot*, Feb. 4, 11, 18, 1972.

164. Sasson to Sharett, Aug. 21, 1949 (*Yedi'ot Aharonot*, Feb. 11, 1972); *DFPI*, vol. 5, no. 125, "Meeting: A. Eban and G. Rafael–M. Abd al-Mun'im Mustafa (Geneva, 27 Feb. 1950)," 170–73.

165. Sela, *Mimaga'im Lemasa 'Umatan*, passim.

166. This account is derived from FO 371, 75345/E14817, Campbell to Kirkbride, Cairo to Amman, Saving tel. no. 180, Dec. 8, 1949; 75345/E14875, Campbell to Strang, Cairo dispatch no. 1/135/490, Nov. 25, 1949, and Nov. 30, 1949; and 75345/E14984, Campbell to Foreign Office, Cairo tel. no. 1340, Dec. 15, 1949.

167. FO 371, 75344/E14717, Foreign Office to Washington, no. 11685, Dec. 22, 1949.

168. *FRUS*, 1950, Ambassador in Egypt (Caffery) to Secretary of State, Jan. 9, 1950, 678–79, and Ambassador in Israel (McDonald) to Secretary of State, Mar. 19, 1950, 796–97.

169. FO 371, 75344/E14375, Kirkbride to Foreign Office, Amman tel. no. 601, Nov. 29, 1949; 75344/E14529, Kirkbride to Foreign Office, Amman tel. no. 611, Dec. 3, 1949.

170. Shlaim, *Collusion*, 527–32.

171. FO 371, 82177/EE1015/21, Kirkbride to Foreign Office, Amman tel. no. 64, Feb. 10, 1950.

172. ISA, 130.02/2453/2, Reuven Shiloah, "Pegisha no. 9 Shel Yisrael-Yarden, February 17, 1950," and "Siha 'Asirit Shel Yisrael-Yarden, February 24, 1950."

173. C. Ernest Dawn rightly points out the delay. But his explanations for it are contradictory. Moreover, they are not borne out by the primary sources now available for perusal. At one point, he states that Egypt's new Wafd government (which took office in mid-January 1950) restrained itself from attacking Jordan because it was awaiting the outcome of Egypt's own probings. These probings were little more than exploratory, however, and thus could not have been an important part of Egypt's calculations. Egyptian hopes may have also been briefly raised, Dawn notes, by the PCC's seeming tilt toward Egypt on Mar. 2. This also does not seem crucial, for the PCC-sponsored negotiations bore scant chance of a breakthrough, and the Egyptians had been made thoroughly aware of Israel's unwillingness to countenance territorial concessions. (Dawn, "Pan-Arabism and the Failure of Israeli-Jordanian Peace Negotiations, 1950," in *Islam and Its Cultural Divergence*, ed. G. L. Tikku (Urbana: Univ. of Illinois Press, 1971), 41–42; see also Schueftan, 231–37.)

174. DOS, 784.00, Caffery to Secretary of State, Cairo dispatch no. 478, Mar. 14, 1950, and enclosure, "Egypt's Attitude to Future Settlement in Palestine."

175. *DFPI*, vol. 5, no. 124, G. Rafael to W. Eytan, Mar. 3, 1950, 168–69; no. 125, "Meeting: A. Eban and G. Rafael–M. Abd al-Mun'im Mustafa (Geneva, 27 Feb. 1950)," 170–73; no. 129, M. Sharett to A. Eban and G. Rafael (Geneva), Mar. 6, 1950, 176–77.

176. FO 371, 82178/EE1015/34, Kirkbride to Foreign Office, Amman tel. no. 89, Mar. 1, 1950, and enclosure, "A Translation of a Decision Taken by the Council of Ministers on the 26th of February, 1950."

177. FO 371, 82178/EE1015/36, Kirkbride to Foreign Office, Amman tel. no. 91, Mar. 2, 1950.

178. FO 371, 82705/ET1016/4, Kirkbride to Bevin, Amman dispatch no. 19, Mar. 6, 1950.

179. *FRUS*, 1950, Ambassador in Israel (McDonald) to Secretary of State, Mar. 9, 1950, 796–77.

180. DOS/684.85, Drew to Secretary of State, Amman dispatch no. 43, Mar. 17, 1950.

181. For a particularly venomous attack on ʿAbdallah, see *al-Misri*, Mar. 19, 1950, cited by Abidi, *Jordan*, 27n. 43.

182. The decision that the invitation should specify a Government of All-Palestine representative, and not just "an Arab representative of Palestine," was made by Nahhas Pasha after intensive lobbying by the mufti and Hilmi Pasha, and over the strong opposition of Nahhas's foreign minister and ʿAzzam Pasha. ʿAzzam characterized it as a "needless wounding" of ʿAbdallah. (DOS/786.00, Caffery to Secretary of State, Cairo dispatch no. 662, Apr. 4, 1950.) Even so, a distinction was made between the League Council and the Political Committee (which often met between Council sessions and at the same level of representation). The Palestinian representative was not invited to the latter's sessions, and it was only on Apr. 13 that a decision was made to invite him to those Committee meetings dealing with Palestine. (DOS/786.00. Caffery to Secretary of State, Cairo tel. no. 969, May 2, 1950.)

183. FO 371, 81930/E1071/11, Kirkbride to Foreign Office, Amman tel. no. 126, Mar. 29, 1950.

184. A translation of the regent's letter of Mar. 28, 1950, is found in enclosure to FO 371, 81930/E1071/20, Mack to Furlonge, Baghdad dispatch no. 1067/70/50, Mar. 29, 1950.

185. DOS/786.00, Caffery to Secretary of State, Cairo tel. no. 307, Mar. 29, 1950; FO 371, 81930/E0171/14, Mack to Foreign Office, Baghdad tel. no. 168, Mar. 29, 1950.

186. DOS/788.00, Crocker to Secretary of State, Baghdad dispatch no. 566, May 9, 1950.

187. FO 371, 81930/E1071/17, Troutbeck to Foreign Office, BMEO tel. no. 81, Mar. 31, 1950.

188. FO 371, 81930/E1071/18, Kirkbride to Foreign Office, Amman tel. no. 127, Apr. 1, 1950.

189. ʿAbdallah immediately told the U.S. ambassador in Amman that he intended to resume negotiations with Israel after the elections. If they did not accept his explanation that the talks concerned an extension of the armistice, he said, he was fully

prepared to face expulsion. (DOS/786.00, Drew to Secretary of State, Amman tel. no. 64, Apr. 3, 1950.)
    190. Text of the resolution is in Khalil, 2: 165–66.
    191. Text of the resolution is in Khalil, 2: 166–67.
    192. DOS/786.00, Caffery to Secretary of State, Cairo tel. no. 353, Apr. 9, 1950.
    193. DOS/786.00, Caffery to Secretary of State, Cairo tel. no. 378, Apr. 13, 1950.
    194. FO 371, 82710/ET1024/21, Campbell to Foreign Office, Cairo tel. no. 327, Apr. 11, 1950.
    195. Text of the resolution is in Khalil, 2:166.
    196. DOS/788.00, Crocker to Secretary of State, Baghdad dispatch no. 566, May 9, 1950.
    197. DOS/786.00, Ireland to Secretary of State, Cairo tel. no. 777, Apr. 17, 1950.
    198. FO 371, 82719/ET1081/6, Kirkbride to Furlonge, Amman dispatch no. S.102/5/50, Apr. 28, 1950.
    199. FO 371, 82718/ET1081/11, Mack to Foreign Office, Baghdad tel. no. 211, Apr. 22, 1950.
    200. ISA, 130.00/24533/2, "Pegisha 'Im 'Hayogev'" (Moshe Sasson), Apr. 24, 1950.
    201. Text of the resolution is in Khalil, 1:54.
    202. Relevant sections of the speech are contained in FO 371, 81932/E1071/60, Kirkbride to Furlonge, Amman dispatch no. S.103/4/50, May 4, 1950, and 81932/E1071/67, trans. from *al-Zaman* (Cairo), May 9, 1950. For British (and Egyptian) embarrassment with the sources of some of Abu al-Huda's comments, see 81932/E1071/58, Campbell to Eastern Department, Cairo dispatch no. 1062/156/50, May 9, 1950; and Kirkbride to Furlonge, May 4, 1950.
    203. RG59/785.022, Howard to Department of State, Cairo tel. no. 1056, May 11, 1950.
    204. A rare public acknowledgment of the contradiction between the Political Committee's resolution of Apr. 12, 1948, and Arab acceptance of the Lausanne Protocol was made by Iraq's minister without portfolio, Khalil Kinna, in a statement to the Iraqi Broadcasting Service on May 16, 1948. (FO 371, 81932/E1071/68, enclosure to Mack to Wright, Baghdad dispatch no. 1077/81/50, May 18, 1950.)
    205. The attacks in early May on Jordan in the pro-palace *Journal d'Égypte* and *Akhbar al-Yawm* were more unyielding than those in the Wafd's *al-Misri*. (Cf. FO 371, 81931/E1071/39, Campbell to Foreign Office, Cairo tel. no. 389, May 2, 1950, and 81931/E1071/42, Campbell to Foreign Office, Cairo tel. no. 398, May 6, 1950.) According to Iraq's Salih Jabr, the Wafd government was giving Faruq more or less a free hand in Arab affairs provided that he left them alone in internal affairs. (FO 371, 81932/E1071/61, Mack to Wright, Baghdad dispatch no. 1077/67/50, May 11, 1950.) This may have been an overstatement.
    206. FO 371, 81931/E1071/41, Campbell to Foreign Office, Cairo tel. no. 396, May 5, 1950.
    207. DOS/786.00, Caffery to Secretary of State, Cairo tel. no. 514, May 15, 1950. FO 371, 81932/E1071/75, Man to Furlonge, Damascus dispatch no. 10709/48/50, May 29, 1950. For the formal arguments presented by the two sides, see Hussein A. Hassouna,

The League of Arab States and Regional Disputes (Dobbs Ferry, N.Y.: Oceana, 1975), 36–37.

208. FO 371, 81931/E1071/53(A), Campbell to Foreign Office, Cairo tel. no. 417, May 15, 1950.

209. The decision not to withdraw from the League was commensurate with Kirkbride's advice. (FO 371, 81931/E1071/49 and 50, Kirkbride to Foreign Office, Amman tel. nos. 184 and 185, May 14, 1950.

210. Text of the resolution is in DOS/786.00, Caffery to Secretary of State, Cairo tel. no. 1119, May 17, 1950.

211. Tawfiq al-Suwaydi's tortuous maneuvering (accepting that the annexation was a violation of a League resolution, abstaining on the expulsion recommendation, and pushing for the Council meeting's postponement) was sharply criticized by Nuri al-Sa'id and his followers, as it did not offer full backing for Jordan. The regent tried to stay aloof while remaining firmly against any notion of agreeing to Jordan's expulsion (FO 371, 81932/E1071/68, Mack to Wright, Baghdad dispatch no. 1077/81/50, and enclosure; 81932/E1071/72, Mack to Bevin, Baghdad dispatch no. 1077/86/50, May 24, 1950).

212. RG59/787.00, Embassy Baghdad to Department of State, no. 51, July 12, 1950; FO 371, 81933/E1071/83, Man to Foreign Office, Damascus tel. no. 154, June 10, 1950.

213. For the correspondence between Ibn Sa'ud and 'Abdallah during this period, see FO 371, 81933/E1071/93, enclosure to Trott to Younger, Jidda dispatch no. 85, June 10, 1950.

214. FO 371, 81932/E1071/75, Man to Furlonge, Damascus dispatch no. 10709/48/50, May 29, 1950.

215. FO 371, 81932, E1071/70, Kirkbride to Foreign Office, Amman tel. no. 209, May 30, 1950.

216. FO 371, 81932/E1071/19, Mack to Foreign Office, Baghdad tel. no. 24, June 7, 1950, and 81932/E1071/80, Mack to Foreign Office, Baghdad tel. no. 314, June 10, 1950.

217. Text of the government communiqué is contained in FO 371, 81932/E1071/71, Kirkbride to Foreign Office, Amman tel. no. 213, May 31, 1950.

218. Text of the resolution is in DOS/784.02, Caffery to Secretary of State, Cairo tel. no. 664, June 19, 1950.

219. RG59/787.00, Embassy Baghdad to Department of State, no. 51, July 12, 1950.

220. FO 371, 81933/E1071/102, Trevelyan to Younger, Baghdad dispatch no. 162, July 13, 1950.

221. FO 371, E1071/101, Kirkbride to Younger, Amman dispatch no. 63, June 29, 1950. The second secretary-general of the Arab League incorrectly states that Jordan accepted the League formula (Hassouna, 40–41).

222. FO 371, 82178/EE1015/53, Helm to Foreign Office, Tel Aviv tel. no. 201, Apr. 27, 1950; DOS/684A.85, McDonald to Secretary of State, Tel Aviv tel. no. 309, Apr. 27, 1950.

223. Sela, *Mimaga'im Lemasa 'Umatan*, 50.

224. FO 371, 82718/EE1015/55, Kirkbride to Foreign Office, Amman tel. no. 172, May 4, 1950.

225. Sinai and Pollack are explicit about this (Anne Sinai and Allen Pollack, eds. *The Hashemite Kingdom of Jordan and the West Bank* [New York: American Academic Association for Peace in the Middle East, 1977], 27). Rubin suggests it (215).

5. SOLIDIFICATION AND TRANSITION, 1950–1954

1. Louis, 322–44; RG59/890B.00, Tuck to Secretary of State, Cairo dispatch no. 156 and enclosure, Feb. 25, 1948; RG59/890B.00, Memminger to Secretary of State, Damascus dispatch no. 69 and enclosures, Feb. 25, 1948; RG59/890B.00, Pinkerton to Secretary of State, Beirut tel. no. A-100, Mar. 9, 1948.

2. In a Nov. 14, 1950, speech, Nuri bluntly advocated an alliance with the West and scorned the idea that Iraqi neutrality between East and West could safeguard Iraq's independence. The speech drew sharply negative reactions from radical-nationalist elements in Iraq. Subsequently, Nuri attempted to conciliate his opponents by stressing the need for a change in Anglo-Iraqi relations and for collective *Arab* defense of the Arab world (FO 371, 82408/1016/32, Mack [Baghdad] to Bevin, Nov. 28, 1950; RG59/787.00, Olcott-Allen to Department of State, Baghdad dispatch no. 822, Feb. 12, 1951).

3. RG59/783.00, Davies to Department of State, Damascus dispatch no. 375, Feb. 27, 1951.

4. Seale, 101–5.

5. Raymond Hare, oral history, Columbia University Oral History Collection, 56, cited in Rubin, 217.

6. FO 371, 81913/E1024/14, Mack to Bevin, Baghdad dispatch no. 253, Nov. 29, 1950.

7. FO 371, 81913/E1024/15, Montagu-Pollock to Bevin, Damascus dispatch no. 199, Dec. 15, 1950.

8. Ibid. Egyptian officials were divided on Qudsi's motives, with some being suspicious that he was fronting for advocates of a Syrian-Iraqi federation and others seeing him as taking a disinterested, businesslike attitude (FO 371, 81935/E1071/62, Chapman-Andrews to Foreign Office, Cairo tel. no. 203, Nov. 11, 1950).

9. For the scathingly negative press reaction in Egypt to the meetings, see DOS, American Embassy, Cairo to Department of State, dispatch no. 1875, Feb. 6, 1951.

10. FO 371, 91205/E1072/2, Stevenson to Foreign Office, Cairo tel. no. 44, Jan. 20, 1951.

11. FO 371, 91202/E1071/20, Stevenson to Foreign Office, Cairo tel. no. 60, Jan. 26, 1951.

12. RG59/787.00, Tenney to Department of State, Baghdad dispatch no. 821, Feb. 2, 1951; ALC protocols, 13th meeting, 3d sess., Feb. 2, 1951, 41–42.

13. RG59/787.00, Tenney to Department of State, Baghdad dispatch no. 821, Feb. 2, 1951.

14. Press reports of Jordan's terms for adhering to the pact varied slightly. In substance, they included (1) the creation of a two-tiered alliance, concentrating on those states adjacent to Israel and capable of military response and (2) modifying ARTICLE 2's definition of armed aggression specifically to limit it to "foreign" aggression. While

the Jordanians explained this by stating that aggression by one Arab state against another was inconceivable and incongruent with the spirit of the pact, the modification was intended to rule out any possible invoking of the pact to block ʿAbdallah's Greater Syria ambitions. Other terms were (3) making the Joint Defense Council's decisions binding only on those states that adhered to them (instead of the two-thirds vote being binding on all); and (4) making sure that the pact did not invalidate the obligations and rights deriving from any existing treaty. (The translation of the purported text, as published by *al-Misri* on Feb. 1, 1951, is contained in FO 371, 91205/E1072/5. See also FO 371, 91202/E1071/22, 28, and 30, Rapp to Foreign Office, Cairo (British Middle East Office) tel. nos. 41, 44, and 53, Jan. 27, 29, and Feb. 1, 1951; RG9/786.00, Fritzlan to Secretary of State, Amman tel. no. 133, Feb. 3, 1951.)

15. RG59/787.00, Olcott-Allen to Department of State, Baghdad dispatch no. 822, Feb. 12, 1951.

16. *FRUS*, 1951, Fritzlan (Amman) to Department of State, Mar. 29, 1951, 977–81.

17. Asher Goren, *Haliga Haʿaravit* (Tel Aviv: ʿEynot, 1954), 287.

18. Ibid, 282–85.

19. PMC members had to be nationals of the participating countries, so as to exclude Glubb Pasha and other British officers in Jordan (RG84/317, box 1 [Dhahran], "Implementation of Arab League Collective Security Pact," WDGS Intelligence Report no. R-234-53, Cairo, Oct. 10, 1953).

20. For example, Egypt delayed an Iraqi-requested discussion on on implementing the pact during the Mar. 1953 Arab League Political Committee meeting. (Goren, 284–86.)

21. According to Iraq's Foreign Minister Tawfiq al-Suwaydi, the chiefs of staff agreed on the establishment of a single Arab command in the event of hostilities (RG59/785.5, Berry to Department of State, Baghdad dispatch no. 216, Sept. 21, 1953).

22. See Daniel Dishon and Bruce Maddy-Weitzman, "Inter-Arab Relations," *Middle East Contemporary Survey* 6 (1981–1982): 235, 256, and Maddy-Weitzman, "Inter-Arab Relations," *Middle East Contemporary Survey* 8 and 9 (1983–1984 and 1984–1985): 119.

23. *FRUS*, 1951, Ambassador in the United Kingdom (Gifford) to Department of State, Oct. 9, 1951, 395–96.; text of the proposal in Khalil, 2: 314–15.

24. Text of statement is contained in Khalil, 2: 316–17. The liaison system was designed not only to bring about Arab participation but also to try to overcome the difficulty of associating the Arab states and Israel under the same umbrella (FO 371, 91635/EQ1022/10, "The Arab States and Middle East Defense," brief prepared for the Secretary of State, n.d.).

25. FO 371, 91204/E1071/111, Stevenson to Foreign Office, Alexandria tel. no. 690, Oct. 10, 1951.

26. *FRUS*, 1951, Acting Secretary of State to Secretary of State, at Paris, and Acting Secretary of State to the Embassy in France, Nov. 18, 1951, 248–49.

27. For Ibn Saʿud's unhappiness with the Egyptians, see DOS 786.00, Kopper to Jones, NEA memorandum, Oct. 22, 1951.

28. Text of the resolution in FO 371, 90141/E1051/287, Montagu-Pollock to Foreign Office, Damascus tel. no. 298, Oct. 10, 1951.

29. FO 371, 91842/EY1015/27, Montagu-Pollock to Eden, Damascus dispatch no. 172, Nov. 20, 1951.

30. Ibid.

31. FO 371, 91850/EY1027/2, 3, Montagu-Pollock to Foreign Office, Damascus tel. nos. 332 and 335, Nov. 5 and 7, 1951.

32. For Hakim's account of the events, including a statement that he retained his respect and esteem for Qudsi, see Hasan al-Hakim, *Mudhakkirati, 1920–1958* (Beirut: Dar al-Kitab al-Jadid, 1966), 2: 64–69.

33. *al-Jil al-Jadid*, the newspaper of the *Parti Populaire Syrien* (PPS), of which Shishakli had previously been a member, was strongly critical during this period of Egypt's opposition to the Four-Power proposals, and its monopolization, in general, of the Arab League. Shishakli was more circumspect, but his views were not significantly at variance with this line (FO 371, 9185/EY1027/1, 6, Montagu-Pollock to Foreign Office, Damascus tel. nos. 319, 360, Oct. 25, Nov. 27, 1951).

34. FO 371, 98279/E1193/59, Samuel to Ross, Damascus dispatch no. 10104/54/52, July 17, 1952.

35. Seale, 122–24.

36. FO 371, 90146/JE1051/413, Stevenson to Foreign Office, Cairo tel. no. 976, Nov. 11, 1951.

37. E.g., the granting of "self-government (Dominion Status)" to the Sudan, to be accompanied by an internationally supervised referendum and a British-Egyptian agreement on the future of their respective military forces there (FO 371, 91246, Harvey to Foreign Office, Paris Saving tel. no. 667, Nov. 10, 1951).

38. FO 371, 90151/JE1051/534, 543, Troutbeck to Foreign Office, Baghdad tel. nos. 977, 991, Dec. 23, 28, 1951; *FRUS*, 1951, Ambassador in Egypt (Caffery) to Department of State, Dec. 18, 1951, 441–42.

39. FO 371, 98278/E1193/2, Bowker (Foreign Office) to Troutbeck, Jan. 11, 1952; "Minute" by J. C. Wardrop, Jan. 3, 1952.

40. FO 371, 91638/EQ10325/1, Troutbeck to Foreign Office, Baghdad tel. no. 657, Aug. 16, 1951; 91638/EQ10325/3, Furlonge to Troutbeck, Foreign Office Confidential, Oct. 11, 1951.

41. Ibid; FO 371/91246, Harvey to Foreign Office, Paris Saving tel. no. 666, Nov. 10, 1951; and 9104/JE1051/426G, "Secretary of State's conversation with the Regent and the Prime Minister of Iraq," Eden to Troutbeck, Foreign Office tel. no. 244, Nov. 17, 1951.

42. DOS/780.5, Crocker to Department of State, Baghdad dispatch no. 822a, Mar. 5, 1952.

43. FO 371, 98278/E1193/1, "Iraq and the Middle East Command," A. D. M. Ross (n.d.). The chiefs of staff later urged the Foreign Office, but without avail, to emphasize to Nuri that all members of the MEC, regardless of when they joined, would be on completely equal terms (FO 371, 98278/E1193/29, Secretary of Chiefs of Staff Committee to Ross, Mar. 5, 1952).

44. RG84/321, box 2 (Amman) "Prospects for an Inclusive Middle East Defense Organization," SE-23, Mar. 17, 1952.

45. Rubin, 216–36.

46. RG84/321, box 2 (Amman) "Prospects for an Inclusive Middle East Defense Organization," SE-23, Mar. 17, 1952.

47. Shanqiti signed the checks transmitted to some of the conspirators (FO 371, 82797/EY1038/1, Montagu-Pollock to Attlee, Damascus dispatch no. 166, Oct. 2, 1950).

48. See the report of the Military Judge examiner, RG59/783.00, enclosure no. 1 to Davies to Department of State, Damascus dispatch no. 256, Dec. 7, 1950.

49. Kirkbride repeated for the umpteenth time his inability to dissuade 'Abdallah from involvement in Syria. (FO 371, 82786/EY1015/45, Kirkbride to Bevin, Amman dispatch no. 110, Oct. 10, 1950.)

50. This was made clear to Lieutenant Colonel Kallas upon his initial overture to the Jordanians in Feb. 1950. (FO 371, 82785/EY1015/10, Kirkbride to Furlonge, Amman Dispatch no. S.103/3/50, May 15, 1950.)

51. For the essential details surrounding the trial, see FO 371, 91851A/EY10380/1, Montagu-Pollock to Bevin, Damascus Dispatch no. 21, Feb. 5, 1951.

52. FO 371, 82797/EY10380/3, Montagu-Pollock to Furlonge, Damascus dispatch 10303/45/50, Nov. 15, 1950.

53. FO 371, 82797/EY10380/1, Montagu-Pollock to Attlee, Oct. 2, 1950.

54. For a sharp official exchange and subsequent media comments, see FO 371, 91875/EY1902/6, and enclosure, Walker to Furlonge, Amman dispatch no. S.190/5/16/51, June 18, 1951; 91875/EY1902/7 and enclosure, Damascus Legation to Eastern Department, dispatch no. 19004/10/51, June 18, 1951; 91875/EY1902/9 and enclosure, Amman Legation to Eastern Department, dispatch no. S.190/5/24/1, July 2, 1951.

55. The accepted French and English translations, *Phalanges de la Redemption Arabe* and Arab Redemption Society, respectively, fail to convey the quasi-religious concept of "sacrifice" embodied in the word *fida'*.

56. Ruwayha later claimed that he possessed certain incriminating evidence against Shishakli. (FO 371, 91842/EY1015/14, Damascus Legation to Eastern Department, dispatch no. 90101/49/51, June 11, 1951.

57. Anwar el-Sadat, *In Search of Identity* (New York: Harper and Row, 1977), 59–67.

58. FO 371, 82786/EY1015/57, Montagu-Pollock to Bevin, Damascus dispatch no. 190, Dec. 4, 1950.

59. FO 371, 81913/E1024/16, British Embassy, Cairo, to Eastern Department, dispatch no. 1077/200/50, Dec. 21, 1950.

60. FO 371, 82786/EY1015/53, Montagu-Pollock to Foreign Office, Damascus tel. no. 309, Nov. 15, 1950.

61. FO 371, 82786/EY1015/51, Montagu-Pollock to Foreign Office, Damascus tel. no. 296, Nov. 7, 1950.

62. RG59/783.00, Hare to Department of State, Jidda tel. no. 198, Dec. 23, 1950; Cannon to Secretary of State, Damascus tel. no. 240, Nov. 15, 1950; al-Hashimi, 319; FO 371, 82784/EY1013/12, "Political Summary No. 11 for the Month of November, 1950," issued by the British Legation, Damascus.

63. FO 371, 91842/EY1015/14, British Legation, Damascus, to Eastern Department, dispatch no. 10101/49/51, June 6, 1951.

64. FO 371, 91842/EY1015/13, Damascus Chancery to Eastern Department, dispatch no. 10101/42/51, May 23, 1951.

65. FO 371, 81913/E1024/8, Montagu-Pollock to Foreign Office, Damascus tel. no. 312, Jan. 17, 1950; RG59/783.00, Cannon to Secretary of State, Damascus tel. no. 250, Nov. 18, 1950; Tenney to Secretary of State, Baghdad tel. no. 301, Nov. 29, 1950.

66. For the text of Qudsi's plan, see Khalil, 2: 40–46.

67. Seale, 105–6.

68. RG59/783.00, Cannon to Secretary of State, Damascus tel. no. 369, Feb. 1, 1951.

69. FO 371, 91842/EY1015/2, Montagu-Pollock to Foreign Office, Damascus tel. no. 52, Mar. 11, 1951.

70. FO 371, 91842/EY1015/778, Montagu-Pollock to Furlonge, Damascus dispatch no. 101/19/51, Mar. 20, 1951; Seale, 106.

71. FO 371, 82785/EY1015/21, Man to Younger, Damascus dispatch no. 91, June 11, 1950.

72. RG59/683.84A, Crocker to Secretary of State, Baghdad tel. no. 721, May 17, 1951.

73. RG59/683.84A, Fritzlan to Secretary of State, Amman tel. no. 203, May 19, 1951.

74. RG59/683.84A, Caffery to Secretary of State, Cairo tel. no. 190, May 18, 1951.

75. RG59/680.84A, Caffery to Secretary of State, Cairo tel. no. 1199, May 20, 1951; ISA, 24/1101, Sasson (Ankara) to Divon, May 30, 1951. Khalid al-'Azm incorrectly states in his memoirs that they in fact did so (268).

76. RG59/683.84A, Cannon to Secretary of State, Damascus tel. no. 636, May 17, 1951; Crocker to Secretary of State, Baghdad tel. no. 750, May 29, 1951.

77. FO 371, 91843/EY1015/34, Montagu-Pollock to Foreign Office, Damascus tel. no. 374, Dec. 4, 1951.

78. FO 371, 91843/EY1015/35, Troutbeck to Foreign Office, Baghdad tel. no. 918, Nov. 4, 1951; 91843/EY1015/52, Foreign Office "Minute" (Furlonge, Bowker), Dec. 4, 1951.

79. This is a more complex version than the one presented by Marr, who emphasizes only Nuri's obstruction of the regent's Syrian scheme (Marr, 109). Her account of the regent's activities in 1953 and his disagreements with Nuri over Syria is more convincing. (113–14).

80. FO 371, 91843/EY1015/34, Troutbeck to Foreign Office, Baghdad tel. no. 915, Dec. 3, 1951.

81. FO 371, 91843/E101/35, Foreign Office to Baghdad, tel. no. 1299, Nov. 5, 1951; 91843/E1015/49, Troutbeck to Foreign Office, Baghdad tel. no. 935, Nov. 7, 1951.

82. FO 371, 91843/EY1015/35, Troutbeck to Foreign Office, Baghdad tel. no. 918, Nov. 4, 1951.

83. FO 371, 91843/EY1015/64, Troutbeck to Foreign Office, Baghdad tel. no. 951, Dec. 13, 1951.

84. RG59/783.00, Hare to Secretary of State, Jidda tel. no. 327, Dec. 22, 1951.

85. RG59/783.00, Drew to Department of State, Amman dispatch no. 141, Dec. 17, 1951.

86. Several issues of *al-Ahram* and *al-Misri* were confiscated on arrival from Egypt by the Syrian authorities because they criticized the delay in restoring parliamentary life in Syria and in releasing political prisoners (FO 371, 98914/EY1013/1, "Political Summary No. 12 for the Month of December, 1951," issued by the British Legation, Damascus).

87. FO 371, 91844/EY1015/80, Troutbeck to Foreign Office, Baghdad tel. no. 980, Nov. 24, 1951.

88. FO 371, 98916/EY1016/18, Chapman-Andrews to Ross, Beirut dispatch no. 1028/4/18/52, Oct. 9, 1952; 98920/EY10393, Samuel to Ross, Damascus dispatch no. 10303/15/2, July 18, 1952.

89. FO 371, 98263/E1071/45, Bromley to Ross, Baghdad dispatch no. 1073/24/52, Oct. 11, 1952.

90. FO 371, 98914/EY1013, "Political Summary No. 9 for the Month of September, 1952," prepared by the British Legation, Damascus; 98916/EY1016/16, Samuel (Damascus) to Foreign Office, Sept. 26, 1952.

91. FO 371, 98920/EY10393/13, Samuel to Foreign Office, Damascus tel. no. 348, Dec. 4, 1952.

92. Marr, 113–14.

93. RG59/783.00, Moose to Secretary of State, Damascus tel. nos. 639, 646, and 648, Apr. 8, 16, 17, 1953; 783.00(W), U.S. Army (Damascus) to Department of Army, tel. no. 368, May 1, 1953; Berry to Secretary of State, Baghdad dispatch no. 830, May 7, 1953 and enclosure ("memorandum of conversation with Col. Taleb Daghestani, Syrian military attaché, Baghdad"); Khalil Mardam, *Taqarir al-Khalil al-Diblumasiyya* (Beirut: Mu'assasat al-Risala, 1982), report no. 24 to Foreign Ministry, 2 Jaziran 1453, 219–25.

94. RG59/783.00, American Embassy, Damascus to Department of State, dispatch no. 489, Feb. 17, 1954.

95. Iraqi activities included payments to a number of Syrian politicians, details of which were revealed in the "People's Court" trials in Iraq following the 1958 military coup there (al-'Azm, 281; Seale, 137–38; Marr, 114). For the text of the proposal, see Khalil, 2:47–49.

96. RG59/783.00, Berry to Secretary of State, Baghdad tel. no. 494, Mar. 3, 1954; RG59/787.00, Berry to Department of State, Baghdad dispatch no. 629, Mar. 9, 1954.

97. RG59/783.00, "Memorandum of Conversation with Syrian Prime Minister Asali," enclosure no. 3 to Damascus to Department of State, Dispatch no. 646, May 15, 1954.

98. In terms of causation, this is a reverse of Malcolm Kerr's dictum that "when the Arabs are in a mood to cooperate, this tends to find expression in an agreement to avoid action on Palestine, but when they choose to quarrel, Palestine policy readily becomes a subject of dispute" (Malcolm Kerr, *The Arab Cold War*, 3d ed. [Oxford: Oxford Univ. Press, 1971]), 114.

99. Aryeh Shalev, *Shituf Pe'ulah Betzel 'Imut: Mishtar Shvitat Haneshek Yisrael-Suriya, 1949–1955* (Tel Aviv: Israel Defense Ministry, 1989).

100. FO 371, 96262/E1071/23, "Interview with Azzam Pasha," Thomas C. Rapp, Mar. 4, 1952.

101. FO 371, 91793/ET10316/1, Kirkbride to Furlonge, Amman dispatch no. S.103/

6/1/51, Feb. 2, 1951. Similarly, the assistant secretary-general of the Arab League, Ahmad al-Shukayri, told a British official that any notion of fashioning the West Bank into an independent Palestinian Arab state was "unrealistic and stupid." Ironically, as first head of the Palestine Liberation Organization in the mid-1960s, Shukayri would be the bitterest foe of Jordan's King Husayn's dominance in the West Bank (FO 371, 98263/E1071/43, Rapp to Foreign Office, Fayid [BMEO] dispatch no. 570, Oct. 4, 1952).

102. For Kirkbride's poignant, even melancholy description of the changes that were occurring in Jordan, see FO 371, 82705/ET1016/21, Kirkbride to Attlee, Amman dispatch no. 109, Oct. 5, 1950.

103. Avi Plascov, *The Palestinian Refugees in Jordan, 1948–1957* (London: Frank Cass, 1981), 29–40; Shaul Mishal, *West Bank–East Bank* (New Haven: Yale Univ. Press, 1978), 1–52.

104. For Jordan's interest in such an agreement, see ISA, 130.02/2453/3, "Siha 'im Ahmad Bey Tuqan," M. Sasson, Jan. 8, 1952. For Abu al-Huda's denial and Israel's disappointment, see FO 371, 98477/EE107/34, Amman Chancery to Eastern Department, May 1, 1952; 98479/EE1073/83, "Conversations with Israeli Officials," A. D. Fritzlan (American diplomat), Oct. 16, 1952; DOS, Tawfiq Abu al-Huda's press release, May 29, 1952, enclosure to Amman dispatch no. 328 (n.d.).

105. Shalev, 215–53.

106. RG59/674.86a, Caffery to Secretary of State, Cairo tel. no. 104, July 25, 1950; FO 371, 90151/JE10151/530, Balfour (secretary, C.O.S. Committee) to Allen (Foreign Office), Dec. 20, 1951, and comments to Allen, Dec. 31, 1951 — and Bowker (Foreign Office) — Jan. 2, 1952.

107. ISA, 4021/Aleph, Biran to Foreign Ministry Director-General, Oct. 28, 1951 (reporting on his conversation with Jordan's Foreign Ministry director-general).

108. For earlier attempts (not connected to a British-Egyptian settlement) to arrive at an Egyptian-Israeli settlement of Gaza's status, see Morris, *Palestinian Refugee Problem*, 266–75, and Pappé, *Britain and the Arab-Israeli Conflict*, 13–40.

109. Jordan's Foreign Ministry director-general, 'Azmi al-Nashashibi, told his Israeli interlocutor that this would be achieved via a road along the Sinai-Negev border (apparently to transverse the southern Negev) to Aqaba. (Biran to Foreign Ministry director-general, Oct. 28, 1951).

110. On the British-Egyptian dispute, Jordan tread very lightly. On the one hand, as a solidarity gesture to Egypt (and fearful of Arab criticism), it refused to allow the recruitment of Palestinian Arab refugee labor for work in the Canal Zone to replace boycotting Egyptian workers. On the other hand, its leadership acted decisively to prevent the passage in the Jordanian Parliament of any resolution supporting Egypt's abrogation of the 1936 treaty with Britain (FO 371, 98865/ET1011/1, "Annual Report of Events in Jordan, 1951," Jan. 26, 1952).

111. In early 1952, Jordanian government officials privately asked the Israelis for information on Egyptian intentions, indicating both the limitations of their own contact with Egypt and their mistrust. In this, the situation was reminiscent of 'Abdallah's concern in early 1949 (FO 371, 98476/EE1073/1, Evans to Foreign Office, Tel Aviv tel. no. 75, Feb. 29, 1952).

112. RG59/785.13, "Meeting of the Arab League Political Committee in Am-

man, October 21–24," Lynch to Department of State, Amman tel. no. 141, Oct. 27, 1953; RG59/674.85, Caffery to Department of State, Cairo tel. nos. 1136, 1182, Nov. 7, 13, 1953.

113. RG59/785.00(W), Seelye to Department of State, Amman tel. no. 346, Apr. 10, 1954.

114. Ibid.

115. RG59/785.00(W), Seelye to Department of State, Amman tel. nos. 88, 95, Sept. 4, 11, 1954. For the festering of Egyptian-Israeli border tension and the deterioration toward the 1956 war, see Michael Oren, "Escalation to Suez: The Egypt-Israel Border War, 1949–1956," *Journal of Contemporary History* 24, no. 2 (1989): 347–73.

116. FO 371, 96262/E1071/23, "Interview with Azzam Pasha," Thomas C. Rapp, Mar. 4, 1952.

117. Maddy-Weitzman, "Jordan and Iraq: Efforts at Intra-Hashimite Unity," *Middle Eastern Studies* 26, no. 1 (1990): 65–75.

118. FO 371, 98333/E1023/2, Stephenson to Eden, BMEO/GHQ/MELF dispatch no. 13, May 20, 1952; EA1023/3, Hay to Eden, Bahrain dispatch no. 64, June 11, 1952.

119. DOS 786.00, More to Department of State, Benghazi dispatch no. 23, Oct. 7, 1952.

CONCLUSION

1. Avi Shlaim, "Israeli Interference in Internal Arab Politics: The Case of Lebanon," in *The Politics of Arab Integration,* ed. Giacomo Luciani and Ghassan Salame (London: Croom Helm, 1988), 232–55.

2. Abdallah, *My Memoirs Completed,* 7.

3. The move was part of a general housecleaning of veteran politicians and the "king's men" in Egyptian political life, categories to which ʿAzzam certainly belonged, even though his own access to and influence with Faruq had declined considerably in recent years. FO 371, 98263/E1071/46, "Recent Developments in the Arab League," Rapp to Eden, Cairo (BMEO) dispatch no. 40, Oct. 7, 1952; DOS, 786.00, Caffery to DOS, Cairo dispatch no. 470, Aug. 24, 1951. For a contemporary analysis of the Arab League's achievements and failures, see Boutrous Boutrous-Ghali, "The Arab League, 1945–1955," *International Organization,* no. 498 (1954): 387–448.

4. The postulation of a link between a certain level of development and the capability to implement any kind of unity plan, whether political or economic, has been made by Gabriel Ben-Dor, "Ihud Vepilug Beʿolam Haʿaravi," *Skira Hodshit* (no. 9, 1973): 3–13.

5. United Nations, Department of Economic and Social Affairs, *Economic Developments in the Middle East, 1945 to 1954* (New York: United Nations, 1955) 152.

6. Charles Issawi, *Egypt at Mid-Century* (London: Oxford Univ. Press, 1954), 257.

7. Yusif A. Sayigh, *The Arab Economy* (New York: Oxford Univ. Press, 1982), viii. In his words, the 1930s and 1940s formed a "period of isolation" (p. 151); he uses the phrase to describe the situation in the hydrocarbon sector, but it is adequate to describe the state of inter-Arab economics as a whole.

8. Daniel H. Garnick, "On the Economic Feasibility of a Middle Eastern Common Market," *Middle East Journal*, 14, no. 3 (1960): 265–76.

9. Issawi, *Egypt*, 256–57.

10. Galal Amin, *The Modernization of Poverty: A Study in the Political Economy of Growth in Nine Arab Countries, 1945–1970* (Leiden, E. J. Brill, 1974), 34.

11. United Nations, 18.

12. Mursey, 62.

13. Ibid., 56.

14. Ibid., 70.

15. Muhammad A. Diab, *Inter-Arab Economic Cooperation, 1951–1960* (Beirut: Economic Research Institute, American Univ. of Beirut, 1963), 12–13, 34.

16. Michael Van Dusen, "Syria: Downfall of a Traditional Elite," in *Political Elites and Political Development in the Middle East*, ed. Frank Tachau (Cambridge, Mass.: Schenkman, 1975): 115–55.

17. Khoury, 620, 622.

18. Israel Be'eri, *Army Officers in Arab Politics and Society* (Jerusalem: Israel Univ. Press, 1969), 364–65.

SOURCES CITED

ARCHIVES

Arab League Council (ALC) Protocols, 1945–1953 (in Arabic). The Harry S. Truman Institute, Hebrew Univ., Jerusalem.
Israel State Archives (ISA) (Jerusalem). Foreign Ministry Files.
Public Record Office (London). FO 371 (General Political Correspondence).
St. Antony's College (Oxford). Middle Eastern Library, Private Papers, Cunningham Papers.
U.S. National Archives (Washington, D.C.).
- DOS (Department of State, obtained under provisions of the Freedom of information Act).
- OSS (Office of Strategic Services), R&A no. 1754, "Notes and Comments on Arab Federation and Arab Unity, Covering August to December 1943."
- RG (Record Group) 59 (Diplomatic Records).
- RG (Record Group) 84 (Diplomatic Posts, Suitland, Md.).

PUBLISHED DOCUMENTS

Egypt, Ministry of Foreign Affairs. *Records of Conversations, Notes and Papers Exchanged Between the Royal Government and the United Kingdom Government, March 1950–November 1951.* Cairo, 1951.
Great Britain. *Parliamentary Debates (Hansard), House of Commons.* Vol. 410, no. 7 (1945). London: His Majesty's Stationery Office, 1945.
Heald, Stephen, ed. *Documents on International Affairs, 1937.* London: Oxford Univ. Press, 1939.
Iraq, Hashimite Kingdom of. *Me'ahorey Haparagod: Va'ada Parlimentarit*

'Iraqit 'al Hamilhama Beyisrael. Translated by Shmuel Segev. Tel Aviv: Ma'arakhot, 1954.
Israel. *Documents on the Foreign Policy of Israel (DFPI)*. Vol. 1, *May 14–September 30, 1948*. Edited by Yehoshua Freundlich. Jerusalem: Government Printer, 1981.
———. *Documents on the Foreign Policy of Israel (DFPI)*. Vol. 2, *October 1948–May 1949*. Edited by Yehoshua Freundlich. Jerusalem: Government Printer, 1984.
———. *Documents on the Foreign Policy of Israel (DFPI)*. Vol. 3, *Armistice Negotiations with the Arab States, December 1948–July 1949*. Edited by Yemima Rosenthal. Jerusalem: Government Printer, 1983.
———. *Documents on the Foreign Policy of Israel (DFPI)*. Vol. 5, *1950*. Edited by Yehoshua Freundlich. Jerusalem: Government Printer, 1988.
Jordan, Royal Jordanian Court. *al-Kitab al-Urduni al-Abyad*. Amman, 1947.
Khalil, Muhammad, ed. *The Arab States and the Arab League*. 2 vols. Beirut: Khayats, 1962.
Mardam, Khalil. *Taqarir al-Khalil al-Diblumasiyya*. Beirut: Mu'assasat al-Risala, 1982.
Moore, John Norton, ed. *The Arab-Israeli Conflict*. Vol. 3. Princeton: Princeton Univ. Press, 1974.
Sasson, Eliahu. "Sasson Letters from Lausanne." *Yedi'ot Aharonot* (Feb. 4, 11, 18, 1972).
United States. *Foreign Relations of the United States (FRUS)*, Vol. 8, *1945*. Washington, D.C.: Government Printing Office, 1969.
———. *Foreign Relations of the United States (FRUS)*. Vol. 7, *1946*. Washington, D.C.: Government Printing Office, 1969.
———. *Foreign Relations of the United States (FRUS)*. Vol. 5, *1947*. Washington, D.C.: Government Printing Office, 1971.
———. *Foreign Relations of the United States (FRUS)*. Vol. 5, *1948*. Washington, D.C.: Government Printing Office, 1976.
———. *Foreign Relations of the United States (FRUS)*. Vol. 6, *1949*. Washington, D.C.: Government Printing Office, 1977.
———. *Foreign Relations of the United States (FRUS)*. Vol. 5, *1950*. Washington, D.C.: Government Printing Office, 1978.
———. *Foreign Relations of the United States (FRUS)*. Vol. 5, *1951*. Washington, D.C.: Government Printing Office, 1982.

PERIODICALS / AGENCIES

(Some of the periodicals cited here can be found in the Shwadran Collection and the archives of the Documentation Center of The Moshe Dayan Center for Middle Eastern and African Studies, Tel Aviv Univ. Translations of others are contained in diplomatic dispatches cited in the notes.)

al-Ahram
Akhbar al-Yawm
al-Asas
Barada
Haboker
al-Hayat
Iraq Times
Istiqlal (Baghdad)
Jewish Telegraph Agency (JTA)
al-Jil al-Jadid
Journal d'Égypte
Le Progres Égyptien
al-Misri
New York Times
al-Nidal (Damascus)
Palestine and the Middle East
al-Sha'b (Damascus)
al-Usbu' al-'Arabi
Yedi'ot Aharonot
al-Zaman (Cairo)
al-Zaman (Baghdad)

MEMOIRS

'Abdallah Bin Husayn (Abdallah, King of Jordan). *Mudhakkirati*. Jerusalem: Matba'at Bayt al-Muqaddas, 1945.
——. *al-Athar al-Kamila li al-Malik 'Abdallah bin-Husayn*. Beirut: Dar al-Muttahida lil-Nashr, n.d.
——. *My Memoirs Completed, "Al-Takmilah."* London: Longman, 1978.
al-'Azm, Khalid. *Mudhakkirat Khalid al-'Azm*. Vol. 2. Beirut: Dar al-Muttahida lil-Nashr, 1973.
'Azzam, 'Abd al-Rahman. "Dhikrayat al-Amin al-'Am Lijami'at al-Duwal al-'Arabiyya 'Azzam Pasha." *al-Usbu' al-'Arabi*, Jan. 31, Feb. 7, 1972.
Ben-Gurion, David. *Yoman Hamilhama*. Vol. 3. Edited by Gershon Rivlin and Elhanan Oren. Tel Aviv: Defense Ministry Publishing House, 1982.
Glubb, Sir John Bagot. *A Soldier with the Arabs*. New York: Harper and Brothers, 1957.

al-Hakim, Hasan. *Mudhakkirati, 1920–1958.* Vol. 2. Beirut: Dar al-Kitab al-Jadid, 1966.
al-Hashimi, Taha. *Mudhakkirat Taha al-Hashimi.* Vol. 2. Edited by Khaldun Sati al-Husri. Beirut: Dar al-Tali'a, 1978.
Haykal, Muhammad Husayn. *Mudhakkirat Fi al-Siyasa al-Misriyya.* Vol. 2. Cairo: Matba'at Misr Sharika Musahima Misriyya, 1953.
Jawdat, 'Ali. *Dhikrayat, 1900–1958.* Beirut: Matba'at al-Wafa', 1967.
Kirkbride, Alec S. *From the Wings.* London: Frank Cass, 1976.
al-Qawuqji, Fawzi. "Memoirs, 1948, Part I." *Journal of Palestine Studies* 1, no. 4 (1972): 27–58.
el-Sadat, Anwar. *In Search of Identity.* New York: Harper and Row, 1977.
Spears, Sir Edward. *Fulfillment of a Mission: The Spears Mission to Syria and Lebanon, 1941–44.* London: Cooper, 1977.
al-Tall, 'Abdallah. *Karithat Falastin.* Cairo: Dar al-Qalam, 1959.
Yusuf, Hasan. *al-Qasr wa-Dawruhu Fi al-Siyasa al-Misriyya, 1922–1952: Mudhakkirat Hasan Yusuf.* Cairo: Markaz al-Dirasat al-Siyasiyya wal-Istratijiyya bi al-Ahram, 1982.

SECONDARY SOURCES

'Abd al-Mun'im, Muhammad Faysal. *Asrar: 1948.* Cairo: Maktabat al-Qahira al-Haditha, 1968.
Abidi, A. Haydar Hassan. *Jordan—A Political Study, 1948–1957.* London: Asia, 1965.
Ajami, Fouad. "The End of Pan-Arabism." *Foreign Affairs* 57, no. 2 (1978–1979): 355–73.
Alami, Musa. "The Lesson of Palestine." *Middle East Journal* 3, no. 4 (1949): 373–405.
Amin, Galal. *The Modernization of Poverty: A Study in the Political Economy of Growth in Nine Arab Countries, 1945–1970.* Leiden: E. J. Brill, 1974.
al-'Arif, 'Arif. *al-Nakba.* Vols. 1 and 2. Sidon: Manshurat al-Maktaba al-'Asriyya, 1956, 1959.
Bar-Josef, Uri. *The Best of Enemies: Israel and Transjordan in the War of 1948.* London: Frank Cass, 1987.
Be'eri, Israel. *Army Officers in Arab Politics and Society.* Jerusalem: Israel Univ. Press, 1969.
Ben-Dor, Gabriel. "Ihud Vepilug Be 'olam Ha 'aravi." *Skira Hodshit* (no. 9, 1973): 3–13.
———. "Inter-Arab Relations and the Arab-Israeli Conflict." *Jerusalem Journal of International Relations* 1, no. 4 (1976): 70–96.
———. *State and Conflict in the Middle East.* New York: Praeger, 1983.

———. "Stateness and Ideology in Contemporary Middle East Politics." *Jerusalem Journal of International Relations* 9, no. 3 (1987): 10–37.
Binder, Leonard. *The Ideological Revolution in the Middle East*. New York: Wiley, 1964.
———. "The Middle East as a Subordinate International System." *World Politics* 10, no. 3 (1958): 408–29.
———. "The Tragedy of Syria," review article. *World Politics* 19, no. 3 (1967): 521–49.
Boutrous-Ghali, Boutrous. "The Arab League, 1945–1955." *International Organization*, no. 498 (1954): 387–448.
Brecher, Michael, and Hemda Ben-Yehuda. "System and Crisis in International Politics." *Review of International Studies* 11 (1985): 17–36.
Bullock, Alan. *Ernest Bevin, Foreign Secretary, 1945–1951*. London: Heinemann, 1983.
Cantori, Louis, and Steven Spiegel. *The International Politics of Regions*. Englewood Cliffs, N.J.: Prentice-Hall, 1970.
Cohen, Gabriel. *Churchill Veshe'elat Eretz Yisrael*. Jerusalem: Ben-Zvi Institute, 1976.
———. "Mediniyut Britanya 'Erev Milhemet Ha'atzma'ut." In *Hayinu Keholmim*, edited by Yehuda Wallach, 13–177. Ramat Gan, Israel: Massada, 1985.
Cohen, Michael J. "A Note on the Mansion House Speech, May 1941." *Asian and African Studies* 2, no. 3 (1977): 375–86.
———. "Origins of the Arab States' Involvement in Palestine." *Middle Eastern Studies* 19, no. 2 (1983): 244–52.
Copeland, Miles. *The Game of Nations*. London: Weidenfeld and Nicholson, 1969.
———. *The Game Player: The Confessions of the CIA's Original Political Operative*. London: Aurum, 1989.
Coury, Ralph M. "Who 'Invented' Egyptian Arab Nationalism?" *International Journal of Middle East Studies* 14, nos. 3–4 (1982): 249–81, 419–34.
al-Dali, Wahid. *Asrar al-Jami'at al-'Arabiyya wa-'Abd al-Rahman 'Azzam*. Cairo: Matabi' Ruz al-Yusuf, 1982.
Dawn, Ernest C. "The Formation of Pan-Arab Ideology in the Inter-War Years." *International Journal of Middle East Studies* 20, no. 1 (1988): 67–91.
———. *From Ottomanism to Arabism*. Urbana: Univ. of Illinois Press, 1973.
———. "Pan-Arabism and the Failure of Israeli-Jordanian Peace Negotiations, 1950." In *Islam and Its Cultural Divergence*, edited by G. L. Tikku, 27–51. Urbana: Univ. of Illinois Press, 1971.
Diab, Muhammad A. *Inter-Arab Economic Cooperation, 1951–1960*. Beirut: Economic Research Institute, American Univ. of Beirut, 1963.

Dishon, Daniel, and Bruce Maddy-Weitzman. "Inter-Arab Relations." *Middle East Contemporary Survey* 6 (1981–1982): 221–71.
el-Edroos, Syed Ali. *The Hashimite Arab Army, 1908–1979.* Amman: Amman Publishing Committee, 1980.
Elpeleg, Zvi. *Falastin 'Atzma'it Besvakh Hayerivut Habeyn-'Aravit, 1946–1948.* Tel Aviv: Shiloah Institute, Tel Aviv Univ., 1982.
———. *Hamufti Hagadol.* Tel Aviv: Defense Ministry Publishing House, 1989.
Eppel, Michael. "The Iraqi Domestic Scene and Its Bearing on the Question of Palestine, 1947." *Asian and African Studies* 24, no. 1 (1990): 51–73.
Evron, Yair. *The Middle East: Nations, Superpowers and Wars.* London: Elek, 1973.
———, and Yaacov Bar Simantov. "Coalitions in the Arab World." *Jerusalem Journal of International Relations* 1, no. 2 (1975): 71–107.
Fabunmi, L. A. *The Sudan in Anglo-Egyptian Relations.* London: Longmans, Green, 1960.
Fansa, Nadhir. *Ayyam Husni al-Za'im.* Beirut: Dar al-Afaq al-Jadida, 1982.
Gallman, Waldemar J. *Iraq under General Nuri.* Baltimore: Johns Hopkins Univ. Press, 1964.
Garnick, Daniel H. "On the Economic Feasibility of a Middle Eastern Common Market." *Middle East Journal* 14, no. 3 (1960): 265–76.
Geertz, Clifford. *The Interpretation of Cultures.* New York: Basic, 1973.
Gelber, Yoav. "The Negotiations Between the Jewish Agency and Transjordan, 1946–1948." *Studies in Zionism* 6, no. 1 (1985): 53–83.
Gellner, Ernest. *Nations and Nationalism.* Ithaca, N.Y.: Cornell Univ. Press, 1983.
Gershoni, Israel. "The Arab League as an Arab Enterprise." *Jerusalem Quarterly* 40 (1986): 88–101.
———. *The Emergence of Pan-Arabism in Egypt.* Tel Aviv: Shiloah Institute, Tel Aviv Univ., 1981.
———. "Hale'om Ha'aravi, Beyt Hashim, VeSuriya Hagedola Bikhtavav shel 'Abdallah." *Hamizrah Hehadash* 25, nos. 1–2, 3 (1975): 1–26, 161–83.
———, and James Janowski. *Egypt, Islam and the Arabs.* New York: Oxford Univ. Press, 1987.
Gilbar, Gad G. *Calcalat Hamizrah Hatikhon Be'et Hahadasha.* Tel Aviv: Defense Ministry Publishing House, 1990.
Gomaa, Ahmad. *Foundation of the League of Arab States.* London: Longman, 1977.
Goren, Asher. *Haliga Ha'aravit.* Tel Aviv: Eynot, 1954.
Haim, Sylvia. *Arab Nationalism: An Anthology.* 2d ed. Berkeley: Univ. of California Press, 1976.
———. "Islam and the Theory of Arab Nationalism." In *The Middle East in*

Transition, edited by Walter Lacquer, 280–307. London: Routledge and Kegan Paul, 1958.

———. "The Palestine Problem in *al-Manar*." In *Egypt and Palestine*, edited by Amnon Cohen and Gabriel Baer, 299–313. Jerusalem: Ben-Zvi Institute, 1984.

Harik, Ilya. "The Origins of the Arab State System." In *The Foundations of the Arab State*, edited by Ghassan Salame, 19–46. London: Croom Helm, 1987.

al-Hasani, ʿAbd al-Razzaq. *Taʾrikh al-Wizarat al-ʿIraqiyya*. Vol. 4. Sidon: Matbaʿt al-Irfan, 1940.

Hassouna, Hussein A. *The League of Arab States and Regional Disputes.* Dobbs Ferry, N.Y.: Oceana, 1975.

Hourani, Albert. *The Emergence of the Modern Middle East*. London: Macmillan, 1981.

———. "Ottoman Reform and the Politics of Notables." In *The Beginnings of Modernization in the Middle East*, edited by William R. Polk and Richard L. Chambers, 41–68. Chicago: Univ. of Chicago Press, 1968.

Hudson, Michael C. *The Search for Legitimacy*. New Haven: Yale Univ. Press, 1977.

Huntington, Samuel. *Political Order in Changing Societies*. New Haven: Yale Univ. Press, 1968.

Hurewitz, J. C. *The Struggle for Palestine*. New York: Shoecken, 1976.

Ibrahim, Saad Eddin. *The New Arab Social Order*. Boulder, Colo.: Westview, 1982.

Ismael, Tareq Y. "The Middle East: A Subordinate System in Global Politics." In *The Middle East in World Politics*, edited by Tareq Y. Ismael, 240–56. Syracuse: Syracuse Univ. Press, 1974.

Issawi, Charles. *An Economic History of the Middle East and North Africa*. New York: Columbia Univ. Press, 1982.

———. *Egypt at Mid-Century*. London: Oxford Univ. Press, 1954.

Jankowski, James. "The Egyptian Wafd and Arab Nationalism, 1918–1944." In *Nationalism and International Politics in the Middle East: Essays in Honour of Elie Kedourie*, edited by Edward Ingram, 164–86. London: Frank Cass, 1988.

———. "Zionism and the Jews in Egyptian National Opinion, 1900–1939." In *Egypt and Palestine*, edited by Amnon Cohen and Gabriel Baer, 314–31. Jerusalem: Ben-Zvi Institute, 1984.

Kedourie, Elie. "The Arab-Israeli Conflict." In *Arabic Political Memoirs*, edited by Elie Kedourie, 218–30. London: Frank Cass, 1974.

———. "Great Britain and Palestine: The Turning Point." In *Islam and the Modern World*, edited by Elie Kedourie, 93–170. London: Mansell, 1980.

———. "The Kingdom of Iraq, a Retrospect," and "Pan-Arabism and British Policy." In *The Chatham House Version and Other Middle Eastern Studies*, edited by Elie Kedourie, 236–85, 213–35. London: Weidenfeld and Nicholson, 1970.

Kerr, Malcolm H. *The Arab Cold War*. 3d ed. Oxford: Oxford Univ. Press, 1971.

Khadduri, Majid. *Arab Contemporaries*. Baltimore: Johns Hopkins Univ. Press, 1973.

———. "General Nuri's Flirtations with the Axis Powers." *Middle East Journal* 6, no. 3 (1962): 328–36.

———. *Independent Iraq*. London: Oxford Univ. Press, 1951.

———. "The Scheme of Fertile Crescent Unity." In *The Near East and the Great Powers*, edited by Richard N. Frye, 137–77. Cambridge, Mass.: Harvard Univ. Press, 1951.

Khalidi, Rashid, Lisa Anderson, Muhammad Muslih, and Reeva S. Simon, eds. *The Origins of Arab Nationalism*. New York: Columbia Univ. Press, 1991.

Khalidi, Walid. "The Arab Perspective." In *The End of the Palestine Mandate*, edited by William Roger Louis and Robert W. Stookey, 104–36. Austin: Univ. of Texas Press, 1986.

Khoury, Phillip. *Syria under the French Mandate*. Cambridge: Cambridge Univ. Press, 1987.

Kimche, Jon, and David Kimche. *Both Sides of the Hill*. London: Secker and Warburg, 1960.

Kirk, George. *The Middle East in the War*. London: Oxford Univ. Press, 1953.

Lerman, Eran. "The Egyptian Question, 1942–1947." Ph.D. diss., Univ. of London, 1982.

Little, Douglas. "Cold War and Covert Action: The United States and Syria, 1945–1958." *Middle East Journal* 44, no. 1 (1990): 51–75.

Louis, William Roger. *The British Empire in the Middle East 1945–1951*. Oxford: Oxford Univ. Press, 1984.

Maddy-Weitzman, Bruce. "Inter-Arab Relations." *Middle East Contemporary Survey* 8–9 (1983–1984, 1984–1985): 123–48, 109–37.

———. "Jordan and Iraq: Efforts at Intra-Hashimite Unity." *Middle Eastern Studies* 26, no. 1 (1990): 65–75.

Marr, Phoebe. *The Modern History of Iraq*. Boulder, Colo.: Westview, 1985.

Mayer, Thomas. "Egypt's 1948 Invasion of Palestine." *Middle Eastern Studies* 22, no. 1 (1986): 20–36.

Mishal, Shaul. *West Bank–East Bank: The Palestinians in Jordan, 1949–1967*. New Haven: Yale Univ. Press, 1978.

Moore, Clement Henry. "On Theory and Practice among Arabs." *World Politics* 24, no. 1 (1971): 106–26.
Morris, Benny. *The Birth of the Palestinian Refugee Problem, 1947–1949.* Cambridge: Cambridge Univ. Press, 1987.
———. "The Crystallization of Israeli Policy Against a Return of the Arab Refugees: April–December 1948." *Studies in Zionism* 6, no. 1 (1985): 85–118.
Mursey, Alfred G. *An Arab Common Market: A Study in Inter-Arab Trade Relations, 1920–1967.* New York: Praeger, 1969.
Nevo, Yosef. *'Abdallah Ve'araviyey Eretz Yisrael.* Tel Aviv: Shiloah Institute, Tel Aviv Univ., 1975.
———. "The Arabs of Palestine 1947–48: Military and Political Activity." *Middle Eastern Studies* 23, no. 1 (1987): 3–38.
Olmert, Yosef. "British Policy Towards the Levant States, 1940–1945." Ph.D. diss., Univ. of London, 1983.
Oren, Elhanan. "Matarot Vetotsa'ot Bemilhemet Ha'atzma'ut," *Ma'arakhot*, nos. 279–80 (1981): 12–22.
Oren, Michael. "Escalation to Suez: The Egypt-Israel Border War, 1949–1956." *Journal of Contemporary History* 24, no. 2 (1989): 347–73.
Pappé, Ilan. *Britain and the Arab-Israeli Conflict, 1948–1951.* London: Macmillan, 1988.
———. "British Foreign Policy Towards the Middle East, 1948–1951: Britain and the Arab-Israeli Conflict." Ph.D. diss., Oxford Univ., 1984.
Persson, Sune O. *Mediation and Assassination: Count Bernadotte's Mission to Palestine in 1948.* London: Ithaca, 1979.
Pipes, Daniel. *Greater Syria.* New York: Oxford Univ. Press, 1990.
———. "Radical Politics and the Syrian Social Nationalist Party." *International Journal of Middle East Studies* 20, no. 3 (1988): 303–24.
Plascov, Avi. *The Palestinian Refugees in Jordan, 1948–1957.* London: Frank Cass, 1981.
Porath, Yehoshua. "Abdallah's Greater Syria Programme." *Middle Eastern Studies* 20, no. 2 (1984): 172–89.
———. "Agada 'Umetzi'ut Betahalikh Hakamat Haliga Ha'aravit." *Zmanim*, no. 5 (1981): 32–43.
———. *In Search of Arab Unity, 1930–1945.* London: Frank Cass, 1986.
———. "Nuri al-Sa'id's Arab Unity Programme." *Middle Eastern Studies* 20, no. 4 (1984): 76–98.
———. *The Palestine-Arab National Movement.* Vol. 2, *1929–1939: From Riots to Rebellion.* London: Frank Cass, 1977.
Rabinovich, Itamar. "Inter-Arab Relations Foreshadowed: The Question of the Syrian Throne in the 1920's and 1930's." In *Festschrift in Honor of Dr.*

George S. Wise, edited by Hayyim Ben-Shahar et al., 237–50. Tel Aviv: Tel Aviv Univ., 1981.

———. *The Road Not Taken*. New York: Oxford Univ. Press, 1991.

———. *The War for Lebanon*. Ithaca, N.Y.: Cornell Univ. Press, 1984.

Richards, Alan, and John Waterbury. *A Political Economy of the Middle East*. Boulder, Colo.: Westview, 1990.

Rubin, Barry. *The Arab States and the Palestine Conflict*. Syracuse: Syracuse Univ. Press, 1981.

Safran, Nadav. *Egypt in Search of Political Community*. Cambridge, Mass.: Harvard Univ. Press, 1961.

Salame, Ghassan. "Integration in the Arab World: The Institutional Framework." In *The Politics of Arab Integration*, edited by Giacomo Luciani and Ghassan Salame, 256–79. London: Croom Helm, 1987.

———. "Inter-Arab Politics: A Return to Geography." In *The Middle East: Ten Years after Camp David*, edited by William B. Quandt, 319–53. Washington, D.C.: Brookings Institution, 1988.

Sayegh, Fayez. *Arab Unity, Hope or Fulfillment?* New York: Devin-Adair, 1958.

Sayigh, Yusif A. *The Arab Economy*. New York: Oxford Univ. Press, 1982.

Schueftan, Dan. *Optzia Yardenit*. Tel Aviv: Hakibbutz Hameuhad, 1986.

Seale, Patrick. *The Struggle for Syria*. London, Oxford Univ. Press, 1965.

Sela, Avraham. "Israel, Transjordan and the 1948 War: Myth, Historiography and Reality." *Middle Eastern Studies* 28, no. 4 (1992): 623–88.

———. *Mimaga'im Lemasa 'Umatan*. Tel Aviv: Dayan Center, Tel Aviv Univ., 1985.

———. "She'elat Eretz Yisrael Bema'arekhet Habeyn-'Aravit Mehakamat Haliga Ha'aravit 'Ad Pelishat Tzva'ot 'Arav Le'eretz Yisrael, 1945–1948." Ph.D. diss., Hebrew Univ., 1986.

Shalev, Aryeh. *Shituf Pe'ulah Betzel 'Imut: Mishtar Shvitat Haneshek Yisrael-Suriya, 1949–1955*. Tel Aviv: Israel Defense Ministry, 1989.

al-Sharif, Kamal Isma'il. "Ha'ahim Hamuslimim Bemilhemet Palastina." In *Be'eyney Ha'oyev*, translated and edited by Shmuel Segev, 69–123. Tel Aviv: Ma'arakhot, 1954.

Shim'oni, Ya'acov. "Ha'aravim Likrat Milhhemet Yisrael-'Arav, 1945–1948. *Hamizrah Hehadash* 12, no. 3 (1962): 189–211.

Shlaim, Avi. *Collusion Across the Jordan*. Oxford: Oxford Univ. Press, 1987.

———. "Israeli Interference in Internal Arab Politics: The Case of Lebanon." In *The Politics of Arab Integration*, edited by Giacomo Luciani and Ghassan Salame, 232–55. London: Croom Helm, 1988.

Simon, Reeva S. "The Hashemite 'Conspiracy': Hashemite Unity Attempts, 1921–1958." *International Journal of Middle East Studies* 5 (1974): 314–27.

Sinai, Anne, and Allen Pollack, eds. *The Hashemite Kingdom of Jordan and the West Bank*. New York: American Academic Association for Peace in the Middle East, 1977.
Susser, Asher. "Western Power Rivalry and Its Interaction with Local Politics in the Levant, 1941–1946." Ph.D. diss., Tel Aviv Univ., 1986.
Tibi, Bassam. *Arab Nationalism: A Critical Inquiry*. London: Macmillan, 1981.
Touval, Saadia. *The Peace Brokers*. Princeton: Princeton Univ. Press, 1982.
United Nations, Department of Economic and Social Affairs. *Economic Developments in the Middle East, 1945 to 1954*. New York: United Nations, 1955.
Van Dusen, Michael. "Syria: Downfall of a Traditional Elite. In *Political Elites and Political Development in the Middle East*, edited by Frank Tachau, 115–55. Cambridge, Mass.: Schenkman, 1975.
Vatikiotis, P. J. *Arab and Regional Politics in the Middle East*. London: Croom Helm, 1984.
———. *The History of Egypt*. 2d ed. London: Weidenfeld and Nicholson, 1980.
Walt, Stephen. *The Formation of Alliances*. Ithaca, N.Y.: Cornell Univ. Press, 1987.
Wilson, Mary C. *King Abdullah, Britain and the Making of Jordan*. Cambridge: Cambridge Univ. Press, 1987.
al-Yunis, 'Abd al-Latif. *Shuqri al-Quwwatli. Ta'rikh Umma Fi Hayat Rajul*. Cairo: Dar al-Ma'arif, 1959.
Zurayq, Qustantin. *Ma'na al-Nakba*. Beirut: Dar al-'Ilm lil-Malayin, 1948. (English translation by R. Bayly Winder, *The Meaning of the Disaster*. Beirut: Khayat's College Book Cooperative, 1956.)

INDEX

'Abd al-Hadi, Ibrahim, 39, 97, 107; and letters with Tawfiq Abu al-Huda, 68, 100–102, 137
'Abd al-Ilah (regent and crown prince of Iraq), 12, 53, 65, 70, 72, 84, 93, 106–7, 116, 118, 123, 125, 134, 140, 153, 162, 164–65, 170; and 'Abdallah, 15, 19, 28; and Inshas summit, 33, 35
'Abdallah Bin Husayn (king of Jordan), 3, 53; and 'Abd al-Ilah, 15, 19; appeals to Britain, 11; and Arab League, 37, 64–70, 81, 177–78; and British reactions to Palestine plans, 58–59; and coronation, 31; and Dar'a meeting, 71–73; and Druze, 38; and Faruq, 64–66, 68–69, 73–75, 84, 86, 98; during first truce, 74–77; and Government of All-Palestine, 80–81; and Great Arab Revolt, 41; and Greater Syria, 11, 15, 17, 25–26, 36, 37–44, 93, 106, 156–57; hostility to Egypt, 79–81; and Ibn Sa'ud, 28, 75, 106; and Inshas summit, 33, 35–36; and Israel, 76, 79, 89–90, 93, 96, 127–37, 141; and Khashaba, 98; and Jewish Agency, 57, 68; and Jericho conference, 84–85; meeting with 'Azzam, 65–66; and mistrust of Egypt, 96; and Mufti, 60, 79, 94; and Nahhas Pasha's diplomacy, 15; and Nuri al-Sa'id, 17, 95; and opposition to Iraq, 126; and Palestine question, 35–36, 51, 57–58, 76–78; and Qawuqji, 62– 63; and Saudi Arabia's rule of Hejaz, 32, 75; and Transjordanian civilian elite, 76–77, 79, 80–81, 84, 93, 131–32, 141, 166; visit to Cairo, 74–75; visit to Riyadh, 75; and Za'im, 106, 114. *See also* Arab-Israeli war (1948); Egypt; Greater Syria; Hashimites; Iraq; Syria; Transjordan

'Abd al-Mun'im Mustafa, Muhammad, 128–29, 131

'Abd al-Nasir, Jamal, x, 1, 3, 170–73, 177, 178

Abu al-Huda, Tawfiq, 40, 57, 62, 73, 74, 76, 80, 81, 97, 128, 132, 167; and 'Abd al-Hadi, 68, 100–102, 128; and meeting with Bevin, 58; and meeting with Khashaba, 98–99; and Nahhas, 15, 85–86; and understanding with Sirri, 128–29, 137

Afrika Corps, 11

Afuleh, 67, 71

Ajami, Fouad, x

al-'Ajlani, Munir, 112, 156

al-'Alami, Musa, 18

Alexandretta, 29, 151

Alexandria, 14, 15, 83, 117; meeting of Preparatory Committee of General Arab Conference, 17–19, 27

Alexandria Protocol, 18–20, 33

Aley, 50

All-Palestine, Government of, 80–82, 166

al-'Alusi, Ibrahim 'Akif, 114

244 INDEX

Amman, 28, 51, 66, 140, 168
Anglo-American Commission of Inquiry, 32–34, 36
Anglo-Egyptian question. *See* Great Britain, relations with Egypt; United Nations, Security Council
Anglo-Egyptian Treaty of 1899, 46
Anglo-Egyptian Treaty of 1936, 149–50
Anglo-Iraqi Oil Company, 95
Anglo-Iraqi treaties, 49–50, 53, 143; and Syrian-Iraqi federation, 119, 126
Anglo-Transjordanian Treaty of Alliance, 31, 58, 141
Ankara, 29
Antonious, George, 11
Aqaba, 32, 69, 75, 87; coast, 129; Gulf of, 97, 102
Arab chiefs of staff, 66, 149
Arab Cooperation Council, 1
Arab Higher Committee, 9, 36, 62, 80. *See also* All-Palestine, Government of
Arabian Peninsula, 41, 75
Arab-Israeli armistice negotiations (Jan.–June 1949), 87, 92, 94–102
Arab-Israeli conflict (1950–1954): as inter-Arab issue, 165–70
Arab-Israeli war (1948), 2; Arab invasion plans of, 64–70; British and Transjordanian plans in, 58–59; "civil war" phase of, 55–70; *and stages of conflict:* first round and truce, 70–77, second round and ceasefire, 72, 77–78, third round, 76, 82–83, ceasefire in Jerusalem, 85, fourth round, 76, 86–87, impact of collective Arab failure, 87
Arab-Israeli war (1967), 141
Arab League, 1–3, 12, 31, 37, 58, 79, 86, 87, 89, 92, 125, 142, 161, 171–72, 175–81; and annexation of West Bank, 135–41; broadcasts of, 45; *Charter (Pact) of:* ix, 19–21, 30, 39, 41–42, 43, 112, 116, 135, 136, 139, 179, and annex on Palestine, 32, 60, 136; *Council Meetings:* June 1945, 27, 31, Dec. 1945, 28, Mar. 1946, 30–31, June 1946, 36–37, Nov. 1946, 39, Mar. 1947, 45–46, 49, Oct. 1947, 50–52, Feb. 1948, 62, July 8, 1948 decisions, 76, Mar. 1949, 103, Oct. 1949, 120–22, 128, Mar.–Apr. 1950, 132–36, June 1950, 139–41, Oct. 1950, 140, Jan.–Feb. 1951, 146–48, 160–61, Sept. 1952, 164; and Egyptian domestic politics, 46; Egyptian-Iraqi differences, 102–4; Egypt's role and, 52, 88–89, 92–93, 99, 102–4; and French challenge, 26–27, 31; and Gulf crisis, ix; Joint Defense Council of, 148–49; and Jordanian-Israeli settlement, 132–35; Military Advisory Committee of, 148–49; and Military Committee on Palestine, 50, 57, 60–62; Palestine Committee of, 62; Permanent Military Committee of, 148–49; *Political Committee meetings:* Mar. 1947, 45, Sept. 1947, 49–50, Feb. 1948, 61–62, Apr.–May 1948, 64–67, 136, June 2, 1948 decision, 73, rejection of Bernadotte's proposals, July 3, 1948, 75, July 1948 call for Palestinian/civil administration, 76, Sept. 1948 declaration of support, 79, Nov. 1948, 83, 89, Oct. 1949, 120–22, 128, Apr. 1950, 135–36, May 1950, 138–39, Jan.–Feb. 1951, 146–47, 159, Oct. 1951, 150, Oct. 1953, 168–69, Jan. 1954, 165; and Qibya, 168–69, 172; Qudsi's critique of, 160–61; West Bank trusteeship proposal of, 138–41. *See also* Joint Defense and Economic Cooperation Treaty
Arab Legion, 57, 64, 72, 77, 82–83, 86, 99–101, 156, 168
Arab nationalism, x, 1–7, 9–11, 20–23, 41, 52–54, 87, 170–73; and Arab elites, 170–71, 175–81
Arab prime ministers' meeting (Dec. 1947), 54–58
Arab Revolt (Palestine, 1936–1939), 9, 48, 62
Arab state system, 9, 22–23, 52–54, 89, 125, 176–81; expansion and, 172; systemic crisis in, 91–92, 103, 142
Arab summit conference, 1, 178
al-Ard, Nash'at, 157, 159
Ardahan, 29

INDEX

al-Arish, 66
Army of Salvation. *See Jaysh al-Inqadh*; al-Qawuqji, Fawzi
al-Asas, 106
Ashkelon, 130
al-Atasi, 'Adnan, 122
al-Atasi, Hashim, 110, 116, 124
'Atfa, 'Abdallah, 114
Atrash (Druze faction), 38
Azerbaijan, 29
al-'Azm, Khalid, 138, 139, 161
al-'Azma, 'Adil, 110
al-'Azma, Nabih, 110
'Azzam, 'Abd al-Rahman, 3, 19, 27, 32, 36, 46, 51, 62, 70, 72, 79, 83, 85, 87–88, 92, 141, 166, 170, 172; cable to UN Secretary-General from, 70; and Egyptian policies, 27, 37, 45, 87; and Iraq, 27–28, 103–5, 112; and meeting with 'Abdallah, 65–66; resignation of, 178; and Za'im, 107, 111

Baban, Ahmad Mukhtar, 118
Baban, Jamil, 106–10, 109
Baghdad, 1, 28, 50, 118
Baghdad Pact, 165, 171–72
al-Barazi, Muhsin, 43, 114
Ba'th, x, 172
Bayt Jalla, 83
Beeley, Harold, 83
Beersheba, 82, 87, 99, 130
Beirut, 26, 98, 101
Ben-Gurion, David, 82–83, 89, 96
Bernadotte, Count Folke, 73, 74, 77; first proposals, 75–76; second proposals, 78–79, 90
Bethlehem, 68, 79, 99, 101
Bevin, Ernest, 44, 48, 58, 73, 76; and agreement with Sidqi, 44, 143
Bilad al-sham, 11
Binder, Leonard, 127
Bludan, 149; Arab League Council resolutions, 34, 36–37, 45–46, 48–50, 61
"Blue Book" (of Nuri al-Sa'id), 12
Bosporus (strait), 29
Bunche, Ralph, 85, 97

Cairo, 14, 15, 19, 28, 30, 33, 49, 58, 64, 65, 100, 103; 'Abdallah's visit to, 74–75; Feb. 1950 conference in, 131
Campbell, Sir Ronald, 86–87
Camp David Accords, x, 96
Casey, P. G., 12
Caucasus (region), 144
Central Intelligence Agency (CIA), 105–6
Chamoun, Camille, 134
Churchill, Winston, 11
Copeland, Miles, 105–6
Crusades, 34
Cyprus, 154

al-Dajani, 'Umar, 57
Damascus, 26, 29, 67, 118, 161
Dar'a meeting, 71–73
al-Dawalibi, Ma'ruf, 151, 163
Dayan, Moshe, 83
Dayr al-Zur, 110
Dead Sea, 99, 130
Defense plans, regional, 143–55
Deuxième Bureau (Syria), 156–59
Druze, 38
Dulles, John Foster, 155

Eden, Sir Anthony, 11–13
Egypt, 3, 7–9, 52–53; and Syria agreement with Iraq, 124–25; and Arab-Israeli conflict, 167–69, 171; and dispute with Great Britain (and implications), 25–27, 32–37, 44–48, 56, 143–54, 167–69, 172; domestic politics and foreign policy of, 46, 56, 61, 139; Faruq's overthrow in, 154; and Hinnawi coup, 115–16; and Huleh Valley clashes, 162; and Military Committee on Palestine, 50; Mufti and Government of All-Palestine and, 61, 74, 80–81, 88–89, 166; and negotiations with Israel, 87, 92, 100; parliament, 44; *relations with Transjordan:* 'Abdallah's coronation, 31, 'Abdallah's visit to Cairo, 74–75, during Arab-Israeli armistice nego-

Egypt (continued)
tiations, 93, 95–102, confiscation of Transjordanian ammunition and, 74, on eve of Palestine invasion, 64–65, 67–70, during first fighting and truce in Palestine, 72–75, and Jordanian-Israeli negotiations, 1949–1950, 127–35, 141–42, during 1950s, 166–68, during second truce and further fighting, 76–92, and West Bank annexation, 135–42; and rivalry with Iraq, 8, 13–14, 16–19, 30, 65, 102–4, 144–50, 152–54, 162, 165, 171–73, 177; role in Arab world and League, 37, 52, 88–89, 92, 93, 99, 102–3, 115–16, 120–22, 124–27, 138–41, 172–77; and Shishakli's first coup, 123–24; Syrian-Iraqi federation and, 120–22, 124–27; and territorial desires in Palestine, 82–84, 86–87, 97–99, 128–30; and Zaʿim, 106, 111–14. See also Faruq; al-Nahhas Pasha, Mustafa

El-Alamein, 10, 12

Euphrates River, 30, 108

Eytan, Walter, 96

Faluja, 82–83, 87

Faruq (king of Egypt), 3, 10, 13, 18, 31, 39, 43, 47, 51, 53, 56, 61, 72, 103, 118, 121, 128, 129, 145, 149, 152, 154, 158; and ʿAbdallah, 66, 73–75, 84, 86; and ʿAzzam, 88, 178; and Hinnawi coup, 115–16; and Ibn Saʿud, 19, 28; and Inshas summit, 33–35; and invasion plans, 33, 64–69; and Zaʿim, 111

Fawzi, Mahmud, 84

Faysal I (king of Syria), 41, 151

Faysal II (king of Iraq), 33, 66, 112, 118, 164–65, 169, 170

Faysal Al Saʿud, 47, 52

Fertile Crescent, 5–6, 8, 12–14, 20, 35, 41, 92, 117, 161. See also ʿAbdallah Bin Husayn; al-Saʿid, Nuri; Syria

France, 2, 9–11, 20, 21, 22, 25–27, 31, 32, 45, 110, 113, 150; and opposition to Syrian-Iraqi federation, 120, 126;
and Tripartite Declaration, 141–42, 161

Free Syria Command, 165

Galilee, 77, 78, 82; Sea of, 68

Gallad Bey, Edgar, 75

al-Gaylani, Rashid ʿAli, 11

al-Gaylani, Yusuf, 122

Gaza, 59, 80, 86, 87, 89, 96–97, 99, 101, 128, 130; "Gaza Plan," 167–68. See also All-Palestine, Government of

Geertz, Clifford, 22

Gellner, Ernest, 6

General Syrian Congress, 41

Geneva, 131

Gilbar, Gad C., 2

Glubb, Sir John Bagot, 69, 70, 72, 112, 149

Gomaa, Ahmed, xii, 10

Great Arab Revolt, 41

Great Britain, 2, 9–10, 22, 34, 36, 48, 88, 90, 95, 113, 118, 129; and ʿAbdallah's Greater Syria aspirations, 11, 43; and ʿAbdallah's Palestine policies, 58–59, 76; and Arab League, 26–27, 37, 42, 45, 54; and Bernadotte plan, 90; Commonwealth and, 117; and dispute with Egypt, 25–27, 32–37, 44–48, 143–54, 167–68, 169, 172; Foreign Office of, 58–59, 83, 96, 130, 154; and Government of All-Palestine, 81; and Huleh Valley clashes, 162; and Ibn Saʿud, 15; and Iraq, 94–95, 97; intervention in French-Arab crisis by, 26; and Middle East regional defense, 152–54; the Negev's strategic importance to, 55–56, 59, 94; Palestine policies of, 48–49, 53; and policies during World War II, 10–17; pressures Arab states into truce, 73; promotion of Egyptian-Transjordanian coordination by, 78–79, 86–87, 90, 130; relations with Arab governments of, 53; and Syrian-Iraqi federation, 126; and Transjordan, 31, 37, 76; and Tripartite Declaration, 141–42; withdrawal from Palestine and Arab views

on, 55–56, 63; and Za'im coup, 105, 107, 111. *See also* Bevin, Ernest; Defense plans, regional; Eden, Sir Anthony; Kirkbride, Sir Alec S.; Middle East Command (MEC); Middle East Defense Organization (MEDO)
Greater Syria, 11, 14–16, 25–26, 36, 37–44. *See also* 'Abdallah
Greece, 146
Gulf crisis (1990), ix–xi

Habash, George, 157
Haganah, 63, 65, 66
Haifa, 63, 67, 95, 131
Haim, Sylvia, 6
al-Hakim, Hasan, 151, 156
Hamza, Fu'ad, 116
Harik, Ilya, 5
Hasan II (king of Morocco), ix
al-Hashimi, Taha, xv, 62, 72
Hashimites, 22; and anti-Hashimite divisions, 2–3, 8, 11, 18–19, 25–28, 31–32, 40, 44, 49, 56, 92, 111–12, 125; and Arab League Charter, 20. *See also* 'Abdallah Bin Husayn; 'Abd al-Ilah; Fertile Crescent; Greater Syria; Iraq; al-Sa'id, Nuri; Transjordan
Hawrani, Akram, 156
Haydar, Muhammad, 86–87
Hebron, 68, 74, 79, 82, 99–101, 130
Hejaz, 8, 32, 38, 75
Hilmi, Ahmad, 133
al-Hinnawi, Sami, 114–16, 123
Homs, 110
Homsey, Edmond, 110–11
Hourani, Albert, 21
Huleh Valley, 149, 161–62, 168
Husayn (king of Jordan), 96
Husayn, Saddam, ix–x
al-Husayni, 'Abd al-Qadir, 62
al-Husayni, Hajj Amin. *See* Mufti of Jerusalem
al-Husayni, Ibrahim, 157
al-Husri, Sati', 6

Ibn [bin] Sa'ud, 'Abd al-'Aziz, 3, 8, 53, 163; and 'Abdallah, 28, 31, 43, 51, 66, 75, 139, 165; and Faruq, 19, 28, 33–34; and Hinnawi coup, 116; and Nahhas Pasha's diplomacy, 15; and Nuri al-Sa'id, 51–52; and preparatory pan-Arab conference, 15, 18; and Quwwatli, 15, 19, 108; and Za'im, 107–8, 111, 113
Imam Yahya, 16, 18, 33
Inshas: Faruq-Za'im meeting at, 111; summit at, 33–35, 45–46, 48
Inter-Arab relations: before 1945, 7–23; and economic links, 22–23, 178–80; and end of "dynastic phase," 170, 172; periodization of, xi, 1–2. *See also* Defense plans, regional
Iran, 8, 59, 149
Iraq, 3, 8–9, 59; and challenge to ruling elite, 180; and Huleh Valley clashes, 161; and Kuwait invasion, ix–x; *and Palestine question:* and Arab-Israeli settlement, 94–95, and autumn 1947 policies, 49–52; at Bludan meeting, 36–37, domestic considerations of, 49–50, 65, 78, and relations with Great Britain, 49–50, and Government of All-Palestine, 81, and Mufti, 60, and parliament, 57, and withdrawal, 92, 95, 100, 102, 106, 108; and relations with Saudi Arabia, 8; and relations with Turkey, 28–29; and rivalry with Egypt, 8, 13–14, 16–19, 30, 65, 93, 102–3, 143–50, 152–54, 162, 171–73, 177; *and Syria:* 29–30, federation proposals of, 118–20, Hinnawi coup and aftermath, 116–23, during 1949 upheaval, 92–93, 106–27, Shishakli's first coup, 123–25, 161, after Shishakli's second coup, 162–65, and Za'im, 106–15; *and Transjordan:* coordination between, 28, 50, 57, 66, differences between, 49, 81–82, 147–48, mediating role of other Arab states, 44, 84–85, 138–40, succession crisis in, 171, treaty with, 31, 37–38, 43–44, and West Bank annexation, 138–40; views of Arab League and 'Azzam, 19, 25–28, 92, 102–5. *See also* 'Abd al-Ilah; Arab-Israeli

Iraq (continued)
    War of 1948; Arab League; Hashimites; al-Sa'id, Nuri
Iraqi Jewry, 95
Iraq-Iran war, 149
Israel, 107, 176; and 'Abdallah, 74, 76, 89–90, 91–92, 96–100, 127–37, 141, 166; and Arab joint defense pact, 145–46; and armistice negotiations, 94–102; balancing role of, 126; and contacts with Arab states, 167; diplomatic possibilities and, 89, 102; and Huleh Valley clashes, 149, 161–62, 168; and negotiations with Jordan, 127–37, 141; and Nuri al-Sa'id's settlement plan, 94–95; and PCC, 129; postwar policy aims of, 92–93; talks with Egypt, 87, 89, 92, 95–97, 100. *See also* Arab-Israeli war (1948); Ben-Gurion, David; Jewish Agency

Jabal Druze, 38
Jabiri, Sa'dallah, 109–10
Jabr, Salih, 43, 49–51, 57, 139–40, 162
Jaffa, 63, 72
al-Jamali, Fadil, 36, 44, 109, 164, 165, 169; and attack on 'Azzam, 104–5, 112, 115, 171
Japan, 23
Jawdat, 'Ali, 123–25
Jaysh al-Inqadh, 50, 59, 63, 104. *See also* al-Qawuqji, Fawzi; Yarmuk Army
Jazira, 122
Jenin, 67, 130
Jericho conference, 84–86
Jerusalem, 49, 63, 69, 74, 77, 79, 85, 94, 97, 101, 130, 166
Jewish Agency, 57, 58, 63, 89
Jezreel Valley, 100
Jidda, 108
Joint Defense and Economic Cooperation Treaty, ix, 142, 169, 172, 179; functioning of, 147–49; Joint Defense Council and ratification, 148–49; and Military Advisory Committee, 148–49; and Permanent Military Committee, 148–49; and Oct. 1949 proposal, 120–22, 126; and Western defense plans, 142–47, 152–54. *See also* Arab League
Jordan. *See* Transjordan
Jordanian White Book, 40
Jordan River, 35

al-Kallas, Bahij, 156
al-Karmi, 'Abd al-Ghani, 136–37
Kata'ib al-Fida' al-'Arabi, 157–59
Kedourie, Elie, 10
Khadduri, Majid, 29
al-Khalidi, 'Awni, 106–7, 109
Khashaba, Ahmad Muhammad, 83–84, 97–99; meeting with Abu al-Huda, 98–99, 137
Khoury, Phillip, 181
al-Khuri, Bishara, 3, 16, 71, 81, 85, 121
al-Khuri, Faris, 47–48, 106, 109
Kirkbride, Sir Alec S., 43, 58, 64, 72, 74, 75, 76, 84, 97, 99, 130, 135, 139; and Qawuqji, 62–63
Korean War, 144, 146–47
Kutla Wataniyya. *See* National Bloc
Kuwait, ix–x, 172

Lampson, Sir Miles, 17
Latrun, 167
Lausanne, 127–29
Lebanon, 5, 39, 82, 85, 119, 148; and 'Abdallah's coronation, 31; and Alexandria Protocol, 18; and Arab League Charter, 20; and crisis of French intervention, 25–27; and inter-Arab diplomacy, 16; and promotion of British-Arab cooperation, 93; and relations with Syria, 16. *See also* al-Khuri, Bishara; al-Sulh, Riyad
LEHI, 78
Lerman, Eran, 44
Levant, 10, 20, 21, 26–27, 32, 40
Libya, 172
Ligue Orientale, 89
Louis, William Roger, xi
Lydda, 72, 77, 78

Ma'an, 32, 75
Mack, Sir Henry, 103, 119
Mafraq, 108
al-Mahdi, 'Abd al-Rahman, 86
Mahmud, Nur al-Din, 66–67, 70
Majdal, 130
Mansion House speech, 11–13
Mardam, Jamil, 16, 17, 45, 47, 50, 62, 64, 70; and 'Abdallah's Greater Syria plan, 42
Maronites, 12
Marshall, George, 52
Meade, Stephen, 105
Mecca, 15
Mediterranean Sea, 59, 96, 130, 168
Middle East Command (MEC), 150–55
Middle East Defense Organization (MEDO), 154–55
Middle East Supply Center, 23, 179
al-Midfa'i, Jamil, 13
Mishmar Ha'emek, 63
al-Misri, 103
Montgomery, Field Marshal Sir Bernard Law, 12
Morocco, ix, 161
Morris, Benny, xi
al-Mufti, Sa'id, 132
Mufti of Jerusalem (Hajj Amin al-Husayni), 9, 36, 56, 74, 79, 80, 96, 98; and Arab League, 50–51, 58, 59–63, 78–81, 89; and Government of All-Palestine, 79–81, 89; and Hebron and Bethlehem followers, 79; and Iraq, 60; and plot to kill 'Abdallah, 94. *See also* All-Palestine, Government of; Arab League; Palestinian Arabs
Muhammad (prophet), 6
al-Mulqi, Fawzi, 80–81, 132, 168
Muslim Brotherhood: in Egypt, 9, 61, 86, 99; in Syria, 151

al-Nahhas Pasha, Mustafa, 13–18, 33, 138–39, 145, 149, 152; and Ibn Sa'ud, 15; and Lebanese leadership, 16; and Nuri al-Sa'id, 14, 93; and Syrian leadership, 15–16; and Tawfiq Abu al-Huda, 15; and Yemen, 16
Najd, 32
Nasir, Muhammad, 157
National Bloc: in Egypt, 46; in Syria, 15
National Pact, 16
National party (Syria), 110, 120, 122. *See also* National Bloc
Nazareth, 67
Negev Desert, 59, 68, 78, 82–84, 86, 94, 97, 98, 102, 129–31
al-Nidal, 112
Nile Valley unity, 13, 37, 41, 46, 117, 150, 171
North Africa, 12–13
North Atlantic Treaty Organization (NATO), 145
North Yemen, 2
al-Nuqrashi, Muhammad Fahmi, 44–48, 50–51, 56, 69, 76, 79–81, 83, 85–87

Operation "'Uvda," 97
Ottoman Empire, 1, 5, 7, 12, 21, 22, 41, 179

al-Pachachi, Hamdi, 28
al-Pachachi, Muzahim, 78, 81, 83–85, 113; and Egyptian agreement on Syria, 124–25
Pakistan, 153
Palestine: and Alexandria Protocol, 18; as all-Arab issue, 8–9, 17, 22, 137–38, 151; Arab Revolt in, 9; British withdrawal from, 70; during 1930s, 8–9; and Fertile Crescent plan, 12; and inter-Arab divisions, 32–37; Popular Front for the Liberation of, 157; reaction to partition proposal about, 55–58; as a U.N. issue (with Arab perspective), 48–54. *See also* Arab-Israeli war (1948); Bernadotte, Count Folke; Palestinian Arabs; United Nations
Palestine Conciliation Commission (PCC), 83, 94, 99, 106, 127–29

Palestine National Council, 80
Palestinian Arabs: and Alexandria conference, 17, 18; and Arab League meetings, 128, 133; eclipsed as political force, 142; and Jericho conference, 84; and proposals for civil administration/provisional government, 56, 58, 60–61, 76, 78–82; and proposals to create army, 79–80; as refugees, 78, 84, 91, 95, 129–31, 166, 168; and relations with Arab states, 60–62. *See also* All-Palestine, Government of; Gaza; Mufti of Jerusalem
Palmyra, 110
Pan-Arabism. *See* Arab nationalism
Pappé, Ilan, xi
Paris, 120, 150
Parti Populaire Syrien, 123
People's party, 110, 116, 122, 151, 161, 162, 163
Persian Gulf, 153, 172. *See also* Gulf crisis
Pirie-Gordon, C. M., 40, 43
Popular Front for the Liberation of Palestine, 157
Porath, Yehoshua, xii, 10, 11
Portsmouth agreement, 50, 119, 143

al-Qadhdhafi, Mu'ammar, 172
al-Qa'im, 113
al-Qawmiyyun al-'Arab, 157
al-Qawuqji, Fawzi, 62–64, 77, 82, 104
Qibya, 168–69, 172
al-Qudsi, Nazim, and all-Arab federation proposal, 144, 159–61, 171; and collective security proposal, 120–21; and federation with Iraq, 117–19; as prime minister, 155, 159–62; and Western defense plans, 144–45, 151
al-Quwwatli, Shukri, 15, 19, 40–41, 43, 47, 66, 70, 71, 93–94, 105, 108, 109, 116, 120, 157–58; and Inshas summit, 34–35

Rabinovich, Itamar, xi
Rafah, 99
Ramadan, Hafiz, 46
Ramadan Proclamation, 40–41
Ramleh, 72, 77, 78
Ra's al-'Ayn, 77
al-Rawi, Najib, 124–25
Red Sea, 59, 130
Rhodes (island), 87, 94, 96, 103, 127
Richards, Alan, 2
al-Rifa'i, 'Abd al-Mun'im, 88
al-Rifa'i, Samir, 40, 43, 50–51, 88, 132
Riyadh, 75, 158
Robertson, General Sir Brian, 153–54
Rommel, Field Marshal Erwin, 10, 11
Rubin, Barry, xi, 37
Ruwallah tribe, 157
Ruwayha, Amin, 157, 159

Saadabad Pact, 30
al-Sadat, Anwar, 1, 96, 158
Safed, 63
Safwat, General Isma'il, 50, 57, 61–62, 64, 66–67
al-Sa'id, Nuri, 8, 53, 84, 125–26; and 'Abdallah, 13, 15, 17, 19, 28; and Arab League views, 28, 30; and attack on 'Azzam, 103–5, 121; Fertile Crescent and confederation plans and, 11–13; and Egypt, 145–50, 152–54; and Hinnawi, 116–23; and Inshas summit, 35; and Jabiri meeting, 29–30, 109–10; and Nahhas Pasha, 13–17, 93; and Palestine question with Ibn Sa'ud, 51–52; and PCC negotiations, 94–95; and proposal for Turkish-Egyptian-Iraqi pact, 30; and regional defense plans, 145–50, 152–54; regional outlook of, 28–30, 35, 143–47, 172; and Shishakli, 162–64; and Sirri meeting, 117; and Syria, 16–17, 29–39, 106–27; and Za'im, 106–15
St. James Conference, 9
Saladin, 34
Salah al-Din, Muhammad, 124–25, 135, 146
Salame, Ghassan, x, 1
Sasson, Eliahu, 89, 96, 100, 128–29

Sa'ud (crown prince), 33, 35, 165
Saudi Arabia, 8–9; and Hashimite ambitions in Syria, 42, 93; and Iraqi relations, 8; and Iraqi-Transjordanian relations, 31, 43–44; and inter-Arab diplomacy during World War II, 15, 18, 19; and intrigues against Shishakli, 157–59; and loan to Syria, 114, 116, 158–59; and reaction to Shishakli's coup, 123–24; and recognition of Shishakli government, 163–64; and U.S. relations, 42, 60–61, 93; and Za'im, 106–8, 111, 113–14. *See also* Ibn Sa'ud, 'Abd al-'Aziz
Sayigh, Yusuf A., 179
Seale, Patrick, xii, 106, 127
Sela, Avraham, xi
Sha'lan, Amir Fawaz, 157
al-Shanqiti, Muhammad Amin, 156
al-Sharabati, Ahmad, 158–59
Sharett, Moshe, 89
Shiloah, Reuven, 141
Shirin, Isma'il, 129–30
Shishakli, Adib, 62, 167, 172; first coup and control, 122–23, 126, 155–62; second coup until overthrow, 151–52, 162–65
Shlaim, Avi, xi, 130
Shtura, 164
al-Shurayki, Muhammad, 39, 40, 138
Sidqi, Isma'il, 32; and agreement with Bevin, 44, 143; and Inshas summit, 34–35
Silu, Fawzi, 158, 164
Sinai Peninsula, 69
Siraj al-Din, Fu'ad, 145, 152
Sirri, Husayn, 115–16, 120–21; and Nuri al-Sa'id meeting, 117; and understanding with Abu al-Huda, 128–29, 137
Sofar, 49–50
South Yemen, 2
Soviet Union, xi, 2, 29, 35, 54, 59, 144–45, 147, 155
Spanish civil war, 111
Spears, Sir Edward, 17
Stern gang. *See* LEHI
Sudan, 13, 25, 44–46, 85–86, 117, 143, 152, 153, 171; Mahdi of, 86

Suez Canal, 25, 59, 131, 143, 145–46, 150, 152, 153, 167
Suez war (1956), 153
al-Sulh, Riyad, 3, 47, 62, 65, 70, 81, 113, 121, 139, 143
Suriyya al-tabi'iyya, 11
al-Suwaydi, Tawfiq, 54, 134, 136, 138, 140
Syria, 3, 5, 29, 102, 103, 172; and 'Abdallah and Mufti, 60–61; and 'Abdallah's coronation, 31; and 'Abdallah's Greater Syria ambitions, 38–44, 62; and Arab invasion plans, 69–70; and Arab League Charter, 20; and armistice negotiations with Israel, 102, 107; and elite competition, 180–81; French intervention in, 25–27; and Huleh Valley clashes, 149, 161–62, 168; and inter-Arab diplomacy during World War II, 15–17, 19; Iraqi relations with, 29–30; and Iraqi-Transjordanian treaty, 43–44; and Israeli diplomatic contacts, 167; Palestine question and, 51; parliament, 40, 42, 109, 115, 116, 119, 123, 150, 163; and Qawuqji, 62; and Saudi loan, 114, 116; *"struggle for":* 2–3, 91, 105–27, 155–65, first coup, 94, 105–6, Hinnawi's coup and aftermath, 114–23, and Iraqi federation proposals (and opposition), 116, 118–20, 123, 126, Shishakli's first coup and control, 122–24, 126, 155–62, Shishakli's second coup and overthrow, 151–52, 162–65, Za'im's rule, 105–14. *See also* Greater Syria; al-Quwwatli, Shukri; al-Za'im, Husni
Syrian Congress. *See* General Syrian Congress
Syrian Desert, 110
Syrian Doctors Organization, 157
Syrian-Lebanese Customs Union, 179

Takla, Phillipe, 39
Talal bin 'Abdallah (crown prince, king of Jordan), 28
al-Tall, 'Abdallah, 133, 168

Tawfiq, Husayn, 158
Tel Aviv, 67, 69, 71, 77
Thabit, Karim, 86, 121
Tiberias, 63
Tibi, Bassam, 6
Tlas, Asad, 113–15, 122
Transjordan (Jordan), xv, 5, 9; and annexation of West Bank, 135–42, 166; and Arab League, 37, 44, 45, 84–85, 88, 92, 133–42; and civilian elite, 40, 76–77, 79, 80–81, 84, 93, 131–32, 141, 166; and *Egypt:* during Arab-Israeli armistice negotiations, 93, 95–102, and common views about invasion, 67–70, and Dar'a understanding, 72, during first fighting and truce in Palestine, 72–75, and government crisis, 132, and Government of All-Palestine, 80–81, and negotiations with Israel, 127–37, 141, reaction to Faruq's declaration, 64–65, during second truce and fighting, 76–90, 91–92; and Great Britain, 31, 37, 58–59; and *Iraq:* common frustrations with Arab League, 28, military coordination, 66, opposition to Syrian-Iraqi federation, 121, and Palestine question, 49–51, and succession crisis, 171, treaty with, 31, 37–38, 43–44; and Israel, 74, 79, 85, 89–90, 91–92, 127–42, 166–68; and Jericho conference, 84–85; and Palestine question, 51; and Palestine occupation plan, 57–59, 64, 67–69; Parliament, 38, 44, 135–37, 141; and Qibya, 168–69; and Syria, 37–44, 62–63, 69–70, 106, 114, 123, 155–57; and treaty with Turkey, 29; and *White Book,* 38. *See also* 'Abdallah Bin Husayn; Abu al-Huda, Tawfiq; Great Britain; Kirkbride, Sir Alec S.
Treaty of Friendship and Arab Brotherhood (Iraq–Saudi Arabia), 8, 117, 120
Tri-Partite Declaration, 141–42, 144, 150, 163
Troupes Speciáles, 27
Tuqan, Jamal, 133, 135–36

Turkey, 107, 110, 144, 146, 150, 153; and Iraq, 28–29; and Syria, 29; and treaty with Transjordan, 29

United Arab Republic, 155, 172
United Nations, 44, 66, 72, 78, 150; appointment of special mediator by, 73; and British fears about Transjordan, 58–59; Charter, 58, 146–47; *Security Council:* 58, 73, 76, 77, 78, 107, 162, and British-Egyptian dispute, 44–48, 53–54; Special Committee on Palestine (UNSCOP), 49–50; Trusteeship Council, 164; vote on partition resolution, 48–49, 51–52, 54, 55, 57, 59. *See also* Bernadotte, Count Folke; Bunche, Ralph
United States, ix, xi, 12, 14, 36, 42, 53–54, 56, 61, 63, 66, 88, 90, 95, 102, 113, 116, 118, 126, 129, 154; and Arab League views, 54; and Huleh Valley clashes, 162; and interagency intelligence assessment, 154–55; and postcoup Egyptian government, 154; State Department, 126; and Tri-Partite Declaration, 141–42; and Za'im coup, 105–6, 111. *See also* Defense plans, regional; Middle East Command (MEC); Middle East Defense Organization (MEDO)
'Uthman, Ahmad, 158

Vatikiotis, P. J., 1
Vichy France, 11

Wadi 'Ara, 100
Wafd party, 13, 20, 25, 124, 131, 152
Wahba, Hafiz, 116

Walt, Stephen, 43
Waterbury, John, 2
West Bank, 107, 127–34; annexation of, 135–42, 166
White Book. *See* Jordanian White Book
White Paper on Palestine, 34
World War I, 41, 175
World War II, 9–10, 23, 175

Yahya. *See* Imam Yahya
Yanbu', 19, 28
Yarmuk Army, 104–5
Yasin, Yusuf, 15, 18, 50, 116

Yemen, 2, 9, 18, 19, 121, 138, 148. *See also* Imam Yahya
Yusuf, Muhammad, 118

al-Za'im, Husni, 102, 105–15, 163, 165; and consolidation of power, 112–14; and crisis with Iraq, 113–15; and emissaries to Ibn Sa'ud, 107–8; and Faruq meeting, 110; and France, 110; and Jordan, 106, 112; and Nuri al-Sa'id meeting, 109–10; overthrow of, 114–15; and presidency, 113–14
Zionist movement, 42, 48, 55, 57, 59

THE CRYSTALLIZATION OF THE ARAB STATE SYSTEM, 1945–1954
was composed in 10 on 13 Trump Medieval on Digital Compugraphic equipment
by Metricomp;
printed by sheet-fed offset on 50-pound, acid-free Natural Hi Bulk
and Smyth-sewn and bound over binder's boards in ICG Arrestox B
by Braun-Brumfield, Inc.;
and published by
Syracuse University Press
Syracuse, New York 13244-5160

Contemporary Issues in the Middle East

This well-established series continues to focus primarily on twentieth-century developments that have current impact and significance throughout the entire region, from North Africa to the borders of Central Asia.

Recent titles in the series include:

Arab Women in the Field: Studying Your Own Society. Soraya Altorki and Camillia Fawzi El-Solh, eds.
The Communist Movement in Egypt, 1920–1988. Tareq Y. Ismael and Rifa'at El Sa'id
Egypt's Other Wars: Epidemics and the Politics of Public Health. Nancy Elizabeth Gallagher
Extremist Shiites: The Ghulat Sects. Matti Moosa
Family in Contemporary Egypt. Andrea B. Rugh
International Relations of the Contemporary Middle East: A Study in World Politics. Tareq Y. Ismael
The Iranian Revolution and the Islamic Republic. Nikki R. Keddie and Eric Hoogland, eds.
Iraq and Iran: Roots of Conflict. Tareq Y. Ismael
Islam and Politics. Third edition. John L. Esposito
Khul-Khaal: Five Egyptian Women Tell Their Stories. Nayra Atiya
Law of Desire: Temporary Marriage in Shi'i Iran. Shahla Haeri
The Middle East from the Iran-Contra Affair to the Intifada. Robert O. Freedman, ed.
Muslim Hausa Women in Nigeria: Tradition and Change. Barbara J. Callaway
Reveal and Conceal: Dress in Contemporary Egypt. Andrea B. Rugh
The Rise of Egyptian Communism, 1939–1970. Selma Botman
The Rushdie File. Lisa Appignanesi and Sara Maitland, eds.
Toward an Islamic Reformation: Civil Liberties, Human Rights, and International Law. Abdullahi Ahmed An-Na'im
Veils and Words: The Emerging Voices of Iranian Women Writers. Farzaneh Milani
Women Farmers in Africa: Rural Development in Mali and the Sahel. Lucy E. Creevey, ed.
Women in Egyptian Public Life. Earl L. Sullivan
Women in Muslim Family Law. John L. Esposito